The Transit of Empire

The Transit of Empire

Indigenous Critiques of Colonialism

Jodi A. Byrd

University of Minnesota Press
Minneapolis | London

FIRST PEOPLES
New Directions in Indigenous Studies

Publication of this book was made possible, in part, with a grant from the Andrew W. Mellon Foundation.

A version of chapter 4 was published as "'Been to the Nation, Lord, but I Couldn't Stay There': American Indian Sovereignty, Cherokee Freedmen, and the Incommensurability of the Internal," *Interventions: International Journal of Postcolonial Studies* 13, no. 1 (2011).

Published by the University of Minnesota Press
111 Third Avenue South, Suite 290
Minneapolis, MN 55401-2520
http://www.upress.umn.edu

Library of Congress Cataloging-in-Publication Data

Byrd, Jodi A.
    The transit of empire : indigenous critiques of colonialism / Jodi A. Byrd.
        p.   cm. — (First peoples : new directions in indigenous studies)
    ISBN 978-0-8166-7640-8 (hardback : acid-free paper)
    ISBN 978-0-8166-7641-5 (paperback : acid-free paper)
    1. Indians of North America—Government relations—History. 2. Indians of North America—Colonization—United States. 3. Imperialism—Social aspects—United States. 4. Racism—United States—History. I. Title.
    E91.B97   2011
    323.1197—dc23

                                                                2011023623

Printed in the United States of America on acid-free paper

The University of Minnesota is an equal-opportunity educator and employer.

17 16 15 14 13   10 9 8 7 6 5 4 3

For Jay

Onward, James, and remember me as a goddess
on your transit. Let this trip be the transit of night—
not the loss of a faint speck in the wilderness of sky . . .
go on, James, and journey for the discovery
of great peoples . . . avoid the misery
of ignorance and sermons, James. Look to history
for harmony—set out well as your acts precede you—
harmony, James, be harmonious with these people:
I am their star too. I know their mana,
their skill in crossing oceans . . .

ROBERT SULLIVAN, *CAPTAIN COOK IN THE UNDERWORLD*

Contents

Full Fathom Five

This book is my attempt to account for the traverse of U.S. empire by resurrecting indigenous presences within cultural, literary, and political contexts. This project is very personal for me as well. My father passed away one week before Barack Obama was elected president and as I was working on this book. While his life had become unlivable through whatever it was that chased him on the roads linking Iowa, Nebraska, Oklahoma, and Texas, I always thought his struggle was, in the end, about home, place, and belonging. We Chickasaws lost our country twice—once through the removals Tocqueville described in *Democracy in America,* and then through allotment and the creation of the state of Oklahoma in 1907. And though the Chickasaw Nation has certainly rebuilt and is today just as unconquerable and unconquered as it ever was, there is a difference between recovered and having never lost in the first place that stands in breach still for those of us attempting to theorize the legacies of colonialism within indigenous worlds. For my dad, I think, that loss was unmappable, ungrievable, and unapproachable within the constraints of U.S. settler society. And though he spent his life as a medical doctor, a family practitioner trying to heal American Indians and white settlers in Valentine, Nebraska, or in Indian Health Service in the Sisseton-Wahpeton community, that loss flitted on the edges, drove him crazy, haunted him, and prompted anger whether toward those he loved or toward those towns and communities that built up rural with a dogged determinism to never admit to any wrongdoing. That loss never allowed the United States to be home, even though the lands the United States was built upon might in fact be so.

Before he died, my dad read parts of my book and many of my articles, and always he had opinions. He would call at 4 o'clock in the morning on the road from the sandhills of Nebraska or on his way back from his horses in Thackerville, Oklahoma, to share his thoughts and insights on what this book and my work should always be about. "Did you know Tocqueville was there at removal?" he would ask. He was obsessed with Tocqueville's

description of the Choctaw dogs who threw themselves into the Mississippi to chase after their owners who were unable to take them on the
boats into Indian Territory. But more often than not, he'd tell me his philosophy about Indians in America. "We didn't have time, money, or power,"
he'd say more than once. "You put that in your book. That's what your work
is missing." And then he'd laugh and tell me he couldn't wait to read more.

Since he last called, I have thought of little else. Indians did not have
time, money, or power. The indigenous critical theory scholar in me wants
to argue with my dad, to point out all the ways the Chickasaws and other
indigenous nations have always had power, time, and resources through
relationship with land, complicity in chattel slavery, negotiations with the
British, French, Spanish, and Americans, or in the very ability to rebuild
one more time out of the destruction the militaries, laws, and legislative
bodies left behind. But there is something also fundamentally true in what
my dad wanted me to say for him, particularly in the ways Indians figure
and do not within the academic, literary, cultural, and political inquiries
that seek to delineate the problems facing so many people, be they settlers,
diasporic immigrants, or natives in those lands stolen from indigenous
peoples. A book like this cannot do much in the way of power or money,
but the one thing it might be able to do is offer some of my time spent
thinking about theory, narrative, and politics and the place of indigenous
peoples within contemporary theories of postcoloniality, queerness, and
race. I hope that was what my dad had in mind when he offered me those
challenges to think through the syllogistic traps of participatory democracy born out of violent occupation of lands.

This book, then, is a journey of sorts, its method mnemonic as it places
seemingly disparate histories, temporalities, and geographies into conversation in the hopes that, through enjambment, it might be possible to perceive how Indianness functions as a transit within empire. My method here
suggests a reading praxis inspired by Blackfeet novelist Stephen Graham
Jones's *Demon Theory*, in which he delineates genre as mnemonic device in
order to retell the Medea story through horror narrative.[1] The story of the
new world is horror, the story of America a crime. To read mnemonically
is to connect the violences and genocides of colonization to cultural productions and political movements in order to disrupt the elisions of multicultural liberal democracy that seek to rationalize the originary historical
traumas that birthed settler colonialism through inclusion. Such a reading

practice understands indigeneity as radical alterity and uses remembrance as a means through which to read counter to the stories empire tells itself. Lumbee scholar Robert A. Williams Jr. has argued that "the American Indian emerges as a distinct problem in Western legal thought," but I contend here that ideas of the Indian and Indianness—the contagion through which U.S. empire orders the place of peoples within its purview—emerge as distinct problems for critical and postcolonial theories.[2] As a transit, Indianness becomes a site through which U.S. empire orients and replicates itself by transforming those to be colonized into "Indians" through continual reiterations of pioneer logics, whether in the Pacific, the Caribbean, or the Middle East. The familiarity of "Indianness" is salve for the liberal multicultural democracy within the settler societies that serve as empire's constituency. In the wake of this transit, and indeed as its quality as colonialist practice, one finds discordant and competing representations of diasporic arrivals and native lived experiences—what I call cacophony throughout this book—that vie for hegemony within the discursive, cultural, and political processes of representation and identity that form the basis for what Wendy Brown has identified as the states of injury and Foucault and others have termed biopolitics. Bringing indigeneity and Indians front and center to discussions of U.S. empire as it has traversed across Atlantic and Pacific worlds is a necessary intervention at this historical moment, precisely because it is through the elisions, erasures, enjambments, and repetitions of Indianness that one might see the stakes in decolonial, restorative justice tied to land, life, and grievability.

As Willow Rosenberg in Joss Whedon's television series *Buffy the Vampire Slayer* once said, "A vague disclaimer is nobody's friend."[3] *The Transit of Empire* is built upon a number of foundational premises that may or may not be givens within critical theory but that are rapidly emerging as foundational to the disciplining of American Indian and indigenous studies. First, that colonization matters. For indigenous peoples, place, land, sovereignty, and memory matter. In a world growing increasingly enamored with faster, flatter, *smooth*, where positionality doesn't matter so much as how it is that we travel there, indigeneity matters. Second, this book temporalizes U.S. empire to the birth of the United States, and within its assumption of European colonialist agendas that sought to appropriate indigenous lands, knowledges, presences, and identities for its own use. Third, that despite cautions against original and originary within poststructuralist theory, this book asserts that there must be the possibility of the originary in the new world, and that it is located within the historical experiences of new world colonizations, genocides, and violences. There is a long line of continuity between the past and the present that has not been disrupted despite the fact that the stories we tell may or may not acknowledge that continuity. And fourth, that indigenous peoples must be central to any theorizations of the conditions of postcoloniality, empire, and death-dealing regimes that arise out of indigenous lands. We are long-memoried peoples, and we remember what happened the last time the world was flat.[4]

Indigenous Critical Theory and the Diminishing Returns of Civilization

*Such is our view of those who we describe as savages or half-savages;
and their mental life must have a peculiar interest for us if we are right
in seeing in it a well-preserved picture of an early stage of our own
development.*

Sigmund Freud, *Totem and Taboo*

What does it mean to be in transit? Mass transit, certificates of transit, and transits of planets across the sun denote movement, security, and rational explanation. Transit evokes the cacophony of traffic jams and exhaust fumes of the everyday workday, or the elegance and easy silence of the morning star rising and falling on the horizon in cycles that help navigators move among islands and allow growers to determine seasons for planting and harvesting. As a word, transit implies fluidity, noise, and instability. In a world of increasing global capital and environmental change, transit can also contradictorily mean responsibility, green liberalism, or the influx of the global South into the global North as certain geographies bear the catastrophes of nations addicted to oil. Transit also connotes death and the impossibilities of grief in first world surveillances that police bodies, urns, and caskets during their final return to family and earth. A certificate of transit provides the authority to transport hazardous materials across state lines; the transit authority is the first line of defense in the war on terror.

What it means to be in transit, then, is to be in motion, to exist liminally in the ungrievable spaces of suspicion and unintelligibility. To be in transit is to be made to move.

The Transit of Empire begins with a network of conflicting definitions to reflect upon the cultural and political modes of "Indianness" regulated and produced by U.S. settler imperialism née colonialism. Primarily, this book is essayistic, provisional, and some of its readings and conclusions often defy the expected affective common sense of liberal multiculturalism invested in acknowledgements, recognitions, equality, and equivalences. Transit is slightly provocative, an incomplete point of entry, and its provenance might be more suited to diaspora studies and border-crossings than to a notion such as indigeneity that is often taken as rooted and static, located in a discrete place. Steven Salaita's *The Holy Land in Transit* denotes transit alternately as the function of an alliance between United States and Israeli settler colonialisms that map old world sacred names onto new world sacred sites, a comparative approach to American Indian and Palestinian literatures, and finally a gesture towards the ways in which peoples have been forced to move and relocate.[1] Gerald Vizenor's work offers another way to frame modes of indigeneity in his concept of transmotion that he defines as a "sense of native motion and an active presence [that] is *sui generis* sovereignty. Native transmotion is survivance, a reciprocal use of nature, not a monotheistic, territorial sovereignty. Native stories of survivance are the creases of transmotion and sovereignty." Those creases, according to Vizenor, are apprehended in the complementarities of stories, associations, intimacies, and reincarnations that resist absence and possession.[2]

The Chickasaws have a migration story that we tell. In search of a new homeland, twin brothers, Chikasah and Chatah, were charged with leading the people as they traveled across the land. Ababinili had given them a sacred pole, the *kohta falaya,* that would point the way. After each day of travel, Chikasah would plant the long pole in the earth, and each morning the brothers would rise to find the pole leaning eastward in the directionthey needed to travel. Led by a white dog and the Milky Way, the brothers and the people traveled for years, always following the direction of the pole. Until one morning. At sunrise, the brothers awoke to find the pole standing almost straight upright. Chatah insisted that the pole confirmed that their travels were done, but Chikasah disagreed and argued that the pole still leaned, that there was still further to go. After continued debate, the question was put to the people—those who agreed with Chatah would stay and make a life there as Choctaws, in the lands that would become central Mississippi, and those who sided with Chikasah would travel further east to finally live in what is now northern Mississippi. Chickasaw sovereignty is, according to our national motto, unconquered and unconquerable. It is contrary and stubborn. But the creases of Chickasaw movement demonstrate how sovereignty is found in diplomacy and disagreement, through relation, kinship, and intimacy. And in an act of interpretation.

To be in transit is to be active presence in a world of relational movements and countermovements. To be in transit is to exist relationally, multiply.

There is more than one way to frame the concerns of *The Transit of Empire* and more than one way to enter into the possibilities that transit might allow for comparative studies. On the one hand, I am seeking to join ongoing conversations about sovereignty, power, and indigeneity—and the epistemological debates that each of these terms engender—within and across disparate and at times incommensurable disciplines and geographies. American studies, queer studies, postcolonial studies, American Indian studies, and area studies have all attempted to apprehend injury and redress, melancholy and grief that exist in the distances and sutures of state recognitions and belongings. Those distances and sutures of recognitions and belongings, melancholy and grief, take this book from the worlds of Southeastern Indians to Hawai'i, from the Poston War Relocation Center to Jonestown, Guyana, in order to consider how ideas of "Indianness" have created conditions of possibility for U. S. empire to manifest its intent. As liberal multicultural settler colonialism attempts to flex the exceptions and exclusions that first constituted the United States to now provisionally include those people othered and abjected from the nation-state's origins, it instead creates a cacophony of moral claims that help to deflect progressive and transformative activism from dismantling the ongoing conditions of colonialism that continue to make the United States a desired state formation within which to be included. That cacophony of competing struggles for hegemony within and outside institutions of power, no matter how those struggles might challenge the state through loci of race, class, gender, and sexuality, serves to misdirect and cloud attention from the underlying structures of settler colonialism that made the United States possible as oppressor in the first place. As a result, the cacophony produced through U.S. colonialism and imperialism domestically and abroad often coerces struggles for social justice for queers, racial minorities, and immigrants into complicity with settler colonialism.

This book, on the other hand, is also interested in the quandaries poststructuralism has left us: the traces of indigenous savagery and "Indianness" that stand a priori prior to theorizations of origin, history, freedom, constraint, and difference.[3] These traces of "Indianness" are vitally important to understanding how power and domination have been articulated and practiced by empire, and yet because they are traces, they have often

remained deactivated as a point of critical inquiry as theory has transit-
ed across disciplines and schools. Indianness can be felt and intuited as
a presence, and yet apprehending it as a process is difficult, if not impossible, precisely because Indianness has served as the field through which
structures have always already been produced. Within the matrix of critical theory, Indianness moves not through absence but through reiteration, through meme, as theories circulate and fracture, quote and build.
The prior ontological concerns that interpellate Indianness and savagery
as ethnographic evidence and example, lamentable and tragic loss, are deferred through repetitions. How we have come to know intimacy, kinship,
and identity within an empire born out of settler colonialism is predicated
upon discourses of indigenous displacements that remain within the present everydayness of settler colonialism, even if its constellations have been
naturalized by hegemony and even as its oppressive logics are expanded to
contain more and more historical experiences. I hope to show through the
juridical, cultural, and literary readings within this book that indigenous
critical theory provides alternatives to the entanglements of race and colonialism, intimacy and relationship that continue to preoccupy poststructuralist and postcolonial studies.

The stakes could not be greater, given that currently U.S. empire has
manifested its face to the world as a war machine that strips life even as
it demands racialized and gendered normativities. The post-9/11 national
rhetorics of grief, homeland, pain, terrorism, and security have given rise
to what Judith Butler describes as a process through which the Other becomes unreal. "The derealization of the 'Other,'" Butler writes, "means that it
is neither alive nor dead, but interminably spectral. The infinite paranoia that
imagines the war against terrorism as a war without end will be one that justifies itself endlessly in relation to the spectral infinity of its enemy, regardless
of whether or not there are established grounds to suspect the continuing
operation of terror cells with violent aims."[4] But this process of derealization
that Butler marks in the post-9/11 grief that swept the United States, one
could argue, has been functioning in Atlantic and Pacific "New Worlds" since
1492. As Geonpul scholar Aileen Moreton-Robinson argues, discourses of
security are "deployed in response to a perceived threat of invasion and dispossession from Indigenous people," and in the process, paranoid patriarchal
white sovereignty manages its anxiety over dispossession and threat through
a "pathological relationship to indigenous sovereignty."[5] In the United States,
the Indian is the original enemy combatant who cannot be grieved.

Within dominant discourses of postracial identity that depend on the derealization of the Other, desires for amnesty and security from the contradictory and violent occupations of colonialist wars exist in a world where, as Gayatri Chakravorty Spivak points out, "metropolitan multiculturalism—the latter phase of dominant postcolonialism—pre-comprehends U.S. manifest destiny as transformed asylum for the rest of the world."[6] As a result, the Indian is left nowhere and everywhere within the ontological premises through which U.S. empire orients, imagines, and critiques itself. *The Transit of Empire,* then, might best be understood as a series of preliminary reflections on how ideas of Indians and Indianness have served as the ontological ground through which U.S. settler colonialism enacts itself as settler imperialism at this crucial moment in history when everything appears to be headed towards collapse.

Transiting Empire

As metropolitan multiculturalism and dominant postcolonialism promise the United States as postracial asylum for the world, the diminishing returns of that asylum meet exactly at the point where diaspora collides with settler colonialism. Of particular concern is how to theorize the degrees to which indigenous peoples, settlers, and arrivants—a term I borrow from African Caribbean poet Kamau Brathwaite to signify those people forced into the Americas through the violence of European and Anglo-American colonialism and imperialism around the globe—have functioned within and have resisted the historical project of the colonization of the "New World." As the administrative colonialisms of European empires dismantled after World War II, the deep settler and arrivant colonialisms continued unabated within the post- and neocolonial geographies of the global South that are now reconfigured to bear the brunt of the economic, environmental, and militaristic needs of the global North. The emphasis in international law on nation-state formations predicates that indigenous peoples remain still colonized liminally within and beside the established geopolitical and biopolitical borders and institutions of (post)colonial governance as stateless entities. As a result, the breakaway settler colonialisms that produced the global North, particularly the United States, have created internally contradictory quagmires where human rights, equal rights, and recognitions are predicated on the very systems that propagate and maintain the dispossession of indigenous peoples for the common good of the world.

Although critical theory has focused much attention on the role of frontiers and Manifest Destiny in the creation and rise of U.S. empire, American Indians and other indigenous peoples have often been evoked in such theorizations as past tense presences. Indians are typically spectral, implied and felt, but remain as lamentable casualties of national progress who haunt the United States on the cusp of empire and are destined to disappear with the frontier itself. Or American Indians are rendered as melancholic citizens dissatisfied with the conditions of inclusion. All too rarely outside American Indian and indigenous studies are American Indians theorized as the field through which U.S. empire became possible at all. Nor is the current multicultural settler colonialism that provides the foundation for U.S. participatory democracy understood as precisely that—the colonization of indigenous peoples and lands by force. As Kahnawake Mohawk scholar Audra Simpson has argued, "the very notion of *indigenous* nationhood which demarcates identity and seizes tradition in ways that may be antagonistic to the encompassing frame of the state, may be simply unintelligible to the western and/or imperial ear."[7]

From the Pacific with the illegal overthrow of the kingdom of Hawai'i to the Caribbean with Guantánamo Bay as a torture center for "enemy combatants," I argue throughout this book that U.S. cultural and political preoccupations with indigeneity and the reproduction of Indianness serve to facilitate, justify, and maintain Anglo-American hegemonic mastery over the significations of justice, democracy, law, and terror. Through nineteenth- and early twentieth-century logics of territorial rights and conquest that have now morphed into late twentieth- and early twenty-first century logics of civil rights and late capitalism, the United States has used executive, legislative, and juridical means to make "Indian" those peoples and nations who stand in the way of U.S. military and economic desires. Activating the Indian as a foundational concept within poststructuralist, postcolonial, and critical race theories leads to one of the overarching questions of this book: How might the terms of current academic and political debates change if the responsibilities of that very real lived condition of colonialism were prioritized as a condition of possibility?

My use of transit refers to a rare astronomical event, the paired transits of Venus across the sun, that served in 1761 and again in 1769 as global moments that moved European conquest toward notions of imperialist planetary that provided the basis for Enlightenment liberalism.[8] The imperial planetarity that sparked scientific rationalism and inspired humanist articulations of freedom, sovereignty, and equality touched four continents and a sea of islands in order to cohere itself. At its center were discourses of savagery, Indianness, discovery, and mapping that served to survey a world into European possession by transforming indigenous peoples into the *homo nullius* inhabitants of lands emptied and awaiting arrival. As I use the term here, transit as a concept suggests the multiple subjectivities and subjugations put into motion and made to move through notions of injury, grievance, and grievability as the United States deploys a paradigmatic Indianness to facilitate its imperial desires. This paradigm of Indianness that functions as the transit of U.S. empire arises from how the United States was constituted from the start, not just in the scientific racisms and territorial mappings inaugurated through Enlightenment voyages for knowledge, but in the very constitutionality that produced the nation.

When read from this perspective, brief textual moments within U.S. founding documents reveal the historical intent of a fledgling nation that pursued happiness through the acquisition of indigenous lands. Of the many grievances enumerated in the Declaration of Independence, one stands out as particularly revealing: "He . . . has endeavored to bring on the inhabitants of our frontiers, the merciless Indian Savages whose known rule of warfare, is an undistinguished destruction of all ages, sexes, and conditions."[9] The non-discriminating, proto-inclusive "merciless Indian Savage" stands as the terrorist, externalized from "our frontiers," and functions as abjected horror through whom civilization is articulated oppositionally. This non-recuperative category, a derealization of the Other, serves as a paranoid foundation for what Jasbir K. Puar defines in *Terrorist Assemblages* as Islamic "monster-terrorist-fags," the affectively produced and queered West Asian (including South Asian, Arab American, and Muslim) body that is targeted for surveillance and destruction by U.S. patriotic pathology.[10]

Just as the Declaration of Independence evokes "merciless Indian savages" upon whom the violences of invasion are abjected in the pursuit of lands, the Commerce Clause of the U.S. Constitution (Article I, Section 8, clause 3) invokes Indianness to operational ends in order to evacuate sovereignty and international recognition from any nation or peoples the United States may one day seek to invade. The clause states that Congress shall have the right "to regulate Commerce with foreign Nations, and among the several States, and with the Indian Tribes." Supreme Court Justice John Marshall used this clause in *Cherokee Nation v. Georgia* (1831) to declare that, since Indian tribes were "contradistinguished" from both "foreign nations" and "the several states" within the clause, Indian tribes must instead be understood as "domestic dependent nations" whose relationship to the United States was that of wards "in a state of pupilage."[11] Essentially, Marshall concluded that because the Constitution delineated "Indian tribes" as a category at all, they inhabited a different space than "foreign nations" external to the United States and "the several states" internal to and subject to U.S. federalism. Marshall's conclusion that such definitional distinctions meant that American Indian nations, despite the concrete evidence that they had entered into treaties with European nations as well as the United States as sovereigns within international law, were somehow *dependent* on the United States for aboriginal title reveals the larger colonialist agenda—to liberate Indians of their lives and lands.

According to Lenape scholar Joanne Barker, "the entire self-fulfilling narrative of legal, moral, and social superiority offered in such claims to doctrine as Marshall's discovery reinvented a sovereignty for indigenous peoples that was void of any of the associated rights to self-government, territorial integrity, and cultural autonomy that would have been affiliated with it in international law at the time."[12] Marshall's juridical focus on "foreign nation," "several states," and "Indian tribes" as the categories for state formations internal and external to U.S. sovereignty elides the contradistinctions of *with* and *among* that delineate relationality within the commerce clause. Precisely because the clause delineates Congress's regulatory power as "with foreign nations" and "with Indian tribes" as relational legal powers different than those "among the several states" that give Congress federal power over the states of the union, its conjunctive and prepositional logics of conquest over Indian tribes provide the United States the means to assert extraterritorial sovereignty over foreign nations as the need arises. The Commerce Clause, now interpreted as providing the United States plenary power over indigenous peoples and nations, has supplied, in the slip between *with* and *among* rather than "foreign nations" and "Indian tribes," the rule of law through which the United States enacts its imperialist agenda. This prepositional possibility that provides the United States its imperialist historical intent is precisely how I define transit throughout this book. As the ghost in the constituting machine of empire, the paradigmatic "Indian tribe" that exists as a parallel to "foreign nation" is not an absence, but rather a sui generis presence that enables the founding of U.S. empire by creating a *with* that facilitates the colonialist administration of foreign nations and Indian tribes alike.

In setting a precedent for U.S. empire through evocations of the doctrine of discovery, the Marshall Trilogy sets into motion the transformation of indigenous sovereign nations into "domestic dependent" nations where, according to Joanne Barker, "the erasure of the sovereign is the racialization of the 'Indian.'"[13] In order to pry apart the now ascendant though contradictory paradigms of liberalism invested in transformative multiculturalism and postracial politics, my book considers the entanglement of colonization and racialization. These two processes of domination have often been conflated (making racism colonialism and vice versa) within the critiques of empire by U.S. postcolonial, comparative area, and queer studies—and for good reason. Racialization and colonization have worked simultaneously to other and abject entire peoples so they can be enslaved, excluded, removed, and killed in the name of progress and capitalism. These historical and political processes have secured white property, citizenship, and privilege, creating a "racial contract," as Charles W. Mills argues, that orders "a world which has been *foundationally shaped for the past five hundred years by the realities of European domination and the gradual consolidation of global white supremacy.*"[14] Racialization and colonization should thus be understood as concomitant global systems that secure white dominance through time, property, and notions of self.

When these two historical processes are so enmeshed that racialization in the United States now often evokes colonization as a metonym, such discursive elisions obfuscate the distinctions between the two systems of dominance and the coerced complicities amid both.[15] The generally accepted theorizations of racialization in the United States have, in the pursuit of equal rights and enfranchisements, tended to be sited along the axis of inclusion/exclusion as the affective critique of the larger project of liberal multiculturalism. When the remediation of the colonization of American Indians is framed through discourses of racialization that can be redressed by further inclusion into the nation-state, there is a significant failure to grapple with the fact that such discourses further reinscribe the original colonial injury.[16] As Kanaka Maoli scholar J. Kēhaulani Kauanui, White Earth Ojibwe scholar Jean M. O'Brien, and other indigenous scholars have noted, the conflation of racialization into colonization and indigeneity into racial categories dependent upon blood logics underwrites the institutions of settler colonialism when they proffer assimilation into the colonizing nation as reparation for genocide and theft of lands and nations.[17] But the larger concern is that this conflation masks the territoriality of conquest by assigning colonization to the racialized body, which is then policed in its degrees from whiteness. Under this paradigm, American Indian national assertions of sovereignty, self-determination, and land rights disappear into U.S. terrioriality as indigenous identity becomes a racial identity and citizens of colonized indigenous nations become internal ethnic minorities within the colonizing nation-state.

As civil rights, queer rights, and other rights struggles have often cathected liberal democracy as the best possible avenue to redress the historical violences of and exclusions from the state, scholars and activists committed to social justice have been left with impossible choices: to articulate freedom at the expense of another, to seek power and recognition in the hopes that we might avoid the syllogisms of democracy created through colonialism. Lisa Lowe provides a useful caution as she reminds us that "the affirmation of the desire for freedom is so inhabited by the forgetting of its condition of possibility that every narrative articulation of freedom is haunted by its burial, by the violence of forgetting."[18] The ethical moment before us is to comprehend "the particular loss of the intimacies of four continents, to engage slavery, genocide, indenture, and liberalism as a conjunction, as an actively acknowledged loss within the present."[19]

In attempting to people the intimacies of four continents, Lowe activates the Chinese indentured laborer in the Caribbean just after Britain abolished the slave trade in 1807 as the affective entry point into "a range of connections, the global *intimacies* out of which emerged not only modern humanism but a modern racialized division of labor."[20] Her turn to the colonial racialized labor force in the Americas helps to reveal the degree to which intimacy—here tracked through the spheres of spatial proximity, privacy, and volatility—among Africa, Asia, and Europe in the Americas has served as the forgotten and disavowed constitutive means through which liberal humanism defines freedom, family, equality, and humanity. In fact, liberal humanism, according to Lowe, depends upon the "'economy of affirmation and forgetting'" not just of particular streams of human history, but of the loss of their geographies, histories, and subjectivities.[21] In the indeterminacies between and among freedom, enslavement, indentureship, interior, and exterior, the recovered Asian contract laborer, functioning as historical site for Lowe, can reveal the processes through which liberalism asserts freedom and forgets enslavement as the condition of possibility for what constitutes "the human." *"Freedom* was," Lowe stresses, "constituted through a narrative dialectic that rested simultaneously on a spatialization of the *unfree* as exteriority and a temporal subsuming of *enslavement* as internal difference or contradiction. The 'overcoming' of internal contradiction resolves in *freedom* within the modern Western political sphere through displacement and elision of the coeval conditions of slavery and indentureship in the Americas."[22]

But what seems to me to be further disavowed, even in Lowe's important figuration of the history of labor in "the intimacies of four continents," is the settler colonialism that such labor underwrites. Asia, Africa, and Europe all meet in the Americas to labor over the dialectics of free and unfree, but what of the Americas themselves and the prior peoples upon whom that labor took place? Lowe includes "native peoples" in her figurations as an addendum when she writes that she hopes "to evoke the political economic logics through which men and women from Africa and Asia were forcibly transported to the Americas, who with native, mixed, and creole peoples constituted slave societies, the profits of which gave rise to bourgeois republican states in Europe and North America."[23] By positioning the conditions of slavery and indentureship in the Americas as coeval contradictions through which Western freedom affirms and resolves itself, and then by collapsing the indigenous Americas into slavery, the fourth continent of settler colonialism through which such intimacy is made to labor is not just forgotten or elided; it becomes the very ground through which the other three continents struggle intimately for freedom, justice, and equality. Within Lowe's formulation, the native peoples of the Americas are collapsed into slavery; their only role within the disavowed intimacies of racialization is either one equivalent to that of African slaves or their ability to die so imported labor can make use of their lands. Thus, within the "intimacies of four continents," indigenous peoples in the new world cannot, in this system, give rise to any historical agency or status within the "economy of affirmation and forgetting," because they are the transit through which the dialectic of subject and object occurs.

In many ways, then, this book argues for a critical reevaluation of the elaboration of these historical processes of oppression within postcolonial, critical race, queer, and American studies at the beginning of the twenty-first century. By foundationally accepting the general premise that racialization (along with the concomitant interlocking oppressions of class, gender, and sexuality) causes the primary violences of U.S. politics in national and international arenas, multicultural liberalism has aligned itself with settler colonialism despite professing the goal to disrupt and intervene in global forms of dominance through investments in colorblind equality. Simply put, prevailing understandings of race and racialization within U.S. postcolonial, area, and queer studies depend upon an historical aphasia of the conquest of indigenous peoples. Further, these framings have forgotten, as Moreton-Robinson has argued, that "the question of how anyone came to be white or black in the United States is inextricably tied to the dispossession of the original owners and the assumption of white possession."[24] Calls to social justice for U.S. racialized, sexualized, immigrant, and diasporic queer communities that include indigenous peoples, if they are not attuned to the ongoing conditions of settler colonialism *of* indigenous peoples, risk deeming colonialism in North America resolved, if not redressed, two cents for 100 billion dollars.

Haksuba, Cacophony, and Other Headaches

Given all these difficulties, how might we place the arrivals of peoples through choice and by force into historical relationship with indigenous peoples and theorize those arrivals in ways that are legible but still attuned to the conditions of settler colonialism? These questions confront indigenous peoples still engaged in anticolonial projects of resistance. Colonialism brought the world, its peoples, and their own structures of power and hegemony to indigenous lands. Our contemporary challenge is to theorize alternative methodologies to address the problems imperialism continues to create. The conflation of racialization and colonization makes such distinctions difficult precisely because discourses of humanism, enfranchisement, and freedom are so compelling within the smooth narrative curves through which the state promises increasing liberty through pluralization. Just as Indianness serves as a transit of empire, analyses of competing oppressions reproduce colonialist discourses even when they attempt to disrupt and transform participatory democracy away from its origins in slavery, genocide, and indentureship. One reason why a "postracial" and just democratic society is a lost cause in the United States is that it is always already conceived through the prior disavowed and misremembered colonization of indigenous lands that cannot be ended by further inclusion or more participation.[25] I hope to disrupt this dilemma by placing indigenous phenomenologies into conversation with critical theory in order to identify indigenous transits and consider possible alternative strategies for legibility.

One such strategy is to read the cacophonies of colonialism as they are rather than to attempt to hierarchize them into coeval or causal order. Southeastern indigenous phenomenologies understand the Middle World (the reality we all inhabit) as a bridge between Upper and Lower Worlds of creation. When the boundaries between worlds break down and the distinctive characteristics of each world begin to collapse upon and bleed into the others, possibilities for rejuvenation and destruction emerge to transform this world radically. The goal is to find balance. To understand the dualistic pairings of this dynamic system is to understand, as Cherokee scholar Daniel Heath Justice has argued, "its necessary complementarity; it is a dynamic and relational perspective, not an assumption of unitary supremacy."[26] Choctaw novelist and scholar LeAnne Howe demonstrates in her writing the ways a phenomenology that draws upon traditional Southeastern cosmologies of balance between worlds might transform written narratives and theorizations to represent the passage of time and the interactions of relationships and kinship differently. In her short story, "A Chaos of Angels," Howe explains that "when the Upper and Lower Worlds collide in the Between World," there are repercussions in this world.[27] The resultant chaos, or what she translates into Choctaw as "*haksuba*," is both a generative, creative force as well as a potentially destructive one. Her story focuses on the collision between the Choctaw, Chickasaw, French, and British worldings that occur in the creation of New Orleans. "*Haksuba* or chaos," she tells us, "occurs when Indians and non-Indians bang their heads together in search of cross-cultural understanding."[28]

When the French, Choctaw, Haitian, Creole, Chickasaw, indigenous, slave, and free identities collide in the lands that will become Louisiana, the "banging together" creates shockwaves that ripple outward from the collision in time, space, and popular culture (so hard that Darth Vader himself feels the impact). Throughout the story, Howe's narrator is tracked by a black Haitian woman and a bullfrog. Both characters taunt her and incessantly remind her of connections and kinship relationships that she has denied or refused. The frog turns out to be the Frenchman Jean-Baptiste Le Moyne de Bienville, whose obsessions are responsible for erecting New Orleans on the mosquito-infested swampland that the Choctaw gave him as a joke; the Haitian woman is the narrator's sister and cousin, a relative of Choctaws stolen by Bienville and sent as slaves to the Caribbean. The *haksuba* that Howe's story presents is not so much chaos as it is the intercontextual relations between histories and lived experiences. The reader learns along with the narrator how to traverse the past and future worlds that begin to bleed into the present through a rebuilding of kinship networks as an interpretive strategy. Howe's evocation of the tattooed, blue-lipped Ancient Ones who watch over the narrator as she floats naked in a primordial swimming pool at the beginning of the story is simultaneously a reference to the Choctaw women's tradition of tattooing their lips with blue ink and a genealogical trace to the African and African-Choctaw ancestors of the Haitian woman. Bienville's presence attests to Choctaw diplomacies in negotiating with those arriving from Europe and reminds the narrator that New Orleans was originally Choctaw land. Through the course of the story, the narrator struggles to understand the densities that surround her and her place within them.

At the end, when the narrator is reunited with her dead grandmother who has traversed life and death, past and future, in the living challenge of a "cross-cultural afterlife," the narrator is told, "'Never forget that we are *all* alive! All people, all animals, all living things; and what you do here affects all of us everywhere. What we do affects you, too."[29] The *haksuba* that Howe's story describes provides a foundational ethos for indigenous critical theories that emphasize the interconnectedness and grievability embodied within and among relational kinships created by histories of oppressions. The narrator learns throughout the story to see that those pieces and elements "banging together" have deeper motivating logics that place and connect them within already established and functioning Choctaw worldings.

By privileging Southeastern indigenous philosophical understandings and bringing them into conversation with Western philosophical traditions, this book responds in part to calls Dale Turner (Teme-Augama Anishnabai), Sandy Grande (Quechua), Robert Warrior (Osage), and Chris Andersen (Michif) have made for an intellectual disciplining of American Indian and indigenous studies with both an inward and outward turn.[30] Ngāti Pūkenga scholar Brendan Hokowhitu has suggested that, "as a canonical field 'Indigenous studies' does not exist. Its genesis," he continues, "has been *ad hoc*, yet organic, in the sense that the amorphous concept of 'Indigenous studies' has arisen out of pre-established local departments, such as Māori studies in New Zealand, Aboriginal studies in Australia and

Native studies departments in the US and Canada."[31] The challenge facing indigenous studies in the academy is not just the need to negotiate the Western colonial biases that render indigenous peoples as precolonial ethnographic purveyors of cultural authenticity instead of scholars capable of research and insight, but also the need to respect the local specificities, histories, and geographies that inform the concept of indigeneity. Despite these pitfalls, however, indigenous critical theory as an emergent undertaking has made strides in comparative indigenous studies attuned to the local conditions of colonialism that might speak across geopolitical boundaries.

Although the United Nations' Working Group on Indigenous Peoples and the 2007 Declaration on the Rights of Indigenous Peoples have resisted defining "indigenous peoples" in order to prevent nation-states from policing the category as a site of exception, Jeff Corntassel (Cherokee) and Taiaiake Alfred (Kahnawake Mohawk) provide a useful provisional definition in their essay "Being Indigenous":

> Indigenousness is an identity constructed, shaped, and lived in the politicized context of contemporary colonialism. The communities, clans, nations and tribes we call *Indigenous peoples* are just that: Indigenous to the lands they inhabit, in contrast to and in contention with the colonial societies and states that have spread out from Europe and other centres of empire. It is this oppositional, place-based existence, along with the consciousness of being in struggle against the dispossessing and demeaning fact of colonization by foreign peoples, that fundamentally distinguishes Indigenous peoples from other peoples of the world.[32]

In their definition there emerges a contentious, oppositional identity and existence to confront imperialism and colonialism. Indigenousness also hinges, in Alfred and Corntassel, on certain Manichean allegories of foreign/native and colonizer/colonized within reclamations of "place-based existence," and these can, at times, tip into a formulation that does not challenge neoliberalism as much as it mirrors it. But despite these potential pitfalls, indigenous critical theory could be said to exist in its best form when it centers itself within indigenous epistemologies and the specificities of the communities and cultures from which it emerges and then looks outward to engage European philosophical, legal, and cultural traditions in order to build upon all the allied tools available. Steeped in anticolonial consciousness that deconstructs and confronts the colonial logics of settler states carved out of and on top of indigenous usual and accustomed lands, indigenous critical theory has the potential in this mode to offer a transformative accountability.

From this vantage, indigenous critical theory might, then, provide a diagnostic way of reading and interpreting the colonial logics that underpin cultural, intellectual, and political discourses. But it asks that settler, native, and arrivant each acknowledge their own positions within empire and then reconceptualize space and history to make visible what imperialism and its resultant settler colonialisms and diasporas have sought to obscure. Within the continental United States, it means imagining an entirely different map and understanding of territory and space: a map constituted by over 565 sovereign indigenous nations, with their own borders and boundaries, that transgress what has been naturalized as contiguous territory divided into 48 states.[33] "There is always," Aileen Moreton-Robinson writes of indigenous peoples' incommensurablity within the postcolonizing settler society, "a subject position that can be thought of as fixed in its inalienable relation to land. This subject position cannot be erased by colonizing processes which seek to position the indigenous as object, inferior, other and its origins are not tied to migration."[34]

While indigenous scholars such as Aileen Moreton-Robinson and Chris Andersen make a compelling case for indigenous critical interventions situated within whiteness studies and scholars such as Craig Womack (Muscogee Creek), Jace Weaver (Cherokee), Robert Warrior, LeAnne Howe, Daniel Heath Justice and others argue for scholarship grounded within local and national knowledges, my views on indigenous critical theory stem from my training in postcolonial studies. Admittedly, the field of postcolonial studies has been met cautiously within American Indian and indigenous studies because, as Robert Warrior has suggested, "the object of its study makes postcolonialism less compelling for Native scholars."[35] And yet, despite how it may or may not have been coopted or transformed by its incorporation into the academic metropoles of the global North, as scholars such as Aijaz Ahmad, E. San Juan Jr., Benita Parry, Anne McClintock, Ella Shohat, and Arif Dirlik have contended, because postcolonial theory arose as a politicized intervention to colonialist knowledge production, it seems worth reconsidering some of its strategies for the continued development of indigenous critical theory. Certainly, though, there are reasons for the hesitancy that I will discuss below.[36]

Indigenous Critical Theory amid the Posts

Gayatri Chakravorty Spivak first posed her now-famous question "Can the Subaltern Speak?" more than twenty-five years ago, and over the intervening years, the challenge of that question has prompted scholars to grapple with, revise, answer, or completely reject her foundational inquiry as absurd—or present themselves as its irrefutable disproof. Still, Spivak's query continues to taunt even as the academy has transformed, however incrementally, to incorporate those very peoples marginalized within Western and imperialist centers of knowledge. Spivak herself has revised and reformulated her essay over the years, and in *A Critique of Postcolonial Reason* she offers a thicker caution against the tendency within the academies of the global North to depend upon those who would position themselves as the native informant. She writes, "The intellectual within globalizing capital, brandishing concrete experience, can help consolidate the international division of labor by making one model of 'concrete experience' *the* model . . . we see the postcolonial *migrant* become the norm, thus occluding the native once again."[37] The question has now become how, and by what and whom, is the subaltern silenced.

When Spivak began formulating her intervention in the then-emerging field of postcolonial studies, American Indian studies had already begun to surface fitfully in universities throughout the United States. As a field, American Indian studies—which shares provenance with the rise of ethnic studies in the United States and with indigenous studies programs in Canada, Australia, Aotearoa (New Zealand), and Central and South America—functioned primarily as an intervention to the settler narratives of multicultural liberal democracy that refuse to acknowledge that colonialism, genocide, and theft of lands, bodies, and cultures have defined the rise of new world nation-states and empires. After more than forty years of existence within the academy, American Indian studies has in many ways come into its own, yet the intervention indigenous scholars offer to theories of colonization and genocide remains marginal at best. Often those outside the field perceive it as a project of recovery, culture, identity, and polemic; indigenous studies is sometimes erroneously read as a nativist project laced with xenophobia in a world that turns increasingly to the potential liberatory spaces of cosmopolitanism and diasporic movements, where place is relinquished for reinvention. Despite the best efforts of indigenous scholars, one thing that many outside the field do not perceive it as (until recently) is a project of intellectual rigor and theory. For those within American Indian and indigenous studies, postcolonial theory has been especially verboten precisely because the "post-," even though its contradictory temporal meanings are often debated, represents a condition of futurity that has not yet been achieved as the United States continues to colonize and occupy indigenous homelands.

Given that postcolonial theory and American Indian studies arose within the academy almost simultaneously and that both fields are concerned with the ramifications of colonial legacies, it is still notable how little the two fields have been in conversation, even though displacement, forced diaspora, and arrival have often made the lands that compose the United States, Australia, New Zealand, and Canada the ground that nurtures the postcolonial scholar. Eric Cheyfitz suggests that the "surprising, then, if not complete scandal" of postcolonial studies is that it has ignored the histories of indigenous struggles within what is now the United States.[38] But why has indigeneity in the global North not taken root within the theories critiquing the colonialist agendas of Europe and its colonies? One reason Cheyfitz posits for the "almost total eclipse" of American Indians within "the firmament of the postcolonial" is that the two fields arise from vastly different geographical and political terrains, and that the "contemporary forms of the European nation-state [are] a model that does not apply to the historic transformation of Native American kinship-based communities under Euro-American imperialism." Another reason for the eclipse, he speculates, "may be the result, at least in part and with a few notable exceptions, of a resistance to critical theory within Native American studies itself."[39]

However, indigenous scholars have been theorizing about colonialism for a while now, although often from the antipodes and ruralities overlooked by the metropole. Teresia Teaiwa (Banaban/I-Kiribati) makes a foundational critique that, within postcolonial and diaspora studies, the indigenous Pacific "is not brought to the table as an equal partner in any conversation about the nature of humanity or society."[40] Teaiwa goes even further when she asserts that the postcolonial abandons the native.[41] Often, in the work by white settler scholars located in Australia, Canada, and New Zealand, postcolonial debate occurs at the site they define as settler oppression, where they see themselves caught between the European metropole and indigenous peoples upon whose lands they reside.[42] Such a move has prompted Aileen Moreton-Robinson to respond that Australia is a "postcolonizing settler culture," in which the postcolonial settler depends upon a possessive whiteness whose ontological premises are tied to dispossessing indigenous peoples of home, land, and sovereignty.[43] Within the global South, scholars such as Gayatri Spivak and Mahasweta Devi, whose work passionately seeks to address the presence of tribals in India, can occasionally refract indigenous peoples through the very discourses their work attempts to disrupt. Spivak, for instance, speaks of indigenous peoples as the impossible prehistoric pterodactyl, and Mahasweta Devi is concerned that indigenous peoples in the United States are present "only in the names of places [where] the Native American legacy survives."[44] While each of these moments are certainly interpretable within the contexts of their texts, they also demonstrate a colonialist trace that continues to prevent indigenous peoples from having agency to transform the assumptions within postcolonial and poststuctrualist conversations, despite the best work of postcolonial scholars to make room. These colonialist traces have prompted Cherokee scholar Jace Weaver to observe that postcolonial studies seems "oddly detached when discussing indigenous peoples and their lives. It often displays—as in the works of Mahasweta Devi about and on behalf of tribal peoples in India—the same sense of patronizing care reflected by those in the dominant, Western culture."[45] At the very least, such moments demonstrate the dualities of global frictions that Anna Tsing describes when she cautions that "universalism is implicated in *both* imperial schemes to control the world and liberatory mobilizations for justice and empowerment."[46]

Often, scholars who try to sustain a conversation between postcolonial studies and indigenous studies end with the assessment that the geographic localities that fall within the purview of subaltern and indigenous theories are too disparate, that the histories are too different to produce meaningful or productive inroads, and that postcolonial scholars are too imbricated within settler agendas when they speak from academic centers in the United States, Canada, Australia, New Zealand, or the Caribbean. And of course, the very idea of indigeneity can be too dangerous and xenophobic when combined with nationalism or anticolonial struggle in a world shaped by forced diapsora, migration, hybridity, and movement.

As Sankaran Krishna illustrates, the problem of postcolonialism for indigenous peoples has real world consequences: "If identities such as the nation or ethnicity, or notions such as 'traditional homelands' of native peoples, can be shown to be historical and social constructions or fictions, governments and elites can use such ideas to deny their responsibility for past crimes or to oppose current claims for reparation or redress."[47] From the other side, Gaurav Desai cautions that

> the politics of indigeneity and autochthony seem defensible enough—how can one reasonably deny the rights of indigenous peoples who have been colonized to the fruits of their own labor and land? On the other hand, in a world that has seen mass migrations across continents over a long period of time, is it reasonable to allow for a strictly regulated indigenous politics, which in its most exclusionary stance can lead to ethnic strife, mass expulsions, civil wars, and genocide?[48]

If anything, bringing indigenous and tribal voices to the fore within postcolonial theory may help us elucidate how liberal colonialist discourses depend upon sublimating indigenous cultures and histories into fictive hybridities and social constructions as they simultaneously trap indigenous peoples within the dialectics of genocide, where the only conditions of possibility imagined are either that indigenous peoples will die through genocidal policies of colonial settler states (thus making room for more open and liberatory societies) or that they will commit heinous genocides in defense of lands and nations.[49]

Methodologically, an indigenous-centric approach to critical theory helps to identify the processes that have kept indigenous peoples as a necessary pre-conditional presence within theories of colonialism and its "post."[50] To engage this point, I read moments of cacophony in political, literary, and cultural productions. Identifying the competing interpretations of geographical spatialities and historicities that inform racial and decolonial identities depends upon an act of interpretation that decenters the vertical interactions of colonizer and colonized and recenters the horizontal struggles among peoples with competing claims to historical oppressions. Those vertical interactions continually foreground the arrival of Europeans as the defining event within settler societies, consistently place horizontal histories of oppressions into zero-sum struggles for hegemony, and distract from the complicities of colonialism and the possibilities for anticolonial action that emerge outside and beyond the Manichean allegories that define oppression. Of particular interest to this book, then, is the development of a more detailed analysis of how cultural, literary, and political assemblages in the United States depend upon a desire to reconcile through deferment the colonization of indigenous peoples within the horizontal scope of settler/arrivant colonialism, racism, homophobia, and sexism, a desire that implicates all those who reside on colonized indigenous lands. The significance, I hope, for both postcolonial studies and American Indian studies as disciplines, and for the nascent indigenous critical theory arising from the work of native scholars grounded in the knowledges of their communities, is to take seriously the lessons of the past and other struggles for decolonization and to then transform how we approach these issues through academic engagement so that our work and research questions reflect the best of our governance and diplomatic traditions.

To that end, the first chapter interrogates the Indian errant at the heart of poststructuralism and considers how that errant has rendered Indianness as the field through which empire transits itself within political, literary, juridical, and cultural productions. Gerald Vizenor writes, "The Indian with an initial capital is a commemoration of an absence—evermore that double absence of simulations by name and stories."[51] But within poststructuralist theories, I argue, the Indian functions as a dense *presence* that cannot be disrupted by deconstruction or Deleuzian lines of flight, because the Indian is the ontological prior through which poststructuralism functions. Turning to the 1769 transit of Venus and the planetary parallax that inaugurated an Enlightenment liberal empire coinciding with the formation of the United States, this chapter reflects upon key thinkers in American studies, queer theory, and poststructuralism to demonstrate that the United States propagates empire not through frontiers but through the production of a paradigmatic Indianness. In the process, U.S. empire discursively and juridically figures American Indian lives as ungrievable in a past tense lament that forecloses futurity. And out of the epistemological logics of possession, poststructuralism depends upon affective and distortive parallactic effects within Slavoj Žižek's parallax gap that stretches a partially apprehendable "Real" and ties critical theory back to its imperialist function. The transit of empire, then, depends upon the language, grammar, and ontological category of Indianness to enact itself as the United States continues its global wars on terror, the environment, and livability.

The second chapter, "'This Island's Mine': The Parallax Logics of Caliban's Cacophony," discusses the historical factors that complicated Coco Fusco and Guillermo Gómez-Peña's performance art piece, *Two Undiscovered Amerindians Visit* . . . and contributed finally to its failed engagement with the colonialist discourses that they sought to resist during the 1992 quincentennial celebrations of Columbus's "discovery." Shakespeare's *The Tempest* and the character of Caliban have long served as touchstones within the development of postcolonial theory. And yet, despite the new world context of the play and Caliban's claim that "this island's mine," most postcolonial engagements with this text have rendered the impact of the indigenous Americas on Shakespeare's colonial imagination as an archaic artifact. By positioning Caliban as one of the first textual examples of what I term colonial cacophony, I take up Gayatri Spivak's claim that Caliban functions as a textual blankness that precludes subaltern representation and argue instead that he is overfilled with consolidated and competing discourses. Reading this character, then, as simultaneously African, Irish, Carib, Arawak, Jewish, and Other, I suggest that Caliban serves as a cacophonous textualization that does not traffic in absence but rather oversignifies presence in informative ways that unravel colonial logics that are dependent on binary constructions of settler/native, black/white, and master/slave. Through this simultaneity, I suggest, we can see the complex dynamics of colonial discourses that exist horizontally among histories of oppression and inform continued complicities as historical narratives vie for ascendancy as the primary and originary oppression within lands shaped by competing histories of slavery, colonialism, arrival, and indigeneity.

The third chapter, "The Masks of Conquest: Wilson Harris's *Jonestown* and the Thresholds of Grievability," engages in a close reading of the Guyanese novelist's 1996 *Jonestown*. In this chapter, I focus on the narrative strategies Wilson Harris employs to represent indigenous cultures in the aftermath of the 1492 moment of contact. Unlike Jamaican poet Kamau Brathwaite, who suggests in his theorization of creolization that African slaves replaced indigenous peoples as the folk tradition of the Caribbean, Wilson Harris draws upon what he terms "Amerindian" influences as a radical imagined source for Caribbean aesthetics and decolonial nationalisms. His work suggests that the Caribbean continues to be influenced by Amerindian traces lingering in the land to shape past and future historical violences that haunt the Americas, from Jim Jones's murderous utopia in

Jonestown, Guyana, to 9/11. By reading the ways Harris imaginatively accesses and represents indigeneity within fictions that break down the consolidations of linear histories which inform the strategies of realism and the divisions between self and other, I argue that uneasy tensions remain in his work that keep indigenous peoples locked in the moment of contact and seen as the savage counter to the promises of liberal democracy. Despite the colonial romanticism that underpins his radical imagination, however, Harris gestures towards those deeper ethical issues that confront the historical presences and violences within the Americas that infiltrate and influence modern politics and aesthetics in order to provide potential avenues for grievability of and accountability to history.

The fourth chapter, "'Been to the Nation, Lord, but I Couldn't Stay There,'" examines the incommensurabilities of the "internal" for indigenous peoples by providing a genealogy of the concept of "internal colonialism" and its emergence as a descriptor for the relationship indigenous peoples have with settler nation-states in conversation with Gramsci and subaltern studies. On March 3, 2007, the Cherokee Nation voted to disenfranchise approximately 2,800 Cherokee Freedmen citizens (African-Cherokee descendants of slaves held by the Cherokee Nation) in violation of the 1866 treaty with the United States, a treaty that gave those freedmen the rights and status of citizens within the Cherokee Nation. In the following months, the Congressional Black Caucus proposed in response legislation that would, in effect, terminate the Cherokee Nation and eventually the Chickasaw, Choctaw, Creek, and Seminole Nations if they did not abide by the rule of U.S. law. Signaling the collision between discourses of race, slavery, colonization and genocide, the problem of slavery and Freedmen status has haunted Southeastern Indian nations since contact. In this chapter, I argue that these competing discourses and histories of racialization and colonization signal the incommensurabilities within the notions of "internal" indigenous nations and disrupt the dialectics of settler/native, master/slave, colonizer/colonized that all too often inform calls for reparations and decolonization.

Chapter 5, "Satisfied with Stones: Native Hawaiian Government Reorganization and the Discourses of Resistance," focuses on how the Native Hawaiian Government Reorganization Act of 2007 has been framed both within Hawai'i and on the continent as a way to understand how the United States, as it develops and contorts federal law to colonize indigenous nations, uses discourses of Indianness to solidify its presence in the Pacific. For American Indians, the word "reorganization" calls to mind the

Indian Reorganization Act of 1934, and this chapter examines how the continual transformation and revision of federal Indian policy becomes, when viewed from over 2,000 miles away in the Pacific, a coherent and inevitable expansionist discourse orchestrated by a seemingly static United States. In the face of these colonial processes that seek to mask the fractures within U.S. boundaries among American Indian nations, it seems important to examine how discourses of Indianness are used both by the imperial U.S. government, which occupies Hawai'i, and by those Native Hawaiian activists who frame "Indianness" as an infection threatening their rights and status as an internationally recognized sovereign state.

The final chapter, "Killing States: Removals, Other Americans, and the 'Pale Promise of Democracy,'" considers Karen Tei Yamashita's *Tropic of Orange* and discussions of multiculturalism in Los Angeles at the end of the twentieth century to understand how narratives of race and indigeneity within the United States have been recycled to provide a justifying logic for the transit of empire mapped onto Asian American bodies. In this chapter, I examine the ways indigenous peoples are discursively transformed into immigrants, while Asian Americans simultaneously become both cowboys and Indians as a means to police difference within liberal multicultural settler colonialism. To demonstrate how these histories collide, I examine John Collier's speech at Poston Relocation Center on the Colorado River Indian Reservation. In the decade after the Indian Reorganization Act of 1934, John Collier, in his role as commissioner of Indian Affairs, was both radically transforming the government structures of many native nations as well as struggling with the War Relocation Authority for administrative control over Japanese American internment. As administrator for the camp at Poston, Arizona—authorized by the signing of Executive Order 9066—John Collier advocated self-governance as a means to exclude and then reincorporate Japanese Americans back into the citizenry of the United States. The chapter ends with a close reading of Gerald Vizenor's *Hiroshima Bugi*. Vizenor's novel considers the linkages between American Indian history (and lands) and the atomic bombs dropped on Hiroshima and Nagasaki to end World War II in order to reframe victim narratives within colonial and imperial logics.

At its core, this book engages colonial discourses pertaining to indigenous peoples, particularly American Indians, Native Hawaiians, and Amerindians in Guyana. But in many ways my concern is much larger. It is all too easy, in critiques of ongoing U.S. settler colonialism, to accuse diasporic migrants, queers, and people of color for participating in and benefiting from indigenous loss of lands, cultures, and lives and subsequently to position indigenous otherness as abject and all other Others as part of the problem, as if they could always consent to or refuse such positions or consequences of history. And though I do critique the elisions and logics that have continued to inform settler colonial politics that have remained deeply rooted within liberal humanism's investments in the individual, in the singular, and in the racializations of white possession, I also want to imagine cacophonously, to understand that the historical processes that have created our contemporary moment have affected everyone at various points along their transits with and against empire. If colonialism has forced the native to "cathect the space of the Other on his home ground" as Spivak tells us, then imperialism has forced settlers and arrivants to cathect the space of the native as their home.[52] In drawing this distinction, my goal is to first activate indigeneity as a condition of possibility within cultural studies and critical theory and then deploy it to avoid the syllogistic traps of equivalencies on the one hand and the economies of racism, homophobia, sexism, and classism that continue to order the place of peoples on indigenous home grounds on the other. Such an approach, I hope, may provide possible entry points into critical theories that do not sacrifice indigenous worlds and futures in the pursuit of the now of the everyday. The pole is still leaning, and there is still further to go. How we get there depends on how we interpret the cacophonies colonialism has left us in the transit of empire.

Is and Was

Poststructural Indians without Ancestry

*But after all the only conclusion they made was that as we had so much
to do with the sun and the rest of the planets whose motions we were
constantly watching by day and night, and which we had informed them
we were guided by on the ocean, we must either have come from thence, or
be some other way particularly connected with those objects . . .*

John Ledyard, *Journal of Captain Cook's Last Voyage*

"Let the Stars Bear Trouble"

In 1768 Captain James Cook sailed towards the Pacific islands of Tahiti,
Aotearoa, and Australia on the good ship *Endeavor* in search of a southern continent and, perhaps more aspirationally, a way to map the universe.
While there is debate as to what colonial contrivance provided the primal impetus to unfurl the sails of the *Endeavor,* Nicholas Thomas suggests that it was the Royal Society's desire to observe the transit of the
planet Venus across the face of the sun that served as the primary motivation, at least initially, for the mission.[1] The transit of Venus is a rare
occurrence—approximately every one hundred and twenty years, Venus
will pass in front of the sun. A second transit occurs eight years later, and
then it is another one hundred and twenty years before the paired transits
reoccur. The eighteenth-century transit pair created a frenzy within the
scientific circles of the European enlightenment. The 1761 transit sent over
one hundred and twenty European astronomers to sixty-two sites around
the globe, including the island of St. Helena, the Cape of Good Hope, New-
foundland, Siberia, and California, to observe the celestial event. Some
of the participants included John Winthrop, professor of mathematics at
Harvard; Charles Mason and Jeremiah Dixon, who would later demarcate
the eponymous boundary line between Pennsylvania and Maryland; and

Charles Green, who would later travel with Captain Cook into the Pacific. The 1769 transit sent one hundred and fifty-one observers to seventy-seven locations around the globe.[2]

The hope in the observation of the Venus transit was that it might help unlock the key to the universe's mapping and offer astronomers the ability to calculate distances between celestial bodies in earth's home galaxy. That this was the purpose, or cover, for what followed Cook reveals, I think, something telling about the nature of British and American colonialism and imperialism that remained allied even during the family squabble that was the American Revolution. The American colonists declared their independence from Britain; but Benjamin Franklin and several other U.S. founding fathers invested themselves and their future nation in Cook's Pacific voyages, going so far as to issue Cook an American passport in March 1779 that would allow him safe passage through the naval battles of the Atlantic. Not content with the boundaries imposed by gravity, oceans, or ice, Europeans sought possession of all their eyes could see. "This act of looking," Nicholas Thomas writes, "was the chief purpose of Cook's voyage."[3]

There were other purposes for Cook's Pacific voyages, which took place between 1768 and 1780. Launched under the auspices of scientific discoveries—whether preventing once and for all the scurvy that plagued sailors during the months-long voyages through the Pacific; mapping and filling in the void that disturbed the need for a *terra australis incognita* revealed; listening for evidence of polyphony within indigenous *mele, waiata,* and chants; or opening negotiations with indigenous peoples to initiate colonial acquisition of lands and markets to underwrite future commercial interests—Cook's initial mission to record the transit of Venus inaugurated a wave of Pacific invasions that would sweep missionaries, merchants, convicts, and military occupations into the lives and lands of the Pacific peoples. But before all that could happen, Captain Cook had to introduce in those indigenous worlds a restructuring that would reshape the land, law, and biopolitics to cater to and maintain the Barthean mythologies of white subjectivity that Geonpul scholar Aileen Moreton-Robinson has identified as the rationalizing structures of governmentality and property ownership within the logics of settler colonialism.[4]

Within imperial critical, literary, and cultural productions, Cook has always been spectral. He is a haunted figure, deified by the Western mind and fore-shrouded by his death even at the beginning of his journey to chase after Venus in her sky. Debates in anthropology, historiography, and cultural studies have overdetermined Cook's "apotheosis," his so-called ascension to god-like status in the eyes of the Hawaiians who reportedly identified him as Lono, to the extent that the secondary meaning of the word—to cross over into death—is forgotten or displaced in European attempts to anoint him a deity.[5] In addressing Cook's oft-debated apotheosis, Kanaka Maoli scholar Noenoe K. Silva reminds us that "the incommensurability of the two terms ... could erase the debate over whether or not Cook was perceived as a god: that is, Cook may or may not have been perceived as the akua Lonoikamakahiki but this fact bears little relation to what English-language speakers of the time meant by 'god.'"[6] The one thing that remains constant in the slip between English and Hawaiian understandings of "god" and "akua," however, is that Cook's apotheosis, whether he was ever rendered a deity by Hawaiians or whether he just imagined himself to be so in his own mind, resides in his liminality between life and death.

Cook's expeditions haunt the nation-building logics of the age of Enlightenment, and although he is not usually considered to be tied to a particularly American project of imperialism, his voyages began as prelude to the Declaration of Independence and his death heralded a world transformed, in which "Indians," "savages," land, and possession would figure across Atlantic and Pacific worlds and constrain and figure how race, colonialism, and imperialism become the primary distinguishing features of settler imperialisms born out of and invested in multicultural liberal democracy. By tracing the mnemonic constellations that underwrite U.S. imperialism and twenty-first-century wars, I hope to consider the problem indigeneity poses to the analyses of a "postcolonial" and imperial United States and to the larger field of poststructuralist theory. Indigenous peoples, our ongoing colonization, and our historical dispossessions and genocide continue to be pushed toward a vanishing point within critical theory and diaspora studies at the same time that our presence calls into question, disturbingly so for some, progressivist politics that continue to produce race and equality as the primary sites for strategic engagement within participatory democracy.

Part of the problem is that empire in the United States is pushed to the vanishing point of the present. The United States sits on the precipice, where empire either is now manifested in a deterritorialized sovereignty or is on the verge of apocalyptic environmental collapse.[7] Indeed, the question of empire within U.S.-based cultural studies, and especially when that question has intersected with American postcolonial studies, has had a pervasively conflicted provenance. After Edward Said published *Orientalism* in 1978, theories arose to confront the cultural legacies of racism and colonialism, especially within the cosmopole, and scholars also returned to question the demarcation of when, exactly, U.S. empire began. Or whether it ever really did. Or whether that empire, if it had indeed emerged, was such a bad thing after all. "Empire," Michael Hardt and Antonio Negri announce, "is materializing before our very eyes."[8]

While there has been much debate about how, where, and upon whose historical oppression to locate the rise of U.S. imperialism, most scholars point to the Spanish-American War of 1898 and the U.S. acquisition of the Philippines, Puerto Rico, Cuba, and Guam; or perhaps they push along the edges of that date back to 1865 and the end of the Civil War; or maybe they identify 1846 and the Mexican-American War as the generally accepted historical moments when something significant shifted within U.S. cultures of dominance, though Alexis de Tocqueville had even before that framed the United States as exceptional in its project. What that shift entailed depends upon the lens through which one approaches the question and definition of empire. As postcolonial studies in the 1980s and 1990s challenged the colonialist historiographies, cultural dominance, and literary canons of the imperial centers, U.S.-based cultural studies began to locate colonialism and imperialism within the United States as it played out on the bodies of its citizens and those it excluded from citizenship, as metaphor and analogy for systemic oppressions at the site of exception. What emerged as a punctuating refrain, however, was the pervasive idea that the United States could be construed as imperialistic only at the moment it became interested in militarily violating the borders of other nation-states or acquiring overseas territories at the turn of the twentieth century. Simultaneously, and here inflected by the intellectual and philosophical works of prominent nonwhite, queer, and feminist thinkers, scholars began to point to the ways the United States transformed, albeit superficially at the end of the Civil War, into a sovereign that imperialistically dominated those who were now its own citizens.

While I am admittedly summarizing the debates about empire in the United States rather broadly, I do so to draw attention to the recurrent assumptions that inform discussions of imperialism and postcolonialism within U.S. academic centers. Along the way, especially during the Columbian quincentennial in the 1990s, a number of notable scholars have challenged the first iterations of American studies that naturalized U.S. exceptionalism, formed within the frontier logics of Frederick Jackson Turner and Theodore Roosevelt, as anything but colonization and empire. Amy Kaplan is perhaps the most cited for her analysis of how American exceptionalism functions within the nation to deny the reality of U.S. imperialism, if not to recast the nation as anti-imperialist altogether.[9] From without, postcolonial theory reproduces exceptionalism, according to Kaplan, by collapsing and reifying the United States into "the West" on the one hand or by treating the continental expansion of the United States "as an entirely separate phenomenon from European colonialism of the nineteenth century."[10] For Peter Hulme exceptionalism serves as a perpetual siting of the United States as future, new. The current preoccupations with the neocolonial power the United States maintains within its hemisphere of influence continue to inflect the place/non-place of the United States within the purview of postcolonial studies. However, debates about its inclusion into the field, according to Hulme, serve to challenge, trouble, and stretch definitions of colonialism and comparative studies.[11]

Though the preceding discussion captures some of the assumptions that have largely shaped the presence and absence of the United States within the domain of postcolonial studies, another refrain has emerged more recently to make empire a predominantly post–Cold War, postmodern phenomenon in what might properly be described as "the fierce urgency of now"—a phrase that originated with Martin Luther King Jr. and defined Barack Obama's 2008 presidential campaign.[12] As scholars articulate rising concerns about how sovereignty functions at the sites of the bio- and necropolitics that define the violences of late modernity, critiques of U.S. empire are tied increasingly to an urgent twenty-first-century present.[13] Embedded in the nation-state's ability to justify states of exception and global wars for democracy as well as to enact the security state against terror are debates about the logics of "civilization" against "savagery" and the limits of that same state to redress injury. As the war against terror continues unabated, the empire of the "now" is temporally tied to the twentieth and twenty-first centuries, in part because the dénouement of this long century has seen the debates that emerged in Europe after World War I and II and the violences of totalitarianism that followed them, and it witnessed the dismantling of European imperial holdings. It has also been defined by antiracist, queer, and anticolonial scholarship and activism that linked the international struggles against imperialism to the domestic struggles for social justice within the nation-state. The twenty-first century has opened with what Jasbir Puar has described as "a commitment to the global dominant ascendancy of whiteness that is implicated in the propagation of the United States as empire," a commitment that has underwritten post-9/11 affective homonationalist investment in the U.S. "war on terror."[14] Judith Butler figures the barbarism of civilization not as aberrant, "but rather the cruel and spectacular logic of U.S. imperial culture as it operates in the context of its current wars."[15] Paul Gilroy moves the discussion of imperialism further into an anticipated post-empire frame even as he emphasizes the necessity to continually refract how "the imperial and colonial past continues to shape political life in the overdeveloped-but-no-longer-imperial countries" in order to create a multiculture that resists what Gilroy terms the "race thinking" of imperialist regimes and moves toward planetary conviviality.[16]

It seems safe to say that this question of when has haunted postcolonial and American studies as much as the question of who and where and has often foreclosed indigenous peoples in the Americas, Caribbean, and Pacific as having already been acknowledged without actually making them active presences. I do not say this lightly, knowing that in fact most people who study imperialism remember Christopher Columbus's discovery, Robinson Crusoe's shipwreck, Caliban's swearing, and Captain Cook's apotheosis as inaugural narratives on the imperial world stage that set in motion the processes that underwrite current global politics. And yet, perhaps because these representational logics are multiply constitutive, indigenous peoples in Atlantic and Pacific new world geographies remain colonized as an ongoing lived experience that is not commensurable with the stories the postcolonial, pluralistic multiculture wants to tell of itself. In other words, indigenous peoples are located outside temporality and presence, even in the face of the very present and ongoing colonization of indigenous lands, resources, and lives.

Despite scholars' acknowledgments of the coterminous processes of imperialism and colonialism located along the axes of racism, capitalism, and territorial expansion, indigenous peoples, especially in lands now occupied by the United States, continue to serve primarily as signposts and grave markers along the roads of empire. At this point, the regrettable colonization and genocide of American Indians is a truth almost universally acknowledged within postcolonial and American studies, and simultaneously effaced and deferred, despite the work American Indian and indigenous scholars have done to change that fact. In the same essay that critiques exceptionalism and the absence of empire in American studies, Kaplan decenters Perry Miller's discussion of the errand into the American Indian "wilderness" to focus instead on the "jungles" in Africa that serve as Miller's crystallization of the meaning of America even as she notes how other scholars tend to erase Indians from their scope of inquiry altogether. And even as Peter Hulme argues for the inclusion of America within post-colonial studies because 1492 marked the advent of European settlement in the new world, he writes that "as a postcolonial nation, the United States continued to colonize North America, completing the genocide of the Native population begun by the Spanish and the British."[17] The teleological and eschatological narrative of postcolonial theory includes indigenous peoples as the ultimate deferral—that of wilderness as metonymy for indigenous presence on the one hand and that of past perfect completion and death on the other.

This chapter is my attempt to consider how and why that might be the case.

Between Chaos and the Untimely

Jacques Derrida begins *Writing and Difference* with a quotation from Gustave Flaubert: "'It might be that we are all tattooed savages since Sophocles. But there is more to Art than the straightness of lines and the perfection of surfaces. Plasticity of style is not as large as the entire idea. . . . We have too many things and not enough forms.'"[18] Derrida's concern with Flaubert in "Force and Signification" is a concern with "phantoms of energy, 'ideas' 'larger than the plasticity of style'" where Flaubert "is sighing, 'Alas! not enough forms'" to contain all the things for which there are not forms.[19] While Derrida is interested here in setting forth the interrelation between reading and writing, form and meaning, creativity and criticism as a means to push beyond structuralism's totality of form, which supposes meaning is found in the lines that are drawn structurally, he is also setting the stage for elaborating deconstruction as attention to enunciation and interpretation. "Meaning must await being said or written in order to inhabit itself, and in order to become, by differing from itself, what it is: meaning."[20] At the same time, he begins to consider how presence and absence function as acts of interpretation when he writes that "only *pure absence*—not the absence of this or that, but the absence of everything in which all presence is announced—can *inspire*, in other words, can *work*, and then make one work."[21] It is this notion of work that Gayatri Spivak uses to pull deconstruction toward postcolonial critique as "the active resistance to the inexorable calculus of globalization."[22] To understand *difference* and *différance*, difference and deferral, within Derrida's riposte to structuralism is to understand that, according to Spivak, "the elaboration of a definition as a theme or an argument was a pushing away" of "all that is was not" even as that which was pushed away remains as trace or supplement.[23] In "Freud and the Scene of Writing," Derrida links the supplement to the symptomatic return of the repressed, defining it as what "seems to be added as a plentitude to a plentitude, is equally that which compensates for a lack (*qui supplée*)."[24] In order words, a surplus overcompensation.

But what of the "tattooed savages" that both Flaubert and Derrida announce but who remain unacknowledged throughout the rest of the text? How might we approach the present absence, the supplemental gap, of their signification? Derrida's body of work questions how Western thought and philosophy have privileged logocentrism and speech as the foundational principles of meaning—it is a system that, according to Derrida, has depended upon the assumption that *logos* is linear, stable, and reliant upon a master-signifier to order meaning. Derrida's critique of logocentrism at the heart of deconstruction opens for literary scholars instability, movement, doubling, and tension as it looks to how writing depends upon repression of "that which threatens presence and the mastering of absence."[25] The verb "to be" as the presence of the present within Western philosophy gestures, Derrida suggests, toward something else, something prior to the act of enunciation. That prior calls into tension the non-presence of that present and the absent Other, past and future, against whom the "present" aligns itself to come into Being. And it raises concerns about the stakes of all presence that depends always already upon that which is absent. The "tattooed savages" function as a prior to *Writing and Difference,* as an ancillary presence that is necessary to make Western philosophy a possible category of consideration. While tattooed savages may evoke and remain as the trace of Claude Lévi-Strauss's work that Derrida discusses later in the essay "Structure, Sign, and Play," as Gerald Vizenor observes, "the Indian," here in the guise of the tattooed savages, "is a mundane romance, the advertisement of the other in narratives."[26] As presence and absence, "tattooed savages" play on the edges of Derrida's text as signs of raw, primal irrationality, primitivism, and myths of dominance.

They might also be said, as savages, to signify the necessary supplement that continually haunts the edges of any evocation of civilization or Western thought, whose destiny, Derrida says in "Force and Signification," "is to extend its domains while the boundaries of the West are drawn back."[27] Alternatively, they might be said to serve, in Žižekian terms, as an element that is "in excess of the global meaning of the work ... which do[es] not fit this meaning, although it is not clear what additional meaning they bring."[28] They stand at the site of lack. In other words, Derrida's "tattooed savages" (by way of Flaubert) remain as an "impossible utterance" that, much like saying "I am dead," is "foreclosed."[29] As David Kazanjian observes, within Western philosophy, and Kant in particular, indigenous peoples reside in the supplement, in the radical alterity of the deferred, continually evoked as counterpoint and difference to an Enlightenment that depends upon "natural man" and rights, speech and history to make meaning and to underwrite dominance and discovery. Characterizing the rhetorical consequence of Kant's evocation of the "Iroquois" in *The Critique of Judgment*, Kazanjian argues that the "verbal oscillation" of the text "forges a certain, provisional equality between the authorial voice and the examples of the cynic, the critic, and the utopian, with whom Kant deigns to identify if only fleetingly, and a certain, matter-of-fact hierarchy between that voice and the Iroquois sachem, in whose role the text's 'I' prefers not to imagine itself."[30]

At the borders between structuralism, poststructuralism, and deconstruction and in Derrida specifically, as Vizenor notes, "the simulation of the *indian* is the absence of the native, and that absence is a presence of the *other*, the eternal scapegoat, but not a native past; the native is a trace of presence."[31] It is then not insignificant that as signifier, the word "tattoo" entered European worlds and lexicons through Captain Cook's Pacific voyages that transliterated the Tahitian word into signification as "tattow."[32] As sign, "tattoo" bears its trace at the nexus between Western systems of knowledge production that seek to solidify its onto-epistemological meaning into "discovery," "mastery," and "savagery," and the Pacific ontologies of genealogy, kinship, and embodied relationships. Its evocation in Flaubert and Derrida is, to borrow from Aileen Moreton-Robinson, more about "western myth making" than Pacific ontologies.[33]

As traces within twenty-first-century articulations of U.S. empire even where they are always already foreclosed as already known, already completed, indigenous peoples serve a similar mythological function to cohere through deferral the United States as a multicultural liberal democracy with anticolonial, anti-imperialist origins that continue on a smooth curve of perfecting inclusivity. In this same vein, as Giorgio Agamben, Lauren Berlant, Wendy Brown, Achille Mbembe, Elizabeth Povinelli, and Judith Butler articulate in their theorizations of the logics of sovereignty that enact and reproduce themselves through the exception, the camp, that dialectically links democracy and fascism, Flaubert, and Derrida by extension, are also gesturing toward an after to Sophocles, to *Antigone* and *Oedipus,* in which we might all be said to become savages now.[34] This notion of becoming savage is what I call the transit of empire, a site through which the United States, with ties to Enlightenment and Victorian colonialisms, propagates itself through a paradigmatic "Indianness" tied now to the global ascendency of liberalism. As indigenous scholars have argued, inclusion into the multicultural cosmopole, built on top of indigenous lands, does not solve colonialism: that inclusion is the very site of the colonization that feeds U.S. empire. But the function of the "tattooed savages after Sophocles" is more than just myth making and more than proof of the lie of inclusion. The presence of the quote at the beginning of Derrida's text signifies a priori the idea of the savage and the "Indian" that serves as the ground and pre-condition for structuralism and formalism, as well as their posts-. The "tattooed savage" and "Indian" supplements persist as trace, and become an undeconstructable core within critical theories that attempt to dismantle how knowledge, power, and language function.

Despite the interventions of scholars in American studies and American Indian studies, the American mythologies of a sequential narrative that traverses wilderness to frontier to plantation to emancipation to cosmopolitanism and finally to imperialism linger at the heart of other discursive and philosophic fields. Philip J. Deloria, the first American Indian scholar to become president of the American Studies Association, made this analogy in his 2008 address: "Mark Twain is to James Fenimore Cooper as Amy Kaplan is to Perry Miller (and by extension, 1940s and 1950s American studies)."[35] The sequential curve of progress where subsequent generations advance and reflect back upon the past performs a normative evolutionary progression, and yet within Deloria's analogy, a subtle critique lingers since each of the analogical pairs depends upon a reiteration of Indianness at its core within literary nationalism and academic critique. The historical narrative American studies repeats to itself is that of a journey into a wilderness defined by whiteness from which the nation emerges as a multicultural, multihistorical cosmopole where convergences and divergences against normativity feed nonrepresentational politics and resistances.

But in order to understand the foundational paradigmatic Indianness that circulates within the narratives U.S. empire tells itself, even as it strives to overcome and distance itself from such dependency, it is necessary to turn here to another poststructuralist movement that has become ascendant within diasporic and queer studies. In *A Thousand Plateaus*, Gilles Deleuze and Félix Guattari reframe Derrida's concern with the verb "to be" with the additional chain "and . . . and . . . and."[36] Their work maps out possibilities for rhizomatic movements, de/re/territorializations, and nomadic assemblages in flattening and smoothing plateaus that give way to new lines of flight and new nomadologies as a way to resist the arborescence of master-signifiers, *logos*-centered thought, and subjectified historiographies. Drawing upon Leslie Fiedler's *The Return of the Vanishing American*, they write:

America is a special case. . . . directions in America are different: the search for arboresence and the return to the Old World occur in the East. But there is the rhizomatic West, with its Indians without ancestry, its ever-receding limit, its shifting and displaced frontiers. There is a whole American "map" in the West, where even the trees form rhizomes. America reversed the directions: it put its Orient in the West, as if it were precisely in America that the earth came full circle, its West is the edge of the East.[37]

America proceeds, they argue, by "internal exterminations and liquidations," in which capitalism is not just capitalism but "neocapitalism by nature," and capital flows in channels to reorient profit in ways that touch individuals no matter how they are invested in or divested of it. In the process, "it invents its eastern face and western face, and reshapes them both—all for the worst."[38]

To their delineation of a Janus America that is rhizomatic as it pushes westward and by supplement eastward, Amy Kaplan's work provides a necessary additive.[39] In her book analyzing the rise of U.S. imperialism, Kaplan attempts to provide a larger frame in which to contextualize U.S. empire along a similarly Deleuzian frontier between foreign and domestic, home assemblages and undifferentiated expanding horizons, by reactivating black/white race relations and North/South axes as the foundational intimate sites for U.S. representational logics of empire. To focus on the westward march of the United States, according to Kaplan, is to risk performing a teleological narrative of empire that "overlooks how intimately the issues of slavery and emancipation and relations between blacks and whites were intertwined at each stage of U.S. imperial expansion."[40] Her discussion of U.S. imperialism explores instead "how the representations of U.S. imperialism were mapped not through a West/East axis of frontier symbols, but instead through a North/South axis around the issue of slavery, Reconstruction, and Jim Crow segregation."[41] The tensions between West/East, North/South, and East/West are instructive here, because they are, ultimately, U.S. national geographies demarcated by similar elisions and competing cacophonies of race, colonialism, and imperialism that enjamb settlers, arrivants, and natives into a competition for hegemonic signification.

Kaplan's West/East, North/South mapping is telling here as well. If she is read through Chickasaw, Choctaw, Cherokee, Muscogee Creek, and Seminole histories, it appears that Kaplan avoids considering that Indians inhabited those Southern lands in her attempts to move towards a Gramscian subaltern critique that transforms West/East (and note Kaplan uses that global construction rather than the East/West movement of U.S. colonial occupation of indigenous lands) into the North/South globalization that is the hallmark of postcolonial theory. In her attempts to circumvent the teleological trap of U.S. frontiers that elides, she claims, issues of race at the heart of U.S. empire, Kaplan runs the risk of replicating another teleology that affectively invests progressivism in the dialectics of race that supersede colonialism as the site of originary violence. Her argument that conquest "cannot be understood separately from the expansion of slavery and the struggle for freedom" is in its reverse also true, that slavery cannot be understood separately from the colonization and theft of indigenous lands that provided struggles for freedom their staging ground.[42] The distinction here is not so much that one prohibits the other or that framing the colonization of indigenous peoples as foundational to U.S. empire repeats a teleological narrative of Manifest Destiny and racial erasure; it is more that U.S. imperialism relied upon both horizontal and vertical axes of colonization, slavery, racism, North, South, East, and West to structure and suture itself to the notion that its very foundational democracy was antithetical to colonialism and imperialism, slavery and incarceration.

Deleuze and Guattari also formulate America, and its becoming-minor literatures, in surprisingly arborescent ways that reflect the narrative American studies still tells itself even as scholars critique the United States and decenter the processes of constructing and reconstructing the field of study. Drawing on the paradigmatic Indian wilderness to encapsulate an America in which arboresence becomes rhizomatic, *A Thousand Plateaus* performs a global, nomadic reframing in which the frontier becomes, again, Frederick Jackson Turner's site of transformation, possibility, and mapping.[43] As Michael J. Shapiro has noted, maps in their cartographic form "represent the modern state's persistent ontological project" that is by its very nature a violent encounter.[44] And while Deleuze and Guattari's thought requires what Shapiro describes as "uncommon sense" and, as a result, positions mapping and frontiers within the rhizome as the process through which to proliferate dominant and resistant overlapping deterritorializations and reterritorializations into motion, and ultimately smooth space out of striated hierarchical order, such processes, it must be acknowledged, are also colonialist even in non-cartographic form.[45] The maps of settler colonialism were always already proliferative, the nation-state's borders were always perforated, and the U.S. lines of flight across the treaties with indigenous nations were always rhizomatic and fluid rather than hierarchical, linear, and coherent, located not just in the nation-state but within the individual settlers and arrivants who saw indigenous lands as profit, fortune, and equality. In many ways, that is their point. Deleuze and Guattari re/deterritorialize America as the world, coming full circle to find its west in its east and its east in its west, a worlding anew, in Gayatri Spivak's terms, that decenters all static, grounded belongings and locates them instead in becomings: becoming-Indian, becoming-woman, becoming-America. At the least, it can be said that *A Thousand Plateaus* answers Cherokee, Choctaw, and Irish American scholar Louis Owens's concerns with the geographic homonym of "Indian" in his critique of postcolonial theory in "As If an Indian Were Really an Indian" with a "Yes they are!"[46]

But the matter of the rhizomatic American West's "Indians without ancestry" still lingers alongside Derrida's "tattooed savages." If they have no genealogy and exist sui generis, how might we account for the historical and colonialist traces that accompany their appearance in Deleuze and Guattarri's theory as sign, while retaining sympathy for the impulse to nonrepresentational philosophy that aligns in a multiplicity of regimes of signs? Elsewhere, Gilles Deleuze writes:

The pharaoh's tomb, with its inert central chamber at the base of the pyramid, gives way to more dynamic models: from the drifting of continents to the migrations of peoples, these are all means through which the unconscious maps the universe. *The Indian model replaces the Egyptian:* the Indians pass into the thickness of the rocks themselves, where aesthetic form is no longer identified with the commemoration of a departure or an arrival, but with the creation of paths without memory.[47]

The Indian model, like the nomad, assembles for Deleuze the site of movement, escape, difference—it is a stateless war machine, existing outside of and rupturing the state. The rhizome, which is described as an orchid in relation with the wasp, their becomings and unbecomings, is transversal scramble, antigenealogical and always proceeding through re/deterritorializations by both the orchid and the wasp.[48] The rhizome, for Deleuze and Guattari, stands in Eastern, Oceanic counterpoint to the linear tree—arborescence—of descent, seed, and Western agriculture, and is short-term rather than long historical memory.[49] One must remember, though, that Gayatri Spivak's question "Can the Subaltern Speak?" was first posed as a critique of Deleuze and Michel Foucault, who seemed in their theorizations to suggest that the subaltern already was speaking through them, through the ventriloquism of the left intellectual.[50] In an aside about the "ferocious motif of 'deterritorialization' in Deleuze and Guattari," Spivak adds, "we have already spoken of the sanctioned ignorance that every critic of imperialism must chart."[51] The Indian model, which disappears into rocks and creates paths without memory, serves as an ontological trap within theorizations that follow those paths to articulate alternative spaces outside processes of recognitions and states, arrivals and departures. What we imagine to be outside of and rupturing to the state, through Deleuze, already depends upon a paradigmatic Indianness that arises from colonialist discourses justifying expropriation of lands through removals and genocide.

However, Deleuze and Guattari's "Indians without ancestry" and their "Indian model" move contradictorily as doubles, multiples along other lines of flight within their work and assemble, on the one hand, as nomads and war machines and serve, on the other, as examples of regulating and normativizing faciality within imperialist signifying regimes of signs. For instance, in Plateau 5 they evoke Robert Lowie's assessment of Crow and Hopi approaches to infidelity and Claude Lévi-Strauss's preface to Don Talayesva's

Sun Chief to discuss the paranoia of the circular, imperial despot-god who "brandishes the solar face that is his entire body, as the body of the signifier" that is the hallmark of what they term the *signifying* regime of the sign.[52] Existing in relation to the *primitive presignifying*, the *countersignifying*, and the *postsignifying* regimes (among others), the *signifying* regime is the site of the master-signifier, the priest or psychoanalyst, who uses faciality as masked deception and serves as the model for the surveillance of the imperial despotic regime that orders concentric circles around the same panoptic center of signification that reigns over "every domestic squabble, and in every State apparatus."[53] It is applicable "to all subjected, arborescent, hierarchical, centered groups: political parties, literary movements, psychoanalytic associations, families, conjugal units, etc."[54] It is the site of the spiral that is not, for Deleuze and Guattari, rhizomatic but regulated:

> The Hopi jump from one circle to another, or from one sign to another on a different spiral. One leaves the village or the city, only to return. The jumps may be regulated not only by presignifying rituals but also by a whole imperial bureaucracy passing judgment on their legitimacy. . . . Not only are they regulated, but some are prohibited: Do not overstep the outermost circle, do not approach the innermost circle . . .[55]

Christopher L. Miller has criticized Deleuze and Guattari for their ethnographic and representational authority here that allows them to speak as and for the Hopi "as if they . . . either were in total control of Hopi thought or were Hopi themselves. Through the power of anthropological borrowing, the authors have achieved a mind-meld with an alien people."[56] The Hopi (who became the site of a national affective investment in multicultural liberal democracy as the 2008 U.S. presidential campaign circulated the faux-Hopi prophecy "We are the ones we've been waiting for") are transformed into the logocentric imperial order that cannot tolerate any systemic line of flight.[57] As the logocentric regime, the Hopi can only exclude, scapegoat, curse, or put to flight that which threatens their structures.[58] In other words, the Hopi in this plane become the colonizing, imperial regime that sacrifices and expels. "Your only choice" in this system, according to Deleuze and Guattari, "will be between a goat's ass and the face of the god, between sorcerers and priests."[59]

Much can be made here of the ironies of the jumping Hopi who is made to serve in Deleuzian thought as the example of the imperial, colonial panoptic order that is abjected back onto the Hopi in order for Deleuze and Guattari to provide a critique of Freud and the psychoanalytic mode of interpretation. Perversely, however, Deleuze and Guattari, in their suspect choice to frame the Hopi as an example of the imperial regime of signs, acknowledge something that the colonizing United States has not, in spite of the treaties and land holdings the Hopi have made and retained—they see the Hopi as a State. And certainly, Deleuze and Guattari's delineation here could be deployed to demonstrate the degree to which indigenous nationalisms depend upon signifying regimes, normativities, and assertions of sovereignty grounded in the ability to include/exclude that is found in the executive and juridical pronunciations of the state of emergency that Giorgio Agamben discusses in *Homo Sacer*.[60] But that is not the function of their Hopi example. Rather, the turn to the Hopi serves a structuralist move that stands in the breach of the real of their own colonialist discursive evocation.

The Hopi, though, are not fixed and static in Deleuze and Guattari but are found on other planes and in other assemblages that move among "Indians without ancestry," "the Indian model" that replaces the Egyptian one, and the "solar face" of the imperial *signifying regime* that tortures and expels. Returning to Leslie Fiedler, Deleuze and Guattari articulate "the poles of the American Dream: cornered between two nightmares, the genocide of the Indians and the slavery of the blacks, Americans constructed a psychically repressed image of the black as force of affect, of the multiplication of affects, but a socially repressed image of the Indian as subtlety of perception, perception made increasingly keen and more finely divided, infinitely slowed or accelerated."[61] This infinitely slowed or accelerated perception stems directly from their use of Carlos Castaneda for understanding the "socially repressed image of the Indian." Carlos Castaneda represents the becoming-Indian as a pathological colonizing condition of faux-Indian, a pathology that haunts any left intellectual who steps forward to ventriloquize the speaking Indian by transforming the becoming- into *replacing*-Indian. And yet, Deleuze and Guattari invest the fraudulent indigenous, drugged world of peyote and shamanism that is Castaneda with a presignifying real that has a curious ability.[62] They write:

> One of the many things of profound interest in Castaneda's books, under the influence of drugs, or other things, and of a change of

atmosphere, is precisely that they show how the Indian manages to combat the mechanisms of interpretation and instill in the disciple a presignifying semiotic, or even an asignifying diagram: Stop! You're making me tired! Experiment, don't signify and interpret! Find your own places, territorialities, deterritorializations, regime, lines of flight! Semiotize yourself instead of rooting around in your prefab childhood and Western semiology.[63]

Further, the Indian has the ability to "'stop the world' … [as] an appropriate rendition of certain awareness in which the reality of everyday life is altered because the flow of interpretation, which ordinarily runs interruptedly, has been stopped by a set of circumstances alien to the flow."[64] Deleuze and Guattari's imagined "Indian" functions as a site of interruption through eruption, the introduction of schizophrenia into psychoanalyis. The "Indian" becomes an event, an "alien," instilling the presignifying semiotic into the despotic signifying regime. Despite its origins in the "primitivist" thought of Western philosophy, the presignifying regime serves in *A Thousand Plateaus* as the delineation of a system of signs characterized by polyvocality, dance, proximity to nature, and "a plurilinear, multidimensional semiotic that wards off any kind of signifying circularity."[65]

The Indian—as a threshold of past and future, regimes of signs, *alea*, becoming, and death—combats mechanisms of interpretation through an asignifying disruption that stops, alters, and redirects flow. This stopping of the world of signification is the same as Derrida's "tattooed savage" at the beginning of deconstruction. The Indian sign is the field through which poststructuralism makes its intervention, and as a result, this paradigmatic and pathological Indianness cannot be circumvented as a colonialist trace. In fact, this colonialist trace is exactly why "the Indian" is so disruptive to flow and to experimentation. Every time flow or a line of flight approaches, touches, or encounters Indianness, it also confronts the colonialist project that has made that flow possible. The choice is to either confront that colonialism or to deflect it. And not being prepared to disrupt the logics of settler colonialism necessary for the *terra nullius* through which to wander, the entire system either freezes or reboots.

It seems slightly ironic, then, that many who pick up Deleuze and Guattari's work use language similar to "Experiment, don't signify and interpret!" to describe the possibilities of reframing the world through affect and affective relationships that move toward the states of enchantment, ecstasy, and the everyday. Brian Massumi's cultivation of deviation and contagion to foster radicalism at the crossroads between science, humanities, and cultural studies contains similar Castanedian staccato imperatives: "Let it. Then reconnect it to other concepts, drawn from other systems, until a whole new system of connection starts to form. Then, take another example. See what happens. Follow the new growth. You end up with many buds. Incipient systems."[66] In a gesture towards "a thousand tiny races" in which he provides an alternative future for race to that of Paul Gilroy's *After Race*, Arun Saldanha writes, "Race should not be eliminated, but *proliferated*, its many energies directed at multiplying racial differences so as to render them joyfully cacophonic."[67] Jasbir Puar's delineation of the biopolitics of the now in *Terrorist Assemblages* depends on

> A cacophony of informational flows, energetic intensities, bodies, and practices that undermine coherent identity and even queer anti-identity narratives . . . assemblages allow for complicities of privilege and the production of new normativities even as they cannot anticipate spaces and moments of resistance, resistance that is not primarily characterized by oppositional stances, but includes frictional forces, discomfiting encounters, and spurts of unsynchronized delinquency.[68]

Each of these cultural studies moments flow from the phrase "Experiment, don't signify and interpret!" that functions as a call for transformational new worlds of relation and relationship that move us toward a joyously cacophonic multiplicity and away from the lived colonial conditions of indigeneity within the postcolonizing settler society.[69]

This Deleuzian and Guattarian motif, even if it acknowledges all the divergent discourses that come into race, gender, sexual, and class assemblages, smoothes once again into uncultivated wilderness that allows any trajectory or cultivation to enter it, but not arise from it. By extension, and even if one cannot access how these evocations of "the Indian" function within the plateaus opened by Deleuze and Guattari, "the Indian" serves as an errant return of the repressed that spreads along its own line of infection once the theory is taken up.[70] For example, Jasbir Puar, by restricting her analysis to the biopolitics of the post-9/11 coming out of U.S. empire as "an event in the Deleuzian sense, privileging lines of flight, an assemblage of spatial and temporal intensities, coming together, dispersing, reconverging," can discuss as sui generis the monster-terrorist-fag that emerges in the twenty-first century as a new phenomenon, despite the Wanted posters in New York the week after 9/11 that compared Osama bin Laden to Geronimo.[71] Additionally, Puar discusses Jessica Lynch as a "heroic girl-next-door" in conversation with a "depraved, cigarette-toting, dark-haired, pregnant and unmarried, racialized" Lynndie England at Abu Ghraib. Puar does not even acknowledge Hopi Lori Piestewa, reportedly the first American Indian woman to die in combat while fighting *for* the United States. Piestewa died in the same attack in which Jessica Lynch was captured, and her absence is a telling amnesia within Puar's discussion of how "nostalgically mourning the loss of the liberal feminist subject" converges "white liberal feminists and white gay men" and "unwittingly reorganizes the Abu Ghraib tragedy around their desires" through the now racialized body of the no longer white Lynndie England.[72] Piestewa's absence is yet another deferral that vanishes the violences done to indigenous women, and those same indigenous soldiers' cathexis of U.S. nationalism and imperialism that signals an indigenationalism compatriot to the homonationalism that Puar defines as "the arrangements of U.S. sexual exceptionalisms [marked] explicitly in relation to the nation" that demobilize queer identities by normativizing certain bodies but not others within the enfranchisements of the state.[73]

To phrase this slightly differently, the Indian is simultaneously, multiply, a colonial, imperial referent that continues to produce knowledge about the indigenous as "primitive" and "savage" otherness within poststructuralist and postcolonial theory and philosophy. As a philosophical sign, the Indian is the transit, the field through which presignifying polyvocality is re/introduced into the signifying regime, and signs begin to proliferate through a series of becomings—becoming-animal, becoming-woman, becoming-Indian, becoming-multiplicity—that serves all regimes of signs. *And* the Indian is a ghost in the system, an errant or virus that disrupts the virtual flows by stopping them, redirecting them, or revealing them to be what they are and will have been all along: colonialist. The Indian, then, is a Deleuzian event within poststructuralism: "To the extent that events are actualized in us," Deleuze writes, "they wait for us and invite us in."[74] For Derrida, as he grieved and mourned the loss of his friend and colleague, and saw in that loss the passing of a generation of thought, the event in Deleuze's work becomes the Event, death, the paradox of humorous conformity of a leaping in place, an apotheosis of will. "'It is in this sense that *Amor fati* is one with the struggle of free men,'" Derrida quotes from Deleuze.[75] Nietzsche's love of fate, the invitation inherent in the will of the event opposes the *ressentiment* of resignation to become the point "at which war is waged against war, the wound would be the living trace of all wounds, and death turned on itself would be willed against all death."[76]

On the threshold, then, of "the necessity with the aleatory, chaos and the *untimely*" that is both the work of Derrida's mourning of Deleuze and the *haksuba* of Southeastern cosmologies that Choctaw scholar LeAnne Howe defines in her work as headache, chaos, the collision of Upper and Lower Worlds initiated by colonialism, the Indian wills against the signifying system.[77] That the Indian represents the violent slamming of worlds in what might otherwise be fluidity and flow helps us frame the problem within a U.S. empire, with ties to Enlightenment liberalism, that continues to transit itself globally along lines put to flight by "the Indian without ancestry" that makes everyone its progeny. It is untimely as a site of the death of signification. That *haksuba* can additionally mean "to be stunned with noise, confused, deafened" signals the degree to which cacophony, whether joyous or colonialist, hinges upon the disruptions caused when "the Indian" collides with the racial, gendered, classed, and sexed normativities of an imperialism that has arisen out of an ongoing settler colonialism.[78] The Southeastern cosmologies of the Chickasaw and Choctaw imagine worlds with relational spirals and a center that does not so much hold as stretches, links, and ties everything within to worlds that look in all directions. It is an ontology that privileges balance, but understands that we are constant movement and exist simultaneously among Upper and Lower Worlds, this world and the next. In her poem "The Place the Musician Became a Bear," Mvskoke poet and musician Joy Harjo sings about how Southeastern Indians have always known "where to go to become ourselves again in the human comedy. / It's the how that baffles, the saxophone can complicate things."[79] Harjo reminds us that there is always a prior "becoming-human" within Southeastern worlds that links us to the complications and improvisations of stars, spirals, and jazz.

Much of the scholarship on U.S. imperialism and its possible postcoloniality sees it as enough to challenge the wilderness as anything but vacant; to list the annihilation of indigenous nations, cultures, and languages in a chain of –isms; and then still to relegate American Indians to the site of the already-doneness that begins to linger as unwelcome guest to the future. This last is particularly relevant to understanding how the United States propagates itself as empire transhemispherically and transoceanically, not just through whiteness, but through the continued settling and colonizing of indigenous peoples' lands, histories, identities, and very lives that implicate all arrivants and settlers regardless of their own experiences of race, class, gender, colonial, and imperial oppressions. My point in tracing the Deleuzian wilderness and the Indian deferred is to detail the ways in which "the Indian" is put to flight within Western philosophical traditions in order to understand how the United States transits itself globally as an imperial project. As Derrida and Deleuze are evoked within affect theories, the "Indian" and "tattooed savages" remain as traces. Any assemblage that arises from such horizons becomes a colonialist one, and it is the work of indigenous critical theory both to rearticulate indigenous phenomenologies and to provide (alter)native interpretative strategies through which to apprehend the colonialist nostalgias that continue to shape affective liberal democracy's investment in state sovereignty as a source of violence, remedy, memory, and grievability.

States of Enchantment

While in Hawai'i and standing on the edges of Kealakekua Bay in July 1866, Mark Twain twinned himself to Captain Cook in an attempt to imagine the violences and fear that "the great circumnavigator" must have felt "struggling in the midst of the multitude of exasperated savages."[80] Just shy of the one hundred year anniversary of Cook's death on February 14, 1778, and in the same month that the United States celebrated its nineteenth birthday—a birthday that had been threatened the last few years by the Civil War—Twain tried to imagine Cook facing down savages, trapped at the edge of the water. "—The," the sentence fragments. "But I discovered that I could not do it," he wrote in *Roughing It*. And though he protested too much his inability to imagine such a scene, given that he spends the next few paragraphs explaining how Kanaka Maoli must have interpreted the event, the fact that he cannot quite approach the violences done to the living Cook is transferred into a fascination with the cannibalistic apotheosis that occurred in Cook's liminality between life and death, man and so-called god: "Perceiving that the people took him for the long vanished and lamented god Lono, he encouraged them in the delusion for the sake of the limitless power it gave him," Twain writes. Once he betrayed "his earthly origin with a groan," Twain continued, the Hawaiians killed him and "his flesh was stripped from the bones and burned (except nine pounds of it which were sent on board the ships)."[81] Cook, whose own name even bears out the trace of what Native Hawaiian poet Brandy Nālani McDougall plays as "to eat, to eat," exists as colonial specter throughout the Pacific and serves in life and death to inaugurate the touristic fascinations and nationalistic narratives that link the Pacific sea of islands to Atlantic imperial sites across an intervening continent that is itself rhizome, oceanic.[82] Cook's surname, then, gives rise to the cannibalistic fetish the Western mind evokes when it thinks of Pacific indigenous worlds.

Cook's expedition, according to Thomas, "was not just a rational plan to fill spaces on a map, but also a symptom of a state of enchantment."[83] The voyage, as well as the man himself, existed between the state of enchantment and the state of possession as a symptom and symptomatic contagion of that which served to first exalt the subjectivity of European nationalism and then project it into lands emptied of any subjectivity except the will of the European imperialist. This idea of enchantment is informed by Sunera Thobani, who explains that "exaltation thus endows ontological coherence and cohesion to the subject *in* its nationality, grounding an abstract humanity into particular governable forms."[84] As exalted subject within Western historiography, Cook's presence inaugurates, according to Aileen Moreton-Robinson, the state of possession dependent on British law to interpellate the exalted subject as the white possessing subject.[85] This state of possession, in which Cook's exalted subjectivity possesses land in the name of the British crown and possesses whiteness as preeminent ownership within the logics of capitalism, is the site of the dialectic of sovereignty that functions similarly to Agamben's state of exception where the state—in contradistinction to indigenous peoples' own ontologies of relationship and power—enacts sovereignty as ontological possession, delineating what is and is not possessed. As death omen and as dead man, Cook, in his state of enchantment as well as his state of possession, exemplified the magical thinking of European imperialism that sought to resurrect "discovered" lands into imperial ownership. The state of enchantment was ultimately the rational plan to empty lands of presence via the discourses of *terra nullius* in order to refill them with British imperial law.

Mark Twain, standing "on the flat rock pressed by Capt. Cook's feet when the blow was dealt which took away his life," becomes a similar exalted subject who enacts a state of nationalistic possession, this time not just through whiteness but through American enchantment.[86] In his account of Cook's death detailed in his letters from Hawai'i that serve as drafts to *Roughing It*, Twain turned not to the official accounts of Cook's death by James King and other British nationals who had accompanied the circumnavigator, but instead to two American sources for his Hawaiian history—John Ledyard's account of Cook's third voyage and James Jackson Jarves's *History of the Hawaiian or Sandwich Islands* (1843). Marine corporal Ledyard was from Connecticut, and before joining Captain Cook on his third voyage, he had attended Dartmouth in the hopes of becoming a missionary to Indians.[87] Often identified as the United States' first great explorer, Ledyard served as inspirational precursor to Thomas Jefferson's plans to send Lewis and Clark westward on the heels of the Louisiana Purchase. In fact, John Ledyard, who was the first Euroamerican to set foot in the Pacific Northwest as Cook made his passage through the region, had hoped to prove the Bering Strait theory shortly after he returned from Hawai'i after Cook's death (and in the process set up a lucrative fur trading business along the way) by walking across Russia, into Alaska, down into the Pacific Northwest, and then eastward across the continent.

For Thomas Jefferson, who sought to secure him permission for such traveling in 1786, Ledyard served as a West/East counterpoint to Lewis and Clark's later voyage East/West into the heart of the continent, a bidirectional Janus imperialism that reflects Deleuze and Guattari's description in *A Thousand Plateaus*.[88] Jefferson's plan would have worked, except that Catherine the Great withdrew her permission when Ledyard was 200 miles away from Kamschatka and had Ledyard deported from the Russian empire. Twain's evocation of Ledyard's accounts allows Twain to exalt and cohere U.S. nationalistic subjectivity at the beginning of white imperial contact with Hawai'i through Ledyard as proxy, and it naturalizes Hawai'i as destined for U.S. dominion in 1866. "Ledyard," Twain writes, was "a Yankee sailor, who was with Cook, and whose journal is considered the most just and reliable account of this eventful period of the voyage."[89] As he considers Ledyard most just and most reliable—read here most *American*—Twain assumes the mantle of American exceptionalism and imperialism through evocations of the impartial justice that is putatively the hallmark of the U.S. founding fathers' democratic vision. In the process, Twain becomes *the* literary personage who cathects U.S. imperialist investment in multiculturalism sited along a black/white continuum, one that erases indigenous colonization altogether.

Amy Kaplan has argued that Mark Twain's investment in Hawai'i caused him to look eastward, and then southward across life and death to return to the uncanny plantations that haunted his childhood in slaveholding Missouri. "Hawaii in fact Americanized Mark Twain," she argues.[90] By allowing Twain to locate his Americanness in Hawai'i through a layering of racial expectation of Southern plantations and blackness into Hawai'i, Kaplan then argues that "Twain both displaced and discovered the origins of his own divided national identity at the intersecting global routes of slavery and empire."[91] Twain's ambivalent literary representations of the antebellum and post-reconstruction South serve as consonance and dissonance to his representations of Hawaiians, who stand as newly configured African Americans struggling with sovereignty, democratic inclusion, enslavement, and savagery. Through his re/constructions of race, Twain becomes the voice of an America struggling to reimagine itself as an inclusive democracy in which all are created equal. In response to Kaplan's discussion of Twain, Western Shoshone scholar Ned Blackhawk has suggested that Twain be read across another imperial transit still functioning alongside the enslaving and emancipatory visions that return to haunt Twain's America:

> "All right, then, I'll go to hell," Twain's most famous character, Huckleberry Finn, decides after deliberating on his friend Jim's continued enslavement; and generations have sought meaning in these hopeful, yearning sentiments. However, as with his portrait of Hawaiians, such visions of potential racial coexistence stand in contradistinction to the "nausea" that Clemens experienced upon encountering Goshute Shoshones. . . . Within a panoply of derisive labels, the most common has been "digger," a debasement of Shoshone gathering practices with strong homophonic resonance with America's most powerful racial epithet, "nigger."[92]

Twain's reference to the Goshute Shoshones—whom he labels "Goshoot Indians" in *Roughing It*—carries another homophone alongside "digger" through which Twain cajoles his readers to go and shoot Indians who stand in as the degraded real to James Fenimore Cooper's imagined literary "red man." "Whenever one finds an Indian tribe," Twain writes in *Roughing It* and in rejection of Cooper, "he has only found Goshoots more or less modified by circumstances and surroundings—but Goshoots, after all."[93] The racialized and genocidal homophones underscore the degree to which Mark Twain's imperial routes depended on a foundational In-dianness to help transit them and inaugurate them around affectability achieved through inclusion and nausea cured by genocide.

At these intersections between postcolonial and U.S. imperial studies, Twain's attitudes towards African Americans and transnational routes of travel are well-acknowledged as ambivalent, and trace through most of his work. His deadpan humor and satirical sketches are typically read as self-reflective and critical of the then-contemporary U.S. discourses about "primitivism," race, and regionalism. What is striking, however, is that his affective response to Indians shifts only in relation to his critique of James Fenimore Cooper, whom he ridicules for investing U.S. literary national-ism in an inaccurate portrait of the "noble red man"—at great peril, too, as the plot to his unfinished *Tom Sawyer and Huck Finn among the Indians* at-tests. Although he was certainly anti-imperialist when it came to the ques-tion of the Philippines after the turn of the twentieth century, Twain often asserted that Hawai'i, like the North American continent, was destined for control by the United States. In part, this predestination had to do with an innate ability that linked Hawaiian people to American Indians—their ability to die.

Just as Twain felt that it was a service to put Indians out of their des-titution through goshooting that would finally and fully trap them in a sanitized and distant past, he observed in the many lectures he gave on "Our Fellow Savages of the Sandwich Isles" that Kanakas "are an odd sort of people, too. They can die whenever they want to. That's a fact. They don't mind dying any more than a jilted Frenchman does. When they take a notion to die they die, and it don't make any difference whether there is anything the matter with them or not, and they can't be persuaded out of it."[94] Documenting the population decrease less than one hundred years after the moment of Cook's arrival, Twain observes: "It isn't the education or civilization that has settled them; it is the imported diseases, and they have all got the consumption and other reliable distempers, and to speak figuratively, they are retiring from business pretty fast. When they pick up and leave we will take possession as lawful heirs."[95] His satire was quick to point out how white civilization was not much different from the con-ditions of "savagery," and he acknowledged the impact missionaries and other settlers had on indigenous peoples. But in the end, the demise of na-tive peoples was inevitable whether deserved or not, and as a result, lamen-table, and necessarily sanitized of any violent intent—indigenous peoples will have to retire from the business of living altogether so that Americans may take up the mantle of possession.

Though it is absolutely necessary to understand Twain through a refraction of southern black/white racial politics, his attitudes towards Indians and other "savages" exist alongside and inform his interpretations of U.S. colonial and imperial destinies. Approximately ninety years after Cook's arrival in Hawai'i, Mark Twain performs an important act of racial and imperial alchemy that transforms the stakes for the racial politics of whiteness within the United States. From 1768 to 1779, the British and American colonial travelers who voyaged through the Pacific sailed through a sea of islands inhabited by peoples they identified as Indians. In Cook's journals, the term "Indian" is used interchangeably with Tahitian, Māori, and Hawaiian. In John Ledyard's account of Cook's death, Indians attack and slay the circumnavigator:

> Acquainting Cook in the mean time of the danger of his situation, and that the Indians in a few minutes would attack him, that he had overheard the man whom he had just stopped from rushing in upon him say that our boats which were out in the harbour had just killed his brother and he would be revenged. Cook attended to what this man said, and desired him to shew him the Indian that had dared to attempt a combat with him, and as soon as he was pointed out Cook fired at him with a blank. The Indian perceived he received no damage from the fire rushed from without the croud a second time, and threatened any one that should oppose him. Cook perceiving this fired a ball, which entering the Indian's groin he fell and was drawn off by the rest.... Cook having at length reached the margin of the water between the fire of the boats waved his hat to cease firing and come in, and while he was doing this a chief from behind stabed him with one of our iron daggers just under the shoulder blade, and passed quite through his body. Cook fell with his face in the water and immediately expired.[96]

Ledyard, who was the first American settler to get a Polynesian tattoo and who penned the account of Cook's demise that Twain felt was the most accurate, wrote in his journal about a Pacific world filled with Indians in a signification process that either attests to the same geographical confusions that informed Christopher Columbus's narratives or speaks to a foundational concept of "Indianness" that aligns it with the savage other that functions as the constitutive rationale for imperial domination. I am inclined to read Cook's and Ledyard's "Indians" through the latter. The racial casting of Pacific Islanders as Indians within the British/American moment of possessive "discovery" serves as an intertextual signpost that is errant from the start. Within Amy Kaplan's North/South U.S. imperial mappings, then, there remains a prior supplement, an a priori and paradigmatic Indianness. As Kaplan argues against the masculinist paradigms of Richard Drinnon and Richard Slotkin, Perry Miller and Leslie Fiedler in order to reorient and engender empire along internal/external domesticities, American empire does not replicate itself through a detachable and remappable "frontier" or "wilderness." Rather, I am arguing as an additive here, it does so through the reproduction of Indianness that exists alongside racializing discourses that slip through the thresholds of whiteness and blackness, inclusion and exclusion, internal and external, that are the necessary conditions of settler colonial sovereignty.

As the night sky and stars themselves are remodeled into English-speaking phenomenologies as imperial and colonial constellations, evidenced in the imperial reconstellating of the Mississippian Starry Hand into Orion, it is fitting then to return to the transit of Venus that Cook set out to observe in 1769 in order to understand how "Indians" function as a transit within U.S. empire and how such an observation might serve to open up methodological approaches for theorizing current global politics sited through indigenous worlds.[97] Not only did Cook's observation of the planet's transit across the face of the sun initiate the Pacific's collision with the Enlightenment liberalisms defined by John Locke, Jean-Jacques Rousseau, Thomas Hobbes, Thomas Paine, and Thomas Jefferson among other Thomases, but the twenty-first century has seen its first transit on June 8, 2004, with the second occurring on June 6, 2012, in a pattern of visibility and trajectory that twins the eighteenth century's imperial transits. Cook's 1769 transit was the second of that century and the last chance for those alive at the time to observe and record the event so they could develop the measurements necessary to map the night sky. The eighteenth-century transits also served to tie Europe to the Pacific Islands imaginatively by linking Europe geographically with Tahiti, Hawai'i, Aotearoa, and Australia through a shared cosmological telemetry and ideal viewing conditions. Cook's observation of the transit from Tahiti's Point Venus, which he named for the occasion, made the globe a world of shared European humanistic and scientific endeavor by providing one of the points on the baseline of the earth necessary to calculate astronomical distances. It also inaugurated a second wave of new world imperialism that depended upon already well-established tropes of Indianness to facilitate the ordering of peoples into imperial landscapes that would be mapped and owned through the logics of colonialism. Mary Louise Pratt describes this type of Enlightenment travel as a process of developing a European "planetary consciousness," and the importance of Cook is that he marks the last formal voyage of external discovery and the shift to interiors.[98] However, those notions of interiority, especially on the North American continent, are inflected already by U.S. nationalistic mappings of lands that cohered and transformed external lands into internal domestic space that now seamlessly exists from the moment the American colonists declared their independence from England.

The Transit of Empire and the Planetary Parallax

As an astronomical event, the transit of Venus is marked by an effect that, given the limits of eighteenth-century astronomy, made it almost impossible to pinpoint the exact moment the transit began and ended. As Cook and others around the world observed together the moment Venus began its journey across the face of the sun, their notes reflected variations in time—differences of seconds to minutes even among viewers at the same location—that made precise calculations of astronomical units from the data difficult. This "black-drop effect," as it became known within those scientific communities, obscured the exact moment Venus fully entered into the sphere of the sun in a distortion that seemed to stretch the planet into a silhouetted band between its own edge and that of the sun. Many observers at the time, Cook included, assumed that the momentary merging and pulling of edges between the two bodies was visible evidence of Venus's atmosphere. However, the effect of Venus's trailing touch of the edge of the sun for moments after full ingress and again as it approaches the edge on egress also results from a distortion that makes silhouetted objects that are brightly backlit appear smaller than they are. The line between the edge of the sun and the edge of Venus, assumed to be the result of atmospheric disturbances and observed as a stretching of the darkened planet, is actually the true size of the planet lingering as a trace.[99] That silhouetted band that stretches between the two bodies, then, is a fraction of the planet made visible at the moment it fully enters into the space of the sun and the moment before it begins the end of its transit. In the sticky stretch between sun and Venus, the trace of the actual Venus remains in spite of the overwhelming totality of the sun's encapsulating embrace.

The second effect, and the one most useful to astronomical observation, is that of parallax—a shift in an observer's perspective of a distant object based on a change in vantage point. By establishing a baseline whose length is known, the unknown length to a distant object can be triangulated based upon the angle of shift between two lines of sight on that known baseline.[100] Eighteenth-century astronomers hypothesized that they could calculate the distance between the earth and the sun by observing the transit of Venus from different points on the earth. Both the 1761 and 1769 transits became the occasion for a race around the globe to position European observers at key locations, in the hopes that the data collected would provide enough information to establish the angle of solar parallax across the earth's radius. Slavoj Žižek offers a different understanding of parallax in his magnum opus *The Parallax View*, defining it as "the illusion of being able to use the same language for phenomena which are mutually untranslatable and can be grasped only in a kind of parallax view, constantly shifting perspective between two points between which no synthesis or mediation is possible." The two points, Žižek emphasizes, are *"two sides* of the same phenomenon which, precisely as two sides, can never meet."[101] In other words, for Žižek parallax is similar to a Möbius strip, where there at first appear to be two sides, but as one traverses it, there is only one side that feeds back into itself.

This parallax differential creates certain dialectical shifts—or what Žižek terms parallax gaps. He structures his argument around three sites of parallax—ontological difference as ultimate parallax (which conditions our access to reality), scientific parallax (which accounts for the gap between phenomenology and scientific explanations), and political parallax (which hinders the creation of common ground through which to mobilize political resistances)—as the sites through which to interrogate biopolitics and class warfare.[102] In order to perceive the difference and to approach the Lacanian Real, Žižek argues that one has to shift perspective to alternate viewing locations and approximate the "Real" in the gap. "The 'truth,'" Žižek explains,

> Is not the "real" state of things, that is, the "direct" view of the object without perspectival distortion, but the very Real of the antagonism

which causes perspectival distortion. The site of truth is not the way "things really are in themselves," beyond their perspectival distortions, but the very gap, passage, which separates one perspective from another, the gap . . . which makes the two perspectives radically *incommensurable.*[103]

The gap between two sides of the same phenomenon "allows us to discern its subversive core" that cuts across the cosmopolitan hybrid/nomad and acknowledges the lived conditions of violence, class, and oppression.[104] Multiple viewing locations of the Real are created, though no single one of them is capable of discerning the Real and there is no possibility of triangulating the Real by taking into consideration all perspectives. Instead, according to Jodi Dean, "the distortion among the differing views . . . indicates the Real of the event. The Realness of the event is what generates the multiplicity, the impossibility of its being encompassed."[105]

Though Žižek wants to recover dialectical materialism through such subversions and shifts, his own work bears a metonymical trace that ties him back to the transit of Venus in pursuit of empire that functions as an errant within the very structures of his own text and chapter headings that depend upon stellar, solar, and lunar parallaxes that emerged from Enlightenment colonialism to map, know, and own the earth and stars. It is here that theorizing the planetary parallax might serve as a useful additive to Žižek's discussion of how ontological and dialectical differences antagonize and oscillate between viewing locations in the gap of the Real. As we have seen in Venus's planetary parallax, the distortive parallactic effect created in the stretch between Venus and the sun serves to antagonize further the perspectival parallax by revealing a sticky edge of the Real, partial though it may be. And that distortive parallactic effect distorts even the distortion of the viewing locations by partially making visible that "Real" to be apprehended. Within the planetary parallax gap, colonialist discourse functions as a distortive effect within critical theory as it apprehends "Indianness," where shifts across space and location serve to distort further whatever trace of the Real lingers and make it even less likely to link such moments back to their discursive colonialist core. For instance, in *First as Tragedy, Then as Farce,* Žižek takes up the faux-Hopi prophecy that circulated in the 2008 U.S. presidential campaigns and proffers it as corrective to leftist intellectuals who "desperately await a new revolutionary agent capable of instigating the long-expected radical social transformation. It takes the form of the old Hopi saying, with a wonderful Hegelian twist from substance to subject: 'We are the ones we have been waiting for.' (This is a version of Gandhi's motto: 'Be yourself the change you want to see in the world.')"[106] The planetary parallax between Indians (Hopi and Gandhi) depends upon the faux-Hopi prophecy becoming the "old Hopi saying," a parallax transformation that shifts from fake to lived "Real" in an enunciation of colonialist desire for the inviting Indian event that is fillable and inhabitable by the European self. The consequences of this unexamined distortive effect within the parallax gap signals the colonialist affective need for Hopi wisdom that might radicalize leftist politics without having to make those politics accountable to and actionable for ending the colonization of the Hopi and other American Indian peoples.

My use of transit to discuss both the trajectory of empire dependent upon Indianness as well as indigeneity's challenge to critical theory is intended to be diagnostic. Though it would be tempting to develop a correlative theory that explains that Indians function as Venus or the sun and that the United States serves the vice versa other, such a correlation would miss the larger stakes of the parallax gap and its concomitant distortive effects. Venus, the sun, and the earth are all in motion during the astronomical event that is the transit of Venus. Each body pulls gravitationally upon the other to distort possible viewing locations and antagonizes any parallax angle to discern coequal or equivalent, static theories of how U.S. empire functions through its deployment of paradigmatic Indianness. Using a concept like transit that has its origins in Enlightenment imperialism at the dawning of Western "democracy," and examining how Indianness serves as the field through which lines of flight become possible as a mechanism of U.S. imperialism, necessitates deploying parallax views attuned to the miscalculations that the stretching of the real introduces into any attempt to apprehend a subversive core that might mobilize transformative politics. That distortive parallactic effect centers on the colonization of indigenous peoples and, at key moments within the ingress or egress of critical theory, reveals the colonialist discursive givens that continue to deny indigenous peoples full agency to theorize the world and have that theorization mobilize change. Within the scope of such transits, indigeneity as an ontological prior challenges postcolonial and critical theories because it serves as a significant parallax view—though certainly not the only one—along the baseline of colonialism through which to trouble the dialectical processes that underwrite colonialist hegemonies of racializations and normativities, subjectivities and subjectifications. As radical alterity, indigeneity functions as a counterpoint that disrupts the fictions of multicultural settler enfranchisement and diasporic arrivals; as event and as horizon, indigeneity is temporal as well as spatial, structural as well as structuring. By detailing the constellations that underwrite U.S. imperialism and twenty-first century wars, it may be possible to show that within the logics that have ordered the United States out of indigenous lands, indigenous peoples can be apprehended through parallax within critical theory that demonstrates just how vital they are to any understanding of how difference orients U.S. bio- and necropolitics.

Is and Was

I want to give you two scenes to hold in your imagination. The first is from Alexis de Tocqueville's *Democracy in America.* In his eyewitness account of the Choctaw removal from their homelands to Indian Territory, he writes:

> At the end of the year 1831, whilst I was on the left bank of the Mississippi at a place named by Europeans, Memphis, there arrived a numerous band of Choctaws .... These savages had left their country, and were endeavoring to gain the right bank of the Mississippi, where they hoped to find an asylum which had been promised them by the American Government. It was then the middle of winter, and the cold was unusually severe; the snow had frozen hard upon the ground, and the river was drifting huge masses of ice. The Indians had their families with them; and they brought in their train the wounded and sick, with children newly born, and old men upon the verge of death. They possessed neither tents nor wagons, but only their arms and some provisions. I saw them embark to pass the mighty river, and never will that solemn spectacle fade from my remembrance. No cry, no sob was heard amongst the assembled crowd; all were silent. Their calamities were of ancient date, and they knew them to be irremediable. The Indians had all stepped into the bark which was to carry them across, but their dogs remained upon the bank. As soon as these animals perceived that their masters were finally leaving the shore, they set up a dismal howl, and, plunging all together into the icy waters of the Mississippi, they swam after the boat.[107]

The second is from Michelle Obama's May 16, 2009, commencement speech at the University of California–Merced as she recognizes and applauds the letter-writing campaigns the students used to get their campus built—and to persuade the First Lady to attend their graduation ceremony:

> This type of activism and optimism speaks volumes about the students here, the faculty, the staff, but also about the character and history of Merced—a town built by laborers and immigrants from all over the world: early settlers who came here as pioneers and trailblazers in the late 1800s as part of the Gold Rush and built the churches and businesses and schools that exist; African Americans who escaped slavery and the racism of the South to work on the railways and as truck drivers up and down Route 99; Mexican Americans who traveled north to find work on the farms and have since become the backbone of our agricultural industry—Asian Americans who arrived in San Francisco and have slowly branched out to become a part of the community in the San Joaquin Valley.[108]

The first scene speaks of a stoic desperation, dismal howls, ancient and irremediable calamities, and an endeavoring hope for asylum in what was once home; the second offers a celebration of the optimism of struggle, a linking of students' lives to the trailblazers who discovered gold, escaped slavery, traveled north, labored on farms, or spread across California valleys in the hope of making homes (with no mention here of the internments that facilitated that spread during the early 1940s, the struggles to end the inequities of the backbreaking work on those farms, or the originary genocide that resulted from the Gold Rush).

Though separated by more than 150 years, these two scenes taken together say something profound about the nature of multicultural liberal democracy and the conditions of empire at two distinct moments of transition for the United States. They are both about the foundational violences that created the towns and communities throughout the new world, and they are both about land, labor, journey, and displacement. Yet in the span between the two, a very significant elision occurs that, by the time First Lady Michelle Obama gives that speech to college students in California, naturalizes narratives of overcoming adversity and links them to the very pioneer spirit that drove the Chickasaw and Choctaw from their homelands.

Lauren Berlant tells us:

> "Cruel optimism" names a relation of attachment to compromised conditions of possibility. What is cruel about these attachments, and not merely inconvenient or tragic, is that the subjects who have *x* in their lives might not well endure the loss of the object or scene of desire, even though its presence threatens their well-being, because whatever the *content* of the attachment, the continuity of the form of it provides something of the continuity of the subject's sense of what it means to keep on living on and to look forward to being in the world.[109]

And while one might be tempted to read the Choctaws' experiences of removal that Tocqueville witnesses as the basest form of optimism at its cruelest—the Choctaws Tocqueville describes have no hope—it seems to me that the actual cruel optimism that Berlant describes resides in the narrative of California history that Michelle Obama provides. Cruel optimism is, Berlant continues, "the condition of maintaining an attachment to a problematic object *in advance* of its loss."[110] The loss to be had here is the surety of colonialist mastery, the wealthy promises of Manifest Destiny, and the possibility of confrontation with the history Tocqueville assures will never fade from his remembrance.

I am fairly confident, however, that Berlant does not mean that when she writes of cruel optimism and its role in forming and maintaining attachments in the face of the risks that come with "reproducing and surviving in zones of compromised ordinariness [that are part of the] impasse of living in the overwhelmingly present moment."[111] In fact, one might read her delineations of cruel optimism as symptomatic of the very conditions she critiques. What constitutes the ordinary life in the overwhelmingly present moment for Berlant? And further, who gets to live that life? Each of her textual examples provides what she sees as the "suspension of the reproduction of habituated or normative life," in which said life has the possibility to break from the conditions—be they homophobia, race and class oppressions that turn people and things into "exchange value," or sexual trauma—that produce the attachments to the promises of bourgeois normativity, wealth, and education, but that ultimately fail in doing so.[112]

Berlant is concerned with the processes of normativity and capitalism that provide optimism in spite of lived conditions that are unlivable—what she has elsewhere described as slow death. And while I could focus on each of her examples and delineate the aesthetics and politics of cruel optimism as she explains them, for my purposes here, the best example is Geoff Ryman's *Was*, a novel that takes its name from L. Frank Baum's *The Wizard of Oz* and has as its four main characters Dorothy Gael as a historical figure living in 1880s Kansas, Judy Garland as she plays Dorothy Gale (like the wind) in the movie, a Midwestern mental health worker who encounters the real Dorothy in a mental home near the end of her life, and a gay man dying of AIDS who stars in a touring company of *The Wizard of Oz* while suffering from dementia. "All of these stories," Berlant writes, "are about the cruelty of optimism for people without control over the material conditions of their lives and whose relation to fantasy is all that protects them from being destroyed by other people and the nation."[113] Berlant focuses her essay on reading an exchange between the 1880s Dorothy Gael and Frank Baum, in which Baum as a substitute teacher becomes a substitute for home, caring, and desire for a Dorothy raped by her uncle and starved by her aunt. The fantasy here for Dorothy, as Berlant interprets it, is the thought that another person could care for her, and after she writes Baum a story in which she describes a happy home with her dog Toto, she has a breakdown in front of him and the rest of her classmates as she screams out her rape, torture, and the brutalization of her dog by her aunt, until she can no longer speak. "To protect her last iota of optimism," Berlant writes, "she goes crazy."[114] In return, Baum provides Dorothy a substitute life, a transplanted self who has family, friends, and Toto all with her as she wanders the roads of Oz.

Though Berlant ends her analysis here with the observation that for Dorothy "the optimism of attachment to another living being is itself the cruelest slap of all," she misses entirely the deeper attachment that provides Dorothy her one link to optimism throughout it all—Indians.[115] After her confrontation with Baum and her mental breakdown, the novel tells us, "she was invisible, like the Indians."[116] A few pages later, Ryman's narrative explains, "Dorothy no longer believed in Indians. Rather, she believed in the hopeless, flat, beardless faces wearing dirty white men's clothes, like her own. Dorothy wore britches and boots like a man."[117] Throughout her life, as things were falling apart, Dorothy held on to the hope that she could escape to the Territory, the Nation (Oklahoma), and become an Indian—she achieves it instead in her abjected state of insanity.[118] As she elaborates and deepens the fantasy escape, Indians become invisible, live underground, represent all the play and possibility of the childhood, freedom, and hope that was stolen from her until finally, in the mental home near the end of her life, she explains, "'All of us here,' she whispered, 'are either Indians or fairies.'" Even the title of the novel is pulled into her fantasy of Indian optimism as Dorothy explains how Was is a place: "You can step in and out of it. Never goes away. Always there."[119]

Within Ryman's novel, Indians become a transit, not only of the frontier violences done to children as they are forced into the stolid, colonial lives that are unlivable under the weight of settler colonial responsibilities, but of the non-normative, queered lives that cross gendered borders and pair fairies—evoked as both ephemeral spirits and radical gay men—with an affective Indianness that functions alongside a subsuming of Indian identities. There is a final irony to explore. Where Berlant and Dorothy see Frank Baum as providing a healing balm offering a substitute for home and a better life, the historical author was full of U.S. genocidal normativity. After the Wounded Knee Massacre on December 29, 1890, Baum wrote two infamous editorials in a South Dakota newspaper, the *Aberdeen Saturday Pioneer,* in which he asserted that it "was better that [Indians] die than live the miserable wretches that they are." He continues: "The nobility of the Redskin is extinguished, and what few are left are a pack of whining curs who lick the hand that smites them. . . . the best safety of the frontier settlements will be secured by the total annihilation of the few remaining Indians."[120] To revise Berlant's earlier statement about fantasy within *Was,* then, the cruel optimism is that many of the characters' inner lives and identities revolve around an attachment to Indians as affective fantasy that will somehow protect them from the destruction the United States wreaked upon actual Indian lives. Their fantasy is constitutive of their nation, and the cruelest cut is that Ryman's children affectively grow into what they most despised adults for being in the novel—harsh, desperate people who inhabit and live through a cruelty towards Indians and otherness that can be escaped only through a radical breach with sanity and signification. What Dorothy experiences as she finally escapes her own oppression by running away from her Aunt Em and Uncle Gulch to Wichita is that she has become invisible like Indians as she moves in and out of Was on the transit of Indianness she has created in her own fantasy world.

In many ways, one might argue that this transit of Indianness is the condition of possibility that informs even Berlant's understanding of the "slow death" of obesity that "refers to the physical wearing out of a population and the deterioration of people in that population that is very nearly a defining condition of their experience and historical existence."[121] Here, in the interstices of affect and queer theory, between Lauren Berlant and Judith Butler, I want to elaborate on what indigenous critical theory might offer to such understandings of "bare life." According to Butler and Berlant, the contemporary present is a necessary condition for affect and relation to draw lives into commensurable vulnerability and may, they hope, restructure governance and help make lives more livable. A core set of questions emerges for me as I read Berlant's discussions of "cruel optimism" and "slow death," and they revolve around her delineations of ordinary life. Judith Butler in *Precarious Life* and *Frames of War* takes up Berlant's concerns with the ordinary life in the overwhelmingly present moment and reframes them in the question "When is life grievable?" The concern for me is to consider whether indigenous peoples are understood to be a part of the present within liberal democracy and within the theories Butler and Berlant are articulating to provide possible reframings of relation to reconcile questions of citizenship, sovereignty, recognition, and nationalism. Do Indians live the ordinary life in the contemporary now? Are Indians part of the present tense? And finally, do Indians live grievable lives?

I may be begging the question here, given that Butler does not really consider Indians and that Berlant avoids indigeneity even when it is a thematic concern within the text, as her reading of *Was* indicates. But because their projects work to dismantle the normative state structures that also oppress indigenous peoples whether they actively involve indigenous peoples in their theorizations or not, here we can see how indigenous critical theory transforms queer theory and critical theory more broadly to intervene in the colonialist structures that continue to underwrite racialized and gendered oppressions despite every attempt to disrupt or refuse those structures. To return to Tocqueville and Michelle Obama, we can notice this problem with tenses present—and that Indians are not present at all in the case of the latter. As Tocqueville describes the Choctaw, "their calamities were of ancient date, and they knew them to be irremediable." Even in the present of their removal, the Choctaws are always already past perfect: they had left, they had stepped, they had been promised. According to Butler, in order for life to be grievable, it needs to be faceable; to exist, it needs to "cast a face, a life, in the tense of the future anterior" in what Barthes has described as the present absolute pastness of the photograph. Butler writes:

"The photograph relays less the present moment than the perspective, the pathos, of a time in which 'this will have been.'"[122] Even for Ryman's Dorothy, who perceives Indians in spite of their invisibility, Indians are "Was." So the most we can say, given the lack of possibility of an Indian future anteriority in which Indians will have been decolonized, is that Indians are lamentable, but not grievable. The dogs howl and throw themselves to their deaths in the frozen waters of the Mississippi, but the humanity of the scene is still: "No cry, no sob was heard amongst the assembled crowd; all were silent." The lamentable is pitiable, but not remediable. It is past and regrettable. Grieving, on the other hand, calls people to acknowledge, to see, and to grapple with lived lives and the commensurable suffering, and in Butler's frame apprehend—in the sense of both its definitions that include to understand and to stop—the policies creating unlivable, ungrievable conditions within the state-sponsored economies of slow death and letting die.

As the queer makes claims to an affective indigenous generosity that can welcome all arrivants in the hope that those moves, those approximations of traditional kinship sovereignties and tribal affiliations will transform the normative and transgress the dialectics of state sovereignty that conscript, expel, and police whose bodies and lives count as full citizens in the United States, the indigenous must be absent both from the contemporary now and from the spaces and tenses of grief. In order to transcend what many theorists engaged in confronting state-sponsored violence perceive as a retrograde return to nativism, claims of indigeneity are read as conservative neoliberal discourses of normativity rather than a reassertion of the basic fundamental principles of restorative justice in the face of colonization and genocide. Given the push toward kinship, affect, and futurity that queer theory troubles as a way to intervene within and through discourses of sovereignty, nationalism, and citizenship, it seems that indigenous strategies should not be just a return push that demonstrates difference—that move is anticipated and already silenced. Possible sites of intervention depend then on interrogating how the impulse to world is the setting-to-work of the colonizer, even if that work is to reconfigure the world so that it might be kinder and gentler and be a world more possible to live, and grieve, within. The future anterior of such a world that exists outside the cruel optimisms and violences constitutive of liberalism's very structures must also be a future in which indigenous peoples will have been and will remain decolonized, if there is to be any hope at all.

"This Island's Mine"

The Parallax Logics of Caliban's Cacophony

Be not afeard; the isle is full of noises,
Sounds, and sweet airs that give delight and hurt not.

William Shakespeare, *The Tempest*

But would this same captain be competent to sit in judgment upon
Shakespeare's seamanship—considering the changes in ships and ship-
talk that have necessarily taken place, unrecorded, unremembered, and
lost to history in the last three hundred years? It is my conviction that
Shakespeare's sailor-talk would be Choctaw to him.

Mark Twain, "Is Shakespeare Dead?"

How did the impulse to constellate the Americas into European colonial alignment come to depend upon the lamentable but ungrievable Indian? How do arrivants and other peoples forced to move through empire use indigeneity as a transit to redress, grieve, and fill the fractures and ruptures created through diaspora and exclusion? What happens to indigeneity within liberal multicultural settler societies when a multitude of historical experiences can each claim themselves as the real and autochthonous experience of originary violence and oppression in lands stolen from original inhabitants? And what happens to indigenous peoples and the stakes of sovereignty, land, and decolonization when conquest is reframed through the global historicities of race? Just as "the Indian" stops the Deleuzean world and redirects flow in a rhizomatic imperative, "Indianness," when located in U.S. empire, unspools within postcolonial and poststructuralist theories that seek from the outset to dismantle the colonial logics of territorializations, racializations, and discursive figurations that render some subject positions visible and heard, others absent and silent on the plateau of difference. Within Chickasaw, Choctaw, Cherokee, and other Southeastern Indian cosmologies, the collision of Upper and Lower Worlds creates *haksuba,* cacophony, in this world; the task is to discern how the noise of competing claims, recognitions, and remediations function to naturalize possession at the site of postracial inclusion, transformative multiculturalism, and cruel optimism.

This chapter considers the representational logics at work in Shakespeare's *The Tempest* to explore how colonialist discourses function primarily through the distortive effects of planetary parallax gaps that produce, in the lingering stretch of the real between and among bodies in motion, a series of deferrals that facilitate the transit of empire at the contesting site of indigeneity. Understanding that system of competing and antagonistic parallax views, which layer and resonate across temporal and geographical localities within empire, as a cacophony of contesting experiences allows for the indigenous to become apprehendable within the discursive and juridical logics that persist within liberal humanism's pursuit of governmentality framed as equality, freedom, and progress. As Jacques Rancière observes, "Politics and art, like forms of knowledge, construct 'fictions,' that is to say *material* rearrangements of signs and images, relationships between what is seen and what is said, between what is done and what can be done."[1] Within postcolonial theory what is seen and said, what is and can be done depend upon the materiality of the constructed fictions of colonialism, and upon a cathexis of liberal egalitarian distribution of signs that serves to defer the colonization of the indigenous Americas precisely because it is the *mise en scène* of U.S. neocolonialism and imperialism around the world.

Undiscoveries and Other Sixth Acts

In 1987 Rob Nixon, in discussing how Shakespeare's *The Tempest* functioned within anticolonial literary nationalisms, asserted that "*The Tempest's* value . . . faded once the plot ran out. The play lacks a sixth act which might have been enlisted for representing relations among Caliban, Ariel, and Prospero once they entered a postcolonial era, or rather . . . an era of 'imperialism without colonies.'"[2] Yet only five years later, precisely because none of these characters had entered an era of "imperialism without colonies," a sixth act did indeed play out in postcolonial studies that examined *The Tempest* and its travels within the context of the Columbus quincentennial. As the historical convergences of the "new world discovery" moment sparked impassioned debate, scholars, writers, and artists within the global North and South returned once again to the island in the hopes of listening to Caliban and gaining deeper insights into how colonial logics dependent on ideas of race, indigeneity, and savagery circulated through an early modern planetarity that constellated European imperial expansion. In gesturing toward possible sixth acts that might still emerge, Ania Loomba cautions that the plasticity of the play presents problems at the site of indigeneity across four continents, but especially because "an American focus narrows, not just our view of early modern race and colonialism as a whole, but also the geographies and histories that resonate with *The Tempest*. The play speaks to Mediterranean, North African, and Irish, as well as Atlantic contexts, often moving between these different regions."[3] The stakes in any return to Shakespeare and the diegetic parallaxes of his island plot center on examining how effectively that American context has been elaborated within the entanglements of colonial projects that stripped humanity and agency from indigenous peoples and from those forced to labor and move within the transatlantic and transpacific diasporas.

Cherokee speculative science fiction author William Sanders wrote his short story "The Undiscovered" in 1993, though it did not appear in print until 1996. The story invents an alternative past in which Shakespeare is shipwrecked in Virginia and through a series of captivities ends up in a Cherokee town where he is finally adopted into the kinship structures that place him, now renamed Spearshaker, into relation with the narrator of the story. In the story, Sanders imagines Shakespeare through Trinculo's first encounter with Caliban, describing him as:

> Not the kind of fish-belly white that I'd always imagined, when people talked about white men—at least where it showed. His face was a strange reddish color, like a boiled crawfish, with little bits of skin peeling from his nose. His arms and legs, where they stuck out from under the single buckskin garment he wore, were so dirty and covered with bruises that it was hard to tell what color the skin was. Of course that was true of all the captives; Bigkiller and his warriors had not been gentle.[4]

Sanders's inversion of the contact moment, which enacts a type of othering in reverse, humorously narrates the Cherokee reaction to a half-wit relative who speaks in tongues and writes "pleis," and captures through fragments of writing Shakespeare's Elizabethan horror at his predicament. As the Cherokee teach the white captive language, observe his abilities to carry firewood, and delight in his songs and dances—the favorite of which is "'Wid-a-he/An-a-ho/An-a-he-na-ni-no"—the story functions primarily to provide subjectivity to new world indigenous peoples who, within the literatures of empire, have been relegated to inarticulate savages. And it sets up a punchline about the nature of Indian humor that culminates when Spearshaker learns that, in the translocation from Denmark to Cherokee political and cultural contexts, his masterpiece *Hamlet* is received as a comedy by his new friends and family who laugh uproariously when everyone dies at the end. He never writes another play.

With the specter of translocation shadowing the Columbian quincentennial and the captivity of the savage "other" haunting performativity as trace, Sanders's "The Undiscovered" satirizes colonial dialectics by making the Cherokee "master." Cuban American performance artist Coco Fusco confronts those same translocations and performances inaugurated by Columbus and commemorated in the quincentennial by inhabiting the other side of the cage. In her collection of essays *English Is Broken Here,* she describes the experiences she and her creative collaborator Guillermo Gómez-Peña had when they toured various American and European cities and museums as captured native specimens. The initial premise, as Fusco describes it, was that they both would live in a cage and present themselves "as undiscovered Amerindians from an island in the Gulf of Mexico that had somehow been overlooked by Europeans for five centuries." "We called our homeland Guatinau," Fusco writes, "and ourselves Guatinauis."[5] In the cage with them was a pastiche of American icons, ranging from Coca-Cola cans and Christopher Columbus coloring books to laptop computers, stereos, and TVs playing images of Hollywood's "savages." Fusco wore a grass skirt, shells, and a dog collar, while Gómez-Peña's outfit consisted primarily of a turkey feather headdress, a leopard skin Lucha Libre mask, and something looking quasi-Aztecan—a hint of Quetzalcoatl crossed with bondage gear. For a small fee, Fusco and Gómez-Peña would perform exotic dances, recite prayers and stories in a gibberish language, reveal genitalia, and pose for pictures. The venues for the performance ranged from public spaces that included the Columbus Plaza of Madrid, Spain, to various art galleries and natural history museums in cities such as Sydney, London, New York, Minneapolis, and Chicago. It was a spectacle reveling in Otherness.

The project began in 1991 as a counter to the upcoming quincentennial celebrations of Columbus's first voyage of "discovery." It was designed as a reverse ethnology through which Gómez-Peña and Fusco could draw attention to the myriad of problems associated with the unquestioning celebrations of the five-hundredth year anniversary. Soon, however, the project evolved into an examination, according to Fusco, of "the limits of the 'happy multiculturalism' that reigned in cultural institutions" which linked the "exoticizing rhetoric of 'world beat' multiculturalism" with "the racism implicit in ethnographic paradigms of discovery."[6] The performance, entitled *Two Undiscovered Amerindians Visit . . .* , was intended to lure audiences with a rare chance to participate in the "discovery" moment that the quincentennial celebrated; once audiences became involved, the performance was supposed to reveal to them the European tradition of exhibiting captive indigenous peoples from the Americas, Asia, and Africa for either entertainment or scientific education. This tradition, which began with Christopher Columbus, continued well into the nineteenth and twentieth centuries, culminating in the 1890s with the World Columbian Fair held in Chicago. These ethnographic displays were, as Fusco writes, "the origins of intercultural performance in the West. The displays," she continues, "were living expressions of colonial fantasies and helped to forge a special place in the European and Euro-American imagination for non-white peoples and their cultures."[7]

Despite the context of the performance, its conscious parody of imperial expectations of "indigenous" cultures, and its challenges to any notion of "authentic" museum display, Fusco and Gómez-Peña were surprised that what they characterized as a "self-conscious commentary on this practice" was frequently received as an authentic exhibition of native Guatinauis by an eager and earnest public.[8] On paper the irony of the piece was clear. All the clues necessary to interpret the parody were there at the outset, including the juxtaposition of contemporary everyday technologies with the expected signifiers of "primitiveness" and the textual clues that ventriloquized the scientific racism of the nineteenth century. Barkers and museum guards helped establish the parameters of behavior between the crowd and the performers and also informed the interpretations available to the public. However, when the project they conceived finally became mediated by a live performance, a setting, and an audience, the dynamic shifted; what was originally clear irony was suddenly transformed into an authorized and authoritative exhibition of exotic otherness that audiences willingly accepted. What Fusco and Gómez-Peña learned as they toured galleries and museums was that their audiences often lacked the historical knowledge and context to interpret or read the parodic signs the artists believed to be threaded throughout their performances. In fact, many in those audiences left the performance believing that they had seen an authentic portrayal of native peoples.

Why did the performance undergo such a transformation and how did it sustain the radically different reactions of the audiences? What shared knowledge (or lack thereof on the part of the participants—spectators and artists) did the performance need to be successful? At some level, the tensions between the desired interpretation and the one that many in the audience had was a result of the project's own collision between the "truth" of the history the performance wanted to represent and the accepted "truth" that its representations of otherness evoked for them. The problem that emerged when these distortive parallactic effects collided within the space of the performance exemplifies the dynamics within postcolonial analyses that privilege the dichotomous relationship between the colonizer and the colonized where the Manichean allegories between white and black, good and evil, civilized and savage are first established and then resisted.

The master narrative of colonial history that Fusco and Gómez-Peña sought to dismantle with their performance depended upon a presumed erasure of indigenous peoples and the subsequent normalization of the history of displaying them, dead or alive, in museums for the benefit of future civilized generations. The performance intended to reveal to and explode for the predominantly white audiences their own complicity with these discourses of colonialism. At the same time, the performance sought to invert those Manichean dichotomies between good and evil, civilized and savage, so that the audiences were suddenly the objects of display and their behaviors were documented and recorded as "savage" by the artists performing as "primitives" inside the cage. But, while the performance began with the lofty ideals of reflecting the faces of the audience back to them as colonizers, the end result was much more ambiguous as the artists' stereotypical markers of Indianness transformed into authentic inauthenticities that could be rationalized as the effect of civilization upon the uncivilized by those wanting to resist essentialized understandings of identity, race, and gender. The performance unraveled not so much because audiences did not interpret it correctly, but because it was impossible to interpret correctly at all.

Determining or demanding a "correct" reaction to the history that Fusco and Gómez-Peña presented in their performance piece implies a static interpretation that relies upon a set number of referents to constitute meaning. In the case of *Two Undiscovered Amerindians Visit . . .* , the face paint, the invented "gibberish" language, and Fusco's "tribal" dancing to rap music, for instance, were all supposed to create a postmodern pastiche that would signal to the audience that the performance was mocking the stereotypes Western colonial culture uses to delineate "primitive" and "uncivilized" at the site of race. However, the two artists did not anticipate that these referents could perhaps speak as much to their own internalized ideas of "Indianness," pre- and post-modern, as to the audience's. I am interested in distilling that moment of parallax between worldviews that creates a mêlée of meanings for Fusco, Gómez-Peña, and their audiences because as one delves into the contradictions that the performance engaged, it becomes clear that the meanings and worldviews at odds are intricately dependent upon each other and that to engage one history runs the very great risk of obscuring another.

But in order to understand how a performance that, according to Diana Taylor, "confronts the viewer with the 'unnatural' and extremely violent history of representation and exhibition of non-Western human beings," reiterated and naturalized that history on the expected and already known indigenous body, it is useful to track how Coco Fusco understood herself in relation to the performance.[9] In her essay "El Diario de Miranda/Miranda's Diary," Fusco documents her experiences as a Cuban exile living in the United States. In the essay, Fusco presents her thoughts, as she struggles with both U.S. officials and the Cuban government when she travels back and forth between countries, as a performance artist, a family member, and a friend. She named her travelogue "El Diario de Miranda," she says, "because of the host of allusions to *The Tempest* in Latin American intellectual history and postcolonial thought. Shakespeare's drama, set on an island, is thought to have been inspired by accounts of voyages and shipwrecks during the early colonial period."[10] Although Fusco allies herself with Miranda, writing that "the Mirandas of the present, myself among them, continue to undertake these journeys, straying far from the fictions of identity imparted to us by our symbolic fathers," she performed the indigenous Caliban on display in 1992.[11] Perhaps the moment of distillation that sets the parameters for misreading their staged intervention resides, in part, in the planetary parallax shifts between Miranda and Caliban, Caliban and Ariel, and

Ariel and Sycorax that circulate unstably at the edges of *Two Undiscovered Amerindians Visit*... and signify the subjectifications of colonialism that worlded empire into the globe.

Authority Effects and the Colonial Undead

Mikhail Bakhtin's theories of polyphony and dialogism prove valuable in isolating some of the difficulties that Fusco and Gómez-Peña faced when they confronted audiences unaware of and invested in colonialist attitudes towards "natives." By its very nature, the piece was heteroglossic, as it involved not only the artists in the cage but evoked scientific discourses of taxonomy and discovery. Even within the cage, Gómez-Peña and Fusco were engaged in enunciating and parodying Western notions of the indigenous other through their clothes, actions, dances, stories, language, and silences. "The Guatinauis, a word echoing Columbus's 'Guanahaní' that sounds like 'What now?' demanded incredulity," Diana Taylor writes. "The point of the performance was to highlight, rather than normalize, the theatricality of colonialism."[12] Parody, as Bakhtin asserts, is "one of the most ancient and widespread forms for representing the direct word of another" and through mimicry "rips the word away from the object." "The process of parodying," Bakhtin continues, "forces us to experience those sides of the object that are not otherwise included in a given corrective of laughter, of a critique on the one-sided seriousness of the lofty, direct word, the corrective of reality that is always richer, more fundamental and most importantly too contradictory and heteroglot to be fit into a high and straightforward genre."[13] By transposing Guanahaní, the indigenous name for one of the islands Columbus first invaded, into Guatinau, Fusco and Gómez-Peña ripped the naming away from the colonial archive to mimic the desire for the original at the moment of signification with a well-placed "what now?"

Several things are important here. First, the structural, formal (or direct) language of high or "literary" genres is ultimately monoglot. The act of parodying those forms, according to Bakhtin, "transforms [language] from the absolute dogma it had been within the narrow framework of a sealed-off and impermeable monoglossia into a working hypothesis for comprehending and expressing reality."[14] Second, such parody is a function of the carnivalesque, an exuberant outburst that ultimately strives to break down the barriers between the different social strata and the language that each uses. Parody is important in that it enters into a dialogue with the object of parody and opens the structured and direct language of the form or genre to a multitude of contexts and readings by bringing to the fore forgotten libidinal desires. Bakhtin's ultimate conclusion is that words and speech acts exist in languages that are always in flux and are always, and by nature, polyglot.

One could argue, then, that through parody Fusco and Gómez-Peña entered into a dialogue with the "other history of intercultural performance" from inside the cage. In true carnivalesque fashion, the artists strove to invert the power dynamics so that the audience became the spectacle of the interactive piece as they enacted their own colonialist attitudes towards the "native" bodies they were viewing. This decentering of the colonial gaze, the colonial power, allowed Fusco and Gómez-Peña to force into the open the contradictory desires that artists of color be "authentic," "exotic," and "primitive," in what José Esteban Muñoz delineates as "the burden of liveness," which encourages minoritarian subjects to perform and entertain, "especially when human and civil rights disintegrate."[15] At the same time, Fusco and Gómez-Peña intended that the experiences be a "surprise or 'uncanny' encounter, one in which the audiences had to undergo their own process of reflection as to what they were seeing, aided only by written information and parodically didactic zoo guards."[16] As Bakhtin points out, however, in order for a satire to work within grotesque realism, it is necessary to know the "social phenomena that are being berated."[17] Laughter, parody, and mimicry have the potential to create a gap within a unified language or genre to reveal the inherent heteroglossia within language, even to the extent that any national language (i.e., the socially stratified language that makes up any state) contains a struggle between meanings that allows for parody to occur in the first place. Dissonance enters into Bakhtin's model of polyphony through parody, but it is a dissonance contained and determined again by the objects, discourses, and knowledges that are parodied. Thus, within the polyphony of national stratified language, parody serves not only to introduce dissonance but also to make coherent the object of parody.

That Fusco and Gómez-Peña engaged the histories and discourses surrounding displays of otherness in the United States and Europe is perhaps the most appealing part of their project. And, as Diana Taylor explains in response to the archived video record documenting the performance, *Two Underdiscovered Amerindians Visit* . . . created affective pleasure in the turning of the gaze back on the spectators. "I personally feel gloriously Latin American when I watch this video, very empowered knowing that I 'get it' and 'they' don't. That's what relajo is all about. Through a disruptive act, relajo creates a community of resistance, a community, as Mexican theorist Jorge Portilla puts it, of underdogs."[18] However, the chosen venues for the performance, many of which were natural history museums, have their own thorny relationship with issues of authority and ownership over the cultural artifacts within their walls and may well have served to overdetermine the available interpretations that their installation intended to evoke. As Taylor also explains, the performance enacted a "testlike quality." Pleasure or anger in the face of the performance misses the point. "No matter what," she says, "we fail. But we fail for different reasons depending on transmission."[19]

Reflecting on the project's aftermath, Fusco states that both she and Gómez-Peña had "underestimated public faith in museums as bastions of truth, and institutional investment in that role. Furthermore, we did not anticipate that literalism would dominate the interpretation of our work."[20] Fusco tells of one instance during their tour when the director of Native American programs for the Smithsonian noted that "she was forced to reflect on the rather disturbing revelation that while she made efforts to provide the most accurate representation of Native cultures she could, [their] 'fake' sparked exactly the same reaction from audiences."[21] Fusco acknowledges, as she reflects upon the repercussion of the performance, that *Two Undiscovered Amerindians Visit . . .* provided various museums and institutions a pretext to discuss among themselves the extent to which they could engage in self-critique, and whether there were ways to escape the colonialist ideologies that permeate their claims of objectivity as bastions of knowledge.[22]

The performance itself, in an attempt to parody the problematic traditions of such institutions, included fabricated maps where the island of Guatinau was drawn into the Gulf of Mexico and informational placards that mimicked the authoritative tone of those used to narrate museum dioramas. The text included lines such as "Anthropologists at the Smithsonian observed (with the help of surveillance cameras) that the Guatinauis enjoy gender role playing after dark, transforming many of their functional objects in the cage into makeshift sex toys by night." Or "[The Guatinau] are a jovial and playful race, with a genuine affection for the debris of Western industrialized popular culture. In former times, however, they committed frequent raids on Spanish ships, disguised as British pirates, whence comes their familiarity with European culture."[23] Such lines, although meant to be a parodic exaggeration of the detached, objective voice employed in such institutions, gained authority when they were read in venues such as the Field Museum of Chicago or the Smithsonian National Museum of Natural History. They also required a level of shared knowledge and shared ethical priorities and moral responsibilities that could provide clues on how to interpret the text and the performance. The quote above, for instance, alludes to the Boston Tea Party and the colonists' use of Indianness as a disguise and outlet for subversive, rebellious protests. The performance, then, walked a fine line from the beginning, and the artists' choice to stage the performance in museums tipped the scale and unintentionally risked that such irony could and would be missed.

Fusco and Gómez-Peña, then, underestimated the extent to which the physical spaces that housed their performance would control how the audiences would interpret the piece. Linda Hutcheon ends her *Irony's Edge* with a cautionary tale about the failed irony of the Royal Ontario Museum's 1989–90 exhibit *Into the Heart of Africa*, and she poses a number of questions about the efficacy of irony to advance political critiques. Much of what she says about that installation applies to Fusco and Gómez-Peña's *Two Undiscovered Amerindians Visit . . .* and the ways in which their own performance created such unexpected reactions. Hutcheon raises important questions about elitism, about the subject position of those making the critique, about the ways institutions and museums assign and are assigned authority, and the effect that each of these elements has on the reception of irony. This authority effect resides within the architectural design of the (often) imposing buildings themselves and in the fact that "the museum and the academy in Europe and North America have traditionally shared an institutionalized faith in reason and method, not to mention an unavoidable intersection with governmental agencies."[24] The combination of architecture with governmentality, then, justifies and authorizes the colonial practice of collecting, preserving, and displaying the cultural artifacts of human "civilizations," and provides the ideological framework that also orders the evolution of said cultures in a trajectory towards what the Eurocentric mind deems civilized.

In 1987, five years before *Two Undiscovered Amerindians Visit . . .*, Luiseño performance artist James Luna staged an intervention at the Museum of Man in San Diego that sought to ally itself with the authority effect that

Hutcheon identifies to make living what museums have deemed artifact and collectible. His *Artifact Piece* presented a quiet critique of the museum's fetish for the native body on display when he laid himself out in a steel and glass case filled with sand; at various times throughout the exhibition, museum goers might find Luna or a ghost imprint of where his body had lain moments before. Clad only in a loincloth, Luna presented his own body—and its ability to move, vanish, and reappear—as documentation of the living Indian in the space of the expected dead one. To drive home the emphasis on indigenous modernity, placards ran alongside his body documenting his various scars from "excessive drinking" and from the intimacies of family. "Skin callus on ring finger remains, along with assorted painful and happy memories," read one placard.[25] Accompanying him were cases that included his divorce papers and high school diploma, juxtaposing a lived contemporary life, a name, and a possibility of agency on his part to intervene in and interpret the narrative even as his body and life were curated as merely "artifact" by the museum. According to Jean Fisher, "there is a diabolic humor in this parody of the 'Indian' in the realm of the 'undead.'" "If the purpose of the undead Indian of colonialism is," she continues, "to secure the self-identity of the onlooker, the shock of his real presence and the possibility that he may indeed be watching and listening disarms the voyeuristic gaze and denies it its structuring power."[26]

Luna's performance borrowed the institution's authority effect to affect a response in the visitor/voyeur. As a result, Luna's piece disrupted both the museum's structuring power and the interpretative power of the gaze that the institution directs and sanctions. In contrast, Fusco and Gómez-Peña constructed a performance that allied the authority effect of the institution with the voice of the parody to sanction and then frustrate the desire for the uncontaminated, newly discovered and captured indigenous specimen. They challenged their audience by using the authority effect of the institution to guarantee the authenticity of the inauthentic postmodern pastiche. Such a move thwarted and disrupted expectations for the real, but in the process Fusco and Gómez-Peña's performance courted the possibility that it could be read incorrectly, that their pastiche might reify those stereotypes of indigenous peoples it was seeking to disrupt.

To bring irony into the authorized contexts of museumification is to invite the very real possibility that meaning and intent could well be constrained and transfigured by institutional power. While Hutcheon acknowledges that irony is a powerful tool, at least when used oppositionally to confront issues of imperialism, racism, and colonialism, she also notes that it is a double-edged sword that must be wielded cautiously. When and if the institutions of modernity mediate the critique—and with this Hutcheon refers to universities, museums, libraries, etc.—there is a sense that the irony is directed at the imperialists at the expense of the "natives."[27] In other words, Hutcheon suggests that when museums house critiques or parodies of the Western world's obsession with collecting and displaying artifacts from "conquered" and colonized cultures, the use of the "native" is merely a means to instigate yet another conversation about the colonialists. The "native" remains an object, a metaphor through which these institutions can confront their complicity in colonialist practices, and is never granted agency or presence beyond its usefulness as sign in the cosmopole of the global North.

Thinking outside the Cage

There is a fine line, then, between deconstructing a process of signification and reinscribing the discourses that continue to justify the codification of knowledge production that orders the native as colonized. Part of the quandary for *Two Undiscovered Amerindians Visit . . .* may also have been that the ideology evoked and the sources it operationalized depended upon the colonialist and imperialist discourses that are still used to narrate the discovery moment in the Americas. The performance relied on what Akwesasne Mohawk scholar Scott Manning Stevens has identified as "the dysphasia of encounter."[28] Some of the text surrounding the display of the caged couple included lines such as "Although the term Amerindian suggests that they were the original inhabitants of this continent, the oldest authorities (e.g., Christopher Columbus in his diaries, and more recently Paul Rivette) regarded them as Asian immigrants, not Americans."[29] Juxtaposing Christopher Columbus, who is still hailed in many quarters as the discoverer of the Americas, with a scholar of ambiguous pedigree, who may or may not be Paul Rivet, founder of the Musée de l'Homme in Paris, to serve as the oldest authorities for learned anthropological theories about the settlement of the Americas reinforced for the audiences the naturalization of the discourses that the performance piece engaged.[30]

In addition to tackling accepted scientific rationales for the peopling of the Americas via the Bering Strait, the lines above complicate matters further by evoking the history of anti-Asian immigration laws and the "yellow peril" racisms that were particularly virulent in the early 1990s.[31] Such amalgamations of anthropological discourses with the often unquestioned "foreignness" of Asian Americans were intended to alert the aware viewer to the calculated political intervention of the artists' performance, which sought to overturn not only the history of displaying native others but also the racist and anti-immigrant xenophobias that have remained since the formation of the United States. Instead, for those audience members who were unaware of such critical resonances, the collapsing of indigenous experience into immigrant experience reiterated those discourses that not only erase the indigeneity of the indigenous peoples of the Americas but implicitly necessitate the reordering of their temporal arrival into a "post-conquest" invasion that threatens white nativity. Such a turn naturalizes the colonization of indigenous peoples into the state formation of the United States, and reframes citizens of externally sovereign nations into racialized ethnic minorities whose oppressions are then remediated through an almost but not quite inclusion. It is a turn that progresses not the promissory dream of a perfecting postracial United States but the colonialist and genocidal intent the nation-state has leveled against indigenous peoples from its beginning. Fusco and Gómez-Peña's *Two Undiscovered Amerindians Visit* . . . relies on racial tropes to express otherness and presents us with an elision between colonization and racialization.

Homi Bhabha's concept of colonial discourse as inherently split and therefore ruptured is useful in understanding the ways in which hybridity reveals the processes behind the discourses of colonialism, even as those splits and ruptures undermine their authority in the "place of enumeration" that "makes the structure of meaning and reference an ambivalent process."[32] While Bhabha's third space allows us to "elude the politics of polarity and emerge as the other to our selves," it also relies upon a breach between the "I" and "you," between colonizer and colonized.[33] That third space may open between and within a rupture, but it does not disrupt the structure in which the third space originates. Such a schema does not emphasize an escape from binaries; instead, even as a third space is opened within the space of the slashed rupture, the dialectical life and death struggle between self/other occurs in the diametric opposites who must then traverse that third space of enumeration to introduce ambivalence into colonial discourses and their resistances.[34] Focused as it is on the dialectics initiated by formal administrative colonialisms, Bhabha's ruptured discourse is more difficult to mobilize along the axes of other/others, where racialized and colonized peoples, existing in the same geographical space, interact with one another as well as the colonizer, in what is, essentially a cacophonous proliferation of third spaces. Anne McClintock, in *Imperial Leather*, touches briefly on such a criticism by pointing out the ways in which Bhabha's theory, which centers on race, fails to fully address the intersectional loci of class or gender.[35]

In geographical localities of the Americas, where histories of settlers and arrivants map themselves into and on top of indigenous peoples, understanding colonialism as a cacophony of contradictorily hegemonic and horizontal struggles offers an alternative way of formulating and addressing the dynamics that continue to affect peoples as they move and are made to move within empire. Not only are colonial discourses always caught in a repetition that must propagate itself with a difference, as Bhabha has argued, those discourses also contain discordant incommensurabilities and misapplied representations that try to pass themselves off as coherent, consistent, and real. As a critical term diagnosing the persistence of racialization, subjugation, and hierarchized subject positionalities within and among those targeted and oppressed by the processes of imperialism and colonialism, war and genocide, cacophony carries allegiances to Bhabha's articulation of ambivalence, but as an intervention, cacophony focuses on those moments where the representational logics of colonial discourses break down in the forced application of them in settler colonial localities that contain multiple colonial experiences grounded not only in race but gender, indigeneity, conquest, and sexuality as well. When the processes of colonialism are framed through the interactions of divergently targeted peoples along the transit of empire, it is possible to see how colonial discourses rupture along the seams in the face of what Michael Rothberg has identified as multidirectional memory: "As subject to ongoing negotiation, cross-referencing, and borrowing; as productive and not privative."[36] This multidirectionality creates the possibility for memory and resistance to forge alliances across historical and cultural experiences in opposition to the competitions upon which colonialism relies.

Framed in this way, then, cacophony exists not only in the desire and fear of the colonizer who needs to continually and repeatedly articulate "true" and "real" representations of the colonized, but it also resides within the ways historical oppressions created by liberal multicultural settler colonies exist relationally and in collusion with the processes of racial, gendered, and sexual otherings that seek to make contesting histories and experiences resonate authochtonously through the lingering touch of the real. Cacophony, therefore, focuses not only vertically on the interactions between the colonizer and colonized, but horizontally between different minority oppressions within settler and arrivant landscapes on the baseline between racialization and conquest that stretches the real in the movement between and among. Cacophony is a form of what Slavoj Žižek defines as the parallax view, in which "we should renounce all attempts to reduce one aspect to the other (or, even more so, to enact a kind of 'dialectical synthesis' of opposites); on the contrary, we should assert antinomy as irreducible, and conceive the point of radical critique not as a certain determinate position as opposed to another position, but as the irreducible gap between the positions themselves."[37] This perspectival shift between colonization and racialization exists in the interstices between parallax viewing locations and is dynamic and relational in order to ascertain how differentiation functions within imperialism at the site of indigenous worlds that interrupt the signifying regimes of domination.

Of course, colonization relies upon racialization to facilitate, justify, and rationalize the state-sponsored violences that tear land, resources, and sovereignty from indigenous peoples, but to reframe colonization as racialization at the site of radical critique risks leaving those very colonial structures intact on the one hand and allowing all experiences of oppression within settler colonialism to step forward as colonized on the other. This transitive fallacy of like can become like creates the conditions for what Chadwick Allen has identified as the enduring struggle between "native indigeneity" and "settler indigeneity" in which indigenous peoples in the global North "have been forced to compete for *indigenous* status with European settlers and their descendants eager to construct new identities that separate them from European antecedents."[38] As the logics of multiculturalism become ascendant within those same settler colonial societies, that struggle between indigeneities multiplies to become "arrivant indigeneity," "homonational indigeneity," "rural indigeneity," "Tea Party indigeneity," et cetera. Because settler colonialism arises from the forced domination of indigenous lands that have been reconstellated as the metropole, indigeneity itself becomes the site of inclusive remediation for all settlers and arrivants.

"Peopled Else This Isle with Calibans"

This dynamic of cacophony should not be read as reiterating postmodern aesthetics nor should it be seen as a joyous repetition of the recognition of differences that is often reified into the "happy multiculturalism" Fusco critiques. The simultaneous antinomic differentiations within the economy of colonial representations that I call cacophony have existed from the beginning, when the discourses of discovery and mastery were first employed in the Americas to conquer and enslave. Perhaps the best textual example of such distortive parallactic effects can be found in Shakespeare's Caliban, a character who, through interpretation, becomes an ontological gap disturbed by the lingering traces of the real. Beginning with Trinculo and Caliban's first encounter, we can sketch a reading:

> What have we here? a man or fish? dead or alive? A fish: he smells like a fish; a very ancient and fish-like smell; a kind of, not of the newest Poor-John. A strange fish! Were I in England now, as once I was, and had but this fish painted, not a holiday fool there but would give a piece of silver: there would this monster make a man; any strange beast there makes a man: when they will not give a doit to relieve a lame beggar, they will lay out ten to see a dead Indian. Legg'd like a man! And his fins like arms! Warm o' my troth! I do now let loose my opinion, hold it no longer: this is no fish, but an islander, that hath lately suffered by a thunderbolt.[39]

In this meeting, Trinculo takes great pains to categorize Caliban, naming him first as fish, then as Poor-John or dried hake, and in the course of the scene constructs a taxonomy that classifies Caliban as dead Indian, and finally as an islander within a generic family. From the beginning of this passage, Caliban exists in a liminal space between man and beast, food and cannibal, alive and dead Indian. This indeterminacy in Trinculo's first encounter with Caliban is mediated further by his thoughts of using Caliban to make money on the streets of London. Whatever else he may be, Caliban is profit.

Despite a separation of at least three hundred years, Fusco, Gómez-Peña, and Shakespeare are referencing the same historical moment, the same cultural obsession, albeit from very different subject positions within empire. For that reason, if for no other, understanding how Caliban functions within Shakespeare's play and within the colonialist discourses and postcolonial rewritings of new world histories may help illuminate some of the difficulties that resulted when Fusco and Gómez-Peña exhibited themselves. It is first necessary to acknowledge that *The Tempest,* along with Shakespeare's other plays, even though his work has come to represent high British imperial culture, was once part of the popular culture of England engaged with the preoccupations of sixteenth- and seventeenth-century Europe, much as Fusco is engaged with the political and social issues that dominate the latter portion of the twentieth century. From the moment *The Tempest* was first staged in England, the character of Caliban has represented the native on display and in that vein could be said to manifest the colonial unconscious that Fusco and Gómez-Peña addressed in their performance when they caged themselves in museums. In outlining the historical and cultural contexts for the performance, Fusco cites *The Tempest* as one of the literary moments to which she and Gómez-Peña responded.[40] As Ronald Takaki has documented, before writing the play Shakespeare had attended one such exhibition, where he encountered a native named Epenew of the lands that were to be remapped as "new" England on display in the streets of London.[41] The fact that Shakespeare, in early seventeenth-century England, had at least one opportunity to see an Indian on display is part of the material and historical conditions that are at stake in revisiting *The Tempest* as an early textual example of the colonial representations that were being formulated soon after the discovery and settlement of the new world.

That Shakespeare's play has been read in light of the history of colonialism is well known. These readings have often used *The Tempest* to delve into the psychology behind the colonizer and the colonized as scholars studied the allegories of domination and resistance that are threaded through the play. According to the authors of *The Empire Writes Back,* "*The Tempest* has been perhaps the most important text used to establish a paradigm for post-colonial readings of canonical works."[42] Returning to *The Tempest* and how it has been taken up in the Americas seems necessary in order to put indigenous critical theory into a conversation with postcolonial theory at the interstices of diaspora and autochthony. I am indebted to a host of other scholars whose work to make visible the colonial contexts of the play has provided the scaffolding through which to make an indigenous critical intervention here at the moment Caliban starts the world rather than stops it.[43] While it is impossible to survey them all, critical readings of *The Tempest* can be broken down into two broad categories. The first tends to focus on the material and cultural conditions surrounding the creation of the characters, plot, setting, etc. These readings primarily focus on evidence that allows one to read the play in terms of the Americas, Ireland, Africa, and/or the Mediterranean. The second category relies upon the play as a metaphor through which the text can be said to describe the experiences of colonizer and colonized, master and slave, oppressor and oppressed.

The idea that *The Tempest* might be read through the "new" world did not gain a strong foothold in American literary circles until the late nineteenth century, when Sidney Lee "argued unequivocally that Caliban was Shakespeare's portrayal of an American native."[44] In the century prior to Lee's reading of Caliban, most critics focused on the incidental aspects of the play, suggesting tentatively that some elements of the text—Caliban's name as an anagram of cannibal, the references to Bermuda, the indigenous origins of Ariel's songs, and Setebos as a name of an Amerindian god, for instance—might re-place the play somewhere in the Americas, but those readings were provisional.[45] By the 1950s and '60s, Leo Marx and Leslie Fiedler followed the trend established by Lee and argued that the play should be connected to the Americas, though neither explicitly connected Caliban to American Indians. The concern in these readings was not so much that Caliban evoked European stereotypes of American Indians per se, but that the text represented a uniquely American experience and therefore was foundational in the creation of an American literary national canon.[46] In such readings, Shakespeare becomes "'the father to the man in America' and hence . . . a virtual founding father" for U.S. culture and identity.[47]

At the same time writers in the United States were claiming *The Tempest* as the first "American" text, South American, Caribbean, and African scholars also began debating how the play might speak to their own experiences in the Americas beyond the boundaries of the U.S. imperial hegemon. Of particular note are the works of Uruguayan philosopher José Enrique Rodó, Madagascar scholar Octave Mannoni, Cuban poet Roberto Fernández Retamar, Barbadian writer George Lamming, and Martinique playwright Aimé Césaire. Rodó, writing at the turn of the twentieth century, suggests that *The Tempest* could and should be read as a metaphor for colonialism. In his essay *Ariel* (1900), Rodó adopts Shakespeare's play as a means to articulate the condition of South American civilization and to cohere a hemispheric identity and literary tradition to counter a U.S. exceptionalism that announces itself as a democracy even as it allies with and promotes fascist regimes. To accomplish this task, Rodó relies upon an allegorical reading in which Caliban represents the United States in a state of "brute sensuality" and Ariel symbolizes "the noble, soaring aspect of the human spirit" in a noble/savage dyad that reiterates rather than overcomes the discourses of racializations.[48]

Fifty years later, Octave Mannoni takes from *The Tempest* allegories of colonial encounters that he uses to discuss what was occurring in Madagascar at the time.[49] His *Prospero and Caliban* provides a psychological study of colonialism that, although not particularly concerned with Shakespeare's play, is one of the first texts to associate Caliban with Africa. In 1971 Retamar draws upon such Calibanesque discourses to assert that "our symbol then is not Ariel, as Rodó thought, but rather Caliban."[50] Retamar provides an extensive survey of the ways Shakespeare's play has been read and used by Latin American scholars, as well as offering his own engagement with the metaphors of colonialism in *The Tempest*. "Caliban is our Carib," Retamar writes in a defiant reframing of José Martí's "Our America," and recasts Caliban as a mestizo revolutionary in the vein of Fidel Castro and Ernesto "Che" Guevara, among others.[51] The fundamental textual indeterminacies surrounding Caliban's racial origins in Shakespeare's original text, then, allows critics, novelists, and poets to interpret Caliban within recognizable historical and racialized subjectivities spanning the Atltantic to the Mediterranean to Africa.

In the process, Ariel, who might correctly be identified in Shakespeare's text as the prior and rightful heir of the island who was displaced and imprisoned in a tree by Sycorax upon her arrival, is displaced once again within the political allegories that have arisen from the play. The shift from Ariel to Caliban as the site of both indigeneity *and* slavery reveals how the stakes of indigeneity fill the space of Caliban in ways that have lingered and been repeated to the present. As Ariel receded from theoretical purview within colonial and postcolonial analyses, Caliban solidified as an allegory for the global conditions of colonialism at the site of race and nation, and created the gateway through which settlers and arrivants articulate their sense of status and belonging. Martinique writer Aimé Césaire's *A Tempest* dramatizes the affective shift from Ariel to Caliban by reframing Ariel as the mulatto slave intellectual who works with Prospero and in "Uncle Tom" opposition to the revolutionary Caliban.[52] For Kamau Brathwaite, Caliban's original song, "'Ban, 'Ban, Cacaliban / Has a new master:—get a new man" becomes "How many bangs how many revolutions?" as Caliban, who likes to play Pan at the carnival, re-members the Middle Passage through limbo.[53] Ariel exits stage right; Caliban steals the show.

Indeed, Ariel is abandoned in such formulations as a productive allegory for settler colonialism within twentieth-century deployments of the play, and in the process, the translocation of indigeneity from the prior Ariel to Caliban and his mother, Sycorax, enacts the machinations of settler discourses that detach indigeneity from the original inhabitants of the Americas and relocate it on settlers and arrivants themselves. Caliban as the embodiment of négritude black nationalism, of revolutionary consciousness, of radical difference within the master/slave dialectic draws upon the settler effacement of the indigenous to enunciate those radical critiques as fulfilling and inhabiting the indigenous as a coming to subjectivity. And even in this moment of ontological translocation, there is a multitude of abandonments that linger as trace. Were Ariel to substitute for Caliban, the abusively violent realities of transatlantic and transpacific slaveries and indentureships would be erased in the character's ascendency as an allegorical model.

And then there is gender. Both Caliban and Ariel, according to Abena Busia, become the site of "prodigal sonships" and "they are held up in the discussion exclusively as *the* representatives of the colonial subject, and their maleness lies not only in the questionable conventional usage of 'he' for the colonial subject but in those attributes which are generally celebrated as quintessentially 'male.'" Sycorax's "unvoicing" casts the woman's voice as void, and debates about Caliban and Ariel "are in danger of continuing the lie that tells the story as if Sycorax had no part, and as if her voice were absent from the debate."[54]

Bearing in mind such cautions, I am locating Caliban here as a point of inquiry to understand how race and colonialism map uniquely onto this textual figure to track a slightly different lie that laying claim to and recovering Ariel or Sycorax does not fully disrupt. Caliban serves as the perspectival parallax of new world exceptions and exceptionalisms within the logics of colonial discourse. To focus on his figuration is to understand how indigeneity collapses into race at the beginning of empire and how his centrality within discussions of postcolonial and poststructural debates continues to replicate the errant. That he, rather than Ariel, has come to dominate the continued analyses of the racializations of colonization in the Americas serves the larger function of indigenizing arrival to the Americas and rendering indigenous peoples absent and foreign in their own lands. "Be not afeard," Caliban says late in the play as he plots against Prospero, "the isle is full of noises, / Sounds and sweet airs, that give delight, and hurt not."[55] In attempting to reorder the isle in the shape of Caliban's own desires and anticolonial resistances, the indigenous is rendered spectral, immaterial, and ineffectual—Ariel's continued presence produces the noise, but it cannot transform the island.

In *The Pleasures of Exile,* George Lamming engages with the paradoxes of *The Tempest* and the tensions between Prospero and all the inhabitants on the island. In his analysis, he stresses colonization as a "reciprocal process," in which to be a colonial is to be defined by one's position as colonized or as colonizer. Prospero, like Caliban, is shaped and determined by the colonial relationship, and both are a condition, "a kind of Universal" that speaks to the relationship of exile that the colonial occupies.[56] Lamming tells us that Caliban "is the very climate in which men encounter the nature of ambiguities, and in which, according to his desire, each man attempts a resolution by trying to slay the past." Within the play, Caliban is not seen as the "possibility of spirit," though he is expected to fulfill Prospero's desires for mastery over the land and its peoples. When Lamming speaks of Caliban as the climate in which to encounter ambiguities, he suggests that Caliban is a fundamental indeterminacy within the play. He lacks any ability to see or represent himself by the very nature of his skin color and his position within the discourses of empire; though he may be "seen as an occasion, a state of existence which can be appropriated and exploited for the purposes of another's own development.... the difficulty is to take from Caliban without suffering the pollution innate in his nature."[57] Caliban is still without history and contaminated by his origins. Yet in spite of all this, Caliban is still the state of existence that is fought over, appropriated, and exploited—either by Prospero as slave master or by Caliban's descendants and neighbors, who see in him a moment of context in which to refigure their own futures.

What begins to emerge from this delineation of *The Tempest* criticism is that as the twentieth century progressed and anticolonial movements arose within the outposts of empire, writers and postcolonial critics demanded that the play speak to their own specific historical conditions. The play should either serve as a sign of the colonial oppression dramatized in a text to which they could then write back, or it should be an intellectual delineation of the conditions of colonialism that they could use to describe the violence and damage caused by the imposition of history in their collision with modernity. Though Lamming warns against Caliban's pollution in his discussions of how he is appropriated, Shakespeare's play provides persistent, compelling representations of colonial experiences. Because those representations within the play and the surrounding criticism are marked by continual displacements and deferments of competing narratives of identification and appropriation within former colonies, responding to the play becomes much more complex. At any given moment within the criticism, we find that Caliban can be understood as Latin American intellectual or militant, as African, as slave, or as founding father of the U.S. literary canon. These continual displacements and reassertions of Caliban's position within empire serve to highlight the ways that Caliban is a projection of the desires that each critic has of the character and the text.

Thus, reading *The Tempest* now opens up the possibility for contesting simultaneities of experiences and subject positions that could be embodied within the text. Whenever another scholar or writer asserts a new meaning for Caliban and the play, the echoes of previous claims remain, even as Caliban is refigured and recast as a postcolonial hero. At the very least, these traces within the play continue to serve a similar function to the displays of otherness that occurred (and still do) in the human dioramas that were part of colonialism, imperialism, and nationalism. Writers from all over the "new" and "old" worlds have used Caliban to understand and to reject Prospero's dream of mastery over his island. But because Caliban is such a central figure in colonial, anticolonial, and even postcolonial discourses, it is important to understand the competitive simultaneities that burden him both as a character within the play and as a representation of the colonial subject.

Caliban Deferred

In linking Caliban to the Caribbean, Peter Hulme has suggested in *Colonial Encounters* that "Caliban's struggle against Prospero in *The Tempest* is one moment of a larger discursive conflict in which a Mediterranean discourse is constantly stretched by the novelty of an Atlantic world."[58] Caliban, caught somewhere between the Mediterranean and the Atlantic, is "doubly inscribed, a discursive monster, a compromise formation bearing the imprint of the conflict that has produced him."[59] He is Shakespeare's attempt to deal discursively and imaginatively with the discovery of the "new" world while at the same time reconfiguring it within the old. Barbara Fuchs argues that the "superimposition" of the colonial contexts of Ireland and the Mediterranean "reflects the way colonialist ideology is 'quoted' from one contact zone to another in the sixteenth and early seventeenth centuries." She builds on Hulme's "first layer of a textual palimpsest" to unpack the "condensed layers of colonialist ideology."[60] Although she states that her reading attempts to "prevent Shakespeare's island play from itself becoming isolated somewhere in the Americas," I am particularly interested in how she discusses the layering of colonial expectations onto the play and onto Caliban as a moment of quotational palimpsest from one colonial moment to another.[61] However, if we read the play not through the lens of "quotation" but through a lens of cacophony, we can begin to see the ramifications of the interactions between discourses or referents as they touch and stretch in an attempt to apprehend the ontological gap of the Real. Not only can we see that the British Empire was unoriginal in the representations that it evoked to naturalize domination, but we can start to perceive the beginnings of the justifying narratives of colonialism that persist still today as Indianness is operationalized and appropriated as the transit of U.S. empire.

This facet of colonial representations that determines Caliban in such a way that he must bear competing burdens of meaning across colonial histories, temporalities, and geographies can be found in Shakespeare's own projection of the character. In the original play, Caliban is the liminal creature, hovering between man and beast, civilized and savage, life and death, that Trinculo first encounters and attempts to classify. As each critic and postcolonial intellectual writes back to Caliban, he becomes increasingly overdetermined. But what causes such a phenomenon? When discussing her performance as an undiscovered Guatinau, Fusco observes that the cage and the two artists within became "a blank screen onto which audiences projected their fantasies of who and what we are." Fusco continues, "as we assumed the stereotypical role of the domesticated savage, many audience members felt entitled to assume the role of the colonizer, only to find themselves uncomfortable with the game."[62] This idea that the "native" might serve as a blank screen to reflect the desires of the colonizer exists along side Comanche scholar, essayist, and curator Paul Chaat Smith's observation that "too much of Indian art settles for the expected protest, and the comforting, pastoral images that for the vast majority of us originate in exactly the same place as they do for non-Indians. Our pre-determined role is to remain within the images of ecology, of anger, of easy celebration."[63]

An extension of this would be Edward Said's arguments in *Orientalism* that signal the foundational role that ideas of the Orient in the West played in Europe's self-definition and self-representation. The mode of representation that Said brands "Orientalism" codifies knowledge about the East (and the language used to express it) into an easily recognized shorthand that attests to the West's ownership and mastery of all things Middle Eastern.[64] Likewise, images of American Indians in Western cultures, images that reify "savageness" and "primitiveness," rely upon emptying them of any tribal manifestation of identity, history, and culture, then filling them instead with those signifiers that assert mastery and control. Thus, Fusco notes from inside the cage the moment of erasure and refiguration that transfigured her parody of "primitiveness" into something "real" or something desired by the colonial institutions and the colonizers themselves.

But the theoretical discussions outlined above focus primarily on the ways in which the colonial and imperial centers have invested in their own constructed images of colonized otherness to justify the structuring and demarcating of social hierarchies. At some fundamental level, this dynamic is different from that which compels postcolonial intellectuals to engage with and write back to Shakespeare through reappropriations of Caliban and the other characters of Shakespeare's play. That postcolonial rewritings of *The Tempest* rely upon some of the same strategies of colonial discourse to codify knowledge about the other, returns us to the core argument of this book, which seeks to understand colonial discourses not only as vertical impositions between colonizer and colonized but also as horizontal interrelations between different colonized peoples within the same geopolitical space. In this vein, Gayatri Spivak argues in *A Critique of Postcolonial Reason* that postcolonial critical claims to the status of "native informant" ultimately reflect the constructions of otherness that play to reified notions of what constitutes the colonized subject. Her argument resonates with the discussion raised by Fusco's observation of blankness. In her critique of Retamar, Gayatri Spivak makes the point that his engagement with Caliban, which "den[ies] the possibility of an identifiable 'Latin American Culture,' recasts the model as Caliban [but] ... still excludes any specific consideration of the civilization of the Maya, the Aztecs, the Incas, or the smaller nations of what is now called Latin America."[65] She is right to level this critique against Retamar, who is engaged in what she sees as "a 'conversation' between Europe and Latin America (without a specific consideration of the political economy of the 'worlding' of the 'native')." Spivak continues: "If . . . we are driven by a nostalgia for lost origins, we too run the risk of effacing the 'native' and stepping forth as 'the real Caliban,' of forgetting that he is a name in a play, an inaccessible blankness circumscribed by an interpretable text. The stagings of Caliban work alongside the narrativization of history: claiming to *be* Caliban legitimizes the very individualism that we must persistently attempt to undermine from within."[66]

To extend Spivak's arguments, Caliban represents one of those textual discursive moments through which Shakespeare is worlding the world of the native. This "worlding of the native" stems from Heidegger's essay "'The Origin of the Work of Art'" and presents us, according to Spivak, with "the ethnocentric and reverse-ethnocentric benevolent double bind (that is, considering the 'native' as object for enthusiastic information-retrieval and thus denying its own 'worlding')."[67] Here she gives us the example of the work of the colonial, this time in the shape of a Captain Geoffrey Birch who was assigned as an assistant to the governor in Calcutta; the letters he writes back home have the discursive power to "consolidate the Self of Europe by obliging the native to cathect the space of the Other on his home ground." Spivak argues further that Birch "is worlding *their own world,* which is far from mere uninscribed earth, anew, by obliging *them* to domesticate the alien as Master." Spivak makes an important intervention when she suggests "that the necessary yet contradictory assumption of an uninscribed earth that is the condition of possibility of the worlding of a world generates the force to make the 'native' see himself as 'other.'"[68]

At the most basic level, what Spivak identifies as the "worlding of a world" is the discursive work of colonialism that enters lands already inhabited by peoples with their own laws, customs, languages, and orderings of the world; declares said lands "uninhabited"; and then proceeds to establish another alien world as the dominant order. Key to this discursive work is the paradigmic uninscribed, uninhabited earth, the *terra nullius* convenient colonial construct that maintained lands were empty of meaning, of language, of presence, and of history before the arrival of the European. For a worlding to take place to such a degree that the native comes to cathect her/himself as other, the native must be rendered as an unknowable blankness that can then be used to reflect back the colonizer's desires and fantasies. And such a worlding is accomplished by denying that an "originary" world or peoples exist. While extending Spivak's observations about the discursive work of colonialism, I would stress further that echoes of such worldings remain even when Caliban is recast as a postcolonial hero, and according to Spivak any attempt to define or claim Caliban (a critique she levels at Retamar in particular), who is always a deferment or erasure of "originary" experience, only serves to cast off the "native" yet again.

To pinpoint more exactly what Spivak is arguing against when she warns us that to step forth as the "real Caliban" runs the risk of effacing the "native," we must return to a discussion of how language functions after Derrida. According to Spivak, Derrida is interested primarily in the ways that philosophical texts have failed to recognize how starting principles or definitions function. The act of defining involves a setting off (differentiation) of meaning from all that it is not. It is possible to trace, according to Spivak's reading of Derrida, how that which it is not has been pushed away from a definition in order to establish meaning.[69] Those traces that exist as deferral—that which is cast off—remain within a given definition because they are precisely necessary in establishing a definition. Further, in order to define the self there has to be the other against whom such definitions occur; the self requires and bears the trace of that other as part of its self. The problem with the search for origins is, according to Spivak, that "all institutions of origin concealed the splitting off from something other than the origin, in order for the origin to be instituted. This was a making indeterminate of any answer to questions of origin, as to what it was from which the supposedly original thing or thought, in description or definition, was being differentiated."[70] According to Spivak, the work of *différance* is a "necessary yet impossible" recognition that the moment an institution or origin is defined, there is a split from that which is not defined. The original Caliban always already contains within his definition a differentiation of what he is not, a setting off and abjection of everything that is "un-Caliban." Any claim to Caliban then activates a definition of not only what he is and what he originally was, but what he cannot be.

Understanding how Caliban functions as an inaccessible blankness made possible through the parallactic entry points into the histories his character charts might prove valuable in positing reasons why it was so hard for Fusco and Gómez-Peña to escape the parameters of the discourses that they engaged in their performance. Cacophony provides a methodology of reading practice towards radicalized critique aimed at dismantling the ontological prior of the colonization of indigenous peoples that is always already deferred when claims to Caliban are made. Cacophony intervenes into the erasures and elisions of indigenous presences that linger as trace to *The Tempest,* especially as they occur within those deployments of critical theories that intersect with the logics of recognition, inclusion, equality, enfranchisement, and access within and to democratic national orders made possible by settler colonialism. In the process of apprehending the interrelationality of discursive figurations, cacophony takes as its scope the contradictions and competitions as diagnostic of that multidirectionality that makes the deferral of indigeneity possible at the start of the colonization project.

The Chickasaw–Choctaw understanding of complementary worlds that interact with and bleed into each other informs *haksuba* as an explosion of additive meaning in which the interrelationships between and among those worlds are made manifest to be diagnosed and addressed towards decolonial justice. What happens if we view Caliban and the attempts to claim him in this light, as not an attempt at exclusionary definition but as addition? As outlined above, the cultural history and developments in the criticism and the reappropriations of Caliban in the United States and throughout the Caribbean, Latin America, and Africa suggest that something other within the construction of Caliban and his position as a part of colonialist discourses allows him to signify black, African, native, Amerindian, Irish, U.S. settler, Latin American, Fidel Castro, and, and, and, in a process of simultaneous signification that activates the Indian as the field of transit and the field of the ontological justification that serves nationalist, anticolonial, and imperial projects.

If Caliban contains all these identities and histories collapsed in his signification within the interpretable body of *The Tempest,* one could argue that he presents in microcosm the forces at work in settler colonialism, which are marked by colonization, racialization, and slavery that have served to multiply worldings that occur *all at the same time.* The effect, it could be argued, is that within colonial manifestations and representations there are worldings of the worlds of settlers, arrivants, and natives that serve to other the other. Caliban, as the signification of one such locus of colonial historicities, performs the tensions, the erasures, and the consolidations of cacophonous discourses. He embodies within the space of what is interpreted as "Caliban" all the contradictions and subject positions produced by conquest, slavery, and genocide. Thus, by reading the significant postcolonial signposts of *The Tempest* and specifically the character of Caliban as cacophonous, we can begin to trace how colonial discourses have functioned in geographies where there are multiple interactions among the different colonialisms, arrivals, and displacements at work. Moreover, cacophony as a critical tool allows us to describe the ways in which, in modern and postmodern cultural productions, representations become so culture-deprived and decontextualized that it is difficult to trace their distortive parallactic effects back to their beginnings as colonial manifestations, let alone to their imperial or neocolonial implications.

The ramification of such consolidations is that every time a claim to Caliban is made from within or without empire, that colonization is maintained with a difference. When Caliban is claimed as a stepping forth of the transatlantic slave trade at the site of the "native," that stepping forth translocates new world indigeneity onto those forced labor diasporas (themselves arising from African indigeneities) that made the colonization of indigenous peoples on both sides of the Atlantic possible in the first place. That history of forced plantation slavery becomes precisely an original and autochthonous experience of violence in the conquest of the Americas, but in the process of such recognitions, a secondary translocation occurs as descendants of the Black Atlantic become, now, the "real" new world native at the site of exception where indigenous peoples in the American South and Caribbean are rendered fossils, specters, relics, or pushed from their homes to the hinterlands and territories beyond. As a result, the distortive parallactic effect of the Calibanesque gap reveals the trace of both indigeneities as they are cast off, disavowed, and misremembered.

Once again, Bakhtin is useful in opening up the cacophonous within Shakespeare's text. In writing of the carnivalesque, Bakhtin notes that the grotesque body, which is a necessary component within literary conventions, serves as a means of satirical commentary on social phenomena. As such, "one of the fundamental tendencies of the grotesque image of the body is to show two bodies in one, the one giving birth and dying, the other conceived, generated, and born."[71] Returning to the scene in which Trinculo and Stephano first encounter Caliban will help chart how Caliban becomes the discursive monster that sets in motion the transit of empire at the site of Indianness. The scene opens with Caliban cursing Prospero and his tormenting spirits as he carries his burden of wood. As soon as he hears Trinculo approaching, he hides himself under his "gaberdine," thinking that Prospero has set out another spirit to punish him. Trinculo enters and spots Caliban's body under the garment. Assuming that he is dead, he first tries to classify Caliban taxonomically as either man, fish, beast, or Indian, calculating how much a profit a dead Indian would turn in the streets of England. A few moments later, he seeks shelter from the storm with Caliban under the cloak, and the joke is begun when Stephano finally enters the stage. Not only do Trinculo and Caliban form "a beast with two backs" (with all the sexual innuendo that phrase implies), but Trinculo must eventually emerge from the four-legged "monster" (Shakespeare's word that conjures "salvages" or "men of Ind") and finally separate the civilized from the uncivilized.[72] Caliban is in this scene referred to as a "moon-calf," a term that connotes "abortion, monstrosity formed imperfectly through the influence of the moon."[73] If we agree with Bakhtin that the grotesque image of the body has two bodies, one conceived, generated and born while the other is dying, then the Indian event of the scene, Trinculo's identification of Caliban as "dead Indian," performs a signifying translocation of new world indigeneity onto Caliban at the moment it is also deferred beyond signification as death. Trinculo is born again into civilization, while Caliban's figuration of "salvage" is aborted so that he can pursue a state of freedom within the Hegelian dialectic that has Caliban always needing a new master to be recognized as a new man at the site of translocated Indianness that becomes the rationale for anticolonial nationalism in postcolonizing settler states.

Caliban's contagion, then, occurs under the cloak when Indianness is both deferred and put to flight. Barbara Fuchs, in her reading of this scene, has interpreted Shakespeare's use of Caliban's gaberdine (as has Ronald Takaki) as a reference to British colonial constructions of the Irish within the literary conventions of the time, suggesting that "Caliban's cloak plays a central part in this complicated series of misrecognitions and discoveries, especially as a signal of the play's Irish context. The presence of the cloak does not prove such a context, but it suggests how English domination of Ireland might *take cover* in the text under precisely such details." The cloak provides the cover for British anxieties "over distinguishing savage from civilized, islander from colonizer in Ireland," so that natives of the new world are read through the lens of that which was already known.[74] Additionally, in the sixteenth century and later, the use of the word "gaberdine" to describe a person's garment evokes anti-Semitism; such "covers" in the text create a series of resonances that fill and refill Caliban at the moment of his reentry into the languages of imperialism.[75] At the threshold between giving birth and dying, then, everything under the cloak is translocated into new world indigeneities.

Caliban is a textual moment of dissonant collapse, his cloak the threshold of deferment through which settler colonial genocidal sovereignty enacts itself in the Americas.

Indian Metonymy and the Errant of False Cartographies

With all these various discourses coming to bear on and collapsing within *The Tempest*, spiraling from Africa, the New World, Ireland, the Mediterranean, and Europe, other questions linger that can perhaps be answered before *The Tempest* plays out its usefulness for indigenous critical theory. What happens when all these different discrete contexts are put together in a single space? Who is dominated? Who is dominant? Have these colonized objects and colonial subjects become so overdetermined that they fail to represent anything other than the colonizer's desire to construct the colonized? How does the emptying and reinscription of these referents facilitate the processes of colonization and racialization in the Americas, where the land had to be physically and psychically emptied of its prior inhabitants and refilled with newly arrived "natives" who compete for subjectivity within the emptied referent? And finally, what do these representational cacophonies mean for those who use the play as a metaphor for understanding the colonial relationships that have shaped various islands in the new world and its planetary reach? Though the focus of postcolonial theory has been on theorizing the future anterior of Prospero's leaving, a thornier question lingers: What happens when Caliban is forced to leave the island so that other Calibans might arrive?

George Lamming pinpoints language as the site through which Prospero establishes mastery and Caliban struggles to make an intervention, be it to escape the prison that the imposed language and culture represent, to curse Prospero and the language learned, or to transform that language into the means to overthrow Prospero's reign. "Prospero has given Caliban Language," Lamming writes, and "this gift of Language meant not English, in particular, but speech and concept as a way, a method, a necessary avenue towards areas of the self which could not be reached in any other way."[76] More importantly, the gift of Language, speech and concept, opens possibilities for Caliban and therefore risks Prospero's eventual downfall. Language and the Word establish the Law of Prospero as he enters Caliban's garden and orders the worlding of the native. The risk to Prospero lies in the fact that the language he employs to other the native is stretched to incorporate typologies of race as well as geographical and political orderings of lands in relation to the colonial center. In the economy of colonial representations, categories and metaphors of race, identity, and otherness come to inhabit single words that can then provide a shorthand for the colonizers to codify and master knowledge of difference. These words ultimately contain fissures and antagonisms within colonial manifestations of naming and representing that exist between and among colonial histories.

To model what such a tracing might enable within the transit of empire, I would like to unpack the myriad of distortive parallactic effects that exist in "Indian" as a structuring event that has particular importance in this discussion of both *Two Undiscovered Amerindians Visit . . .* and *Caliban*. Spivak, in her many contributions to postcolonial studies, attempts to place within the field "Aboriginal" issues, though American Indians and indigenous peoples are not intended to be the center of her critique. And yet she does reference indigenous and aboriginal issues at key moments throughout her argument, sometimes in brief asides and sometimes in a gesture to a deeper logic and history of colonial worldings of worlds. In her *Critique of Postcolonial Reason,* for example, she makes three gestures against the use of "American Indian" as a mnemonic device to signal how misnaming has functioned in the colonial archive. The first appears in a discussion of "sati" and the way it "commemorates a grammatical error on the part of the British, quite as the nomenclature 'American Indian' commemorates a factual error on the part of Columbus."[77] In another passage, a footnote discussing, among other things, monotheist tradition, Spivak enacts, as she admits in a parenthetical, a colonial misnaming: "Latin American Indian (what a multiple errant history in that naming)."[78]

The third appears in her analysis of a geographical palimpsest in Baudelaire's two poems "Le Cygne" and "A une Malabaraise," in which his repetition of lines from one poem to the next creates a cacophonous parallax between the islands of Réunion and Mauritius off the coast of Africa and the Malabar coast of India. Spivak writes: "The islands of Mauritius and Reunion, terrains of military colonial exchange between France and Britain, have a sizeable population of Indian origin as a result of the British import of Indian indentured labor. These people are not necessarily, not even largely, from India's Malabar coast. Their naming is like 'American Indian' or 'turkey cock,' products of hegemonic false cartography."[79] All these instances of what she deems false cartography, whether the synecdoche in the usage of "sati"—which translates as "good wife"—as a British grammatical errant for "the burning of the sati" or metonymy for Columbus's errant in which "the only good Indian is a dead Indian," circulate within empire. And though Spivak is primarily interested in the errant inherent within the misnamings that create the impossibility of either origin or the "real" within Baudelaire's palimpsest between India and Africa in the two poems, a refractive parallax occurs through which the Indian indentured laborer and the native African oscillate as afterimage of each other, creating parallactic distortions that interpellate and stop the other, filling the space between them with the possibility that both, instead of neither, are the real.[80] Within the transits of empire, such cacophonous afterimages become the space for coerced complicity within colonialist occupations, where the Indian indentured laborer becomes the affective site of a critique of colonialism in Africa and the Indian in America becomes a geographical palimpsest that carries the trace of indigenous peoples into postcolonial theory.

Such palimpsests within postcolonial theory have prompted Louis Owens to ponder those conditions of impossibility in "As If an Indian Were Really an Indian." In this essay he asks, "what must the colonial, or postcolonial, writer—in this case specifically the indigenous Native American, mixedblood or fullblood—do to be allowed a voice like Shakespeare's cursing Caliban?"[81] Despite Spivak's own critique of stepping forth as Caliban because he represents an inaccessible blankness inscribed by text, she assumes an inherent stability in "Indian," that is, perhaps because of international recognitions following decolonization, an identity one can step forward and claim within and against the errant. Even here, the terms of deconstruction are useful in making an intervention to Spivak's asides that delineate and define "Indian" as errant outside certain geographies. The minute "Indian" is defined within the transit of empire, there is a casting off at that moment of what is not "Indian." Such moments in Spivak's text, which serve to stabilize that identity by referencing a misnaming, additionally raise important questions that are useful in understanding cacophonous colonial discourses: What exactly is the proper use of "Indian" in a world marked (and mapped) by European colonialism? How can "American Indians" exist if they are always under erasure, always deferred by "Indian Americans"?

To answer the first question, because the "discovery" of the "new world" had to be reinterpreted within the old and within Western discourses, its peoples had to be accounted for in terms that were already familiar. Not only did Columbus misname the peoples he encountered, but intellectuals have struggled through the years to determine exactly where "they" came from, a debate that rages today in spite of indigenous peoples asserting continually and repeatedly their scientific knowledges of origins. One of the problems with Columbus is that it is not clear whether he believed he had reached the East Indies. The well-known narrative of Columbus's voyage is that he, in the name of Spain, set out for the East Indies and the Kerala (Malabar) coast to open markets and establish trade, and though there was no priest on board, to bring Christianity to the heathens. He was primarily looking for a less dangerous route to India than the existing ones: a land route that was rife with bandits and an oceanic route controlled by Portugal. When he sailed west and encountered land, we are told, he thought he had reached his destination, a factual error he believed until his death. Hence, the peoples he encountered were named "Indians" for better or worse.

However, with the quincentennial scholars began to challenged that assumption. There are glimmers of another narrative that suggests that, first, the peoples Columbus encountered in the "new world" were familiar to him because indigenous peoples from the "Americas" had traveled across the ocean many times and landed in the port cities of various nations.[82] Second, there were already maps and word-of-mouth stories that described islands such as Barbados in the Atlantic.[83] By 1424 the Antilles already existed on a map as a mythical island of refuge, and scholars have suggested that the name derives from "two Portuguese words, *ante*, meaning 'before', 'in front of', and *ilha*, 'island.'" Such an etymology suggests that "it was given the name *Ante-ilha* because they knew that behind it lay something else, i.e., the American mainland."[84] The question about where Columbus thought he was when he reached land is not important necessarily—the reality here is that the "new world" Columbus entered in 1492 had already been settled for tens of thousands of years. What is important is that the unquestioning dismissal of the term "Indian" when it is used to signify indigenous peoples in the Americas at some level breaks modern U.S. imperialism away from the legacy established by Columbus. There was violence embedded in the naming. And slavery. And genocide. It is today a marker of that legacy. Clarifying the use of "Indian" and "Indies" in the old world and new suggests that these words were not merely a misnaming or a factual error on the part of a deluded latecomer. They already involved and evoked the narratives of Orientalism that were circulating by the time Columbus set sail. It is an "Orientalism" transplanted and re-mapped onto the indigenous peoples of the Americas, and it carries with it all the discursive attempts to control and to narrate the place of peoples into an already established world.

At some level, it is beside the point to critique Spivak for her dismissal of the errant naming of the indigenous peoples of North America. She is right, after all, that the term is a misnomer. It is, as Gerald Vizenor has stated, "an occidental invention that became a bankable simulation; the word has no referent in tribal languages or cultures."[85] The very word signifies a colonial enactment. The problem is that "Native American" is equally untenable under the rubric of political correctness and posses-sion. Anyone who is born in the United States and is a citizen identifies as "Native American." And it does not even touch the reality that America signifies landmasses that exist outside the U.S. geopolitical border. Further, the landmasses were named for another Italian cartographer/explorer, Amerigo Vespucci, and that naming as well has little to do with the names indigenous peoples have for themselves or their lands.

All this still leaves a slight problem regarding the use of "Indian" in the American context. Beyond the fact that it derives from a geographically challenged explorer, it suggests a cultural and racial homogeneity that does not exist. There are over five hundred and sixty indigenous nations and/or communities and hundreds of language stocks within the lands that con-stitute the United States alone that would fall under the category "Indian." Jack Forbes suggests that "the term 'Indian' (or indio) has been applied to many peoples including the Indians of South Asia as well as all groups found in the 'West' Indies (the Americas) and the 'East' Indies (Filipinos, Chinese, Japanese, etc.)."[86] The term 'Negro' has been applied to Black Afri-cans, the Indians of India, Native Americans, Japanese, and slaves of what-ever ancestry."[87] These slippages suggest that such usages before, during, and after the "discovery" of the new world were flexible and indiscrimi-nant, that "Indian" signified non-Western or anything that was "East"; such significations and indeterminacies remain as traces that can still be seen and felt today.[88] "Indian," at least in the context of the United States, can be seen simultaneously as an empty referent—an errant as Spivak points out—and as overdetermined and therefore carrying multiple significa-tions that stretch and silhouette the real within the planetary parallax of imperialism.

Within postcolonial theory, it brings an additional quandary to the fore, given that South Asians have become the signposts of the condition of postcoloniality within the academic centers of the global North. Within an increasingly canonized discipline that is still innovating the language to account for deep settler colonialism within (post)colonized localities, the slippages inherent in "Indian" bear the complications of indigenous peoples in the Americas, whether they are ever fully acknowledged. "From the beginning of this history the specialized vocabulary created by Europeans for 'Indians' ensured our status as strange and primitive," Paul Chaat Smith writes in *Everything You Know about Indians Is Wrong.* "Language became and remains a tool by which we are made the 'Other'; the Lakota name Tatanka Iyotanka becomes Sitting Bull."[89]

New World Borders

It would be easy to end the discussion of *Two Undiscovered Amerindians Visit*... here with an accusation that when Fusco and Gómez-Peña placed themselves as "natives" behind bars in a cage, they stepped forward as "the real Caliban" and in the process, intentionally or not, deferred the "native history" they were trying to represent. Fusco and Gómez-Peña, for all their effort, conflated indigenous issues of sovereignty and self-determination, which came to the fore during the quincentennial when the United Nations declared 1993 the Year of Indigenous Peoples, into issues of multiculturalism and racism so that, in the end, the bars symbolized for Fusco the racism and sexism she experienced on a daily basis as an artist and a woman of color. At the end of her essay, Fusco discusses the impact and aftermath of the show:

> Over the past year, I have felt trapped in a frightful chapter of history that had resurfaced before my eyes. There were the circus and freak show managers of yore, claiming that they had "made us" into Guatinauis and that without them we were nothing. There were the anthropologists of the early century insisting that we had performed our identity without knowing, that we had no proper concept of how to record our culture and represent ourselves and therefore needed them to find an order in our madness. And there were the myriad pseudo-liberal documentarians who believed that

the "reality" they capture is always spontaneously generated, only to be formed into something meaningful by their magic touch.[90]

Fusco here reframes the history of human dioramas and museum exhibitions into a very personal assertion that, because the attitudes that arose when she put herself on display as a form of performance and the attitudes justifying the capturing, caging, and displaying of indigenous peoples are linked, she therefore knows what it means to be an indigenous person from a culture that anthropologists make careers of studying.

Throughout her essay on the performance, Fusco makes similar moves, reducing the cage to a metaphor for racism and pointing out the need of the audiences for "authenticity" and the savage, of which she is particularly critical. Despite this critical distance, the slippages remain in her own understanding of the piece. Even when she notes that the concern over their "'realness' revealed a need for reassurance that a 'true primitive' did exist, whether we fit the bill or not, and that she or he [be] visually identifiable," there is a sense she and Gómez-Peña did fit the bill and there was something "real" in their performance, despite its overt parody and inauthenticity.[91] Those tensions between "real" and "inauthentic," in and of themselves, undermine Fusco's own position and reveal her own complicity with colonialist understandings of indigenous peoples.

By tracing the historical and cultural uses of the term "Indian" within the discourses of discovery and Orientalism and by looking at Caliban (who is simultaneously slave, Irish, African, "Indian," and "native"), cacophony makes inroads into a parallactic postcolonial theory that could then be used to critique ongoing settler colonialisms that coerce arrivants into complicity through reifications of racism, rather than colonization, as the site for political intervention. *Two Undiscovered Amerindians Visit* . . . ultimately unraveled precisely because it was too structured, too controlled, and too insistent on a specific narrative where the lines between colonizer and colonized were drawn too sharply. Despite allowing multiplicity and polyphony in the discourses surrounding the history of displaying others, Fusco and Gómez-Peña's project was ultimately monotonic because it all occurred under the rubric of "oppression" as defined by a specific narrative timeline that allowed them to collapse the distinctions between divergent histories and colonialisms into a larger history of European racism. It created exactly the response that was expected—and although it confronted and resisted certain colonialist practices, it maintained others, namely the subjugation of indigenous peoples. There was no way for the cage to be torn down, no way for the audiences or the performers to resist the dialectic that had been established so effectively. There was no way for indigenous peoples to be anything other than dominated others upon whom this history was enacted.

Thus, although Gómez-Peña stated that the only correct response to their performance would be for the audience to let them out of the cage, the only people who did try to open the cage door were the skinheads who sought to kill him. Rather than revealing all the cacophonic histories and resistances embedded within the colonialist practice of displaying otherness either within museums or traveling exhibitions, in the end *Two Undiscovered Amerindians Visit . . .* unwittingly re-created discourses of colonialism that trap indigenous peoples within the other history of conquest, death, and lamentable tragedy. One goal, then, for indigenous critical theory as it intersects with postcolonial theory might be to develop critical readings that consider the complicities of racializations, where stepping forth to fill the parallax gap of the other as the "real" reinscribes the colonization of indigenous peoples through whom that "real" becomes unfixed and transferrable to settlers and arrivants alike. Indigenous critical theory is the necessary baseline from which to measure the violences produced as empire transits through the field of Indianness.

3

The Masks of Conquest

Wilson Harris's Jonestown *and the Thresholds of Grievability*

Conventionality is not morality; self-righteousness is not religion.

Charlotte Brontë, *Jane Eyre*

Parallax View

On November 18, 1978, the United States and Guyana were shaken by news that U.S. Congressman Leo Ryan and several of those traveling with him had been assassinated on an airstrip in Port Kaituma shortly after having visited the Peoples Temple Agricultural Project in Jonestown, Guyana. And while that event was shocking enough within the neocolonial international relations between the two countries, a deeper horror emerged as news came of the mass suicide and murder of over 900 people, most of them U.S. citizens, who lived in Jonestown and followed the Reverend Jim Jones's teachings. On the twentieth anniversary of the Jonestown suicides, *Stabroek News* reflected on the event's meanings within the Guyanese national imaginary, observing that "to this day, Guyanese hardly regard the mass suicide/murder as being part of their own local history, and in a sense they are right. While the Jonestown residents occupied a portion of Guyana's land space, they were not incorporated into its body politic."[1] Jim Jones's Peoples Temple played out as an American tragedy in a Guyanese national space, an imperial imposition upon a postcolonial Caribbean country. Neville Annibourne observed on the thirtieth anniversary of the tragedy, however, that "you really cannot make that kind of argument when 912 people die suddenly and violently in your country having been invited to settle there by the government of the day."[2] Guyana has been left to grapple with the complicities and realities of that American tragedy which occurred within its borders.

In the United States the lessons of that day have been harder to track. Certainly Jonestown informed a growing public concern about cults and charismatic leaders who had the power to brainwash susceptible believers into dying for a self-proclaimed messiah's cause. In many ways, however, the lessons of Jonestown have been repressed, cast to the fringes, and exported to the emotional labor of other nations. The thirtieth anniversary of the Jonestown deaths in 2008 passed unnoticed by a nation celebrating the recent presidential election of Barack Obama. Jonestown, when it was evoked at all, was misremembered in the form of a glib political critique, the invocation of "Kool-Aid drinkers" who would believe anything Republican or Democratic candidates might promise in pursuit of office.[3] According to Rebecca Moore, professor of religious studies at San Diego State University: "It is unlikely that many people who use the expression know of its origins in Jonestown, however. If they do, they have dissociated the deaths of more than 900 people from their thinking. Or they have consciously or unconsciously repressed the events so that they can talk about Kool-Aid without evoking memories of Jonestown."[4] As the religious, political, and technological spheres collided in the public sphere, "Kool-Aid drinkers" and "drinking the Kool-Aid" circulated as a meme that challenged the hubris of politicians, dot-commers, and charismatic cult leaders that enticed their followers to indoctrinated idealism and devotion. As the United States grappled with the collision of historical events that ultimately eclipsed Jonestown, the largest loss of U.S. civilian life prior to 9/11, "Kool-Aid drinkers" deflected learning from and understanding of the seductive narratives that culminate in disaster through an arch turn of gallows humor that erased the human suffering and loss of life that is and was Jonestown.

This chapter examines the compelling and contradictory impulses of social justice within imperial contexts. How might Jonestown be placed within the transits of empire arising out of abjected concerns in the United States about Indianness, racial justice, and the ethics and morality underpinning cultural and political practices and critiques of colonialism and imperialism? What might it mean to be responsible to history and the temporal densities that the collision of old and new world philosophies set in motion? The methodological frames of both cacophony and transit, I argue, can provide tools with which to discuss Caribbean literary aesthetics that seek to reimagine the present through Amerindian presences. I begin with Jonestown as a location through which to parse its conflicting and disjunctive meanings. The implosion of Peoples Temple becomes a gruesome reminder of the stakes for anticolonial justice and the strong need for scholars to not only disrupt imperialist logics but imagine other possible avenues of intervention attuned to the violences of the past and resistant to the narratives of freedom and equality built on Enlightenment enslavements and colonialisms. To that end, the chapter will read closely Wilson Harris's novel *Jonestown*, which is located at the interstices of national identity and postcolonial resistances that imagine a turn to the interior as redemption for the world. What does the activation of indigenous and tribal presences mean for interpretive strategies at the moment postcolonial multiculturalism fails?

The cacophonous competitions of what it might mean to remember Jonestown transpire in the parallax between incommensurable national imaginaries and colonial histories. In Guyana's national memory, Jonestown represents a U.S. state within their state, an unwanted global North encampment of quasi-sovereignty that existed liminally between the borders of the national and the international. For the United States, Jonestown represents and remains an aberrant and maniacal utopian commune at odds with the sanity and the rationality of the state. The repeated deferrals of meanings created in the shift between and among irreconcilable interpretations exist in the parallax gap of competing attempts to perceive the "Real." The versions of Jonestowns remembered and abjected across colonial and international divides, following Slavoj Žižek, "are not consecutive, [but] they should be read structurally.... The gap between the two versions is irreducible, it is the 'truth' of both of them, the traumatic core around which they circulate; there is no way to resolve the tension, to find a 'proper' solution."[5] Those competing Jonestowns, then, circulate around a traumatic core in search of meaning within the planetary parallax of distortive effects: the "truth" touches and stretches between them both but neither encapsulates nor reduces to that truth even though the U.S. and Guyanese Jonestowns signify simultaneously the violent and excess capitalistic accretion of imperialism that exports death and grief to other nations and the colonialist violations of borders and boundaries that overwrite and disrupt state sovereignties.

The continued search for meaning has produced a series of narratives about Jonestown that remain irreducible and irreconcilable within the United States and Guyana. For Moore, possible alternative narratives to the canonized cult mindlessness plot include placing Peoples Temple in the context of black religion in America. She suggests that "its large African American membership, coupled with its message of social justice and racial equality, all reflected the activism of urban black churches in the 1960s and 1970s."[6] Moore reminds us that Peoples Temple was actively involved in the political struggles for social justice in the heart of San Francisco and drew support from Harvey Milk, Dianne Feinstein, Jane Fonda, and Rosalynn Carter, as well as from members of the American Indian Movement and the Black Panthers. Peoples Temple members were at the International Hotel in 1977, adding their voices to the protests against the impending evictions from a site that for many Asian Americans had been a staging ground for Yellow Power consciousness in the face of diaspora, demolition, and displacement. "Jonestown is enormous," Moore concludes, "by which I mean it looms large in the repository of human consciousness, in the history of religions, in the study of new religions, in the understanding of religion in America, and in the consideration of ethics and morality."[7]

For others Jim Jones and Jonestown represent a culmination of imperial and racist trajectories that targeted African Americans and Korean transnational adoptees left brutalized by segregation and war.[8] Guyanese poet Fred D'Aguiar critiques the false consciousness of Jones's utopian experiment in the long narrative poem *Bill of Rights,* in which he writes, "Jim Jones doesn't know his okra / From his bora; / His guava from his sapodilla; / His stinking-toe from his tamarind."[9] In D'Aguiar's work, Jones's project to create a socialist utopia within the Guyana hinterland was inherently colonialist, an imperial imposition that replayed the U.S. Thanksgiving holiday at the founding of Jonestown, where the inhabitants of the city upon the hill starved "until the locals took pity on us" and brought food and skills to build the community.[10] That the Jonestown deaths occurred during Thanksgiving week in November 1978 underscores the collision of the founding myths of the United States rewritten onto the national space of Guyana—a nation that has its own errand into the wilderness and its own colonialist agendas played out on top of and against Amerindian communities, including the Arekuna, Akawaio, Arawak, Carib, Macusi, Patamona, WaiWai, Warau, and Wapishiana.[11]

Discourses of Indianness circulate uneasily within and around Jonestown, but that might be expected because, as Moore explains, Peoples Temple was not so much a cult as it was "a home-grown religion and, at its heart, reflected American institutions."[12] Though Peoples Temple was focused on racial justice in the face of the dissolution of America's promise to vast sectors of the population excluded from the purview of democracy and freedom, Jim Jones often claimed, according to Tim Reiterman, "Indian blood, sometimes attributing it to his mother, other times to his father."[13] Other sources said Jones claimed Cherokee ancestry through his father, though they were quick to add that "like many stories he told, it apparently was not true. 'There wasn't an ounce of Indian in our family,' Barbara Shaffer, a cousin, said this week."[14] American Indian Movement leader Dennis Banks, a friend of Jim Jones who benefited from Peoples Temple's political activism in San Francisco, says Jones "was part Choctaw and very sympathetic to the Indian cause."[15] Indeed, in 1976 Jim Jones and Peoples Temple raised tens of thousands of dollars to help Dennis Banks post bail for his wife Kamook and to fight "extradition to South Dakota for trial on weapons charges indirectly related to the 1973 Wounded Knee uprising."[16]

In *Ojibwa Warrior*, Banks reflects on Jim Jones's Guyana experiment, reporting that Jones had said: "In Guyana I'll rebuild my temple and create a community. I'd like you to come with me. You can build your sweat lodge down there and do whatever you want, but I need your help. I need your spiritual support. All of these people are leaning on me, depending on me as their spiritual guide. I can't carry this burden by myself. I need you as a friend. Remember, I'm Choctaw, so you must do this for me."[17] Philip J. Deloria has argued that playing Indian was endemic to the counterculture movements and communes of the 1960s and 1970s, and certainly Jim Jones's assertions of an Indian identity exemplify Deloria's point that "being Indian offered one an identity as a critic of empire."[18] In the slippages between "Indian," "Cherokee," and "Choctaw" that circulate around the traumatic core of that event, Jim Jones becomes what Anishinaabe writer Gerald Vizenor describes as a simulation, "an absence of the tribal real" in service to manifest manners of dominance.[19] Such simulations are, according to Vizenor, terminal creeds, static, death-dealing constructions that stand counter to survivance, a word Vizenor uses to denote tribal sovereignties as "more than survival, more than endurance or mere response; the stories of survivance are an active presence."[20]

But Jones's evocations of Indianness did not just provide an identity for himself; they also served as the basis for his narratives that in the end coerced over 900 members of Peoples Temple to follow him into death. In Mary McCormick Maaga's transcription of the "death tapes" from Jonestown's final White Night, there is evidence that Jones deployed the terminal creeds of Indian simulations to manage dissent and convince his followers that the only recourse available to them was "revolutionary suicide." The tapes document an exchange between Jones and Christine Miller as she tries to argue with him about the necessity for suicide. Scholars on the tragedy at Jonestown have often highlighted this exchange as a heroic moment in which "only a single person opposed him, at least according to the audiotape. Christine Miller, a sixty-year-old black woman, asked if it was too late for Russia," in the hopes of preventing the suicides that night by reminding him of his commitment to the Soviet Union as a possible haven for Peoples Temple.[21]

In arguing for life, Miller tried to convince Jones that "when we destroy ourselves, we're defeated. We let them, the enemies, defeat us."[22] Jones responded by asking Miller if she remembered *I Will Fight No More Forever*, a 1976 made-for-television film about the Nez Perce and Chief Joseph that takes its title from his speech of surrender to the U.S. military in 1877. That film, along with over two hundred others—*The Parallax View* (1974), *The Battle of Algiers* (1966), and *Billy Jack* (1971) among them—was included in the Jonestown video inventories that Jim Jones screened in the months prior to November 1978.[23] In the chaos of that final White Night as members prepared the cyanide-laced Flavor Aid, Jones and Miller debated the film's meaning and the options facing Chief Joseph's band as they attempted to make it to the Canadian border with the U.S. military giving chase; Miller argued that if the Nez Perce had not stopped for rest, they would have reached Canada and safety. Jones countered that, because of the violence at the Port Kaituma airstrip, the Peoples Temple was locked into an inevitable plot. Predicting a U.S. invasion of the settlement, Jones implicitly positions the members of Peoples Temple as Indians, and he uses as evidence the history of U.S. military massacres of Indians to justify his decision that every child and adult at the settlement should die by her or his own hand rather than wait for the death and destruction the U.S. government would instigate. These irreducible tensions reside at the interstices of imperial transversals, where the charismatic promises of revolutionary suicide collide with the imagined transits of empire that produce Indianness as an anticipated genocidal outcome of a failed militant idealism.

Jigsaw Multitudes

"What does it mean," David L. Eng asks in *The Feeling of Kinship*, "to take responsibility for a historical event one never actually experienced?"[24] The question frames exactly the problems posed to modernity in the face of overthrows, genocides, internments, slavery, and removals. But it prompts another question: How might one even begin to cohere a historical event for which to be responsible, especially in the *longue durée* of slavery and conquest that created the American South and the Caribbean? What does it mean to take responsibility for a historical present dependent upon Middle Passages, indentured labor, and the violences of conquest in which the explicit goal was not just to rupture in the name of enforced labor, but to chart the direct transit from life to death for certain peoples and not for others? These questions haunt the islands and continents brought into modernity through Atlantic forced diasporas, and they inform Caribbean ontologies struggling with and against the need for origins. Such questions also produce the need for more than just an affective turn—they depend upon memory and imagination to grapple with and create the possibility for grievability in the face of mass death. How might one redress such histories where dislocated arrivals facilitated dislocated removals? How might one imagine radical justice that addresses the cacophonies of colonialism?

Guyanese author Wilson Harris—knighted by Queen Elizabeth II as part of her Birthday Honours in June 2010—attempts to answer such questions by articulating the need to find new possibilities for narrative where "the paradoxes of emphasis born of necessity as sliced being revolves nevertheless into a new configuration or complex evolution, complex regeneration, sound yet sight woven together." Weaving together "sound yet sight" into configurations of grief that might address the sliced being that emerged out of conquest and slavery, Harris seeks throughout his twenty-five novels and numerous essays to generate "a fiction that seeks to consume its own biases."[25] "It is essential to create a jigsaw," Harris writes, "in which 'pasts' and 'presents' and likely or unlikely 'futures' are the pieces that multitudes in the self employ in order to bridge chasms in historical memory."[26] Instead of playing out the expected alienated turns of postmodernism, where the fractured self struggles to cohere, Harris presents us with characters struggling with intuitive knowledges and imagistic worlds, in which it is possible to be deemed a terrorist and shot in the back in the post-9/11, post-Katrina world, fall into a painting hung on a museum wall, and find Christopher Columbus. Harris's philosophic fictions tap the unconscious in order to consider the implications of the questions posed above turned topsy-turvy. How can there be, Harris asks readers to imagine, a historical event that one never actually experienced? This final question stands on the precipice and marks a postcolonial Guyana caught within the dialectics of mass death and suicide facilitated by U.S. imperialism on the one hand and generating the colonial discourses through which to legitimate the continued colonization of Amerindians on the other.[27]

Wilson Harris is in many ways a unique figure within the canon of Caribbean literature. His fictions resist easy categorization and interpretation and they often frustrate readers in search of linear narratives and accessible literary allusions through which to read his texts. In a career spanning over fifty years, he has helped to create what Paget Henry has defined as a "mythopoetic phenomenology" for a region struggling with the legacies that liberal humanism brought to bear on the four continents of British and American imperial hegemony.[28] Each of his fictions rehearses Harris's foundational ideas about imagination and the interventions that can be made to articulate and grasp the forces shaping current modes of consciousness and unconsciousness of self and Other in the Anglophone Americas. And if Harris might be positioned as integral to discussions of colonialisms and their aftermaths for those peoples impacted by Columbus's arrival, then it would be at least in part due to his quest to transform his own fictions to narrate the collisions between the histories and experiences of slavery, genocide, and colonization. His work serves as an example through which one might explore what an aesthetic that consciously engages the conditions of colonial cacophony might entail. His narrative transformations, or rehearsals as he terms them, fundamentally strive to engage Caribbean history with all its competing struggles for hegemonic representations. He writes to resolve the worldings of worlds that exist among Amerindian, African, Asian, and European presences and arrivals. To make such an intervention, Harris depends upon a "decentered ontology in which quantum worlds merge seamlessly into each other, establishing and relativizing each other at the same time."[29]

Wilson Harris's 1996 *Jonestown* enters the historical event of Jim Jones's utopian nightmare with his own imaginative intervention when his protagonist and narrator, Francisco Bone—a fictional witness to and survivor of the Jonestown massacre—adds his voice to the archive in order to reconcile Jones's own inevitable movement towards destruction with alternative futures in what Harris narrates as a "Memory Theatre." This theater of memory, which Harris evokes in many of his novels, could be understood as a performance of remembrance that offers, as Paula Burnett has stated, "an alternative to the annihilations which history records."[30] These alternatives manifest as repentance in *Jonestown*: the narrator rushes towards a resolution and presents himself, at the end of the novel, as a sacrificial victim to heal the contrapuntal responsibilities the self and other have to the histories of slavery, conquest, and genocide. As far as plot goes, the story is this: Francisco Bone, one of the Reverend Jonah Jones's trusted advisors, hides during the Jonestown suicides to cheat death. From the bushes at the edge of the settlement, he watches as Jones's second-in-command, Deacon, shoots Jones with a gun, and in the process Bone is hit by the same bullet and loses two fingers. He splits from his skeleton self (who falls into the grave), and the living spirit Francisco (as narrator) begins a seven-year spiral through quantum time back to himself as a child on the eve of his mother Marie's death in 1939, and then to Deacon's marriage ceremony to his wife Marie in 1954. These are not the same Maries (even though they are), and a third Marie appears as Jonah's mistress Circe. In the process, the boundaries between past/future, self/other, and Bone/Deacon break down as the narrative tries to triangulate and measure the ontological gap or void of Caribbean history.

But any plot summary of Harris's work is partial and limiting. Nor is it even advisable, since the narrative exists in the experiential motion of among and between. In Harris's novels, history cannot be accessed through plot, "fact," or realism, and responsibility to history has wide-reaching ramifications beyond assigning guilt or innocence, or reconciling victim and oppressor. Mr. Mageye, Bone's childhood teacher who serves as his Dantean guide through the realms of memory and un-memory, tells Bone:

> One is in the dark, Francisco. But I would venture to say that this is a question that runs beyond all man-made frames or realisms or commandments. We need to adventure into intangible graces in counterpoint with terrors in nature. Not beauty for beauty's sake, or realism for social realism's sake. These are often disguised kingdoms of dominion that we would chart in nature and in history. There are intangible graces that we cannot seize but whose tracery exists in a web or a vein or the music of a bird or some other creature.[31]

Francisco Bone is in the process of documenting the "intangible graces" within a "Dream-book" that explores the spiritual, cultural, and historical counterpoints leading to and extending from Jonestown. These counterpoints link through "Memory Theatre" and through imagination the conquests and collapses of what Harris deems unknown civilizations before and after the arrival of Europeans in the Americas. *Jonestown* is the manifestation of that "Dream-book," and while a "finished" document, it might also be understood as an incarnation of processes ongoing. Harris is interested in things larger than landscapes and geopolitical boundaries, and the events in the old world also have resonances within the new. Jonestown becomes a utopian ripple from Atlantis; the fall of the Maya empire echoes the fall of Rome; the deaths at Jonestown resonate with other genocides of the twentieth century. All are connected within the imaginative links that seek the prior within Harris's worlds of African, Indian, Amerindian, and European active presences.

Harris's *Jonestown* is not so much concerned, then, with representing the discrete actions and reasons that led up to and spiraled away from the events at Jonestown on November 18, 1978. Rather, his novel is more interested in understanding the Events, the ontological nature of ego and consciousness that made Jim Jones possible within a "Memory Theatre" that encompasses known and unknown, remembered and forgotten, grieved and ungrievable histories that work on the unconsciousness of a collective humanity and manifest themselves in art. Harris eschews realism in the hopes of accessing the Real within a Jungian mythos that taps humanity's unconscious genesis.

Tradition and the Limits of Realism

The faith Harris has in the imagination to grasp something deeper than history or culture, something more fundamentally divine and humane, compels and drives his explorations of language and narrative. It makes his work exceptional and difficult to categorize, and critics continue to debate whether Harris should be classified as a modernist, postmodernist, or postcolonial writer. Hena Maes-Jelinek and Stuart Murray both suggest that he might be, reservedly, characterized as a postcolonial writer, while someone like Sandra Drake might place Harris more fully within the modernist tradition.[32] Others read Harris as a Caribbean science fiction author through his transformation of linear narrative to represent the naturalized world outside the consideration of perceived space and time. Admittedly, Harris's writing is such that it demands that the reader think, reflect, perhaps even revere. To read Wilson Harris, as Mary Lou Emery has described it, is to enter into an incomplete conversation in which "one improvises. Becomes more than one—two readers, three readers—whose 'hidden ties' to others multiply, diffusing perceptions and activating ghosts of other selves, who read excitedly or indulgently or confusedly or, at times, are carried to a threshold, through a doorway."[33] Through novelistic and essayistic narrative, Harris has tried to create a way of writing (and seeing) that, in his words, "possesses a re-visionary capacity itself as if the text possesses an intentionality of its own to uncover connections that lie in other and deeper layers of what appears to be lost, areas that can be recovered to assist us in reading reality in a new way."[34] Such a re-vision of writing seeks to embody the connections, the complexities, the voices, the histories, the pasts, presents, and futures that have been called into motion in the Americas by greed, love, power, lust, and everything imaginable. Though it cannot and does not necessarily always escape the logics of enchantment and possession, Harris's narrative strategies are often considered destabilizing and disorienting—the reader and the critic focus on understanding and interpreting rather than critiquing.

It is this last point that Glyne A. Griffith posits as he critiques Harris's divergence of form as reifying the problems inherent in nineteenth-century novels of empire. Griffith suggests that rather than challenging how realism as narrative has, from the outset, depended upon bourgeois ideologies of class and race, Harris's novels, in their textual distance from recognizable forms and structures, often fall back into a reinscription of imperialist assumptions.[35] Thus, Griffith argues, the pitfall of writing outside realism's conventions (as opposed to within and against them) results in a failed engagement with imperialist hegemonies and the class interests inherent in realism's conventions. By the end of his investigation of deconstruction and the West Indian novel, Griffith concludes that Jean Rhys's *Wide Sargasso Sea* achieves what few other Caribbean works can claim in its recognition of and resistance to the dominant ideological structures of imperialism. Rhys's novel, more than any of Harris's novels according to Griffith, is the truly engaged West Indian text because of its *rapprochement* with Charlotte Brontë's *Jane Eyre* and its ability to address domination. "The force and presence of Caribbean *obeah* (orality and prophesy)," he tells us, "engage the power of European *obeah* (literacy and the law) to destabilize the authority of the latter." He continues, "[Rhys's] novel examines the anti-hegemonic resistances which threaten the security of dominant ideology" as it rewrites and rereads *Jane Eyre*.[36]

According to Griffith, Harris's failure to achieve what Rhys accomplished in *Wide Sargasso Sea* stems from his refusal to allow that realism's forms influence and determine the narrative choices he is ultimately allowed to make, even in his complete disavowal of those forms. "When Harris attempts to emphasise universal humanity by de-emphasising the strategic positionings of realism's classifications, he misses an opportunity to deconstruct the ideological foundation on which these classifications are built."[37] The insidious ramification of these missed opportunities, Griffith continues, can be found in the ways in which the stereotypes that ground realism go unchecked in *Palace of the Peacock* and the tensions between Donne and his crew. "The aboriginal 'folk' are constituted as the repository of some essential innocence and redemptive spirit. This is an unabashedly conventional and romanticised view of the 'folk'. They exist in the narrative as a stereotype, oppressed and hunted by the crew and yet retaining the solution to the crew's psychic conflicts."[38] This view of the "folk," Griffith maintains, builds upon imperialist and colonialist hegemonies that position them as noble savages outside civilization while simultaneously investing them with the solution for all the problems of Western society.

Griffith's final complaint is that Harris's refusal to recognize the degree to which he himself is always already steeped within realism's trajectory undermines any attempt he may make to break out of those narratives. In Harris's essays, as in his fictions, there is a sense that the Amerindian presence is not a fully realized one, that it (and it is always singular for Harris, always "the Amerindian legacy," "the native presence") is a latency that the conquering cultures and descendants of enslaved cultures must learn to access, to channel, and to recognize in order to fully grapple with modernity. That native presence has no agency of its own, in its own right. It is forever frozen on the precipice of conquest, crouching over campfires, sharing a morsel of flesh played, as Harris might write, on a scrap of music from a bone flute. The Carib and Arawak are forever trapped and doomed by the catastrophic moment of European arrival, and that moment, in Harris's work, forever exists as a possibility of difference that is accessible only obliquely—or rather, opaquely.

I agree with Griffith that Harris relies upon stereotypes about the Amerindian other, but the question that remains is whether those stereotypes are the result of realism in the first place. By approaching Harris's texts through an expectation of and resistance to realism, Griffith sets his argument against and counter to the interventions that Harris attempts to achieve in his fictions. Harris might respond that because the foundations upon which realism has been built—namely the consolidation of character and narrative—depend a priori upon empire and death-dealing regimes, it is impossible, therefore, to write within the form to critique realism. In his essay "Tradition and the West Indian Novel," Harris writes:

> The consolidation of character is, to a major extent, the preoccupa-
> tion of most novelists who work in the twentieth century within
> the framework of the nineteenth-century novel. And this is not
> surprising after all since the rise of the novel in its conventional
> and historical mould coincides in Europe with states of society
> which were involved in consolidating their class and other vested
> interests.... The novel of persuasion rests on grounds of appar-
> ent common sense: a certain "selection" is made by the writer, the
> selection of items, manners, uniform conversation, historical situa-
> tions, etc., all lending themselves to build and present an individual
> span of life which yields self-conscious and fashionable judgments,
> self-conscious and fashionable moralities.[39]

Though Harris concludes that there is an apparent element of freedom within realism's method, he determines that "this freedom—in the con-vention which distinguishes it, however liberal this may appear—is an illusion."[40]

In Harris's eyes, realism is always already rigid, selective, determinative, and steeped in the residue of conquest. Realism as form denies associa-tive links that must be made to recover and reactivate lost histories, cul-tures, peoples, images, metaphors, and archetypes in order to understand fully the consequences of colonialism. Harris would argue, then, that real-ism in the novel orders narrative to such a degree that its very structures encode biases even before they could be employed to deconstruct them-selves. There is a conversation to be had between Harris's narrative choices and the forms of realism; however, Harris is more interested in finding a third and a fourth option to either existing within or outside of his literary inheritances. He seeks to supplement and transform the British novel of empire by existing within the space opened through deconstruction rather than tracing the specter to which deconstruction gestures. At some level, to read Wilson Harris is to take a leap of faith with him and enter the chasms of narrative and space that Western civilization has struggled to sublimate and hide. One must trust that there is an alternative.

The Shadow Texts of Counterpoint

But what alternative does Harris provide and how, more importantly, does it depend upon indigeneity as the site of European imperial transits to consume biases without cannibalizing the other? In writing about Wilson Harris's *Palace of the Peacock,* Antonio Benítez-Rojo suggests that the novel performs, through Donne's and his crew's expedition into interior, the "historic search of Guyanese society, looking for a root to link it to the country's vast and intricate land." The search for El Dorado, Benítez-Rojo tells us, continues today in Guyana "beneath the slogan of 'repossessing the interior,' which refers to the economic exploitation of the inland territory, potentially rich in natural resources, as well as to the discovery of a collective psychic state which would allow a feeling of cultural identity, extended toward the hinterland, which Guyanese society has lacked."[41] For Harris, who spent the 1940s in service to the possessing of the hinterland as a land surveyor, the experiences he had in the interior of Guyana were transformative and, according to Maes-Jelinek, served to "stimulate his conception of the human personality as a cluster of inner selves." Futher, Maes-Jelinek tells us, "this experience in the Guyanese interior was the seed of his original art of fiction, making him reject realism as inadequate to represent its complex, living, ever-changing landscapes as well as the depths of the human psyche."[42] His obsession with the interior, and particularly the quest for El Dorado (the quest on the one hand for wealth and material goods and on the other for the divine) that Guyana evokes as it looks to the hinterlands to cohere a national identity, culminates in *Jonestown*'s reengagement with Jim Jones's doomed and tragic agrarian experiment on the border between Guyana and Venezuela.

Harris's notion that all the world's cultures are partialities that are presumed to be wholeness in themselves provides a foundation for conversations across and through traditions that have often been assumed to be discrete and isolated, or framed within the logics of colonial politics that suture worlds into hierarchies of access to capital and resources. His work is situated within a kind of planetary conviviality that Paul Gilroy imagines—one whose postracial, postimperial soundscapes are attuned to historical violences but not determined by them.[43] But also at play in Harris's reconfiguration of historical events within the Caribbean are the individual characters' connections to those histories, even if at first they seem random and unrelated. Thus Harris, through a narrator like Francisco Bone, can ask whether Jonestown's final destruction was "the latest manifestation of the breakdown of populations within the hidden flexibilities and inflexibilities of pre-Columbian civilizations?" at the same time that he can link those breakdowns to his narrator's witnessing of his mother's death in 1939 or to Deacon's wedding in 1954.[44] Harris's sense that cultures exist only partially, that they are neither whole, complete, or consolidated in and of themselves, manifests itself in his fiction through his evocation of quantum mechanics. Each character is incomplete and often split and divided among other fractured and partial existences; the effect of such fragmented partialities is that Harris's characters (like the cultures they cross) seek fulfillment in relation to other characters and other histories and moments. The challenge is to perform through language these interstitial connections of sidereal matter.

The Amerindian absent presence that links moments past and future cannot necessarily be, Harris tells us, perceived visually nor felt physically or tangibly. Rather, they are heard and experienced obliquely, at the margins of sensory perception. As a result, Harris is interested in a critique of realism that goes deeper than a dismantling of stereotypes. One of Harris's significant contributions to Caribbean literature is his desire to reconfigure the legacies of colonial history by incorporating Amerindians into a conversation that, through the work of writers such as Kamau Brathwaite, C.L.R. James, George Lamming, and Derek Walcott, was already taking place between Africa and Europe and within the Black Atlantic. His insistence on complicating identities of the self disrupts the binary that can emerge when discussing Caribbean histories of colonization and slavery. Within Caribbean and postcolonial studies, "African" signifies "native," and in the elision, such distortive parallactic effects, which stretch the real between transatlantic indigeneities and diasporas and then evacuate signifying agency from Amerindian perspective points, inform Guyana's nationalistic endeavors to control and incorporate indigenous lands and peoples into the body politic of the settler-arrivant nation-state for the good of all.

Harris's novels and critical work make it possible for Benítez-Rojo to write:

Of course it's always possible to try to wipe the Indian out, which unfortunately would be nothing new in America. But nothing of this kind could be the theme of a Caribbean novel. The ordinary thing, the almost arithmetical constant in the Caribbean is never a matter of *subtracting*, but always of *adding*, for the Caribbean discourse carries, as I've said before, a myth or desire for social, cultural, and psychic integration to compensate for the fragmentation and provisionality of the collective Being.[45]

Harris indeed takes to heart the lessons of addition within Caribbean literature. But Benítez-Rojo's observation that the subtraction of the Amerindian is not a theme in Caribbean literature is not necessarily always true—the theme is more the mathematical principle of substitution. Jamaica Kincaid has in the past imaginatively rendered Amerindians as "living fossils," and Kamau Brathwaite, in *Contradictory Omens,* replaces the Amerindian indigenous "folk" traditions with African "native" traditions when he delineates the distinctions within creolizations.[46] One might at least allow, then, that the stereotypical images of Amerindians that rest on the surface of Harris's narrative discourse hint at a deeper commitment to apprehension, a deeper responsibility to access (at least imaginatively) what he thinks is lost or hidden from Caribbean society in order to first grieve and then be transformed in the process. And in contradistinction to Deleuze and Guattari's "Indians without ancestry" who move along a line of flight without memory, the Amerindian in Harris becomes *the* assemblage, the ancestral machine within the transits of empire that created Caribbean national literatures at the site of memory.[47]

Musical metaphors provide Harris with a tool to tap many of these hidden landscapes, hidden densities. Songs, flutes, and chords/cords trace throughout Harris's fictions and essays and have come to represent at some level his attempts to distill discourses of colonialism and resolve them into something that compensates for the "fragmentation and provisionality of the collective Being" that Benítez-Rojo identifies as part of the Caribbean psychic wound. In his essay "Merlin and Parsifal," Harris writes that "music in fiction, in my estimation, reaches through and beyond poetic ornament or metaphor into a real engagement with unfathomable coherency in the body of an entire creation."[48] In *Jonestown* Harris remains interested in the coherency of creation, but what also emerges is the dissonance between and among histories and cultures at the discrete levels of their quantum partialities. It is the "*shadow of music*" that Harris emphasizes in *Jonestown*, the ability to carry "what is virtually unseen but not unhearable or unseeable, even as sheer quantity and number lose their claustrophobic tyranny."[49]

In his fiction Harris always rehearses a reading praxis that attempts to engage the "concordances and dissonances" of the vocabulary of death-dealing regimes and their interrelations that resulted when Renaissance Europe encountered pre-Columbian civilizations.[50] As he writes into and through the thresholds of correspondence to show how one moment can touch upon a multiplicity of other historical, cultural, and individual moments, he attempts to narrate his fictions through the principles of musical counterpoint as a mode of seeing through to the contextual and relational dynamic between specific notes, histories, and cultures. In *Culture and Imperialism,* Edward W. Said defines "contrapuntal reading" as a praxis that "must take account of both processes, that of imperialism and that of resistance to it, which can be done by extending our reading of the texts to include what was once forcibly excluded."[51] Harris deploys a related impulse to aesthetic ends where the unknown histories, the hidden texts that underscore known texts, shadow each moment to reveal a deeper logic, a more subtle disruptive pull. Harris writes that "dissonances in music lie in depth within all harmonies to acquaint us with unwritten relationships that disturb our Sleep. Or else harmony would consolidate itself into an illusion."[52] For Harris, counterpoint is not just a matter of including what was once excluded; it is a process of entering into the relational dialectic that exists in cacophony, where "'death's vocabulary is rooted in human discourse...'" as Francisco starts and Deacon finishes, "*in counterpoint with the extra-human dissonances of the victim soul, the long suppressed, plaintive and wonderful music of the victim soul.*"[53]

As a musical form, counterpoint emphasizes dependent lines that exist relationally with rules to resolve harmoniously; and though counterpoint can entail secondary lines independent of the first, original line, counterpoint always relies on tension with the original melody to determine its existence and options. The imperial ear is trained to hear intervals and chords as either harmonious or dissonant, with the melodic structure dependent on recognized harmonic progressions. Counterpoint can build on scales of whole tones and semitones, but the additional voices in the piece stay in the home tonic of a composition. Tensions and divergences are controlled, predictable, and expected within intervals of whole and semitones, major and minor progressions that in imperial musical traditions determine which sounds are consonant in their interrelations. For Harris, counterpoint is the tool with which to engage those seemingly consolidated and coherent narratives of colonialism and imperialism and force them into the parallactic breaches that exist on the margins of dissonance. Harris's dream narratives are haunted by the dissonances that counterpoint linear narratives. And his emphasis on disruption provides his characters the means to identify the conquistadorial logics underpinning utopian projects and postcolonizing Caribbean societies alike.[54] "Jones's brand of religion, Jones's split between the dead past (so-called) and the future (so-called), Jones's irredeemable universe, can prove a killing dogma, a killing manifesto directed at the heart of originality."[55]

Perhaps one should then approach Harris's fictions in *Jonestown* as rehearsals of contrapuntal texts that seek to reflect within the linear narratives and arguments that are his inheritance from the Age of Reason. He adds lines and perspectives to the structures of realism to seize and transform the impulse toward character consolidation into character fulfillment, from strictly controlled and coherent narrative into a more dialogic interaction among partialities. There are a few ways to traverse the tensions that emerge as Harris figures narrative in musical and cultural metaphors of bone-spirit. The first comes from the very questions that Bone asks in his Dream-book that he eventually sends to W.H. to publish: "Does music inhabit a quest for self-knowledge beyond all conventional framework?" This question is followed by the more elaborate rumination: "Wherein lies the mystery of music in the densities of space, the live fossil solidity of music in the song of a blackbird or reflected rhythms and compositions in the mirrored throat of a South American apparitional mocking-bird? Did the bone in a wing of the mind, a wing of the brain, inhabit a treasonable space beyond fixtures which sanction extinguished species, poisoned landscapes?" (16). These questions, though ultimately left for the narrator and reader alike to reflect upon, do advance Harris's own concerns with the dialectic within and between self and other as they grapple with the cacophonies and deferments that we have seen emerge in figures like Shakespeare's Caliban.

It is Deacon, however, who offers Bone a means to transform these dialectical confines. He interrupts Bone's musings to ask "Is it not time—when time seems to be ending—to unravel that counterpoint, varieties of counterpoint between priest and sacrificial victim, between huntsman and hunted species, between lovers and Virgins of the wild . . . ?" (19). The bone flute, which comes from, according to Harris, the Carib tradition of consuming a morsel of enemy flesh in order to embody the enemy other within the self, is finally transformed into a flute made of the enemy's bone. The resulting music bears not only the cannibal morsel, as Harris phrases it, but performs the breakdown of the dialectic established when cultures and peoples collide. The music played by the bone flute mirrors and twins the act of consuming flesh—the song and notes themselves become the morsel that the spirit and the ear cannibalize.

The Carib spirit twins—exists in counterpoint to—that of the European: "The evil conquest in the invader smarts and exacerbates a sensation of mutual horror in the Carib spirit which entertains an identical lust for triumphal victory" (54). For Harris, the true understanding of the horrors of conquest are felt precisely because the Carib themselves seek victory over their environment, over other native peoples, and (when they wash up on shore) the Europeans. There is a moment, then, whether it is through the eating of flesh or the listening to the bone-flute, in which the Carib other merges with and corresponds to the European self as their desires align in parallax. Despite the destruction and horror that resulted from the collision between these cultures, Harris identifies a distinctly human impulse to conquer and control; in that moment, neither side is victim. The fundamental crisis of sameness rather than otherness that Harris identifies as the chasm opened in the collision between old and new worlds—the breach with all its seeming dissonances—presents a foundational harmony to the cannibal bone flute music that traces throughout Harris's imagination. Counterpoint becomes the means through which Harris is able to deconsolidate the European and Amerindian selves and place them into kinship. While neither side necessarily acknowledges the other, perceived or heard together they provide fertile imaginative vistas for Harris to trace other possible means of human interaction that do not depend upon genocide or slavery.

Thus, while Harris stresses the dissonances within harmonies and counterpoints to break down the dialectics that exist within Caribbean landscapes and between peoples and histories, a distinct relationship emerges in his use of musical metaphors to transform consciousness. As Deacon phrases it in *Jonestown*, there is counterpoint in the role of the priest and the sacrificial victim, for example, so that their individual trajectories are to some extent independent of one another but simultaneously are also fundamentally dependent upon each other—the act of sacrificial offering can only be understood through the counterpoint of both experiences. Both of these subject/subjected positions are intricately bound up in each other and forever caught in that interaction. But the overall score that encapsulates the contrapuntal ceremony bears other traces and calls into the space of land and imagination the violence and terror of death and sacrifice. Harris is concerned not just with the interpersonal relationships between and among priest/sacrifice, master/slave, or colonizer/colonized. He emphasizes the violence that those relationships activate in the land, the traces and webs that extend beyond the mass destruction of Amerindians by first the Spanish and then the British, the mass terror and oppression that extends from British plantation economies and the Middle Passage of peoples torn from families and forced into new worlds and new relationships. Those violences themselves counterpoint each other—the destruction of Amerindian societies has a counterpoint in African slavery; Jonestown has counterpoints in the sacrificial ceremonies of the Maya and other unknown but still present violences that occurred centuries before and are set to occur in the future.

Cities of Gold, Cities of God

In attempting to understand Jonestown on the quantum level of interspersed textual secretions, Harris, writing through his main character Francisco Bone, seeks ways to break the composite epics of empires that structure themselves through linearity and consolidation. Bone writes in his Dream-book that "models of fiction cemented in the eighteenth and the nineteenth century are sacred in the twentieth. Sacred eighteenth-century, nineteenth-century linearity. But I was attempting to rewrite the past from the funny side of sacred, imperial time, from a futuristic angle that breached linearity" (89). An important aspect of Bone's imaginative work here is that he seeks to dissolve that monolithic linearity through a fracturing of his Dream-book characters, by splitting and then doubling, tripling, and twinning them. They enter an archetypal, mythic realm where their individuality breaks down, as do the boundaries between historical moments. What this means for *Jonestown* is that "one becomes, it seems, a vessel of composite epic, imbued with many voices, one is a multitude. That multitude is housed paradoxically in the diminutive surviving entity of community and self that one is" (5). Francisco Bone, as a diminutive survivor of Jonestown, is, according to the Virgin Oracle from whom he seeks guidance, "the embodiment of lost tribes, or peoples, Atlantean peoples," and such embodiments necessarily contain the extinction of peoples—it is the extinctions of species that provide "*a mystical unity with all creatures*" (131, 132). Bone's imaginative voyage through the history leading up to and beyond Jonestown centers, in part, on Bone's ability to apprehend and see himself not only in, but through Jones and what he represents, to see in his own near-death experiences a counterpoint to other extinctions, other deaths.

The intimacies between and through characters are an important dynamic in Harris's novel. Through the hidden and woven kinships between characters, Harris creates composite archetypes with which to understand the capacities for destructive and regenerative movements through space and time. As composite characters built out of partial selves, partial others, the people contained within the chasm between Jonestown and its pasts and futures are fragments, broken and in some ways trapped between being free and being determined by the events they are trying to escape, or paradoxically, inescapably cause. Jonah Jones, the charismatic madman who is trapped within the Classics of Anger that U.S. society feeds its citizens, is flanked by Francisco Bone, the idealist dreamer made flesh who is haunted by past civilizations and by his own forgotten memories, and Deacon, the fallen angel who is responsible for killing Jonah at the beginning of the book and at the end, the figure who is held responsible for violating the Arawak shaman's ceremony that rendered him immune to scorpion venom. For Jones, those Classics of Anger depend upon composite evocations of the savage other as "a stick with which to beat my cursed society. Use the heathen savage as a clarion call when you wish to upbraid your civilization. Pretend to be black," Jonah explains to Francisco, "or red or yellow. Say you understand what black South Africans have suffered under apartheid regimes. Eskimos, South Sea islanders, whatever" (118–19).

Francisco finds himself inexorably drawn to Jones's anger, could "see Jonah in myself, suffer him in myself, with a dark humor." The push-pull counterpoints that the novel charts allow Francisco to realize that Jones's *ressentiment* sought to mold Bone "into Dickensian flesh-and-blood. A liberality that made me invisible to him and ripe therefore (who knows) for salvation! Such is the predicament of savage conscience in seeking to lay bare the transgression and transfiguration of anger that I sought to achieve in my Dream-book, the transgression of anger's compulsive frame to damn and use others forever" (119). As Bone attempts to transgress and transfigure anger away from the stick Jones created to Calibanesquely beat at his society, Bone's Dream-book seeks to use counterpoint to make visible all that liberality seeks to hide in the name of salvation.

Each of these three archetypal men has a Marie, or a Virgin Goddess (Animal Goddess or Fury) who accompanies, guides, and shapes their composite journeys to, through, and beyond Jonestown and the moments that determined its outcome. This archetypal trinity is a fragmented version or rehearsal of Jim Jones, who sets up a settlement in Guyana's interior only to watch it implode before he himself dies. Bone is central to the novel, in some ways the word made flesh—flesh because in the aftermath that followed his survival at Jonestown, he "dreamt [he] was dead." A ghastly skeletal twin splits from Bone at the precipice of the grave that Bone does not fall into, and Bone is told later in the novel by one of his guides that "you need that twin to orchestrate Bone—the Bone or survivor that you are—into the Carnival news of a futher re-entry into Jonestown. On that day of the holocaust you survived, Francisco Bone, but something integral to the fabric of yourself remained behind within the trauma of the grave" (109). That act of escaping death, or more accurately, because Harris never makes these things simple, the act of dying and splitting from his dead self into his living self, transforms Bone into a "diminutive survivor" and as such, he bears the sign of all who have narrowly escaped extinction through genocide. Harris disrupts consolidation through exponentials, and as a character Bone already embodies the partialities and counterpoints that Harris seeks to represent—his dead self corresponds to his live self and both must be felt and perceived together in order to fulfill or "orchestrate" the character struggling with survivor's guilt.

The first section of the novel, entitled "Virgin Ship," is mainly a philosophical engagement with what survival might mean in the aftermath of unspeakable horror and the collapse of a utopian dream. How does one understand survival of the self after so many others have vanished? For seven years after his survival (what he terms his betrayal of Jonah Jones), Bone wanders through memory and "un-memory" on the Virgin Ship until his mental wanderings bring him to question and confront the meaning of history, violence, terror, and the forces that separate self from strangers. Such questions finally force Francisco from his self-imposed stasis, and he realizes that the way through the legacies he inherited from his own colonial ancestors and from Jonah Jones is to confront the terror that they represent. He begins to understand that the first step beyond the survival of the self is a recognition of that self embedded within others, a glimmer of which Bone perceived during the final moments within Jonestown, when he, Jones, and Deacon became one. He fired Deacon's gun that killed Jones and took two of his own fingers just as much as he realized that he had died there on the forest floor with Jones.

In many ways, the recognition that he formed a "deadly circuit" connecting himself to Deacon and Jones is the source of his initial break with reality and the basis for his wanderings through his own personal history. As the character recognizes that he is himself Jones and Deacon, this realization calls into question his own inactions, his own failure to prevent the murders in Jonestown. This "deadly circuit" that Bone grasps at the threshold of the grave stems from the womb of space and creation that connects all life: the reason Bone is set wandering at the beginning of the novel is that he has refused to relinquish his self and give himself up to the void the grave represents. That raging against the relinquishment of self to the abyss prompts Bone to begin constructing his Virgin Ship. This vessel embodies both the womb of creation that Stephanos Stephanides articulates as maternal necessity within Bone's psyche, and the deeper evocation of the Middle Passage and the arrival of peoples in the new world.[56]

To recover his lost self after the tragedy at Jonestown, Bone draws the first nail in his Virgin Ship, a ship that he believes can be converted into "'a new architecture born of profoundest self-confessional, self-judgmental nails and materials and fabrics ...'" that will allow him to traverse without losing himself to the void gaping before him.[57] Maes-Jelinek has linked Harris's use of the Virgin Ship throughout *Jonestown* to a quote by Norman O. Brown that appears as an epigraph to Harris's *The Carnival Trilogy*: "The wanderings of the soul after death are prenatal adventures; a journey by water, in a ship which is itself a Goddess, to the gates of rebirth...." According to Maes-Jelinek, Harris's use of the ship here in *Jonestown* "validates the saving role of the female."[58] Harris too writes that the Virgin Ship in his novel "is a way of incorporating everything, for example, the energy of the fire that destroys becomes regenerative."[59] And while the ship serves to transport Bone between 1939, when he witnessed his mother's death, 1978 and his witnessing of the deaths at Jonestown, and 1954 when he witnessed Deacon's marriage (and when he revisits it, he himself becomes the groom as masked Deacon) to Marie, a woman he also loved, the Virgin Ship may also represent the arrival of Europeans within the new world when Christopher Columbus sailed out of Spain in 1492 on his flagship, the *Santa Maria*. The Marian trinity that forms between the Maries associated with the three main players in the "Memory Theatre" (Marie Antoinette, the Virgin Ship and Mother Marie, and virgin bride Marie) counterpoints the trinity that Jones, Bone, and Deacon form as a "deadly circuit." The movement toward redemption that Bone seeks is presented in the text as a composite epic; Bone must finally be held accountable not only for his own action/inactions, but he must also be held accountable for Deacon's and Jones's choices. Through fractures and through breaks, Bone himself contains partialities of self that exist in counterpoint to each other; the transubstantiation of self into multitude, of flesh into bone, bone into flesh, gestures toward other composite characterizations that, when taken only on their face as coherent, stagnate and control.

Through Bone's incomplete understandings, Harris makes the point here that the character lacks a fundamental ability at the beginning of the novel to perceive the hidden shadow texts of his own experiences. Bone believes he is a discrete individual at the beginning, and through the course of the novel he must learn not only to fracture and represent himself/selves as partialities, but also to see that his journey is a composite narrative of arrivals and deferrals. Linking Bone's transgressive recovery of memory of self to the building of the Virgin Ship echoes the self's struggle for coherence within composite partialities within the new world arrival, an arrival that shattered both new and old world historical trajectories and splintered them into that random system chaos strives to resolve. The importance of the discovery moment, the arrival of the Europeans and the destruction that followed in their wake, cannot be underestimated in Harris's imaginative explorations of cultures, myths, and narratives. The moment when Columbus first set foot on one of the islands of the Caribbean delineates for Harris a privileged moment of creation-through-destruction that set modernity into motion; its haunting refrain in Harris is an elaboration of what was lost and what was gained through that violent arrival. It is the transformative moment within the Americas, and all Harris's novels and much of his nonfiction engage this rupture in one way or another. In *Jonestown*, one can see how the rupture that separates the pre-Columbian from the post-emerges as the medium for imaginative engagement. The Virgin Ship, for instance, evokes both the womb of creation as well as Columbus's ship of death named for the Virgin Mother. This narrative association is evidenced as well when Bone writes that "my fluctuations of memory, in my wanderings for seven years in the wake of the 'tragedy of Jonestown,' are rooted as well, I am sure, in the amnesiac fate that haunts the South and Central and North Americas across many generations overshadowed by implicit conquest."[60]

These seven years of wandering that separate Bone from the escaped grave of Jonestown and the movement towards historical self-reflection themselves bear the mark of conquest—the number seven here speaks not just to the Christian story of creation but also to the seven generations that have passed since conquest and the seven yet to come that perform Harris's notion of life-in-death, creation-in-destruction. Bone reflects, "The Maya speak of Dateless Days that become a medium of living Shadows in which history retrieves an emotionality, a Passion, to unveil the facts and go deeper into processions into the body of the womb."[61] Such reflections spur Bone to retrieve a deeper past as he struggles to make meaning from Jonestown, and as the narrative progresses, Jonestown is refigured as "Conquest Mission," a more recent manifestation of the violent and often disastrous policies that the Europeans' mission of civilization and Christianization inflicted on indigenous peoples. Here, too, in Francisco Bone's name, are references to not only San Francisco, the city where he and Jones first meet, but also the Spanish Franciscan priests who used enslaved Indian labor to built their missions throughout Central, South, and North America. Francisco Bone writes at the beginning of his Dream-book that he "was obsessed—let me confess—by cities and settlements in the Central and South Americas that are an enigma to many scholars," and one could go so far as to say that Harris's narrative stalks these Columbian moments that mark the transformation of the old world/Renaissance world and the new world/Amerindian world. And then there is El Dorado, the mythic City of Go(l)d that runs through all of Harris's writing. In *Jonestown* El Dorado begins to take on a multifaceted dynamic as Harris plays with its meaning—El Dorado, a place (Golden City) or a person (Golden King), affects Bone-in-Deacon at the end of the novel as he becomes a tainted Scorpion Midas.

But these associative gestures are not an end in and of themselves—they are not the sole justification Harris uses to break nineteenth-century consolidated narratives into self- and inter-referential partialities. Harris's break with linear, structured progressions within fiction lies in the foregrounding of associations, conscious and unconscious, that exist relationally and dependently on any other association that can be accessed imaginatively.

Harris strives to write fictions within the aesthetics of the parallax gap, fictions that will represent differently and pull the reader to the margins, where all the sublimated experiences and perspectives resistant to colonialism and destruction still reside. Associative resonances that are activated once counterpoint intervenes in the nineteenth-century narrative plainsong provide the foundation for cross-culturalism that is so central to Harris's political interventions.

Harris's cross-culturalism differs significantly from multiculturalism. Harris writes, "multi-culturality at best—exercised by a reasonable establishment—signifies an umbrella of tolerance over many different cultures. But reason at times wears thin and that umbrella may be dashed by violent conflict. There is an incorrigible force in multi-culturality. Each culture regards itself as intact (including the dominant establishment) and the quest for wholeness lies solely within itself." This seeming coherence isolates each culture within itself and that "multi"cultural impulse masks a fundamentally detached tolerance towards all as long as they keep to themselves. "Cross-culturality is utterly different," Harris continues. "It is of the conviction that cultures are partial in themselves."⁶² Harris has a strong conviction, however, in the ability of these partialities to provide a larger coherency: The Amerindian trace serves as the focal note for the counterpoints that resist the consolidated linearity of dominant, imperial trajectories. "I glued my eyes to Mr Mageye's global Camera," Bone confesses at one point in *Jonestown*, "in order to see the detail of Aboriginal genius in sculpting the evolutions of mutated holocaust, altered spectres of holocaust into the sacrifices (voluntary and involuntary) that humanity makes in striking a chord linking Devil's Isle to Botany Bay to Port Mourant to dread Jonestown."⁶³ The indigenous trace in Harris's imagination provides the transit between the nineteenth-century penal colony off the coast of French Guiana to Captain Cook's first landing of the *HMS Endeavour* in Australia to the birthplace of Cheddi Jagan to Jonestown.

The final section of the novel, entitled "Roraima's Scorpions," performs this distinction between multiculturalism and cross-culturalism as Francisco Bone begins translating "the Mayan Itzá or Izté Oracle at Chichén and other places of sacrifice."⁶⁴ On his journey of dissolution of self in partiality, Bone has begun to see or unsee the hidden connections that Harris identifies as key to fully grasping and transcending the monolithic linearities that mask such interconnectedness between individuals and cultures. Bone observes:

In the hollow of God—whether water or fire—there is no discrimination. Everyone arrives and departs in mutual body and mutual ghost. This is the "architecture of pilgrimages." The pilgrims come and go "seven times in a minute."

What is a minute or a number (whether seven or zero on the Earth)? It is above and below, it is diversity and uncanny twinships, in the creation and fall and rehabilitation of time.[65]

Bone here links his own Virgin Ship, the hollow of God, to the "architecture of pilgrimages" that is on a quantum, internal level, "above and below" the large-scale movement of peoples. The seven and zero activate not only the twinning between the teleology of Amerindian and Christian creation stories but also the cross-culturalities that Harris demands his narrators and readers make. The "seven" here, as I have said, refers both to Genesis and to the conquest moment; the zero too speaks of destruction, of annihilation, of nothing, of void, but because it was a mathematical concept theorized by the Maya, it also represents another moment of creation. Rather than viewing the zero as nothingness, there is again a cross-culturality that originates with the Maya and allows "zero" to achieve fulfillment as yet another representation of creation-in-destruction that ghosts much of *Jonestown*. For ancient Amerindians, "zero" was neither void nor emptiness alone. Rather, it gestured to creation, the circular movement between life and death, the repetitive progression of history that connects and interweaves past futures and future presents.

The passage quoted above appears near the end of the novel and testifies to the development in Bone's comprehension of the events and cultures folding and unfolding around him as he sails on his ship through time to return finally to 1954 and the scene of Deacon's marriage to Marie. Bone, in his journey through and on the Virgin Ship towards some kind of re-membered "Memory Theatre," dons the head and mask of Deacon and finds himself fulfilling, and at the same time transforming, Deacon's actions prior to Jonestown. Bone finally apprehends his role in the counterpoints and composite epics that have been shaping his journey all along: he must fulfill Deacon's crimes and redemptions because Deacon is unable to do so. Deacon on his own cannot escape himself, but Deacon-in-Bone, Bone-in-Deacon can accept full responsibility for past and future actions. The scenes at the end of the novel culminate all the partialities of selves, cultures, and histories that Bone has documented in his journey. The

Amerindian in the contact moment serves as the catalyst, the presence/
absence that can be used to activate other texualities within African and
European arrivals and set them into contextual motion. The culmination
of this reaction occurs in the text with the carnival circus performance
that represents the wedding between Deacon and Marie. The wedding is a
mess of images and associations within a chaotic orchestration of the final
score. Cross-culturalities—between African Legba and Greek Hephaestus;
Amerindian prisoner/sacrificial victim and Prometheus; Christian, colonial Marie and Indian Kali—are all cacophonous, partial compositions in
the final masque that transforms Bone into Deacon and prepares him for
his final trial, judgment, and sacrifice.

All of these associative partialities exist relationally to Amerindian
conquests and destructions, but as the scene progresses, the Amerindian
catalytic presence that initiated the first movement slowly recedes as other
cultures come to the fore. If the Amerindian presence fractures realism's
linearity into thousands of partialities, then it is the African god Legba
who, Harris tells us, stands at the crossroads between India, Africa, and
the Caribbean to close the gap "between rich nations and poor nations."[66]
Harris invokes other African tricksters in the wedding ceremony, including Anansi, to force Bone to comprehend finally his own responsibility
in the plot that has already unfolded. He has slept with the Virgin and
must therefore pay the price, force society into a redemptive mode to "test
every fragment of a biased humanities, [to] break the Void by sifting the
fabric of ruin for living doorways into an open universe."[67] Through the
transformative moment of the wedding night, when Marie manifests as a
Virgin Goddess guarded by and containing Kali, Bone himself has become
a trickster within the narratives of, around, and through Jonestown, and as
a result, Mr. Mageye reminds him, he has entered into pacts not only with
Jonah Jones and Deacon, but with other realms and other gods, including
at this point Anansi, Legba, Kali, Hephaestus, and Prometheus. Bone had
already violated the pact with Jones at the beginning of the book, when he
did not die in Jonestown. Bone, because of terror and dread, has throughout the course of the novel and his journeys through time, limbo, and the
netherworld, refused repeatedly the Void for fear that it would consume
him entirely and require of him the final relinquishment of conquest that
underpins his own distinctive individuality.

The last few pages of the novel accompany Bone in the Dream-book
of Memory Theatre to Mount Roraima, a *tepui* or geological formation of

sandstone deposits that rises into the air 9,094 feet and sits on the border between Guyana, Venezuela, and Brazil.[68] Supposedly its name translates as "mother of all waters," and Harris's description of the place as "an Eagle's fierce perch, within and upon the watershed between the floodwaters of the Amazon and the torrential rapids of the Orinoco" evokes such a hidden text.[69] The Roraima within Harris's imagination is infested with scorpions that parallel the constellation Scorpio, and in order to climb to its summit in 1954, Deacon had undergone a ceremony to inoculate himself against their venom. Bone-in-Deacon shares in that inoculation at the end of the novel when he sets out to climb Roraima, and he traces Deacon's actions after the wedding and banquet. Mr. Mageye, before he is finally consumed by the narrative of the novel, tells Bone:

> Society is adamant. It rarely forgives. One has to start from within in order to bestow—as each garment falls—another page in Memory theatre's Dream-book on which to assemble new traces or traceries of repentance in the fictionality and actuality of the Dark soul. That is why, Francisco, I shall leave you the skin of the Predator when I go. *Write upon it, Francisco.* Write the last (or is it the first?) epic of repentance. Society tends to be unforgiving. Murderers never change, do they? They must be punished to the end of time. Under lock and key if not on the gallows or the electric chair. [...] You are a diminutive survivor, Francisco, in whom live multitudes, prey and predators and victims alike. [...] We are unconscious of the debts we owe others in history, we are unconscious of the crimes that we have committed in ourselves or through our antecedents. No medium can help us except *life* in the Precipice of the Dark. No word can help us except another music that we blindly see or hear in the computerized grave of the globe or cape of rhythmic numbers. (215–16)

Mr. Mageye's final gift to Bone is the skin of the Predator upon which to write the redemptive fictions that will transform the world, a skin that will allow Bone to "write upon the walls of rotting, colonial institutions, [to] test every fragment of a biased humanities, [to] break the Void by sifting the fabric for living doorways into an open universe" (216). The final moments of the novel gesture towards these redemptive narratives and return to some of the themes common in Harris's other fictions. Bone-as-Deacon finds himself on

a Virgin Ship transformed through the Wedding Banquet into the Ship of
Bread—a ship which finally at the end of the novel invokes Christian communion and transubstantiation as well as symbolizes the moment of transcendence that occurs when the host is taken into the body and consumed,
and a moment in which otherness becomes self through remembrance.

This trope of cannibal communion has appeared before in the novel.
At the beginning, before his escape from death and before his first journey on the Virgin Ship, Bone remembers the "eve of the holocaust" where
he, Jones, and Deacon consumed a Carib morsel in order to gain insight
into and awareness about themselves and their enemies. Jones rejected the
sacrament, though Bone found it terrifying and ecstatic (and here Harris
refers to the idea of ecstasy that results from spiritual transcendence). That
Carib morsel that Bone consumed and Jones rejected bears a "terrifying
conscience within the furies of history." It is one of the things Bone has
forgotten but finally remembers: "I had forgotten that the Caribs were the
authors of the American feast beneath the Virgin statue of Liberty, authors
of asymmetric hospitality granted to aliens and strangers despite their suspicion of, and antagonism to, one another" (18). In the associative realm
that Harris's imaginative canvas creates, the Last Supper before Bone,
Deacon, and Jones confront each other on the battlefield of the Jonestown
genocide is a contrapuntal Thanksgiving, a Carib feast beneath the "Virgin statue of Liberty." He performs Judas's betrayal against the charismatic
leader he had joined, even as he shares in the Caribs' feast as they offer
hospitality to strangers from across the ocean.

The novel begins with Bone's violation; that violation haunts Bone as he
tries to outrun the Huntsman and to outsail the void as he resists and fears
fulfillment (of the pact, of character, of fate). I am tempted to say that the
course of the novel—the trajectory of the associative counterpoints that
reveal hidden histories and consume the biases of narrative and empire—is
an allegory for Bone's passage from refusal of to acceptance of fate. Bone's
survival at Jonestown at some level unsettled the frames of reality and introduced chaos (in the mathematical sense) into the patterns of history
that had emerged before and since conquest. All histories, all moments,
all events are, for Harris, in flux; they are contextual and relational and
therefore accessible. Bone's violation of his pact with Jones unleashes the
threshold void of the novel, a void that symbolizes both destruction and
creation, fulfillment and rejection of character, a void first called into being

by the arrival of Europeans. The redemptive motion of the novel resides in Bone's struggle to comprehend the forces at work in events that shape him.

The final accessible point within the Jonestown composite is Deacon's betrayal of the Amerindians. Forty years before the start of the novel, Deacon had traveled to Roraima in search of wealth, and the natives, who return to judge Bone-in-Deacon at the end of the novel, helped him gain his wealth from Roraima by performing a ceremony to inoculate him from the scorpion venom. We learn that one hidden text within Jonestown's history is Deacon's climb and fall, Deacon's ultimate betrayal of the pact he had made with the native shaman of Roraima who performed that ceremony:

> "Oh my God," I cried to heaven. "*I remember now.* I see now through Deacon's blind eyes in the Play on the other side of Dream. He forgot the shaman's warning. I remember. I see through his blind eyes in the Play. The Play's the thing, the real world beyond all real worlds. *That is the innermost, outermost vocation of trial and judgment in fiction.* Or else fiction is dead. One must re-imagine death as a live fossil apparition. Imagination Dead Imagine. Deacon returned on the day that the Child was born, he lifted it into his arms. He felt himself superior to all curses. And the infant stiffened in his arms. A stone leaf grew where its face was, the face of the Child at the edge of Roraima." (232)

The judges as chorus tell Bone that someone in the Play must step forward to be tried and judged, someone must be held accountable and responsible. With startling clarity Bone realizes that he has come to the "other side of Dream," and has in a way run head on into the histories that earlier, he had been warned by the Giants of Chaos, were necessary for "self-confessional, self-judgmental art" (161). "Deacon," the Giants who twin the judicial chorus at the end tell Bone, "fell from the stars to expose centuries and generations in conquistadorial regimes in which populations were decimated and buried yet liberated in colonial history books. The legacy is strong." Bone responds in counterpoint that "everything depends . . . on how we shoulder such legacies in order to take responsibility for our own fate enmeshed into the fate of others in ourselves" (160).

At the time, he did not understand why the Giants mocked his naïveté, but by the end of the novel, when he is confronted by the masked indigenous judges on Roraima, Bone finally understands the questions that had been posed to him in response by the Giants of Chaos. They had asked:

> "How can the rich save the poor," they demanded, "the poor the rich, the thief the saint, the saint the thief, the judge the judged, the judged the judge, unless they discard contentment, or self-righteous creed, self-righteous parasitism, and build dimensions of self-confessional, self-judgmental art, that take them into recesses and spaces that may pull them *into* and *beyond* themselves? Unless this happens in the theatre of civilizations evolution remains a WASTE LAND and religion contracts into a Void. Yes, the Prisoner sometimes seems the architect of the Void in his uncertainties as to the nature of freedom in art, in science." (160–61)

When Bone faces his masked accusers, his masked judges at the end, he remarks that he is poor, that he has nothing, that it is no accident. And he understands that he "was a mere Colonial. Not an Imperialist. . . . Are Colonials the only potential creators of the genius of Memory?" (233). His moment of self-understanding, of willingness to pay Deacon's debt, fulfills the Giants of Chaos's call for self-confessional, self-judgmental art that takes humanity "into recesses and spaces that may pull them into and beyond themselves." Bone's fulfillment of character comes when he submits himself to Arawak judgment and is held responsible for Deacon's crimes, regardless of whether he was the "diminutive survivor" of holocausts or the embodiment of aboriginal survivors and histories. The native judges on Roraima accept his confession and push him over the edge and into the void of creation-destruction through which he moves closer and closer to the far removed "body of the Creator." The novel ends with Bone finally succumbing to the void he had been trying to escape all along—in that moment he learns that his willing descent was not so much the relinquishment of self, but an offering of himself to cosmic nets of music that capture him and allow him to finally open new doorways and thresholds beyond the Void and into the ineffable of creation.

Plainsong Counterpoints to the Void

Maes-Jelinek has read the final moment of Bone's descent as the re-enactment of the fall of man, "experiencing what Harris calls 'the gravity of freedom,' at once its serious, sometimes terrifying responsibilities and a fall into the 'womb of space' and 'the unfinished genesis of space.'"[70] She notes that Bone is the first of all Harris's characters to take the leap into the void of his own accord, though I find myself wondering what it means here that Bone is judged for the conquest of El Dorado through Deacon by the Amerindians, for whom Mount Roraima is sacred. Should this moment be read as a self-motivated leap into the void when he is tried, convicted, and pushed over the edge for his crimes? Perhaps Bone might be understood as the sacrificial victim that twins the Maya cultural traditions Harris evoked earlier in the novel. But there is an implied interconnectedness between priest and victim within Harris's text, a tension between the one who performs the sacrifice and the one who is sacrificed. I would argue that an interpretation that suggests that Bone descends into the void of his own volition misreads the significance of the reciprocity that the narrative within *Jonestown* seeks. Bone does indeed submit himself to judgment by the Arawak court, and in that act recognizes the moral if not sovereign authority of that court to judge him as Deacon.

It is important to note here that the Arawak judges hold the agency and power to determine the price Bone will pay and not the other way around. If there is a leap that Bone takes, it is a leap of recognition counter to the imperialist agendas of Hegelian dialectics. To say Bone's submission to judgment is a casting of himself into the void, then, implies a paternalistic attitude towards Amerindian agency. It suggests that the Amerindians themselves are a void, merely an absence. And that equivalence is possible only from and within the imperial worlding of Amerindians, in which they gain validity only through the sanction of the colonial juridical order. Further, it is in that moment of judgment that Bone must recognize he is only a mere colonial and relinquish himself to the other side of the dream where he can finally be fulfilled through judgment. The indigenous judges ask: "Who then is to be tried and judged? If not Deacon, who? Does no one claim the part? Is everyone innocent, no one guilty or responsible?" In response, Bone relinquishes his self in a moment of being-for-the-other that reconciles that past through the centrality of indigenous agency to demand and enact judgment counter to the desires of Enlightenment liberalism's constituted subject when he says "Judge me."[71]

In many ways, Harris's fictions call for an accountability within reading and writing inasmuch as he seeks to "consume biases" within language and within narrative. Such a task is daunting, not just for Harris but for the reader, who must enter into her/his own pact with Harris's vision and trust the imaginative and latent possibilities that he opens up and then offers as redemptive resurrections. Part of Harris's intervention lies in his invocation of counterpoints to challenge accepted Caribbean narratives of arrival, be they European "discovery" or African Middle Passage, in which the Black Atlantic figures as the active colonial "native" experience in layered histories of indigenous, African, Asian, and European interactions that leave, as Elizabeth DeLoughrey has observed, "a residue of social stratification in the imagined historical landscape."[72] These historical arrivals serve in the consolidation of Caribbean identity—as colonial, creole, or descendants of slaves and indentured laborers—that stems, Harris would argue, from the disavowal of other hidden traces that originate in Amerindian absences and remain in the indigenous prior of land, languages, and cultures. That precolonial past has been sublimated to such a degree that even to gesture towards its effect upon Guyanese presents and futures is a transgressive move, especially as the Guyana nation-state targets the indigenous interior for resource development and seeks to wrest indigeneity away from the Amerindian communities and peoples who continue to live in their traditional lands.[73]

More than any other Caribbean author of his generation, Harris is committed to accessing imaginatively and narratively those Amerindian pasts that, for him, were significant in resisting consolidations of self and other. In many ways, the triads that Harris uses in his fictions attest to his own sense that the Caribbean is shaped primarily by the interactions among European, African, and Asian/Amerindian histories, even before other cultures and nationalities arrived to complicate Caribbean identities further. Harris posits that the imagination must engage each of these cross-cultural interactions in order to disrupt the consolidation of nationality and racial identity that gains its coherency through an abjection of the Amerindian and an Indianization of the Caribbean nation-state that, in DeLoughrey's reading of Edouard Glissant, runs the risk of displacing African origins and slavery, and supplanting African heritage within the Caribbean.[74] But the Indianization of postcolonizing settler and arrivant nation-states in the Americas not only elides and effaces the histories of African slaveries and resistances; Indianization serves to cohere the settler and arrivant nation-state around a supplanted indigeneity that elides and effaces the indigenous peoples upon whose lands the nation-state is now located.

Signifiers and representations arising in colonial moments—especially within Anglophone settler colonies—bear resonances and discourses that exist simultaneously as they vie for primacy to determine indigenous absences and presences. Those cacophonous discourses render indigenous peoples and referents simultaneously blank and distorted within the parallax of competing narratives of arrival, indigeneity, and otherness. Harris seeks to write fictions that can interrogate densities within densities and access the native within the colonial discourses that shape nineteenth- and twentieth-century narratives. Often he returns to the colonial referents that stem from his British literary and educational inheritances, depicting Amerindians as "bucks," as "noble savages," and as the primal solution to the dissolutions of modern, colonial society. He evokes repeatedly the Bering Strait theory in his fiction and essays as he struggles to extend the 1492 rupture in a gesture to older and, for him, unfathomable movements of peoples.

For instance, in *The Dark Jester* he writes that "the Incas ... had descended into the Amazon in Brazil," or in *Resurrection at Sorrow Hill,* he links the "migration" narrative of "mongoloid" peoples across the Siberian land bridge to the arrival of English pilgrims when he notes that "the earliest pilgrim fathers and mothers from Siberia in the gateway of the New World were bitten by ice and fire and were subject to dismemberment."[75] The fictions Harris writes are in "unfinished genesis" and "infinite rehearsal" as he repeats again and again an evocation of an originary movement southwards of peoples across an ice bridge. It is a trajectory that unfetters the other monolithic movements of more "modern" peoples even as it resists the inheritances of realism, which deny that such linearities are truly associative and contrapuntal. When Harris leaves Amerindian arrivals within a set narrative in which movements of people only occur north to south across a narrow ice age bridge connecting America and Asia, it hints to deeper biases that Harris has only begun to access and engage about Amerindian presences prior to European arrivals. They remain unconsumed within his text as he grapples with the void created in the distortive parallactic effects that attempt to apprehend the Real in those moments when it is partially discernable. The possibility of other migrations, other narratives, other origins, and other knowledges are excluded from his imaginative rehearsals even as he reconfigures presences for native peoples within the Americas prior to contact. This point does not so much diminish the strength of Harris's intervention as it posits the limitations of the individual imagination to consume bias fully.

Harris tries to write himself out of the narratives of consolidation, the condensation of histories that emphasize linearity and favor imperialist agendas, and we are to understand his Guyanese imaginative landscape as a primordial blending of past, present, and future by referencing Amerindian horizons and trajectories that were disrupted by the arrival of the European. Harris's Amerindians are indeed presences that activate other cultures into more complicated cross-culturalities, but to some degree they remain in the pre-/post-Columbian schism that opens in 1492. Amerindians must always be incorporated into the self and into a Caribbean cross-culturality and never the other way around. The transformative alchemy that Harris performs in his writing to achieve the *cauda pavonis* (the peacock's tail)—which according to Harris "may be equated with all the variable possibilities or colours of fulfillment we can never totally realize"—depends upon a "host native" to precipitate transformations, to transit possibilities within the trajectories of empire.[76] This "host native" or paradigmatic Indianness that is the transit of empire allows transformations to take place, but Amerindians, it must be stressed, precipitate out of the transformations they facilitate and are not a part of the future perfect of postcolonizing Caribbean societies.

Thus Amerindians serve as the catalyst for Harris's imaginative interventions, but as such they remain trapped in the past as new culturalities are formed to propel Caribbean identities into the future. It is this tension in Harris, this notion that Amerindian legacies are at some level present but still absent and unknowable, that undermines his ability to break fully from the narratives of colonialism. However much Harris seeks to incorporate the self into being-for-the-native-other, the fact remains that the native remains always othered. In his fiction Harris does not or cannot represent an imaginative space that allows for Amerindian horizons of knowing to determine the possibilities of imagination. Amerindian peoples are always descending across the Bering Strait into the Caribbean—they are always part of a past, always determined by the threshold of discovery. Such imaginings leave Amerindians within a narrative of a priori arrival that does not and cannot activate, as Shona N. Jackson argues, any agency for indigenous peoples within the contemporary Guyana nation-state. "Since 'prior arrival theory' can only be understood as a racial essentialist theory, they must as the original indigenes, be kept in their place in order for subsequent ethnic groups—the former majority black and Indian groups during British rule—to justify their present claims to land and power."[77] As indigenous peoples struggle for agency and authority on their own lands through discourses of antecedent and originary rights, such articulations are perceived by others as exclusionary, essentialist, and counter to a pluralistic society that proffers indigenous peoples cohabitation within a liberal nation-state on the lands that had been stolen from them as remediation for their ongoing colonization. What is seen and what is said, what is heard and not heard continue to haunt the imagined posts of settler colonialisms in the Americas.

The end of *Jonestown* illustrates this threshold between the imagined and unimaginable with Francisco Bone standing on the precipice awaiting judgment. In a letter that Francisco Bone sends to W.H. on a dateless day from somewhere on Trinity Street in New Amsterdam, he writes of his obsession with "cities and settlements in the Central and South Americas that are an enigma to many scholars." In a "precipitate breakdown," the Caribs disappeared mysteriously from British Guiana, and their absence remains an unsolved riddle that still haunts the land according to Harris. But what Bone is most fascinated by is "the amazing story of the Arekuna Indian Awakaipu." Awakaipu, Bone tells W.H. and us in the letter, "persuaded representatives from many Indian peoples to offer themselves as a sacrifice at the foot of Mount Roraima in order to recover an 'enchanted kingdom.'"[78] In the counterpoint that Harris seeks to elucidate, that Arekuna sacrifice prefigures and coincides with the suicide that the victims at Jonestown committed to attain paradise. But on a deeper level, Harris is himself obsessed by what that possible "enchanted kingdom" might have looked like from the other side. That Harris imagines Awakaipu's call in the 1840s to his people to sacrifice themselves to be a similar call answered by the members of the Peoples Temple in the 1970s illustrates his own imaginative struggles to formulate what might lead people to kill themselves. But while the movement of both Bone and Jones towards death remains central to *Jonestown*'s narrative, Awakaipu's sacrifice remains inaccessible. It serves as a shadow, or perhaps a catalyst that initiates Bone's own embrace of the void. Bone is both priest/sacrifice, predator/prey in that moment, both Awakaipu/Jim Jones and the Arekuna/members of Peoples Temple who sacrificed themselves. But is the "enchanted kingdom" that, in Awakaipu's promise, waited on the other side the same as the afterlife that Jones sought?

Such observations, then, lead me to a fundamental concern about how Harris is using Amerindians within his imagination and how his readers' imaginations interact with them. If readers are asked to relinquish and suspend their disbelief for the course of a novel, there is a deeper, more heavily fraught demand that Harris makes as well. The reader, through the course of interpreting Harris's work, must accept the imaginative terms that Harris presents. And to accept the transformations Harris seeks to narrate, the reader must agree with Harris that Amerindian histories are hidden and inaccessible, unknowable and lost, or knowable and accessible only through counterpoint and twinning. As a result, critics often fail to engage the Amerindian at all in Harris's writing, or if they do, they refer to Amerindians in paternalistic and colonialist ways. Hena Maes-Jelinek's reading of the ending of *Jonestown* is one example of this unfinished transformation. It occurs elsewhere in her work. She writes of Harris's idea of cross-culturalism that it is "deeply rooted in a perception in depth of lost, 'alien' experience, of vanished, supposedly 'savage' cultures (e.g. the pre-Columbian) with which the 'civilized' must enter into a dialogue as they retrieve them from the abyss of oblivion."[79] Alfred J. López identifies Harris's boundaries and abysses as fissures that propel us through and beyond freedom, fissures that, López finally explains, are the "*frontier.*"[80] It is a space, López writes, fully informed by Harris's need to "find a space within the monolithic categorizations and taxonomies of Western thought in which to reinscribe the alterity always suppressed with such systems—to find a place, in other words, in which to begin to address the Other."[81] While López acknowledges the "frontier's" highly suspicious history of meanings, it also becomes a replacement for "margin" in his argument, a reappropriation of the "undiscovered space and place up ahead" in which "we have at least found a place to begin, a space or index from which to start reading and writing a future for Africa, the Caribbean, and the rest of the postcolonial world which may reconcile Harris's term 'meaningful paradox' to its contradictorily coherent parts."[82] But that "undiscovered space" of the frontier, at least in the Americas and within Harris's own imagination, has always already been inhabited by Amerindians.

On its surface, such a beginning for a space from which to read futures for Africa, the Caribbean, and the rest of the postcolonial world seems utopic. However, when Maes-Jelinek's argument that what Harris seeks to resolve in the breach between postmodernism and postcolonialism are those lost, vanished, and "savage" cultures is juxtaposed with López's identification of that breach as frontier, the juxtaposition illuminates another meaningful paradox within the disconnect between Harris's own acknowledgments of the limits of his imagination and his readers's assumptions: the belief that because they can see that Amerindians are now present, they are finally knowable and accessible—and that the ongoing present of settler colonialism is finally a part of the past that is reconciled through a past tensing of those presences. And here we begin to see what is at stake for my arguments about cacophony and colonialism within deep settler and arrivant landscapes. If Harris's works ineffably challenge and embody a nuance heretofore never experienced, why do discussions of Amerindian presences continue to be framed within terms delineated—however much they are also under erasure—as "alien," "lost," and "vanished"? Alien to whom? Lost to whom? Vanished by whom? How could the introduction to a collection of Wilson Harris's essays suggest that "for Harris, the indigenous peoples and their *habitat* would make definitive ingress in his language and literary imagination" without recognizing the degree to which "habitat" dehumanizes Amerindians?[83] There is already embedded in certain discussions within Harris scholarship a presumed center from which these experiences have been "lost" or "vanished." The tensions that emerge in the critical engagements with Harris's writings stem from naturalized biases that have yet to be consumed.

Harris himself is aware of the limits of his own narrative to achieve fully such a goal—it is why his fictions are "unfinished" and "rehearsals." At the end of *Jonestown*, the void that Bone finally embraces is both the Arekuna "enchanted kingdom" and the void in which, by the time that Harris writes *The Dark Jester*, Atahualpa is "a supreme being."[84] The abyss is a space that is completely unimaginable at the same time that it is, Harris's fictions insist, necessary for true transformation. *Jonestown* ends at the moment Bone finally relinquishes his own biases and embraces the contrapuntal sacrifices that Awakaipu promised and Jim Jones inflicted as shadows of one another. Harris's imagination leaves us upon the precipice, at the threshold, that Bone is able to move beyond. There is a promised transformation within Harris's fictions, but it exists in the work we as scholars and readers do with the tools Harris has given us to dismantle biases and revise rehearsals. He opens the door, and the question that faces those who read after him is where do we go from here?

4

"Been to the Nation, Lord, but I Couldn't Stay There"

Cherokee Freedmen, Internal Colonialism, and the Racialization of Citizenship

But freedom was also to be found in the West of the old Indian Territory.
Bessie Smith gave voice to this knowledge when she sang of "Goin' to
the Nation, Going to the Terr'tor," and it is no accident that much of
the symbolism of our folklore is rooted in the imagery of geography. . . .
Long before it became the State of Oklahoma the Territory had been
a sanctuary for runaway slaves who sought there the protection of the
Five Great Indian Nations.

Ralph Ellison, "Going to the Territory"

Blues Nation

In 1924 physicist Niels Bohr reportedly remarked upon his visit to Kronborg Castle in Demark, "Isn't it strange how this castle changes as soon as
one imagines that Hamlet lived here?"[1] The possibility of transformation,
of "retrospective world-building" based upon the usual suspects of narrative and remembrance—the who, what, why, and when of a location—is
something that Keith Basso discusses in his analysis of Western Apache
spatial knowledges as place-making. Basso writes, "What is remembered
about a particular place—including, prominently, verbal and visual accounts of what has transpired there—guides and constrains how it will
be imagined by delimiting a field of workable possibilities." These place-
makings, according to Basso, "consist in an adventitious fleshing out of
historical material that culminates in a posited state of affairs, a particular
universe of objects and events—in short, a *place-world*—wherein portions
of the past are brought into being."[2] But what is remembered about a place
is itself a location, a site within a series of locatable historical processes that
stage, particularly in lands shaped and mapped by a Western European
settler colonialism dependent upon slavery and plantation economies, a

contest of remembrances that each strive to bring a past into being as the real past.

Within American Indian epistemologies *where* something takes place is more important than when, and the land itself, according to Cree scholar Winona Wheeler, is "mnemonic, it has it own set of memories."[3] A land that remembers is a land that constructs kinship relations with all living beings who inhabit it, creating what Abenaki scholar Lisa Brooks has described as "the common pot," a reciprocal conceptualization of land dependent on shared resources and responsibility.[4] For American Indians, who have lived for tens of thousands of years on the lands that became the United States two hundred and thirty years ago, the land both remembers life and its loss and serves itself as a mnemonic device that triggers the ethics of relationality with the sacred geographies that constitute indigenous peoples' histories. Such mnemonics inform Joy Harjo's poetry when she writes, "I think of the lush stillness of the end of a world, sung into place by / singers and the rattle of turtles in the dark morning."[5] Her poem "The Place the Musician Became a Bear" is dedicated to Creek saxophonist Jim Pepper and reflects on the processes of renewing a place-world defined through spatial relations brought into being by aurality.

In the notes that follow the poem, Joy Harjo writes, "I've always believed us Creeks ('Creek' is the more common name for the Muscogee people) had something to do with the origins of jazz. After all, when the African peoples were forced here for slavery they were brought to the traditional lands of the Muscogee peoples. Of course there was interaction between Africans and Muscogees."[6] And yet, most of the history books and musicologists who discuss the birth of the blues (and later, its influence in the creation of jazz) understand it as primarily emerging out of the crucible of slavery that filled a Mississippi Delta emptied of any prior indigenous presences to link West African traditions with European Christianity.[7] The blues that surfaced out of this specific land and history fused trauma and redemption with the harsh lived experiences of slavery and Jim Crow oppression. The expansion of what Clyde Woods delineates as blues epistemology was "the full expression of the rise of an African American culture that was self-conscious of its space and time and, therefore, fully indigenous. The South was a space of origin, the African American hearth."[8] Building off a model that positions African American "folk culture" as fully indigenous to the Mississippi Delta, he argues that "If we are to build a society where working-class knowledge and participatory democracy are truly treasured we must understand that the South is the center of African American culture, not its periphery. The Delta then becomes understood as a Mecca."[9]

One of the earliest descriptions of the blues comes from archaeologist Charles Peabody who in 1901 traveled on a mission from the Harvard Peabody Museum to Coahoma County, Mississippi, to grave rob Southeastern mounds, most likely Chickasaw and Choctaw, at the Dorr and Edwards sites south of Clarksdale.[10] Those mounds Peabody excavated were part of the larger Mississippian Ceremonial Complex and represented huge earthworks—the Dorr Mound had a north-south length of 90 feet, an east-west width of 60 feet and rose 9 feet, 6½ inches above the surrounding ground. The largest of the twenty-three mounds at the Edwards site measured 190 feet north to south, 180 feet east to west, and was 26 feet high.[11] The mounds date from at least 3500 BCE to DeSoto's arrival in the 1530s, though Peabody's excavations found contemporary burials, which demonstrate that the Choctaws and Chickasaws continued to use the mounds until they were forcibly removed to Indian Territory in the 1830s. According to Southeastern cosmologies, Mississippian mounds played a significant cultural and symbolic role, representing in the case of the Nanih Waiya mound the site of creation itself for the Choctaw. Other mounds served as "navels," sites of birth, death, and renewal that linked the Upper and Lower Worlds of complementary balance to manifest in this world.

The black workers Peabody hired in Clarksdale, Mississippi, sang as they performed the labor of cutting into the mounds with their shovels and stirring up those who rested there. Peabody found himself fascinated by what he heard—so much so that he published an essay in 1903 in the *Journal of American Folk-Lore* that documented some of the lyrics and music that those laborers sang as they worked. Though he referred to what he was hearing as ragtime, most scholars now suggest that what he documented was the blues, and what is fascinating about his essay is the underlying signifying heteroglossia and improvisation that Peabody narrated without realizing. In the brief essay documenting the birth of the blues into white academic consideration, he attempts to catalog and remark upon the function of the music he was hearing, figuring it as alternating between spirituals and work songs to distract from the back-breaking labor he was demanding. Organized as call and response with leaders improvising and riffing on identity, history, community, and politics, the songs gesture to prior forms of musical presences in the South that tie to African traditions and to Southeastern Indian stomp dance songs that are also call and response, with leaders singing about the politics, concerns, and spiritual matters of the community.

Predictably, Peabody's discussion in his essay abjects the labor and the performances as well as infantilizes the African American men working for him. However, the laborers themselves leave a trace of critical intervention to Peabody's presence and task. For instance, when Peabody describes the last day of work, when he and a friend are sitting outside their tent playing mumble-the-peg, from the trenches in the mounds he hears the lyrics: "I'm so tired I'm most dead / Sittin' up there playin' mumbley-peg."[12] The song leaders and their improvisational play here make a critical comment upon Peabody and pointedly reflect that he must be "so tired [he's] almost dead," from sitting and tossing a jackknife into the ground with his friend while they are the ones digging through the mounds in the hot, humid Mississippi sun.

Even more suggestive are the lyrics from the only whole song that Peabody documents in his essay:

Some folks say preachers won't steal;
But I found two in my cornfield.
One with a shovel and t'other with a hoe,
A-diggin' up my taters row by row.

Old Brudder Jones setten on de log.
His hand on de trigger and his eyes on the hog.

Old Dan Tucker he got drunk,
Fell in de fire and kicked up a chunk.

I don't gamble but I don't see
How my money gets away from me.

When I look up over my head
Makes me think of my corn and bread.[13]

Though Peabody does not provide much (if any) context for the song he records, the lyrics are an improvisation upon "The Paterroller Song," the origins of which trace back to plantation slaves singing about the white slave patrols that surveilled the South after Nat Turner's 1831 rebellion and how fast one needed to run in order to escape them. Over time the song became reinscribed within Tin Pan Alley minstrelsy that emphasizes the violence of capture rather than hope of escape, and by the twentieth century, the song transforms yet again into "Run Children Run" or "Run Johnny Run." The lyrics recorded by Peabody, however, document another turn in the song where the laborers locate preachers as the source of theft and comment directly upon Peabody's project in the mounds. There is evidence within the evocations of corn and fire on the one hand, and a critique of the preachers in the cornfield digging up "taters row by row" on the other, that those laborers and their songs provide resistant traces that acknowledge the desecration that is occurring—and a positioning of themselves as tied to the people buried in the mounds. The corn and potatoes reveal the bundles of bodies and skulls of those Choctaws buried at the site. As Peabody forced the laborers to disinter the mounds through terraced rows, each blow of the shovel exposed the dirt-encrusted whiteness of human bones that are evoked so provocatively by these singers as the white flesh of shovel-scored potatoes in the ground.

Such lyrical play, which depends upon a linking of corn to "look[ing] up over my head," also acknowledges the possibility that those singers reference Chickasaw and Choctaw stories such as those about Ohoyo Osh Chishba (or Ohoyo Chishba Osh), the mysterious, unknown woman who brought corn to the Choctaws by leaving seeds on top of the mounds.[14] Horatio Bardwell Cushman published a version of the story in 1899 that detailed how two Choctaw hunters encounter a mysterious woman who appears on the top of one of the nearby mounds. She tells them she is hungry, and when they give her the hawk they have just cooked for themselves, despite their own gnawing hunger, she eats only a small amount, thanks them, and then tells them to look for her at the exact spot she is standing next year. When they return a year later, at first they cannot find her. After they remember the charge to return to the exact spot, they find the top of the mound covered in a "strange plant which yielded an excellent food, which was ever afterwards cultivated by the Choctaws and named by them Tunchi (corn)."[15] Within the different versions of the story, the hunters are drawn by strange noises, "low but distinct tones, strange yet soft and plaintive as the melancholy notes of the dove, but produced by what they were unable to even conjecture. At different intervals it broke the deep silence of the early night with its seemingly muffled notes of woe."[16] That those mounds that linked Chickasaws and Choctaws in the Mississippi Delta back to ancestors and sacred geographies could serve as the site of food, grief, and perhaps, evocatively, the birth of the blues echoes Bohr's remarks on Kronborg Castle.

The intertextual play and resistance, in which the African American men hired by Peabody sing back to the violences of his jackknife tossing and surveillance of their labor at the same time that they provide a musical reflection on the actual labor of disturbing burial sites they have been hired to do, testify to the agency of those workers and their resistance to violating the sacred space of the mounds. Clyde Woods's construction of the Mississippi Delta that contains these mounds and sites of creation for Southeastern Indians as a Mecca for African American culture that refills a newly made *terra nullius,* however, hints at a rising antagonistic cacophony that figures these spaces as the affective site for participatory democracy. And it speaks to a deeper caution that emerges in Steven Salaita's discussion of *The Holy Land in Transit* that pulls out comparisons between Palestinian and American Indian literatures to analyze the problems of settler colonialism born out of the competing claims to indigeneity, the mapping of settler and arrivant sacred sites onto prior indigenous ones, and the violent expulsions of the other.[17] My point here is not to make a prior claim to the blues for Southeastern Indians. Rather, I am interested in the lessons that blues epistemologies and blues aesthetics might teach us in order to transform the participatory democracy that Woods evokes into a radical reimagining of how peoples exist relationally within the place-worlds located in the stories we tell and the songs we sing. What sorts of possibilities might the blues gesture toward as our communities—settler, arrivant, and American Indian—try to come to terms with the histories of violence, slavery, and removal? How might the blues epistemology of grievability teach us to rethink how indigenous articulations of sovereignty have been sutured to and cut away from the dictates of the colonizing nation-state, where indigenous nations now police the imperial transit of Indianness as the only way to enact the real?

Pride and Prejudice

That the continued colonization of American Indian nations, peoples, and lands provides the United States the economic and material resources needed to cast its imperialist gaze globally is a fact that is simultaneously obvious within—and yet continually obscured by—what is essentially a settler colony's national construction of itself as an ever more perfect multicultural, multiracial democracy. As the United States constructs a Manichean allegory of settler democracy through which imperialism can finally be brought humanely and justifiably to the world through discourses of "fighting them there so we don't fight them here," the status of American Indians as sovereign nations colonized by the United States continues to haunt and inflect its raison d'être. Or as American Indian scholar Elizabeth Cook-Lynn explains:

> The current mission of the United States to become the center of political enlightenment to be taught to the rest of the world began with the Indian wars and has become the dangerous provocation of this nation's historical intent. The historical connection between the Little Big Horn event and the "uprising" in Baghdad must become part of the political dialogue of America if the fiction of decolonization is to happen and the hoped-for deconstruction of the colonial story is to come about.[18]

Cook-Lynn here refers at least in part to the invasive military intent of Custer's Seventh Cavalry that confronted and then lost to Cheyenne and Lakota warriors at the Battle of the Little Bighorn in 1876, went on to massacre Big Foot's band at Wounded Knee in 1890, stayed in Japan as part of the occupation after World War II, participated in U.S. military engagements in Vietnam, and most recently helped secure the March 20, 2003, invasion of Iraq. The Third Infantry Division–Seventh Cavalry was one of the first military units to reach Baghdad in the initial push into Iraq during spring 2003, and throughout late March and April of that year, CNN ran reports from embedded journalists who traveled with them to highlight the shock and awe of U.S. military prowess. The continued presence of the 7th Cavalry, which was constituted in 1866 for the express purpose of fighting Indians, demonstrates the degree to which the United States' twenty-first-century imperialist-military desires the world over depend upon discourses and policies that were catalyzed in the nineteenth-century campaigns to colonize and "domesticate" external American Indian nations *within* a United States that consumed a wide swath of the North American continent.[19]

Drawing upon that historical memory, which arises from indigenous lived experiences of colonization and genocide and which links those experiences with globalization and imperialism, indigenous critical theory prioritizes indigenous ontologies to read symptomatically against the colonialist discourses of settler societies. By foregrounding how colonialist discourses justify the legal, political, economic, and physical dispossession of American Indian lives, lands, and cultures, and by centering indigenous subjectivities and epistemologies through which we might theorize the violences of the United States' "manifest destiny," scholars interested in developing a conversation among postcolonial, subaltern, and transnational indigenous studies might begin by understanding how the United States' global imperialist projects are underwritten by the continued colonization of American Indian, Alaska Native, and Hawaiian lands. Here, I would suggest, indigenous critical theory might make some important contributions to critical race and postcolonial studies through a sustained exploration of the incommensurability of the "internal" for the over 560 sovereign Indigenous nations that consolidate under the U.S. umbrella designation as "Native American." As Gayatri Spivak argues, the work of the colonizer is at some level "consolidating the Self of Europe by obliging the native to cathect the space of the Other on his home ground." Within the context of indigenous nations in North America, that cathexis of the space of the Other demands at the same time a capitulation to the self as assimilated possibility, an obligation, in Spivak's words, to "domesticate the alien [settler] as Master." In other words, according to Spivak, colonialism functions dialectically as a process of "worlding" that obliges the native to imagine and invest herself counter to her own world.[20] As indigenous nations colonized by the United States are continually worlded into the more perfect union, the United States—which has only existed as fifty states for just over fifty years—gains hegemonic authority to enact paternalistic policies that seek to protect U.S. "homelands" by expanding control and markets in an ever-widening net of influence.

In this chapter, I am particularly interested in how the idea of "internal" as modifier to "colonialism" has emerged as a critical race and postcolonial theoretical category through which to engage U.S. systems of disenfranchisement on the North American continent. Taking the Cherokee Nation of Oklahoma's 2007 popular vote to disenfranchise descendants of Cherokee slaves—some who and some who do not have Cherokee "blood"—as my occasion to elucidate the dialectics of race and colonialism still at play in the United States, I hope to begin to provide a means through which the radical inclusion of the Cherokee Freedmen in the Cherokee Nation does not have to result in the radical exclusion of the Cherokee Nation from itself. The problem is that, as the concept of "internal colonialism" to discuss race in the United States continues to circulate, the distinctions between indigenous political sovereignty recognized by treaties and the individual sovereignty that forms the basis for inclusive personhood within U.S. multicultural democracy collapse as the United States is cathected as master.[21] Thus, when colonialism is used to describe indigenous peoples' experiences of land loss and genocide, often the "internal" is layered as supplement onto such discussions by a U.S. hegemony that asserts the internal within the symbolic order of juridical colonization at the expense of the external "real" for indigenous nations. Interrogating the emergence of and limits to "internal colonialism," which many scholars acknowledge as a not always sufficient analogy even for race, may allow a site of intervention through which scholars might center indigenous experiences of U.S. colonialism as that which exceeds discussions of race. Doing so may help point the way for more robust intersections between postcolonial, subaltern, and indigenous worlds.

In many ways, then, one might argue that the idea of "internal colonialism" services the construction of the United States as a multicultural nation that is struggling with the legacies of racism rather than as a colonialist power engaged in territorial expansion since its beginning. Seen in this light, American Indians might be apprehended as subaltern if we take Antonio Gramsci's "Some Aspects of the Southern Question" as one of the theoretical genealogical entry points for subaltern studies, especially given that the theoretical notion of "internal colonialism" stems from that same discussion of North/South divisions within a state's territory. However, the emphasis on the in as condition of subalternity presents fundamental problems when applied to understanding American Indian nations vis-à-vis the United States, precisely because that in reifies the United States as the overarching state authority and is always already a colonial spatialization.[22] This transformation of more than five hundred and sixty indigenous nations into a single racial minority within the national borders of the United States is folded a priori into postcolonial and racial critiques of what Patrick Wolfe has identified as "regimes of difference" within deep settler societies.[23] This presumed self-evidentiary process of minoritization, of making racial what is international, continues to infect competing understandings of citizenship, identity, inclusion, and exclusion with, among, and outside the intersections of sovereignty, race, land, and labor. The processes by which citizens of American Indian nations become minorities within the United States, with no prior claim to nation or territory that exceeds the U.S.'s will, further inform current struggles over citizenship and historical reconciliation within the indigenous nations colonized by the United States and is nowhere more striking than in Indian Territory—what is now Oklahoma—where unresolved histories of removal, slavery, racialization, allotment, settlement, and sovereignty threaten to make internal once and for all that which is external: native space.

As citizens of the Chickasaw, Choctaw, Cherokee, Creek, and Seminole Nations—often identified as the "Five Civilized Tribes"—continue to struggle with the legacies of colonialism and racism that also inform their refusals to recognize the status of African American Freedmen Indians, those Southeastern Freedmen find themselves triangulated by histories of race, colonialism, and slavery and expelled from the very nations they call home.[24] The problem for indigenous nations colonized by the United States and in the face of the continual forced migrations and diasporas arising from U.S. capitalistic and militaristic policies abroad is that the world—its problems, complicities, and oppressions—has been brought to our lands. If, as Cook-Lynn says, we need to make the connections between Iraq and federal Indian relations part of the political dialogue, then I would add that indigenous nations on lands that are now currently part of U.S.-controlled territories need also to address the world in ways that do not replicate the fictions of U.S. multicultural settler democracy and reinscribe the very discourses and policies we seek to overcome for ourselves.

These incommensurabilities are particularly relevant as they continue to play out over the one hundred and fifty years of struggles among the Southeastern Indian nations to define not only who counts as citizens in their own nations but how those nations will continue to assert sovereignty tied to land after the radical breaches of removal and allotment as well as address their own national complicities with the historical violences of slavery. The most recent development in this long historical struggle emerged in 2007. On March 3 of that year, the Cherokee Nation voted to disenfranchise approximately 2,800 Cherokee Freedmen citizens, in violation of the 1866 treaty with the United States that gave Freedmen the rights and status as citizens within the Cherokee nation. That status was in perpetuity and extended not only to the slaves the Cherokee had owned, but to those Freedmen born in the Cherokee Nation as well as any descendants they would have.[25] The March 2007 vote amended the Cherokee Constitution to define Cherokee citizenship through the 1906 Dawes rolls that purported to document the blood quantum of Cherokee citizens at the time, and those who can now trace ancestry to those rolls. As a result, the Nation expelled the Freedmen who traced their citizenship through the Freedmen rolls that listed the former slaves living within the nation at the time of enrollment even though, as many scholars have noted, there were a number of Cherokee descendants with black ancestry who, because of racism, were placed on the Freedmen rolls instead of the Cherokee by blood rolls.[26]

In the months that followed the Cherokee vote in March 2007 and the resultant disenfranchisement of the Freedmen, a number of Congressional leaders and members of the Congressional Black Caucus worked to draw U.S. legislative attention to the Cherokee Nation's decision.[27] Melvin Watt, a Democratic representative from North Carolina, proposed an amendment to HR 2786, the Native American Housing Assistance and Self-Determination Reauthorization Act of 2007, that provided for funding appropriations to support housing assistance for American Indians, Alaska Natives, and Native Hawaiians. Representative Watt's amendment sought to prevent allocation of funds provided by the act from being extended to the Cherokee Nation until it complied fully with the Treaty of 1866, and on October 14, 2008, that amendment became law when President Bush signed the Native American Housing Assistance and Self-Determination Reauthorization Act of 2008. Title VIII, Section 801 of Public Law 110–411 affirms that "no funds authorized under this Act, or the amendments made by this Act…shall be expended for the Cherokee Nation" pending the continuance of the temporary injunction reinstating Freedmen citizenship rights, a restoration of citizenship to the Freedmen, or a settlement of the issue within the Cherokee courts.[28]

In addition, on June 21, 2007, Representative Diane Watson of California's 33rd District introduced legislation in the form of HR 2824 to sever the United States government's relationship with the Cherokee Nation of Oklahoma until they restored full tribal citizenship to the Cherokee Freedmen. Watson's bill sought to stop the expenditure of $300 million in federal funding to support the health care, education, and housing services the Cherokee Nation provides, and to subsequently terminate their recognized status as a nation until they comply with the terms of the 1866 treaty.[29] Though Representative Watson's bill never made it out of committee in the 110th Congress, she reintroduced the bill as House Resolution 2761 on June 8, 2009, and while her legislation stalled again, and she has since not sought reelection, Watson has continued to call publicly for governmental sanctions against the Cherokee, Choctaw, Chickasaw, Creek, and Seminole Nations.[30]

The Cherokee decision and the legislation proposed in the U.S. Congress have created a maelstrom of responses within the U.S. and American Indian media. Responses both inside and outside Indian Country have ranged from assertions that, while unfortunate, the Cherokee Nation of Oklahoma as a sovereign political entity has the right to define its own citizenship to outcries in major news outlets that the Cherokees are unreformed neoconfederates who have enacted policies of "ethnic cleansing" and Jim Crow segregation against the Freedmen.[31] More nuanced opinions emerged within publications such as *Indian Country Today* and *News from Indian Country* as Eric Cheyfitz and Robert Warrior discussed the decision and the U.S. Congressional response. Warrior explains how the Cherokee have "fle[d] the moral high ground" when he writes, "morality, however, has been the missing topic in the wrangling thus far, and I would argue is the basis for why it is important for everyone, especially American Indian people who have been silent thus far, to support efforts like those of Representative Watt." Warrior continues: "The moral case against the Cherokee is straightforward. As a duly constituted nation in the nineteenth century, they legally embraced and promoted African slavery, a position they maintained after Removal to Indian Territory in the 1830s."[32] For Eric Cheyfitz, the Cherokee Nation's decision "is a moral and legal issue that concerns us all." And both morally and legally the issue is quite clear: the Cherokee stand in violation of their own rule of law and ethics. However, Cheyfitz points out, the irony of the U.S. Congressional legislation is that the relationship between the federal government and the Cherokee Nation is a colonial one. "One can only understand [HR 2824], then, if one understands that the history driving it is not only the violent and troubled history of race in the United States but also the violent and troubled history of the struggle for sovereignty of colonized Indian nations with the colonizer."[33]

The censuring of the Cherokee Nation of Oklahoma for its historical and continual racist complicities with the legacies of slavery coincided with the centenary celebration of the creation of the state of Oklahoma in 1907 that also marks one of the most disastrous federal Indian policies in the history of disastrous policies. The 1887 Dawes General Allotment Act, followed by the 1898 Curtis Act, broke up the collective land holdings of the nations in Indian Territory and allotted lands to individuals in an attempt to transform the citizens of those nations into farmers within the United States. In the nineteenth century, Freedmen's struggle for rights within those nations collided with those nations' struggles against colonialism, now in the form of allotment and termination that would lead to incorporation into the United States. What ultimately emerges is a competition between racist ideologies of exclusion that deny Southeastern Freedmen within the "Five Civilized Tribes" and colonialist hegemonies of inclusion to the United States that seek to deny utterly those nations' inherent rights to sovereignty and land. Part of the problem is that, caught within the incommensurable binds of colonialism/racism, indigenous/minority, and external/internal, the calls for sovereignty by the Cherokee Nation of Oklahoma are heard by the colonizing nation as the mimesis of white Southern demands for states' rights that immorally justified Jim Crow segregationist policies. Meanwhile, Democratic members of Congress are heard by the colonized Cherokee Nation as the ventriloquism of U.S. colonial policies that led to termination and assimilation when they frame the Cherokee Nation and Freedmen within the teleology of racial struggle within the United States. In a letter to U.S. Attorney General Eric Holder, members of Congress wrote in May 2009: "Over forty years after the enactment of the landmark Civil Rights and Voting Rights Acts, there is a place in the United States that African Americans cannot vote or receive federal benefits as a matter of law."[34] There are in fact currently over 565 places in the United States where African Americans, Euro-Americans, Asian Americans, Latino/as and citizens of at least 564 indigenous nations cannot vote as a matter of law, and those are the indigenous nations in which they are not citizens. But that is not what they mean. The problem is that these perceived mimeses and ventriloquisms foreclose the radical alterity of "Indianness" as site of identity and sovereignty for the Freedmen, who become African American, and for the "Five Civilized Tribes" of Oklahoma, who become "the United States."

North/South Divides: Definitions and Origins of "Internal Colonialism"

Following Cheyfitz's observation that the histories of race and colonialism collide within the U.S. federal response to the Cherokees' vote, then, it seems important to examine the discourses within conceptual models of "internal colonialism" that maintain a racialized multiculturalism at the heart of U.S. liberal democracy. Gayatri Spivak provides us with a methodological starting point when she calls for us to "learn to distinguish between 'internal colonization'—the patterns of exploitation and domination of disenfranchised groups within a metropolitan country like the United States or Britain—and the colonization of other spaces, of which Robinson Crusoe's island is a 'pure' example."[35] But she leaves open the question of whether American Indians, who are currently circumscribed by the boundaries of the United States, are located within the metropole or whether they constitute the "pure" colonization of other spaces. Spivak's methodological concern as it is phrased presents us with the originary double bind that has heretofore silenced American Indian histories, presences, and lived conditions in subaltern and postcolonial studies. Particularly when we consider that Robinson Crusoe's island is imaginatively situated in the Americas off the coast of what is now Brazil, this unanswered question becomes especially frustrating for an American Indian scholar committed to understanding the colonial discourses that postcolonial studies interrogates.

Most of the current scholarship defining internal colonialism within the United States begins by tracing the origins of the term as it was defined first by Marxism and then transformed through civil rights activism. Standard delineations of the concept's origins assert that it is a term used first in late nineteenth-century and early twentieth-century Europe and appeared in writings by Vladimir Ilyich Lenin and Antonio Gramsci. Their use of "internal colonialism" articulated the systemic economic and political inequalities that emerged within a state and were used to extract resources from the margins/peripheries/souths to the center/core/norths of a single polity. According to Michael Hechter, Lenin first evokes the concept, though not the actual phrase, in *The Development of Capitalism in Russia* as a means to investigate economic disparities that emerge between regions and affect nationalisms among different classes within a nation.[36] With the attribution to Gramsci, most scholars look to his "Some Aspects of the Southern Question," in which the concept of internal colonies informs how the northern bourgeoisie has reduced the southern Italian proletariat to "exploitable colonies."[37] He uses the concept to spatialize the ways in which the north continued to draw resources and wealth from the south to maintain control by limiting access to power. His analysis of economic exploitation between regions has shaped current debates in subaltern studies and arguments that shift the First World/Third World divide to a global North/South paradigm of exploitation, capital, and imperialism. In the United States, the echoes of the global North/South divide are reiterated through the lingering regionalisms of the Civil War that continue to underscore current discourses of racism as well as frame U.S. dominant culture's attempts to grapple with and disavow the legacies of slavery, segregation, and Jim Crow abject racism. And in many ways, this doubly inflected North/South might help inform how the "Five Civilized" nations, whose original lands in what is now Tennessee, Mississippi, North Carolina, and Georgia were stolen to create the U.S. regional South, are disavowed in relation to their historic land claims and reframed in relation to their own attempts to reconcile their participation in and maintenance of slavery up to and after removal in the late 1830s, in what is their triply inflected North/South divides.

Perhaps the most extended engagement with the concept of internal colonization emerged in Michael Hechter's *Internal Colonialism: The Celtic Fringe in British National Development.* While the work looks primarily at how the Irish, Scottish, and Welsh continue to assert oppositional ethnic identities to British nationalism, his work has also been influential for scholars in critical race and postcolonial studies in North America. In his text, Hechter defines the model of internal colonialism as a process through which the national development of a state's economic power progresses unevenly and disparately, with the center dominating the periphery and the periphery remaining within a condition of economic dependency. "The spatially uneven wave of modernization over state territory," Hechter writes, "creates relatively advanced and less advanced groups."[38] According to Hechter, it is through this process of consolidating the stratification and institutionalization of modernization and technology that ethnic and cultural markers begin to emerge to define those with power and those without, those with access to institutions and those without. Part of what has made internal colonialism appealing as a model to describe the economic and political inequities that develop within a state is that it is largely a spatial model that stretches not only to incorporate uneven access to resources, markets, and exchanges, but also accounts for emergent and sustained cultural and ethnic identity markers to stand as signs of economic oppressions.

While Hechter is primarily interested in defining internal colonialism within the Western European context as a means to analogize England's domination of Ireland, Scotland, and Wales, the subtext of some of the sources he works with suggests a clear connection with overseas projects of colonialism that shaped European nation-states through the seventeenth, eighteenth, and nineteenth centuries. It is important here to notice that the metaphors Hechter uses to explain the process of industrialization and modernization in Europe rely upon U.S. notions of what Perry Miller has described as an errand into the wilderness. "The internal campaigns were not in any sense," Hechter assures us, "coincidental to overseas colonization."[39] Drawing upon Fernand Braudel's discussion of the Mediterranean struggle against the wilderness in which he observes "the Mediterranean found its new world, its own Americas in the plains," Hechter refers to the internal process of colonialism in Europe as "a quest for 'internal Americas.'"[40] This parallax view within the scholarship engaging the processes through which the economic periphery is oppressed politically and culturally ties "internal colonialism" to the quest for new worlds and frontiers, or in Hechter's terms, the internal peripheral hinterlands that make up the endogenous colonies within a nation-state who lack sovereignty to affect their own economic development.[41]

What emerges out of this transit of meaning is a colonialist recursive. And it seems, then, that after Lenin and Gramsci, "internal colonialism" as a concept was an also-and that mapped the imperial European projects of colonialism in the Americas back into Europe itself, creating "internal Americas" out of the very hinterlands that provided Europe with the means to colonize the Americas in the first place. It fundamentally acknowledges the colonization of indigenous peoples at the same time that it disavows that colonization by making economic disparities stand in for "Indians" within the newly analogized frontier mythos of Europe. These nascent links that draw an analogy between "internal colonialism" as operational model and "internal Americas" as a European metaphor for regional economic disparities were inspired by the social justice movements of the 1960s and 1970s, including activists such as Malcolm X, Martin Luther King Jr., Che Guevara, and Stokely Carmichael.[42] And it is here that a second recursion begins to emerge and gives shape to the racialized discourses that, as I will argue below, inflect the national debates over the Cherokee Nation's decision to disenfranchise the Cherokee Freedmen. For Hechter, understanding the lasting ethnic identities embedded within Irish, Scottish, and Welsh articulations of national struggle within the larger frame of British national (colonialist) development stemmed from his own observations of the growing debate surrounding nationalism or assimilationism as modes of resistance within the political mobilization of ethnic groups, particularly African Americans, within the United States. While most scholars at the time Hechter wrote his text might have expected discourses of inclusion and access to emerge as a primary mode of resistance, what came to the fore were black, Chicano, and American Indian nationalist movements. The radicalism of the late 1960s certainly shapes his analysis, and he acknowledges that much of his insight on British nationalism comes from observing how ethnic groups in the United States defined "their situation as that of an 'internal colony.'"[43]

This idea that racial minorities are internally colonized by the United States is further elaborated by sociologist Robert Blauner, who argues that the U.S. white–black relationship is an exceptional form of internal colonization. Distinguishing it from "classical colonialism," Blauner asserts that white colonization of blacks in urban centers functions as a process of racism as internal colonialism that retains features of the classic form centering on land, natural resources, and sovereignty. Because both forms, according to Blauner, "developed out of a similar balance of technological, cultural, and power relations, a common *process* of social oppression characterized the racial patterns in the two contexts—despite the variation in political and social structure."[44] Though Blauner briefly acknowledges that American Indians occupied the land and fall more fully under the categorization of classic colonialism, he is more concerned with delineating a kind of exceptionalism that might be used to address the processes of political, social, and economic exploitation that continue to persist due to white racism and disrupt the possible avenues for African Americans to gain access to power within the United States. Internal colonialism then, in the U.S. context, refers primarily and originally to African American oppression that then over the course of time serves to erase indigenous peoples altogether as it is thought to account for the indigenous within the racial paradigms it critiques.

Building off ideas that African Americans are internally colonized within the United States, but eschewing land as the sign of difference between classic and internal colonialism, bell hooks writes that "even though African Americans in the United States had no country, whites took over and colonized; as a structure of domination that is defined as ownership of a people by another, colonialism aptly describes the process by which blacks were and continue to be subordinated by white supremacy."[45] By identifying slavery as the original sin of the United States' colonialist project, bell hooks is able to foreground how racism continues to perpetuate the economic, social, and political oppressions African Americans face every day within the United States, but in the process she perpetuates the colonialist narratives that deny that the land ever belonged to anyone prior to the United States. Over the last thirty years, theories of internal colonialism shifted from locating it first as an analysis of the economic processes that necessitated the maintenance of ethnic difference to a primarily racialized analysis of how economic, social, and political inequalities came to be naturalized. To come at this another way, "internal colonialism" was initially operationalized in Europe to describe the economic disparities that serve to make ethnic identities within a nation-state matter. Within U.S. critical race studies, "internal colonialism" describes how racial and ethnic identities create economic and political disparities and in the process racism becomes homologous to U.S. colonialism in North America. It is this shift that allows bell hooks to write:

> Just as many white Americans deny both the prevalence of racism in the United States and the role they play in perpetuating and maintaining white supremacy, non-white, non-black groups, Native, Asian, Hispanic Americans, all deny their investment in anti-black sentiment even as they consistently seek to distance themselves from blackness so that they will not be seen as residing at the bottom of this society's totem pole, in the category reserved for the most despised group.[46]

"Native" here is grouped with "Asian" and "Hispanic" Americans, and through the enjambment American Indians are made newcomers in hooks's racial paradigms that create a white/black binary in the United States. As Aileen Moreton-Robinson has shown in her critique of whiteness studies, "blackness becomes an epistemological possession . . . which forecloses the possibility that the dispossession of Native Americans was tied to migration and the establishment of slavery driven by the logics of capital."[47] Ironically, hooks's framings of white/black paradigms refract a similar foreclosure with regards to indigenous dispossession. But certainly, in the case of the Southeastern Indian nations and their continued disenfranchisement and oppression of Freedmen, those indigenous nations have denied their investment in the logics of capital underscoring slavery and in anti-black racism. Often, this denial evolves out of fears that blackness will somehow undermine indigenous claims of sovereignty and authenticity and will allow further U.S. encroachments on land, culture, and identity. However, indigenous dispossession is foreclosed for hooks, given that her metaphor for understanding the hierarchies of oppression in the U.S. is projected on top of a stereotypical reference to "totem pole," which in indigenous worlds is neither hierarchical nor oppressive. It is this turn that finally allows hooks to reposition African American bodies as the foundational site of colonization rather than American Indian lands.

The justification for framing the colonization of American Indians as internal, despite the problems that emerge, might have been that it resists the United Nations' definitions of colonialism that depend upon the "blue water" or salt water thesis, which states that the colony must be separated from the colonizing country by water or noncontiguous territory.[48] In the United States, where the dominant society and much of dominant academia disavow that American Indians faced any colonialism, internal or otherwise, the use of "internal" has often allowed indigenous scholars a means to analyze the ongoing logics of colonialism still functioning for the United States. The "internal," however, reifies colonized indigenous peoples as "minorities within" countries such as New Zealand, Canada, Australia, and the United States, and according to Will Kymlicka, "not . . . as separate 'peoples' with their own right of self-determination, even if they have been subject to similar processes of territorial conquest and colonization as overseas colonies."[49] And given that the colonization of American Indians has, particularly within postcolonial theoretical models, been glossed or ignored in what Anne McClintock has framed as "historical amnesia," understanding the ongoing processes of colonialism that continue to affect American Indians and other indigenous peoples in break-away settler societies has been useful in driving the point home that the "post-" has not yet arrived.[50]

It is then, with some amount of that historical amnesia yet with an awareness of the problems inherent within Hechter, Blauner, hooks, and others who have tried to frame race as colonialism in the U.S., that Jenny Sharpe reminds us in her essay, "Is the United States Postcolonial?" that "*internal colonialism* is only an analogy for describing the economic marginalization of racial minorities."[51] However, she herself reintroduces the same problems of those scholars she critiques, as she collapses "Native Americans" into a list of racial minorities that now include voluntary and involuntary migrants to the United States. The "postcolonial," if it can diagnose the United States at all, according to Sharpe, does so only uneasily and inadequately because the "colonial" is an inaccurate metaphor to describe the internal workings of the United States. Rather, "postcolonial" for Sharpe must transform to "be theorized as the point at which internal social relations intersect with global capital and the international division of labor. In other words, I want us to define the 'after' to colonialism as the neocolonial relations into which the United States entered with decolonized nations."[52] Nativism, along with the notion that ethnic minorities constitute a "nation of nations," is a growing concern for Sharpe as she argues that "the nation of nations paradigm blurs the distinction between a racial identity formed in opposition to the idea of the United States as a nation of immigrants and an ethnic identity formed around the idea of the United States as a nation of unmeltable immigrants."[53] The incommensurability of the internal for American Indians resides now in an irresolvable dialectic that always already evokes anti-immigrant nativism whenever indigenous rights to sovereign nations are asserted. Moreover, the only "after to colonialism" that Sharpe provides is not the decolonization of indigenous nations that made the United States possible in the first place and that Elizabeth Cook-Lynn defines as the hoped-for deconstruction of colonialist stories, but the United States' neocolonial relationship with already decolonized nations in the global South.

Since the creation of the United States as a political entity, American Indians have existed in a space of liminality, where what was external was repeatedly and violently reimagined and remade as internal in order to disavow the ongoing colonization of indigenous peoples that is necessary for the United States to exist. Kevin Bruyneel brings postcolonial theory into conversation with indigenous critical theory to argue that colonialism in the United States and indigenous struggles against it produce a "third space of sovereignty" that resides in the borders neither inside nor outside the United States.[54] Though Bruyneel locates the postcolonial "third space" spatially and temporally in the United States after the Civil War, the legal processes through which this liminality is enacted are tied directly to the removal of the Cherokees from the South. In the 1831 ruling on the legality of the Indian Removal Act, Chief Justice John Marshall opined that American Indians constituted "domestic dependent nations" and through that ruling transformed the foreign sovereign status of native nations that the U.S. had previously recognized into the internal domestic within the United States.[55] In 1832 Marshall reiterated the external as he affirmed that tribes maintained the sovereign right to protect their homelands from intrusions.[56]

These tensions and slippages within the law continue to haunt federal legislation and court rulings, and yet within dominant cultural imaginings, the borders between the United States and native nations are endlessly transgressable to the point that native peoples no longer exist as political entities at all. Transforming American Indians into a minority within a country of minorities is the fait accompli of the colonial project that disappears sovereignty, land rights, and self-governance as American Indians are finally, if not quite fully, assimilated *into* the United States. As a theoretical concept within critical race and postcolonial theories, "internal colonialism" continually stretches from the United States to Europe and back again, fulfilling in the transit the need for "internal Americas" and frontiers. It creates the conditions for the "internal" to emerge as a modifier to colonization in the first place and then provides the discursive means through which "internal colonialism" becomes analogy for race and class differentials within a nation-state. As a result, "internal colonialism" becomes an empty referent that can be claimed by any marginalized group; to use it to describe the historical and spatial positionality of indigenous nations is a colonial violence that undermines sovereignty and self-determination.

Going to the Territory: Multiculturalism vs. Sovereignty, Round 150 Years

The process through which the borders of the United States become ineluctable or natural is the same process through which American Indians become invisibilized and minoritorized within the United States. And this might, in part, be understood as a process of colonialist expansion founded upon legal ideologies that continually oscillate between recognizing and disavowing the presence of the native other internal and external to the imperial project. As Ann Laura Stoler argues, the politics of comparison, in which the commonalities "particular (racialized) entities ... were *made* to share and that made such comparisons pertinent and possible," also risk flattening out historical specificities.[57] One might argue that the incommensurability of the internal stems in part from the concept of "Native Nation," which directly contradicts nationalist ideals of justice, democracy, and civilization that are foundational to the image the United States currently has of itself. Through this assimilationist mode of "made to share,"

U.S. slavery, as a colonial institution that stripped the bodies of Africans away from themselves to facilitate European and U.S. colonization of the "New World," becomes commensurable with the loss of lands that stripped native nations away from the peoples who had lived upon those lands for tens of thousands of years, and in turn, casts both as equally internal to the United States. Neither balances the other, nor can they account fully for the historical violences embedded within the Cherokees' institution of slavery within their own colonized nation and the Cherokees' 2007 decision to disenfranchise the Freedmen and refusal to recognize their own agency and responsibility in perpetuating racist ideologies.

The incommensurabilities of the internal stem in part, too, from the competitions embedded within the politics of comparison that Stoler cautions against. Bell hooks's metaphor of "totem pole" to rank hierarchical oppressions performs a spatial reorganization that accounts for how the Cherokee have benefited from and perpetuated racism against African Americans. However, the analogy breaks down because, by figuring black oppression as foundational, it cannot address colonialist gestures within the paradigmatic "Indianness" upon which it relies. The difficulty in the case of the Cherokee Freedmen is that within these hierarchical models of racial and colonialist imaginings, and like hooks's totem pole, the myths of multiculturalism and racial inclusion deconstruct in the face of the material body of the Cherokee Freedmen who historically carry the supplemental traces of Indian and slave and who then slip between the two, depending upon the agenda of the colonizing and enslaving discourses that the Freedmen's presence confronts. Such analogies leave the Southeastern Freedmen with nowhere to stand, with no claim, and with no recognition.

Because the Cherokee Nation is in violation of the U.S. national imaginary of its own racial inclusions and multiculturalism as well as the 1866 treaty, and because its principal chief has argued in essence the Nation's sovereign right to make immoral decisions, Congress has responded by threatening to cease all federal recognition of the tribe in what is, in effect, termination of their status under federal law. Included within Representative Watson's HR 2761 is a further provision that, should such a bill ever pass, will allow the United States to initiate six months later a similar process with the Chickasaw, Choctaw, Creek, and Seminole, each of whom have very different colonial histories and treaties addressing the Freedmen question. Discursively, the legislation Watson has proposed delineates a one-size-fits-all response to the Southeastern Indian nations and conceptually denies their distinct national and cultural sovereignties from the start, collapsing all five nations into the treaty the Cherokee negotiated in 1866, and then into the United States itself. At the same time, the issue is framed as one over which all Americans have a say, because monies appropriated to provide services to the Cherokees are, according to standard politician rhetoric, "taxpayer's dollars." The tensions and competitions between racist and colonialist ideologies refracting around the Cherokee's vote and the U.S. congressional response have brought the impossibilities of domestic sovereign nations into sharp focus, along with all the discourses of race and identity, sovereignty and colonization, civilization and savagery that fuel dominant notions of "Indianness," which have haunted native and African native peoples for centuries.

Further, the questions that continue to surround the Cherokees' decision to define identity through citizenship based on certain rolls and not others underscore the competing understandings of how native identity is articulated. When the Cherokee Nation argues that "you have to be Indian to be Indian," embedded within that statement is an essentialism that runs counter to prevailing U.S. understandings of self and race.[58] Does an Indian ancestor, whether or not that person can be documented within the historical record, constitute a valid claim to a tribal identity? How are kinship and relation traditionally understood within tribal ontologies? And are they shaped in any way by the colonial imposition of the Dawes rolls that transformed community identity into an individualistic self traced through a paper trail? Alternatively, does African American ancestry invalidate any other claims to what is now, at its core, an indigenous identity defined as citizenship within the Cherokee Nation?

The ways in which the U.S. colonial, national, and racial imaginary has framed this issue are further elucidated by Representative Diane Watson who, when asked during an interview on National Public Radio why she, as a California congresswoman, had any interest or right to intervene in the Cherokee Nation of Oklahoma's political decisions, responded: "Because I have Indian blood. We're descendants of Pocahontas. Not the Pocahontas that's part of the Cherokees, but since we have Indian blood, it could happen among our nation as well."[59] One could read this moment as an example of "playing Indian," where claiming "Indianness" is part of a core process through which U.S. nonnative national identities form.[60] But a fear that "it could happen among our nation as well" seems to complicate such an interpretation. Though one assumes she is referring here to

Pocahontas's nation—the Powhatan—to whom Watson traces her Indian blood, her delineation of a nation refers back to the Pocahontas that is not "part of the Cherokees." The Pocahontas in the Cherokee Nation to whom she refers through deferral could be interpreted as a reference to the Indian Women's Cherokee Pocahontas Club, but that would not constitute an indigenous identity nor would it provide a historical person through whom one might trace ancestry within the Cherokee Nation.

While Representative Watson's ellipsis is telling in that it reveals a claim to Indian blood based on an incomplete story that then provides an explanation for her congressional activism on the part of Cherokee Freedmen, more interesting and significant, I think, is her slippage at the end when she refers to "our nation." Given the context of her answer, it seems she is expressing concern about the possibility of African American disenfranchisement from the nation to which Pocahontas belonged. However, the turn to "our nation" also resonates with her role as an elected U.S. Representative and member of the Congressional Black Caucus who is committed to passing socially just legislation within the United States. Such an elision in the ways she articulates what is at stake for her might be read as an implicit acknowledgement that such disenfranchisement, which has already happened in her nation—the United States—during the 2000 and 2004 presidential elections, has yet to be confronted and dealt with morally or legally. In many ways, the call for sanctions against the Cherokee might be said to function additionally as a call for social justice in the face of the same disenfranchisement that occurs within the U.S. liberal multicultural state.

The controversy around the Cherokee Nation's decision to disenfranchise Freedmen who were citizens is framed as a moral issue for the United States to address precisely because it adheres to the constitutive hegemonic illusion of the U.S. myth of multicultural inclusion in which Freedmen, within the logics of the incommensurable internal, are first African American and then Indian. In its projection of itself as civilized and civilizing, the United States propagates the fiction that it has already resolved these issues for itself by sanctioning the Cherokees for their racism and participation in slavery. In the process, the Cherokee Nation, once referred to as one of the "Five Civilized Tribes" and now reframed as one of the "Five Slaveholding Tribes," is rewritten back into the discourses of savagery as Congress chastises them for violating the rule of law, even though in the summer of 2007 the Cherokee Court issued an injunction against the Cherokee Nation, temporarily halting the disenfranchisement of the

Freedmen as it considered the constitutionality of the vote. The sense of Cherokee lawlessness must at some level be redressed in order to redeem the larger colonizing United States. Meanwhile, the Cherokee who voted to disenfranchise the Freedmen are in the process of mirroring the colonial racisms embedded within discourses of multiculturalism as a means to deny their own immoral and racist disenfranchisement of a group of people because they are descendants of their forebears' slaves. They justify the North/South divisions within their own nation through a cathexis of U.S. rhetorics of multicultural inclusion:

> The Cherokee Nation is a great Indian nation that embraces our mixed-race heritage. We are proud of our thousands of citizens who share African-American, Latino, Asian, Caucasian and other ancestry. Our sole purpose is to weave together a great Indian nation, made up of many ethnic groups which are knit together through one common cultural thread—a shared bond to an Indian ancestor on the base roll.[61]

In their attempts to weave a thread of diversity to knit a defense of the indefensible, repeating the "great Indian nation" twice and echoing U.S. evocations of patriotic "founding documents," the Cherokee here deploy this lofty language only to uphold as a cultural thread "the base roll" that was used to dispossess Cherokee of their lands during the allotment period and create the "by blood" racial category in the first place.

Gayatri Spivak significantly warns about nationalism when she argues "that just as nationalism in many ways is a displaced or reversed legitimation of colonialism, this approach is a displacement of what we have, metonymically, named 'Hegel.'"[62] In other words, for Spivak, colonialism produces nationalism in the ways in which anticolonialist action comes into the world and that action, moreover, reifies that colonialism even in its resistances. Within Spivakian theoretical figurations, positing hybridity as salve for the excessive thresholds of exclusions that form the basis for calls to national identity results in another problem: "too uncritical a celebration of the 'hybrid' . . . inadvertently legitimizes the 'pure' by reversal." In many ways, Spivak's observation that hybridity creates purity, especially for what she terms the "generalized indigenous soul," seems particularly relevant to the disenfranchisement of the Cherokee Freedmen. Despite all attempts to stave off Manichean dichotomies of "authentic/inauthentic," "mixed/full," "hybrid/pure," we are still caught in a Hegelian dialectic of self/other that has already occurred through colonization.[63] One can read this as a caution, as I think Spivak intends, over a zero-sum game. In this dialectic, one discovers that one can only counter hybridity with claims to pureness or wholeness that lead to totalitarianism as one possible disastrous outcome of nationalism.

Nowhere do the problematics of nationalism become more evident than in the ways in which the United States constructed for itself a national literature. In 1818 British critic Sidney Smith wrote:

> Literature the Americans have none—no native literature, we mean. It is all imported. They had a Franklin, indeed; and may afford to live for half a century on his fame.... There is also a small account of Virginia, by Jefferson, and an epic by Joel Barlow; and some pieces of pleasantry by Mr. Irving. But why should the Americans write books, when a six weeks' passage brings them, in their own tongue, our sense, science, and genius, in bales and hogsheads?[64]

In many ways, Smith's imperialist critique of American literary culture (or rather the lack thereof) draws upon already well-established colonialist discourses that figure the emergent United States as "American," a crucible of naming transformations that ultimately serves to supplant indigenous peoples with settlers and figures colonialists as the "natives" of the land, all the while erasing American Indians from consciousness at all in a process Jean M. O'Brien has described as firsting and lasting.[65] Smith's dismissal of the uncultured "American" creates the need for a "nativist" national literature, and in October 1837 journalist and nationalist John L. O'Sullivan takes up the cause of wedding literature and politics in his inaugural issue of *The United States Democratic Review*, when he writes:

> But a more potent influence than any yet noticed is that of our national literature. Or rather we have no national literature. We depend almost wholly on Europe, and particularly England, to think and write for us, or at least to furnish materials and models after which we shall mold our own humble attempts. We have a considerable number of writers; but not in that consists a national literature. The vital principle of an American national literature must be democracy.[66]

This essay, which also famously included the phrase "The best government is that which governs least" that Thoreau espoused over a decade later, begins a monthly magazine that, according to Robert Scholnick, serves as "a unique site to explore the interconnections and contradictions of politics, rhetoric, literature, race, empire, and print culture during the antebellum years."[67] Part of the Young America movement, O'Sullivan's monthly published writings and essays by Henry David Thoreau, Walt Whitman, Ralph Waldo Emerson, and Nathaniel Hawthorne in addition to reflections upon the political struggles of the Democratic Party—it is in the pages of this magazine that O'Sullivan coins the phrase "manifest destiny" in 1845. In 1858 Whitman reflects back on its contribution as "'a monthly magazine of profounder quality of talent than any since.'"[68] In spite of such praise, however, "the larger cultural work was," Scholnick reminds us, "to legitimize and naturalize a social order that included slavery, Indian extermination, and territorial conquest."[69]

Scholnick is particularly concerned with the ways in which periodicals underwrote political power in the antebellum United States and as a result focuses primarily on the ways in which the *Democratic Review*'s political commentary supported the "gag rule" to keep Congress from debating slavery, in addition to praising the minority judges Johnson and Baldwin in opposition to Marshall in his decision in *Worcester v. Georgia* as "dissentient against a minatory opinion, which rather brandished than hurled the veto; but next session the lightning went with the thunder, striking a sovereign State lifeless, at the feet of a savage tribe adjudged a nation."[70] That the magazine emanated out of Jacksonian politics and the entire project was undergirded by ideologies of slavery and celebrations of removal underscores what is key to understand here in relation to "literary nationalism." If, as Craig Womack argues in *Red on Red*, "Tribal literatures are not some branch waiting to be grafted onto the main trunk [of American literature]. Tribal literatures are the *tree*, the oldest literatures in the Americas, the most American of American literatures. We *are* the canon," then how should we understand the implications of these competing visions of "literary nationalism," especially when they intersect with the politics of disenfranchisement and exclusion within indigenous nations and the larger colonizing one?[71]

Linda Tuhiwai Smith compellingly argues that "'we,' indigenous peoples, people 'of colour,' the Other, however we are named, have a presence in the Western imagination, in its fibre and texture, in its sense of itself, in its language, in its silences and shadows, its margins and intersections."[72] O'Sullivan's manifest destiny and literary nationalism exist simultaneously to Chickasaw, Choctaw, Creek, Seminole, and Cherokee struggles to retain sovereignty in the face of an overriding U.S. nation that ultimately legislates and enforces removal. I am not trying to overdetermine how O'Sullivan's magazine functions as doppelganger in calls for nationalism, but it seems to create, in that moment of deconstruction, the native response. O'Sullivan's assertion of a U.S. literary nationalism as justification and rationale for removal creates the possibility that there is another nationalism or other nationalisms that exist as shadow because the antecedent nationalism arose exactly to carve out and ennunciate the United States in relation to native peoples and lands. And through adaptation as resistance strategy, the "Five Civilized Tribes" are swept up in the recognitions and misrecognitions that not only provide the United States "its fibre and texture" but finally compel removal and genocide juridically and militarily.

A troubling trend within indigenous nationalism has been the reification of colonization and imperialism that situates outsiders, and anyone who might be identified as such depending on political agendas, as always already oppressive "others," and here I am thinking specifically of the ways in which indigenous arrivants enter other indigenous lands as a consequence of colonization and diaspora. One of the key components of national self-determination and sovereignty involves the nation's ability to define for itself the self and other, the inside and out. These boundaries are absolutely necessary, first and foremost for indigenous peoples because of the genocidal ethnic fraud, and the concomitant speaking as, not to mention the exploitation and mining of indigenous intellectual and cultural subjectivities. However, as Robert Warrior's essay "Native Critics in the World" points out, there have always been intellectual epistemologies within tribal communities that work against such otherings and that strive to define responsible and right relations that reframe recognitions and ethical encounters that are not dependent upon what Giorgio Agamben has delimited as the state of exception.[73]

The racial and colonial discourses arising from the Cherokee Freedmen issue reveal some of the incommensurabilities embedded within the concept of U.S. "internal colonialism," because the Freedmen themselves represent impossible "internals" within the United States and Cherokee nation. As Diane Watson's proposed legislation demonstrates, the fact that the Cherokee Freedmen are black and descendants of slaves places them firmly within the tautology of American progress towards racial equality and therefore constructs them first and foremost as citizens of the United States. Their alterity stems from the fact that they seek citizenship within a sovereign, though colonized, nation that transforms them into refugees from their own histories and identities. Such multicultural poses cannot hold up to the question of how Indian identity is constituted culturally or juridically, nor can those poses ever enact justice within a system through which the ongoing colonization of North America depends upon all the inhabitants on the continent cathecting the United States as home.

Away to a World Unknown

The title of this chapter is taken from Charley Patton's 1929 song, "Down the Dirt Road Blues," in which he sings about the liminality of his own African, Mississippi Choctaw, and white ancestry.[74] With lyrics such as "I'm going away to a world unknown," "I've been to the Nation, mmm Lord, but I couldn't stay there," "Some people say them overseas blues ain't bad," and "Every day seem like murder here," the song is structured around stanzas about the impossible triple binds of his own history. The song testifies to his inability to be at home in this world, be it the "Nation" or Indian Territory, living overseas, or surviving the murder that is the Mississippi Delta. While the song engages the incommensurabilites of identity, place, and belonging for an African American whose identity triangulates internally and externally to the United States, Europe, and indigenous nations, a subtler subtext plays out within the song and the ways it attempts to resolve some possibility of finding community through musical structure and the call and response that arise out of the confluence between slaves and Choctaws within the Mississippi Delta where he was born. Tuscarora artist Pura Fé sings back to Charley Patton and other African Indian blues musicians in her song, "Going Home/Stomp Dance." Recalling Patton as a Choctaw blues musician, she attempts to sing him home by linking Southeastern Indian stomp dance music with the other musical influences that gave birth to the blues. "Tell the world the blues where it comes from," she sings. "I hear Nigerian chains, they say are buried real deep. Tobacco fields, Trail of Tears, stolen people on stolen lands."[75] The syncretic exchanges that arise from the interpellations of racial and colonial identities within the United States provide both Patton and Pura Fé a vibrant soundscape through which to reimagine community that transcends the current limitations of a landscape mapped and owned through colonization. While Patton's search for identity and belonging never reaches resolution in the song, he initiates a journey to a world unknown in the hopes that it might someday be.

Though the Cherokee Nation and its Principal Chief Chad Smith argue that Freedmen citizenship is a matter of sovereignty and a matter for the Cherokees to handle themselves through their own legislative and juridical systems of governance, the Nation could equally resolve the issue through a radical act of sovereignty that restores the Freedmen to full citizenship status immediately. As Robert Warrior rejoins, "Chad Smith could save us all the trouble by following some of the best examples of Cherokee history rather than the morally corrupting and exclusionary ones he and his supporters have chosen thus far."[76] Instead, on February 3, 2009, the Cherokee Nation filed a lawsuit in the U.S. federal court in Tulsa, listing several Freedmen, Secretary of the Interior Ken Salazar, and the Department of the Interior as defendants and asking the court to rule that the Five Tribes Act of 1906 amended the 1866 Treaty to strip "non-Indian" Freedmen of their rights to citizenship. In a statement about the case, Chad Smith said, "The Cherokee Nation [is] keeping its word, and letting the federal courts have a clear path to reaching a decision on the merits without compromising the nation's sovereign immunity."[77] On January 14, 2011, a Cherokee Nation district court judge overruled the 2007 vote and reaffirmed that the Treaty of 1866 granted full citizenship rights to Freedmen and their descendants. As the federal cases still pend, an attorney for the Cherokee Nation has indicated that they are considering an appeal to the Cherokee Nation's district court decision.[78] The inclusion of the Freedmen in the Five Southeastern Nations, however, does not need to be framed as an issue of competition over scarce resources, an attack on indigenous sovereignty, or a reenactment of the removal from traditional homelands that casts Freedmen as intruders threatening the rights and lands of traditional peoples. Rather, it is a unique opportunity for the colonized Southeastern Indian nations to enact the kinship sovereignties that have for so long been part of our governance structures in order to form the kind of relations that will not only reconcile the violences of the past but move us towards a decolonial future where we can finally go to the nation and know that we can stay.

5

Satisfied with Stones

Native Hawaiian Government Reorganization and the Discourses of Resistance

Ua lawa mākou i ka pōhaku,
I ka 'ai kamaha'o o ka 'āina.
(We are satisfied with the stones,
Astonishing food of the land.)

Ellen Wright Prendergast, "Kaulana Nā Pua"

Sin of Annexation

For a while now, as discussed in the first chapter, literary scholars, historians, and American studies scholars have perennially debated when and how U.S. empire emerged to reveal its face to the rest of the world. Often in these discussions, 1898 circulates, Victor Bascara explains in *Model-Minority Imperialism,* as "aberration," "a moment of decision to take up imperialism," and "an unburdening of empire, the removal of the ideological and material encumbrances that make expansion hard to legitimate."[1] The nineteenth-century fin de siècle marked, Bascara says, the moment "the United States first became an old-style empire, forcibly acquiring lands beyond its borders and unfurling Old Glory conspicuously above them."[2] Within such formulations, the year 1898 signals the point at which the United States' nascent ability to militarily slip from the "internal" occupations of race to "external" overthrows and annexations of Pacific and Caribbean islands, and that year stands as time-stamp despite the work of scholars to reframe 1898 through the Mexican-American War, the Civil War, and other burgeoning imperialist endeavors. It is a date that accommodates, certainly, Native Hawaiian critiques of U.S. empire, and one that obscures and denies what American Indian nations have known and experienced since the onset of the United States. Such recurrent tendencies to mark the United States as imperial only after it encounters salt water stem from a foundational U.S. exceptionalism that declared the lands between the Atlantic and the Pacific to be somehow uninhabited and miraculously part of the United States whether any citizen of that nation had ever set foot on the soil there. As Manifest Destiny declared its intent to slide from one shining city upon a hill to the next as it progressed westward towards Hawai'i and the Philippines, those intervening lands initially deemed external and terrifying were continually remade and remapped as internal in an attempt to obliterate any other possible spatial, historical, or sovereign memory.

One feature of U.S. imperialism (if one wants to phrase it as if marketing a new product for purchase) has been the discursive machinery it has deployed to confront, contain, and abject difference and alterity. As we all know, upon those external-made-internal lands that predate the creation of U.S. empire live those indigenous nations who have, for centuries, fought, negotiated, and struggled to remain in charge of their own destinies in spite of the overarching wave of colonialism that swept over and across North America. Simultaneously, the constructed Indian became a utilitarian transit of empire within U.S. discourses—those against the United States at the turn of the twentieth century or the turn of the twenty-first century are always already "savage," "terrifying," "heathen," "uncivilized," or inhabitants of "Indian Country." While such examples can be discussed across the U.S. military-industrial complex from Okinawa and Vietnam to Iraq and Nicaragua, this chapter centers on Hawai'i and the ways in which Indianness functions as imperial sign and infection within the contact zones of what have become, through colonization and occupation, "U.S. indigeneities." Taking as my entry point, then, the current debates over federal recognition for Native Hawaiians that continue to play out in the local politics of Hawai'i and that have stretched into U.S. continental presidential and congressional elections, I interrogate how the United States has deployed "Indianness" as a function of colonial incorporation at the same time that I consider the ways in which resistance to those discourses of "Indianness" further entrench U.S. control over American Indian nations.

For American Indians and scholars familiar with U.S. federal Indian policies, the word "reorganization" most likely calls to mind the Indian Reorganization Act, also known as the Wheeler-Howard Act, of 1934. That act, under the guidance of John Collier, has sometimes been dubbed the "Indian New Deal." In the most generous reading, it halted the disas-

trous allotment policies of the late nineteenth century, reestablished government-to-government relationships between Indian nations and the
United States, and granted authority to the Department of the Interior to
reconstruct tribal governance against traditional forms of government to
reflect the United States' model of liberal democracy as a means of civilizing through self-governance. Though the principles of the Act shaped
a broad legislative agenda for the U.S. Congress in the 1930s and 1940s,
ultimately less than half of American Indian nations reorganized under
its auspices. Yet in Hawai'i, where the proposed Native Hawaiian Government Reorganization Act is more commonly referred to as the "Akaka bill,"
that context and layering on of continental federal Indian policy is often
sublimated or forgotten even as the Office of Hawaiian Affairs, court cases
such as *Rice v. Cayetano* (2000) and *Doe v. Kamehameha* (2005), and the
U.S. Congress debate whether Hawaiians have the same status as American Indian nations under the commerce clause of the U.S. Constitution.[3]
Sometimes, and understandably, attempts to contextualize U.S. colonization of Hawai'i through American Indian histories are criticized as yet
another form of U.S. hegemonic imperialism that seeks to transform subjects of an independent Hawaiian kingdom into "Native Americans." Many
Hawaiian activists, and especially kingdom sovereignty nationalists, focus
on understanding the Hawaiian archipelago as the site of exceptionalism
within the trajectory of U.S. empire-building. Hawai'i is in this view a militarily occupied territory logically outside the bounds of American control,
while American Indian nations are naturalized as wholly belonging to and
within the colonizing logics of the United States.[4]

This chapter will focus particularly on how the Native Hawaiian Government Reorganization Act of 2007 has been framed discursively within
Hawai'i and within the continental United States as a way to understand how
the United States, as it develops and contorts its own federal laws to control
indigenous nations, uses discourses of Indianness to solidify and extend its
boundaries. In the face of these colonial processes that seek to mask the fractures within the United States' boundaries at the site where they overlap and
overwrite American Indian nations, it seems important to relocate the pending legislation within the larger history of U.S. concerns about where Indian
nations figure, whether internal or external, as the United States extends its
imperialist gaze towards Hawai'i. Foundationally, the United States' colonization of American Indian nations throughout the nineteenth and twentieth
centuries provided the impetus for the imperial turn that stretched and then

naturalized the United States across the continent and into the Pacific. Native Hawaiian activists, more frequently than they intend, mirror U.S. hegemonic and colonizing discourses used to maintain control over American Indian lands and resources as they struggle to find a way out of that imperial grasp for their own island nation and kingdom.

What is at stake for me in this chapter is twofold. First, I want to emphasize in unequivocal terms my abiding support for Hawaiian independence struggles against the United States as they are argued in international forums. There is no singular indigenous sovereignty, nor is there a singular history that contains the specificities of U.S. imperialism as it has affected Alaska Native villages, American Indian nations, unincorporated, insular, and incorporated territories, Hawai'i, Iraq, Okinawa, and Afghanistan, to name just a few. There is, however, a United States government that uses precedent and the "rule of law" to colonize through the unification of the bureaucratic and militaristic systems of colonial administration and control. I argue for the decolonization of Hawai'i, but I also argue for the decolonization of North America, which leads me to the second concern of this chapter: to find ways for activists and scholars to resist the processes through which the U.S. government pits indigenous and Hawaiian struggles against each other in what Taiaiake Alfred and Jeff Corntassel have identified as "the politics of distraction."[5] Such politics emerge in the context of certain discourses of "Indianness," constructed juridically and legislatively by U.S. law to further underwrite U.S. empire and ensure that the forms of protest that rise up in resistance to that empire are limited, constrained by affective normativities, and self-policing. By pitting indigenous peoples against each other, or making them fight for scraps to avoid the larger structuring problems of settler colonialism, the politics of distraction that I want to interrogate serve to maintain U.S. control over colonized indigenous peoples, lands, and resources on the continent and in the Pacific by naturalizing that control as the a priori condition to any anticolonial critique. To that end, this chapter examines the cacophony of "Indianness" underscoring the legal logics of various iterations of the Native Hawaiian Government Reorganization Act considered by the U.S. Congress and the state of Hawai'i. In addition I will consider how a paradigmatic "Indianness" has functioned within resistances, indigenous and haole, radical and conservative, to that legislation—resistances that pull between racial and national identities, threat and contagion, and the internal and external imaginings upon which U.S. colonialist discourses transit.

Unexpected Hawaiians in Indian Places

In the March 16, 1935, issue of the *New Yorker*, a short vignette appears in the "Talk of the Town," a section that reports gossip on happenings around town, functioning much the same way then as now. The piece reported on the opening of a new restaurant called the Versailles, and while news of a new French restaurant is not usually cause for gossip, the restaurant's featured specialty was. The authors decided to investigate, and when they arrived, they found the scene exactly as it had been reported to them. The restaurant, to distinguish itself from others in the area, was featuring an Indian dish, prepared by a real Indian. The Indian in this moment was a woman dressed in beaded buckskin, complete with braids and moccasins. The writers, curious as to what an Indian dish might be—and they could only imagine corn-meal mush—decided to give the cook carte blanche to prepare whatever she liked for them. As soon as the meal was presented, the piece continues, they were struck by the fact that it was indeed an Indian dish—an excellent meal featuring curried lamb, rice, chutney, and grated coconut. Disturbed by the discrepancy between Indians, but not willing to challenge anyone in person, the writers headed across the street to call the restaurant under the assumed identity of a curator at the Museum of the American Indian. They asked the headwaiter if he could inform them what tribe the woman belonged to; when he returned, he told them, "Well, she's Hawaiian, but she *looks* Indian." With the mystery deepening, they continued to push the waiter until they got the full story: "The lady in question is Miss Alice Tong. She was born in Hawaii, the gateway to the Far East and naturally picked up a thorough knowledge of Indian cooking. When she went to work at the Versailles, they sent her to a costumer's to get an Indian costume, and she came back rigged out as a squaw. She looked so nice in the outfit, and seemed so pleased with it, that the management didn't have the courage to tell her anything was wrong."[6]

By the time that this squib appeared in 1935, John Collier and Franklin D. Roosevelt had successfully passed the Indian New Deal and had begun reorganizing American Indian governments. Hawai'i had already been annexed as a U.S. territory for thirty-seven years, and debates had been under way for almost as long about admitting the islands as a state. However, since the 1900s, Republican senators and their southern Democratic allies blocked such proposals for fear of admitting a state with such a strong ethnic minority composed primarily of Asians, particularly after several Chinese exclusion acts had been passed starting in 1882.[7] The scene exemplifies the discourses and confusions of race, nation, and Indianness spiraling around the colonization of Hawai'i. There are a number of ways to unpack these historical collisions, but for my purposes, what is interesting is the ways in which Native Hawaiians are seemingly haunted by an Indianness that simultaneously includes and excludes them within U.S. modernity. Moreover, that Indianness in which Asians and Hawaiians—collapsed into the form of Miss Alice Tong who could be either one or a combination of both (the story never clarifies)—pass as exotic domestic foreignness within the fractures played out upon the signification of "Indian," continues to ghost Hawaiians as they slip between Asian, American, and Indian as well as between a racial and political identity in the decades leading up to the admission of Hawai'i as the fiftieth state.

As all these anxieties about internal and external, indigenous and domestic foreignness play out on the body of a woman identified as Hawaiian passing as Indian, the story in the *New Yorker* speaks to deeper concerns about authenticity, "the real," and performativity. What emerges in the parallax gap between and among Hawaiians, Asians, and American Indians, as well as their potential interchangeability, is not so much a dynamic between native and arrivant per se, but rather the product of colonial discourses, in which the particulars of distinct colonial encounters are flattened into equivalencies that then pit one colonial history against another as each tries to claim a parallactic real from which to resist. Rather than understanding those histories as absolutely interconnected by United States imperialism, what occurs, not only in the story but in Native Hawaiian resistance some seventy years later, is the seemingly absolute incommensurability of the historical processes that created "Indians" as domestic dependents belonging to the United States and Native Hawaiians as something else entirely. Through the tensions between vying claims to indigenous colonial positionality—pulled out into competition in the reification and creation of a "Native American" that Native Hawaiians now resist as they assert their rights to self-determination and sovereignty—we can see how the stages of U.S. policies that transformed American Indian nations from foreign nations into domestic peoples become stabilized and naturalized in the distance between the "mainland" and its Pacific colonies.

In 1993, one hundred years after the U.S.-backed overthrow of Queen Lili'uokalani by local white businessmen and missionaries and one year after the triumphalism of the Columbus quincentennial, President Clinton signed into law the Apology Resolution, in which the U.S. acknowledged its role in the dissolution of the Hawaiian kingdom. While the apology, like much the United States does, is not legally binding and served only as a mea culpa, it did set the stage and indeed called for a process of reconciliation between the United States and citizens of the Hawaiian kingdom. It was also an attempt to acknowledge a formal relationship between the United States government and the indigenous people of Hawai'i through a recognition that the United States had deprived Hawaiians of their innate rights to sovereignty and self-determination. However, the 1993 Apology Bill did nothing to redress the legal indeterminacies swirling around Hawai'i and did not resolve the question about where Hawaiians fit within or outside of the larger U.S. imperial society or colonialist legal structures.[8]

And because the Apology Resolution did nothing to restore the Hawaiian kingdom, nor did it even attempt to resolve the legal indeterminacies of race, indigeneity, and sovereignty affecting Native Hawaiians and their relationship to the United States, Hawai'i senators Daniel Inouye and Daniel Akaka proposed a bill in 2000, initially conceived as a form of federal recognition, that would incorporate Native Hawaiians into the same legal category of domestic dependence that subsumes American Indian sovereignties. Senators Inouye and Akaka framed the bill as a legislative initiative to follow up on the process of reconciliation between the United States and Native Hawaiians begun with the Apology Resolution. Part of President Clinton's 1993 "Acknowledgement and Apology" expressed a "commitment to acknowledge the ramifications of the overthrow of the Kingdom of Hawai'i," in addition to acknowledging that the agents and citizens of the United States deprived Native Hawaiians of their rights to self-determination.[9] However, much of the initial urgency to move forward on federal recognition seven years after the official U.S. apology stemmed from the then recent rulings in cases such as *Rice v. Cayetano* and the legal challenges facing other programs administered by Kanaka Maoli in Hawai'i, including the administration of Hawaiian Homelands. In the late 1990s and early 2000s, the state of Hawai'i became a test ground for virulent anti–affirmative action cases that sought to establish precedent within U.S. law by taking advantage of those legal indeterminacies that left Native Hawaiians somewhere between a racial category and a political entity. The first blow came in the 2000 *Rice v. Cayetano* case when the U.S. Supreme Court ruled in favor of Harold F. Rice, a fourth-generation nonnative resident of the Hawaiian islands who challenged the legality of a native-only vote, arguing that the exclusionary, "race-based" vote for representatives in the Office of Hawaiian Affairs (OHA) that oversees Native Hawaiian trusts violated the Fifteenth Amendment.[10] That ruling, along with cases challenging the right of Kamehameha Schools to use race as a basis for admission and the legality of Hawaiian Homelands to lease lands only to native Hawaiians, Kānaka Maoli with 50 percent blood quantum or more, provides some of the impetus for federal recognition and reorganization.

Support for the Akaka bill has spanned the political spectrum in Washington and in the Hawaiʻi state legislature. Both Republican and Democratic members of Congress have backed the bill, and at various times during her tenure as the Republican governor of Hawaiʻi, Linda Lingle promised to push the Bush II and Obama administrations to move forward on the bill with the weight of full White House approval. However, some Republicans such as John McCain, who has served as chairman of the Senate Committee on Indian Affairs, have expressed "reservations" concerning the impact of the bill on current federal Indian law and the future possibility of gaming within Hawaiʻi, while still other Republicans object to the creation of a separate government in the state of Hawaiʻi on the grounds that it is unconstitutional.[11] The core political concern expressed by Republicans who oppose the bill is that it would, in their view, create a distinct and sovereign government within an already established state in the United States whose rights and power would ultimately supersede those of the state. Further, they argue, establishing a government based solely upon what they see to be claims to ethnic identity excludes outsiders from any access to lands, funds, resources, and decision-making power while also creating "special rights" for a racial, in this case Native Hawaiian, minority.[12]

The bill itself provides the structure through which the United States recognizes that "despite the overthrow of the government of the Kingdom of Hawaiʻi, Native Hawaiians have continued to maintain their separate identity as a distinct native community through cultural, social, and political institutions, and to give expression to their rights as native people to self-determination, self-governance, and economic self-sufficiency."[13] In order to further those claims to self-determination and self-governance, the Akaka bill authorizes the establishment of additional bureaucracies (and here bureaucracy is indeed the point) that outnumber those that currently exist to administer Indian trusts and treaty annuities. Some of the departments that would be created by the Akaka bill include the United

States Office for Native Hawaiian Relations within the Office of the Secretary of the Interior, as well as the Native Hawaiian Interagency Coordinating Group within the Department of the Interior.

Additionally, the bill provides a mind-numbingly latticed framework through which Native Hawaiians will establish a "Native Hawaiian Governing Entity" (NHGE) that will work closely with the Office for Native Hawaiian Relations and the Native Hawaiian Interagency Coordinating Group to maintain and facilitate the "special relationship" between the United States and the reorganized Hawaiian government. In order to establish such a governing entity, the bill provides for the creation of a commission of nine adult members of the Native Hawaiian community who would oversee the creation and maintenance of a roll, similar to those created as part of the Dawes Act, of "each adult member of the Native Hawaiian community who elects to participate in the reorganization of the Native Hawaiian governing entity."[14] The bill further defines Native Hawaiians eligible for enrollment as

(i) An individual who is one of the indigenous, native people of Hawaii and who is a direct lineal descendant of the aboriginal, indigenous people who (I) resided in the islands that now comprise the State of Hawaii on or before January 1, 1893; and (II) occupied and exercised sovereignty in the Hawaiian archipelago, including the area that now constitutes the State of Hawaii; or (ii) an individual who is 1 of the indigenous, native people of Hawaii and who was eligible in 1921 for the programs authorized by the Hawaiian Homes Commission Act (42 Stat. 108, chapter 42) or a direct lineal descendant of that individual.[15]

Although the Akaka bill does not impose a blood quantum per se, the Hawaiian Homes Commission Act did set blood requirements for those who could be awarded lands at 50 percent or more (referred to in state law as "native Hawaiians" in distinction from the generalized "Native Hawaiian" who traces direct lineal descent regardless of blood quantum). Any movement towards membership rolls raises fears of blood quantum requirements that, should they be instituted within the "Native Hawaiian governing entity," would violate Hawaiian cultural protocols of descent and genealogy.[16] Once the community of Native Hawaiians enrolls and the Secretary of the Interior approves the final document, they will then be authorized to establish a governing council whose duties will include the creation of the organic documents of governance that will form the basis for the NHGE. The intricacies of interoperative agencies and government offices hint at the number of vested interests jockeying for power in the structures that federal recognition will create. OHA, for instance, assumes that its agency will quickly transform into the new Office of Native Hawaiian Relations that will supposedly have similar responsibilities as the Bureau of Indian Affairs (BIA). What is notable, and a bit stunning, is the number of interagency groups that will be created and exist alongside the BIA within the Department of the Interior should such a bill ever pass.

The racial and legal indeterminacies that haunt Native Hawaiians within the current logics of U.S. colonialism and threaten to impose a specter of additionally bureaucratized federal policy upon them have prompted Senator Jon Kyl from Arizona to complain that Native Hawaiian reorganization is a preferential and unconstitutional creation of a race-based government that will balkanize the United States when, he fears, other racial groups like Mexican Americans, Asian Americans, and African Americans will follow suit and claim rights to establish for themselves sovereign nations within the U.S. based upon historical oppression.[17] Radically reframing the recognition of American Indian sovereignty that is at the heart of the impetus to "recognize" Hawai'i as a form of racial "special rights," Kyl signals a deeper fear that somehow "Indianness" in the form of indigenous sovereignty and self-determination will spread to other minorities, who will then argue for similar recognitions and thereby break the United States into pockets of racial nations in the pursuit for social justice.

As the specter of federal Indian policy looms for Senator Kyl as a trope of historical and "special" racial entitlement rather than a long history of treaty recognitions and state diplomacies with and among indigenous nations, what accompanies the layering of federal Indian policy into the Pacific is a similar sense of contagion. Senator Daniel Inouye, in a report on the Akaka Bill to the 107th Congress ten days after the events of 9/11, went to great lengths to argue that words like "Indian" and "tribe" within the Commerce Clause and the "Indians not Taxed" clause of the Constitution denote an understanding of the place of aboriginal nations within U.S. borders and laws. In effect, Inouye argues that Hawaiians are "Indians," that "the Framers of the Constitution did not import a meaning to those terms as a limitation upon the authority of Congress, but as descriptions of the native people who occupied and possessed the lands that were later to become the United States."[18] As such, Inouye continues, Hawaiians fall under the jurisdiction of the federal government, where a formal acknowledgment of the domestic dependent nature of Hawaiians living within the United States is the same as American Indians.

Within Hawai'i, Kanaka Maoli resistance to the bill prompted community member Anna Reeves to state at the initial public hearings regarding the possibility of federal recognition that "I express my ohana, because of the changes. We have to do this. I stand before the committee, and I am born and raised in Hawai'i for generations. I am 100 percent Hawaiian, kanaka maoli. I do not have any other blood, not even Indian. I want the committee to know you are not going to inject Indian in my blood."[19] Reeves's resistances to being injected with "Indian blood" diagnoses U.S. imperialism as depending upon a catchable "Indianness" to justify continued colonial occupation of and control over others' lands and bodies. But what is troublesome to me is that such constructions of Indianness as infection depend upon a series of misrecognitions about federal Indian law and the diverse histories of American Indian nations that in these discussions are both feared and contaminating.

"Indian," as the radical otherness structuring the multicultural liberal settler state, threatens the entire foundation of the United States precisely because it is the ongoing colonization of indigenous nations and their lands that made the U.S. possible at all. Senator Kyl's fear that nonindigenous minorities will somehow catch "Indianness" to become sovereign themselves as a means to disrupt the coherency of white dominance over the naturalized borders of the North American continent speaks not just to the deeper colonial architecture of those borders, but to a sense that colonial coherency is only maintained through white supremacy. The creation of non-indigenous minority "nations" that Kyl fears would not end colonization in North America, it would proliferate it. Indianness as an injected contagion serves to erase the transnational distinctions of all the peoples who collapse under its sign and as it is refied, the sign itself—which now bears indigeneity, sovereignty, and racial minority—becomes the site of contention as indigenous and occupied peoples throughout the empire struggle to resist U.S. hegemony. In the process, and precisely because "Indianness" serves as the ontological scaffolding for colonialist domination, anticolonial resistances such as those articulated by Anna Reeves outside the continental United States, which align themselves against "Indianness" as a manifestation of empire, risk reflecting and reinscribing the very colonialist discourses used to possess and contain American Indian nations back onto the abjected "Indian" yet again.

Reorganization not Recognition

"Indian" as sign within U.S. colonial discourses, then, serves as a deracinated supplement that signifies the underside of imperial dominance. As a result, in the midst of all these concerns about Indian contagion, an unidentified American Indian man, attending the same hearings as Anna Reeves and given the floor by Harry Wasson a few minutes after she spoke, is recorded as saying in response, "I understand everybody here does not want to be Indian. I do not know anybody who wants to be Indian. It is not easy being Indian. Why you would want to be Indian, I do not know."[20] The rest of the unidentified man's words are recorded in the hearing documents as "inaudible," and Senator Inouye quickly closes the floor to his statement. It is difficult to interpret exactly what "Why you would want to be Indian, I do not know" means in its context. And such interpretation would depend upon tone. But one possible meaning that emerges from this moment in the testimonies is that Indianness has been abjected into a category that no one would want to claim.[21] Certainly, the United States, by discursively forcing peoples into the objectified category of "Indian," signals its intent to exploit at the same time that it reinscribes its own mastery over indigenous nations on the continent. As long as the United States continues to construct itself as cowboy, it must designate or infect those to be vanquished as "Indians"—not an easy position of subjectification within empire. The consequence of such infections is that they disrupt the possibility of forming what Leela Gandhi has identified as the improbable affective communities that emerge on the horizontal trajectories within and across empire that might, through friendship and shared political resistances, disrupt self/other and other/other binaries and forge new transits of resistance.[22]

In a government that looks to precedent in order to effectively and legally colonize a people, it is not a coincidence that the "Native Hawaiian Government Reorganization Act" that was initially proposed as a recognition bill now carries the sign of "reorganization" rather than the "federal recognition" title that many people associate with it when the Akaka bill is discussed in Hawai'i.[23] In fact, it is striking how blatantly both namings—which solidified to "reorganization" as the bill moved from the House to the Senate between February 14, 2001, and April 6, 2001—locate the bill within the history of federal Indian policy and provide important insights into the legal and colonial oscillations that Native Hawaiian struggles for sovereignty now resist. The language of "federal recognition" that the Akaka bill attempts to ally itself with draws upon the Bureau of Indian Affairs' 1978 regulations and criteria outlining a community's ability to pursue recognition through a congressional or presidential act, and reflects the push/pull between U.S. political, legislative, and juridical colonization of American Indian nations on the one hand and resistances to that colonization by American Indians on the other, especially after the disastrous effects of the 1954 Termination Act. What resonates in the slippage between "recognition" and "reorganization" in the Akaka bill is the degree to which it draws upon the policies of the 1930s and not the post-termination policy era of the late twentieth century to incorporate Native Hawaiians further into the structures already established to maintain power over Indian lands and peoples under the rubric of "reorganization."[24]

This history of "reorganization" as federal policy requires contextualization. By the 1920s, it was clear even to white politicians in Washington that the Dawes General Allotment Act of 1887 had failed to solve once and for all the "Indian Problem" that faced the colonizing United States, who wanted the problem and Indians to go away once and for all. Despite parceling up reservation lands and allotting acres to individuals in a systematic effort to assimilate Indians into farmers (and opening up "surplus" lands for white settlement), Indians had not disappeared into the mass-producing heartland farming culture as hoped. Conditions on remaining reservations were deplorable, and corruption and greed rife in the allotment process, with non-native Indian agents, settlers, and arrivants gaining more and more power with access to more and more indigenous lands. The Meriam Report, published in 1928 by the Brookings Institute, identified the Dawes Act as the primary source of the further impoverishment of native peoples and implicated allotment in increasing the rates of disease and infant mortality. In an attempt to convince Congress to take the findings and suggestions of the Meriam Report seriously and to reform the disastrous federal Indian policies of allotment, John Collier pushed for the Senate Indian Committee to conduct its own investigations. By 1934 Collier had been appointed as commissioner of Indian Affairs by Franklin D. Roosevelt, and with the help of Representative Edgar Howard and Senator Burton K. Wheeler, presented a reformed Indian policy to Congress that same year. The Wheeler-Howard Act sought to repair the damage of previous policies and made a significant intervention by halting the Allotment Act and, in some cases, returned "surplus" lands to tribes; however, its primary agenda reiterated the long-term goal of "humane" assimilation and dissolution of native nations to end treaty obligations under the lofty desire to acknowledge and "atone" for "wrongs" that had been committed in the past.[25]

At the center of the Indian Reorganization Act was John Collier's pet project of "self-governance," a project he that sought to implement again in the 1940s when the BIA briefly controlled the Japanese American internment camp at Poston, Arizona.[26] Under the auspices of "reorganization," the Wheeler-Howard Act sought to centralize tribal governance within a Western democratic structure in order to streamline the annuities paid to a tribe under treaty agreements and to effectively control land deals for non-native prospectors interested in natural resources and eventually nuclear-waste dumping. Tribes targeted by the Act were offered a cookie-cutter model of government that featured a top-down structure, in which the elected leader or governor and his handpicked council controlled all branches of government and resources. If tribes wanted an alternative government, they were given a set time limit (sometimes only thirty days) to construct their own that then had to be approved by the Department of the Interior. The end result was that the IRA governmental structure was pushed and implemented as a number of tribes were brought under the jurisdiction of the act. Citizenship was determined through blood quantum and enrollment, and traditional government and values were subsumed within a corporate model that set the stage for termination in the 1940s and 1950s and the struggles of the 1970s.

At the time the IRA was implemented, many Indian scholars and activists challenged the Act because of its implications for treaty rights, land claims, and sovereignty—challenges that are today echoed in Kanaka Maoli resistances to the Akaka bill. There was concern that the act would further erode self-determination as well as provide the United States the opportunity to end treaty obligations, and a number of tribes, including the Navajo, Seneca, and Crow, refused to ratify the Act altogether. Today, American Indian scholars still struggle with the meanings of "reorganization" and the ramifications it has had for tribal self-governance. Forty years after Collier's reform bill passed, however, Vine Deloria Jr. (Standing Rock Sioux) observed that "far from limiting the political powers of the tribe, the Indian Reorganization Act seems to have either added powers or defined existing powers more specifically."[27] The IRA, despite its underlying agenda of assimilation and in spite of the hierarchized governmental structures that could too often become corrupt puppets for U.S. and corporate interests, ironically reaffirmed self-governance and laid the legal foundation through which tribes have been able to reassert sovereignty and challenge Chief Justice Marshall's decision that indigenous nations are somehow "domestic dependent nations."[28] Deloria, writing from the vantage point provided by the American Indian Movement's reassertion of treaty rights and sovereignty in the 1970s, identified within the IRA and the federal government's self-interested consolidation of "tribal councils" to serve as mouthpieces for the colonialist agenda, the possibility of turning the IRA into an affirmation of the implicit sovereignty that underlies the right to self-governance.

The irony, then, in the transformation of the initial discussions of a possible Native Hawaiian recognition process into a government reorganization bill is that the Hawaiian kingdom up until the overthrow had international recognition as a nation-state within the family of nations that is now being exchanged for a process that would incorporate Hawaiians into U.S. legal structures as a newly created political entity. President Clinton's Apology Resolution makes clear exactly why Hawaiians are being forced to politically reorganize, but by instituting a majority vote in the process of establishing the council to oversee the creation of the governing entity, the Akaka bill already frames government as democracy rather than as constitutional monarchy or as traditional consensus governance.[29] The thorny issues between reorganization and recognition as federal Indian policy, mediated through the processes of termination and relocation in the 1950s, drive home the point that Hawai'i is distinct and differs in significant ways from the status and history of American Indian nations on the continent.

As Bruce Granville Miller points out, with the overthrow of Queen Lili'uokalani in 1893, the United States created the legal fiction that Hawaiian sovereignty was somehow extinguished when it was admitted as a territory in 1898. With statehood in 1959, Native Hawaiians were considered wards of the state of Hawai'i and not the federal government.[30] As part of that process, the United States also ordered that the United Nations remove Hawai'i from its list of non-self-governing territories in a clear violation of international norms and Kanaka Maoli claims to sovereignty and self-determination.[31] Miller argues that "unlike Indian tribes, the Hawaiians, as a nation or a people, have had no federal recognition and have remained, in effect, in the stage of termination, as some Indian tribes were in the 1950s under then current U.S. policy," a contention that is contraindicated by the international recognitions of the Kingdom of Hawai'i that supersede those of the United States.[32]

Yet, when representatives from the Office of Hawaiian Affairs, the Council for Native Hawaiian Advancement, and the State of Hawai'i presented their case in front of the Senate Committee on Indian Affairs on March 1, 2005, they argued vehemently for federal recognition as a tonic to termination, claiming that it "is one of the most successful policies" for Alaska Natives and American Indians and that it helps strengthen democracy at home.[33] The slippage between federal recognition and government reorganization becomes increasingly problematic when one remembers Queen Lili'uokalani's emphatic words that *"I was recognized by the United States as the constitutional sovereign of the Hawaiian Islands."*[34]

The Akaka bill, as it is currently framed and debated, refracts tensions present from the beginning of Hawai'i's incorporation into the United States through its continual parallactic distortions between Hawaiian and Indian in relation to this question of recognition and reorganization. At the time of the overthrow in 1893, one of the Queen's concerns was that "overawed by the power of the United States to the extent that they can neither themselves throw off the usurpers, nor obtain assistance from other friendly states, the people of the Islands [would] have no voice in determining their future" and would be "virtually relegated to the condition of the aborigines of the American continent."[35] Political cartoons at the time of the overthrow had already begun the process of transforming Hawaiians into African, African American, and Indian "savages," and these images illustrate how the United States understood expansion into the Pacific and Caribbean.[36]

Queen Lili'uokalani worried that her people might be relegated to the condition of American Indians, a condition that Native Hawaiian historian Samuel Manaiakalani Kamakau and the first Hawaiian Historical Association in 1841 described as "a race without a history."[37] Justifiably concerned that her people would become voiceless in determining their own future (or past) like "the aborigines of the American continent," Queen Lili'uokalani herself relegates American Indian nations to a teleological and completed narrative that not only absented the ongoing conditions of colonialism at the time, but negated any possible usable past or future for indigenous peoples on the continent. Though she could see how Hawaiians were threatened by the usurping power of the United States, she could not see how the United States' policies towards Indians might ultimately inform how the nation-state would perceive the people of Hawai'i, despite the international recognitions of her status as monarch and her island nation as a kingdom.

Instead, she marvels in her book *Hawaii's Story by Hawaii's Queen* at the miles and miles of rich country laid out before her as she travels across the continent to make her case to President Cleveland in Washington, D.C. "Here were," she writes, "thousands of acres of uncultivated, uninhabited, but rich and fertile lands, soil, capable of producing anything which grows, plenty of water, floods of it running to waste, everything needed for pleasant towns and quiet homesteads, except population."[38] She goes on to ask:

> And yet this great and powerful nation must go across two thousand miles of sea, and take from the poor Hawaiians their little spots in the broad Pacific, must covet our islands of Hawaii Nei, and extinguish the nationality of my poor people, many of whom have now not a foot of land which can be called their own. And for what? In order that another race problem shall be injected into the social and political perplexities with which the United States in the great experiment of popular government is already struggling? In order that a novel and inconsistent foreign and colonial policy shall be grafted upon its hitherto impregnable diplomacy?[39]

In that journey eastward to Washington and in her stays in D.C., Lili'uokalani made her way through what she perceived as a *terra nullius* paradisiacal landscape of water running to waste which was, in reality, haunted by massacres that indicted an assailable U.S. foreign policy toward American Indian nations.

What is particularly striking about her observations that "colonies and colonies could be established here, and never interfere with each other in the least, the vast extent of unoccupied land is so enormous" is not so much that it plays out U.S. colonial narratives of expansion into the wilderness, but that she cannot see that what she deems empty space is actually full of peoples. Those lands only appear empty because they have yet to be inscribed *within* the United States, and such *terra nullius* illusions speak to the concerns of the U.S. master narrative of Manifest Destiny which sought to internalize Indians as part of the nation through the Dawes Act that was still allotting traditional, communal lands to individual Indian families in the hopes of transforming them into gentlemen farmers. Even as Queen Lili'uokalani rides the rails eastward to Washington to defend her Hawaiian islands from becoming part of the United States and to regain her rightful place as sovereign of an independent nation-state, she is traveling through the juggernaut of U.S. empire struggling juridically and militarily with Indian nations who remained painfully external to the United States, particularly in the tensions that emerged prior to and following the Wounded Knee massacre of 1890 that occurred just three years before the overthrow of the queen.

In *Indians in Unexpected Places,* Philip J. Deloria delineates the mid-1890s as shaped predominantly by violence, and his treatment of Lakota struggles against the encroaching U.S. military interrogates how violence functions within U.S. national imaginings. Wounded Knee represented, according to Deloria, "a global sign of military defeat."[40] And yet, as he demonstrates in the case of Plenty Horses's attack on and killing of Lieutenant Edward Casey in 1891, Indians were still capable of engaging in acts of war against the United States, and indeed violence and military engagement through outbreak retained, up until 1903 at least, the possibility to disrupt narratives of pacification that the United States was intent upon preserving at the turn of the twentieth century even as the United States remained in a state of war with American Indian nations. For Deloria, violence in the very lands that the queen travels through signals how very much Indians remained external to U.S. imaginings about its citizenship and polity. The queen's cathexion of *terra nullius* discourses invisiblizes those indigenous nations external to the United States as the queen herself naturalizes the lands she travels through as rightfully belonging to the colonizing nation-state.

In the process of naturalizing U.S. hegemony on the North American continent, she reifies Indians as internal to a government that has overstepped its bounds only, in her view, by entering the Pacific and extinguishing "the nationality of her poor people." Her second turn in the questions she poses to her readers draws out the solidifying discourses of racialization that had, by the late 1890s, consolidated into the predominant and "original" sin of the United States that evacuated colonization as a process. In persuading American readers that Hawai'i's incorporation into the

United States risks adding to that sin, she ventriloquizes the discourses of race in an attempt to redirect U.S. nationalistic hegemony to support the Hawaiian cause by strategically reframing the overthrow as an injection of another race problem into the perplexities with which "the great experiment of popular government is already struggling." Her query is echoed one hundred years later when Anna Reeves asserts that "you are not going to inject Indian into my blood."

Her final question draws upon the United States' own discourses of exceptionalism by attempting to righteously prevent the United States from grafting "a novel and inconsistent foreign and colonial policy" upon "its hitherto impregnable diplomacy" as if the United States had not already grafted a very mundane and consistent foreign and colonial policy towards American Indian nations since 1776. By making the United States exceptional, she positions the overthrow and colonization of Hawai'i as exceptional and counter to U.S. foreign diplomacy, an argument that seeks to indict the United States for its injurious and wrongful acts. And though the queen is by no means colonizing continental indigenous nations, the discourses she draws upon to argue her case render indigenous peoples lamentable victims whose case is unactionable. These framing questions continue to inflect how Hawaiians apprehend the overthrow and U.S. policy; additionally, these questions project the negation of the colonization of American Indian nations into the past and future as the foundational premise upon which to build an anti-imperial, anticolonial critique.

In contradistinction, at the same time that Queen Lili'uokalani articulates her concern that her people will be treated like "Indians," Southeastern diplomats from the Muscogee Creek Nation, for instance, were acutely aware of what was occurring in the Pacific and used it as a way to articulate nationalist resistance during the allotment period. In 1893 Creek delegate and nationalist George Washington Grayson approached President Cleveland and reminded him of his commitment to the queen. He used the occasion to draw parallels between her nation and his. According to Mary Jane Warde, "Grayson suggested that the terms 'boomer' and 'intruder' covered the alien element in the Pacific island kingdom as well as the Creek Nation."[41] The struggle over "alien," "intruders," and "citizens" within the Southeastern nations in Indian Territory reflected similar tensions in the United States as it maneuvered the tribes to relinquish land holdings and assimilate once and for all.

Aliens in Paradise

By the early 1920s, many of these concerns with violence in the United States as marker of external Indian nations had been settled; however, the status of Indians remained less settled despite continued assertions that indigenous peoples constituted "domestic dependent nations" and were assimilable through allotment and incorporation into the U.S. body politic, even though the United States did not extend full citizenship to American Indians until 1924. In Hawai'i these oscillating discourses of internal/external, racial minority and political entity, emerged at the site of blood, land, and welfare with the creation of the Hawaiian Homes Commission that began a process of leasing lands to native Hawaiians as a means to assimilate through rehabilitation. J. Kēhaulani Kauanui explains that this process was significantly different than the General Allotment Act of 1887 on the United States continent: "Unlike the explicit push to *detribalize* Indians through the Dawes plan—with individual land title vulnerable to alienation—the initial aim of the HHCA proposal was to rehabilitate urban Kānaka Maoli by *returning* them to the land 'for their own good.'"[42] In 1921, as U.S. senators were debating the constitutionality of the Hawaiian Homes Commission that would lease homestead lands to native Hawaiians, A. G. M. Robertson, the lawyer representing the interests of Parker Ranch that stood to profit from the dispossession of Hawaiian land entitlements, testified before Congress about his concerns about setting aside lands solely for Hawaiians. He argued:

> The Hawaiians are not Indians. The status of Hawaiians is diametrically opposed to that of the Indians on the mainland. The Indians have been regarded as aliens. They get their rights, such as they have, by treaties between them and the federal government. They have no right to vote, unless under subsequent circumstances they become naturalized. As I understand it, they are aliens and not citizens; and their inherent character is by no means that of Hawaiians. The Indians were a roving, nomadic race of people. They did not take to civilization the way the Hawaiians did.[43]

Robertson's declaration depends upon the differentiation of Hawaiians from Indians through the very structures of treaties and the fact that Indians were not across-the-board citizens of the United States at the time that he makes his testimony. The logic of Robertson's argument, then, is that Indians have rights to certain resources and lands because of their treaties and because they are aliens outside the citizenry of the United States—Indians are citizens of external nations governed by external political communities whose rights derive from their foreign status. Hawaiians, on the other hand, became American citizens in 1900 after the Republic of Hawai'i was illegally incorporated into the United States, and therefore, he argues to his own benefit and against Hawaiian land claims, they have the rights that all citizens of the United States should have and no more.

Rona Tamiko Halualani in her reading of this passage emphasizes the last two sentences of Robertson's testimony, noting the distinction between Indians as "a roving, nomadic race of people" compared to Hawaiians who "take to civilization." "It is curious," she notes, "that two indigenous groups, who have strong ties to the land and are similarly constructed through 'barbaric prehumanity' rhetoric, are in the end identified differently from one another: Hawaiians as 'citizens' and Indians as 'aliens.'" She accounts for Robertson's distinguishing of Hawaiian from Indian on the basis of citizenship by speculating that "perhaps, the colonial fetish with a geographical paradise and the supposed inherent generosity of Hawaiian people ('Hawaiianness at heart' or normative benevolence) redeems and elevates Hawaiians over Native American Indians, who are remembered as 'barbaric, unassimilable' and 'forever alien' savages in frequent political confrontations."[44] She interprets Robertson's ploy as evidence of a racial abjection of American Indians that forever marks them as unassimilable nomads in contradistinction to the elevated and redeemed Hawaiian marker of civilization in a moment when Robertson is doing something much more insidious. In his testimony, he discursively attempts to dissolve Hawaiian political status in the face of their incorporation into the citizenry of the United States and marks Indians as the sign of exteriority to the nation-state, in recognition of American Indian treaties and national status as externally sovereign, unincorporated territories and peoples.[45]

Dudley O. McGovney, writing in 1911, explains that individual American Indians are not citizens of the United States and are perhaps better understood as *heimatlos,* stateless aliens outside of their own tribal and national affiliations.[46] Congress could incorporate Indian aliens into the United States and retained the right, he argues, to make them citizens so that "they shall enjoy less than the full special privileges of the citizen, or to make them citizens reserving by way of qualification a special guardianship for their benefit."[47] On the other hand, Hawaiians were, according to McGovney, "collectively made citizens of the United States by the act of Congress, April 30, 1900; moreover, that act 'incorporated' the Hawaiian Islands and made them 'a part of the United States in the fullest sense,' so that there is no question but that any person born therein is a citizen of the United States by virtue of the Fourteenth Amendment, including doubtless *antenati* as well as *post-nati*."[48] In his argument, Indian nations and Indian country might be understood similarly to the Insular Cases that extended U.S. constitutional power over the unincorporated territories of the Philippines, Guam, and Puerto Rico.[49] Non-naturalized tribal Indians, according to McGovney, exist in a liminal space between "incorporated" and "unincorporated" territories, and that oscillation between "incorporated" and "unincorporated" provides Congress the precedent through which to legitimate a seemingly paradoxical democratic colonialist agenda after 1898 and the Spanish-American War.

When Robertson insidiously evokes Indians as aliens in his opposition to the creation of Hawaiian Homelands, he is drawing out a juridical parallax through which to make an argument that ultimately politically allies with Chief Justice Taney's decision in *Dred Scott v. Sandford* (1857). In ruling against Dred Scott's case for freedom, Taney deploys American Indians as the legal precedent through which to argue that the situation of African American slaves

> was altogether unlike that of the Indian race. The latter, it is true, formed no part of the colonial communities, and never amalgamated with them in social connections or in government. But although they were uncivilized, they were yet a free and independent people, associated together in nations or tribes, and governed by their own laws. Many of these political communities were situated in territories to which the white race claimed the ultimate right of dominion. But that claim was acknowledged to be subject to the right of the Indians to occupy it as long as they thought proper.... These Indian Governments were regarded and treated as foreign Governments, as much so as if an ocean had separated the red man from the white....[50]

He goes on to argue that Indians, unlike slaves and descendants of slaves, "may, without doubt, like the subjects of any other foreign Government, be naturalized by the authority of Congress, and become citizens of a State, and of the United States; and if an individual should leave his nation or tribe, and take up his abode among the white population, he would be entitled to all the rights and privileges which would belong to an emigrant from any other foreign people."[51]

Taney, in framing "Indian Governments" as "foreign Governments" for the purposes in *Dred Scott* to justify and legalize the enslavement of African Americans, was contradicting a series of previous juridical rulings about the status American Indian nations had in U.S. colonial law in order to maintain whiteness as the superior, possessive site of entitlement within the United States. Frederick E. Hoxie, in trying to ascertain what Taney was thinking, suggests in the end that "Taney's pronouncement—his statements about both Blacks and Indians—marks a moment in the history of struggles over racial and political hierarchies."[52] And part of those racial and political hierarchies that Taney's decision inaugurated, according to Left Quarter Collective, are "the constructions of politically unequal spaces, including states, incorporated and unincorporated territories, and Indian reservations. Clear and stable demarcations between metropole and colony, domestic and foreign, citizen and subject, and colonized and other imperial subjects proved impossible, made impossible by the very efforts to stabilize them."[53]

In this juridical moment, Taney deploys the notion of the free and independent Indian-government-as-foreign-government not to recognize Indian nations but to reprehensibly secure and cohere white supremacy by distinguishing African Americans as "a subordinate and inferior class of beings, who had been subjugated by the dominant race, and, whether emancipated or not, yet remained subject to their authority, and had no rights or privileges but such as those who held the power and the Government might choose to grant them."[54] These continual arguments for and against Indian naturalization and U.S. citizenship serve as the juridical, legislative, and executive means to justify and legalize the subordination of other peoples within the imperial grasp of the United States. Thus, when Robertson invokes Hawaiian citizens in contradistinction to alien Indians external to the nation-state, he performs a similar consolidation of white haole power through the transit of a paradigmatic Indianness as rationale for further subordination of Hawaiians through full incorporation into the United States.

When Halualani reads Robertson's statement through the language of elevated and redeemed Hawaiian civility on the one hand and barbaric

Indian savagery on the other, she falls into the epistemological trap that Robertson sets up within the racializing logics that supersede and deflect the colonialist logics the United States continues to deploy against Native Hawaiians *and* American Indian nations alike. In some ways, her framing of Robertson's delineation of difference between Indians and Hawaiians as a matter of contrapuntal savage discourses naturalizes U.S. dominion over the continent through a deployment of paradigmatic Indianness that is always already assumed to desire—or perhaps, never escape—the internal within the U.S. nation-state, so that "alien" and "inassimilable" are read as injuries that, according to Wendy Brown, solidify "the identities of the injured and the injuring as social positions, and codifies as well the meanings of their actions against all possibilities of indeterminacy, ambiguity, and struggle for resignification or repositioning." In the process, the colonizing liberalism of the United States enacts and reproduces itself at the sites of law and adjudication as "neutral arbiters of injury rather than as themselves invested with the power to injure."⁵⁵ Robertson's acknowledgement of Indians as aliens outside U.S. citizenry is read as an injury of exclusion from the United States when, in fact, his statement is a recognition of treaty-rights that establish Indian nations as external sovereigns to the United States. The epistemological trap that Taney and Robertson set up in their momentary recognition of American Indian sovereignty and external national status serves to systematize inclusion/exclusion as the site through which liberalism encodes colonization as racialization. Exclusion rather than inclusion becomes the perceived injury in order to remediate and assimilate colonized indigenous nations *into* the borders of the colonizing nation-state.

Native Hawaiians, on the other hand, are naturally externalized outside the United States because their kingdom is over 2,000 miles from the California coast and separated from the North American continent by a vast stretch of the Pacific Ocean. This distinction is important, particularly in the ways in which contemporary Native Hawaiian scholars and activists engage U.S. colonization and military occupation. Queen Lili'uokalani embodies the external colonized subject, while American Indian nations come to bear the sign of the objectification of *nations within.* The hierarchical ordering of peoples initiated by U.S. empire and adjudicated through racialized recognitions and disavowals in cases such as *Dred Scott* creates a struggle for status within those selfsame colonial recognitions that juridically across the board dispossess indigenous peoples in the Pacific and on the continent of resources and land rights. The U.S. colonial misnaming of external indigenous nations on the continent as well as the Pacific and Alaska as "Native Americans" disrupts the diplomatic boundaries of indigenous nations that existed before and well after the arrival of Europeans by subsuming them within the logics and justifications of U.S. imperial mastery that depend upon racial and political hierarchies to maintain and police hegemonic normativity at the site of inclusion.

The effect of these kinds of reinscriptions, in which Indians as "Native American" are always already naturalized as internal, colonized, abjected, and defeated, is that they erase the larger historical processes that are still at work in maintaining U.S. hegemonic control over the continent by reproducing through force the discursive juridical fiction of "domestic dependent." Forced via the same U.S. colonial grinding engine to inhabit a parallax gap, Indianness, as it is projected out into the Pacific by the United States to facilitate U.S. military occupations and conspicuous touristic consumption, transits empire and, as a result, that Indianness serves as the faciality of the vested interests of a settler colonialism that dresses itself in democratic, rehabilitating clothes. Hawaiians, faced with the paradigmatic Indianness that seems to justify U.S. illegal occupations, resist Indianness as a way to resist U.S. imperialism. It is a move that makes complete sense—Hawaiians are not Indians—but that leaves us with the unnamed American Indian man at the Akaka hearings saying in response: "Why you would want to be Indian, I do not know" in a moment of self-denial that stands as a haunting indictment of the discourses of genocide and empire that have signified Indianness as radical alterity, oppression, and death of agency.

From the North American continent, indigenous nations appear in and around the edges where the machinations of settler colonialism are revealed in distortive parallactic effects as the sticky, affective, and lingering planetary stretches of the truth of colonization that are the cascading effect of the Indian transit. Within that transit of U.S. empire, Indianness in dialectical relation to Hawaiian creates a Möbius strip of parallelisms that never intersect, that mirror but remain in competition even as they are forced into a flattened horizon through juridical, legislative, and executive processes. U.S. colonialism enforces affinities between indigenous nations on the continent and in the Pacific that those nations might not have chosen for themselves, and anticolonial resistances create responsibilities to the other as those nations colonized by the United States throughout its imperium struggle to overturn, end, and dismantle the lived conditions that consume human life, land, resources, languages, and cultures in the name of capitalistic production and profit.

Always Look a Trojan Horse in the Mouth

When Republican governor of Hawai'i Linda Lingle testified in front of the Senate Committee on Indian Affairs on March 1, 2005, she asserted that Native Hawaiians, by not being incorporated into federal Indian law, have been historically excluded from the benefits American Indians receive from the government trust relationship. "There are three groups of indigenous people in America," she argued. "Two of the groups have been recognized by the American Government, and one has not. The failure to pass this bill will continue the discrimination that exists against Native Hawaiian peoples."[56] The collapsing of hundreds of disparate and distinct American Indian nations, each with their own histories of extensive treaty relations with the U.S. government, into one group and then making that group indistinctly equivalent to a similarly collapsed grouping of Alaska Native villages and corporations that are then parallel to the singular Hawaiian kingdom to compose the "three groups of indigenous people in America" commits a logical fallacy of epic proportions. Not only does it take 565 American Indian nations and Alaska Native villages to equal one "group" of Native Hawaiians, but these newly constituted "three groups" racialize indigeneity into minority groups within the United States whose injury can and will somehow then be remedied by the colonizing state's recognition in spite of the fact that such recognitions do not end colonialism but rather enact it again and repeatedly. Lingle's testimony gestures towards a common discursive argument that circulates among Hawaiian, haole, and American Indian supporters of the bill—that the problem of Hawaiian status within the United States can be resolved by transforming Hawaiians into American Indians. She further evokes some of the nineteenth century's rhetoric of "saving the Indian" when she observes that residents of the state of Hawai'i must support the Akaka bill as a means to "preserve the Native Hawaiian culture, which is the foundation for our being in Hawaii. It is the essence of who we are as a people and a State. It is also an economic imperative to our State because our State's largest industry, the tourist industry, is really dependent upon the preservation of Native Hawaiian culture."[57] Lingle here performs in conservative, egregious excess the ventriloquism of the speaking subaltern as she argues against the injurious discrimination Hawaiians will continue to face if they are excluded from the recognitions and "benefits" the other two groups enjoy.[58] She then code-switches back to white possession to reveal the true stakes: the continued economic profit off of Hawaiians as exotic tourist capital that is the foundation for "our" being in Hawai'i.

The discourses of Indianness around the Akaka bill and federal recognition of Native Hawaiians discussed in this chapter have prompted those opposed to continued U.S. military occupation in Hawai'i to assert in response that they are not Indians, did not live in tribes, did not hunt buffalo, and do not want to be treated as such as if all indigenous peoples on the North American continent did hunt buffalo and deserve to be colonized. The distancing from the rhetoric Senators Inouye and Akaka evoke to transform Hawaiians into "Native Americans" is absolutely necessary to resist the discursive "Manifest Destiny" that has Inouye arguing that the founding fathers and Chief Justice Marshall prognosticated control of all indigenous peoples whose lands the United States may one day invade by designating such people "Indians." However, arguments that transform American Indians into always already "domestic dependent nations" internal to the United States reify the boundaries of U.S. expansion into the now contiguous 48 states. From Hawai'i, looking across the ocean to the North American continent, the borders of the United States are consolidated, and the colonization and encapsulation of American Indian nations within the United States are complete.

During the Indian Affairs committee meeting at the beginning of March 2005, Senator Daniel Akaka acknowledged that "some of my colleagues have expressed concern that providing Federal recognition will be harmful to American Indians and Alaska Natives," as he turned the floor back to the participants.[59] Though Governor Lingle, Jade Danner, and representatives for the Office of Hawaiian Affairs, the Council for Native Hawaiian Advancement, the National Congress of American Indians, and the Alaska Federation of Natives testified that no BIA funding would be diverted into the structures the bill proposes and assured the committee, in the words of Tex Hall, then president of NCAI, that "federal recognition, self-determination clearly is great," the concern still stands.[60] While the effect on Indian Country may not be monetary, there are significant discursive, cultural, and legal issues that impact how sovereignty, self-determination, and decolonization are framed both within the United States and within the international courts. Arguments for and against the Akaka bill hinge on historical and legal distortions of federal Indian law and reflect competing understandings of what self-determination and sovereignty really mean within the colonizing logics of U.S. juridical biopolitics. Given that states are continually trying to assert jurisdiction over Indian nations within their "borders" while conservative politicians of both parties attack treaty rights and sovereignty on the basis that they are un-American and discriminatory, it seems to me that whittling away at terminologies and structures to further colonize Hawaiians culturally and legally can only be detrimental to all nations currently occupied by the United States. In fact, the Akaka bill, if passed, will put into Indian law a dangerous precedent, particularly in the ways in which it positions the state of Hawai'i as having a prominent and controlling role in how and what the Native Hawaiian Governing Entity will be allowed to govern.

According to a PowerPoint presentation on Senator Daniel Akaka's website, "this bill represents a new paradigm in the government-to-government relationship because it provides a process for negotiation between the Native Hawaiian governing entity and the State and Federal governments to determine how the Native Hawaiian governing entity will exercise its governmental powers and authorities."[61] Such a move comes at a moment in U.S. juridical and legislative colonialism when states are attempting to wrestle Indian policy from the federal government to assert control over nations within their jurisdiction. The 2005 Oneida rulings over land-into-trust exemplify this push for state control over casino earnings and tax collection, and time will tell how the courts will continue to address the push from states to insert themselves more powerfully into the government-to-government relationship between native nations and the federal government. Over the last few years, new amendments have been added to the Akaka bill that would settle all land claims related to breach of trust between Native Hawaiians and the United States. The state and federal governments would retain the civil and criminal jurisdiction they currently enjoy, and the bill would exempt the Department of Defense from the Native American Graves Protection and Repatriation Act and the National Historic Preservation Act, an exemption that, if passed, will have devastating effects as the military expands its presence in Hawai'i and on American Indian trust lands.

This reading of the stakes for continental American Indian nations as they continue to fend off the encroachments of states' rights advocates is, I think, borne out by Governor Lingle's withdrawal of support for the bill in late 2009. Concerned with revisions that Democratic Senators Inouye and Akaka and Representative Abercrombie were able to incorporate when the Democratic Party controlled both the executive and legislative branches of Congress, Lingle said that she could no longer back the bill and demanded a return to the language of the 2007 version that has been, so far, retained in HR 2314. That version very clearly spells out the relationship between the federal government, the state of Hawai'i, and the Native Hawaiian Governing Entity in Sec. 8(b):

> (3) Governmental Authority and Power—Any governmental authority or power to be exercised by the Native Hawaiian governing entity which is currently exercised by the State or Federal Governments shall be exercised by the Native Hawaiian governing entity only as agreed to in negotiations pursuant to section 8(b)(1) of this Act and beginning on the date on which legislation to implement such agreement has been enacted by the United States Congress, when applicable, and by the State of Hawaii, when applicable.[62]

On December 17, 2009, new language was introduced to S 1011 in the Senate Committee for Indian Affairs that changed the 2007 text of the proposed legislation to what is now Sec. 9(b) to the following:

> (3) Governmental Authority and Power—The Native Hawaiian governing entity shall be vested with the inherent powers and privileges of self-government of a native government under existing law, except as set forth in section 10(a). Said powers and privileges may be modified by agreement between the Native Hawaiian governing entity, the United States, and the State pursuant to paragraph (1), subject to the limit described by section 10(a).[63]

The first version of the proposed bill makes it clear that the Native Hawaiian Governing Entity (NHGE), whatever its final form, would be required to accept the results of bilateral negotiations between the federal government and the state of Hawai'i that would legislate the ability of the NHGE to exercise any possible governmental authority and power still allowed it after the federal government and state delimited its powers. In the second version of the bill, the language states that the NHGE would be "vested with the inherent powers and privileges of self-government of a native government" and declares even more explicitly later in section 10(c) that "the Council and the subsequent governing entity recognized under this Act shall be an Indian tribe."

According to the *Honolulu Star-Bulletin,* the primary concern that Governor Lingle and state attorney general Mark Bennett had over the changes was that they "would immediately give the native *[sic]* Hawaiian entity many of the rights that American Indian tribal governments enjoy. That change has 'enormous potential to negatively impact Hawaii and its citizens,' Bennett said."[64] In other words, despite their neoliberal arguments that Native Hawaiians are injured and must be protected by the arbitration of the nation-state that injured them in the first place by excluding them from the recognitions American Indian nations "enjoy," Lingle and Bennett found this version of American Indian sovereignty and governmental power as transit to be too much, too excessive, and too threatening to the state of Hawai'i. Here is colonialism laid bare through the shift from the negative impact on indigenous Hawaiians back to the negative impact on "Hawaii and its citizens" in a move that not just ventriloquizes Native Hawaiian subjectivities, but linguistically evokes the language of state, sovereignty, and citizenry to overthrow yet again the Hawaiian kingdom. While possibilities for a U.S. federal bill ebb and flow as the Republican and Democratic parties vie for dominance in Washington, D.C., Democratic representatives in Hawai'i introduced HB 1627 into the Hawai'i state legislature in 2011 to start a discussion about possible state alternatives to federal recognition. Though amendments have changed the bill's effective-by date to July 1, 2093, in a discussion that is still ongoing, the continued persistence of some form of state or federal recognition suggests a deep neoliberal investment to maintain and entrench colonial administration of Native Hawaiian lands, resources, and governance structures.

The current relationship between Native Hawaiians and American Indian nations has been overdetermined by the discourses of Indianness circulated within the rhetorical economies of U.S. imperial justifications for expansion, racial exclusions, and militarization. The goal in anticolonial struggles against the United States need not be freedom at the expense of another people. Rather, framing our understandings of these concurrent historical oppressions through an awareness of how the United States depends upon a paradigmatic Indianness to underwrite its oppressive policies may provide us with new avenues for anticolonial resistances across and beyond the reach of the United States and may help us resist the tendency towards rivalry in the decolonial process. If the actions of U.S. imperial courts necessitate competitions within indigenous resistances that ultimately replicate colonialist discourses as we are pitted against each other, then what alternatives might exist for American Indian and Hawaiian assertions of sovereignty to ally against those paradigmatic discourses of Indianness that serve as the transit of empire without reinscribing the very colonial logics we hope to disrupt?

Traversing a Sea of Islands

These competing conceptions of indigeneity traced here in this chapter that slip between confronting racializing discourses on the one hand and bringing disparate indigenous locatednesses into conversation on the other, serve, within imperialistic legalities, to force relatedness and recognitions that violate indigenous knowledges that may have once provided the grounds for cross-continental, cross-Pacific exchanges. As Epeli Hau'ofa has argued, "there is a world of difference between viewing the Pacific as 'islands in a far sea' and as 'a sea of islands.' The first emphasizes dry surfaces in a vast ocean far from the centers of power. Focusing in this way stresses the smallness and remoteness of the islands. The second is a more holistic perspective in which things are seen in the totality of their relations."[65] To follow after Hau'ofa, there is a world of difference between seeing American Indian nations as islands of reservations within and belonging to the United States and understanding the ways in which our nations articulate a network of relationships that provide the basis for kinship sovereignties and diplomacies as traditional governance and as strategy in the face of encroaching formal colonialism.

This turn foregrounds the transnational within American Indian studies as a means to resist comparative and contesting parallelisms and to underscore the diplomatic and outward protocols that are rooted in the specific geographies and place-based existences of our communities. The possibilities for such exchanges are not just ideologically hopeful or polemical, they exist alongside of and within these competitions over civilized and savage, and such exchanges inflect the ways in which our ancestors articulated sovereignty and nationalism as resistance to U.S. hegemonic imperialism. On August 9, 1866, Dowager Queen Emma of Hawai'i arrived in the United

States after traveling to England on a diplomatic mission to strengthen ties with Queen Victoria, to solicit Britain's support and friendship in order to protect the Hawaiian Islands from U.S. imperial interests, and to raise funds to build St. Andrew's Cathedral after she and her late husband King Kamehameha IV had invited Anglican missions into Hawai'i.[66] On her way home, she sailed from Europe to the United States, where she made a tour of New York, Niagara Falls, Boston, and Washington, D.C. Newspapers marked her arrival with pronouncements that she was the first queen to visit the United States, and with some fascination, they followed her progress through New England's landscape.[67] While in D.C., she was invited to dinner with President Andrew Johnson who, in a speech welcoming her to the White House, said: "If I were disposed to be facetious on this occasion I might say that, while none of the people of the United States wear crowns, while no man is acknowledged as a King, and no woman as Queen, yet while you are here in these United States you will have none but Queens to associate with. None of our citizens wear crowns, but all are sovereigns." In the *Chicago Tribune's* account of the president's welcome, the writer observes that "the reply of Queen Emma was inaudible, and we do not wonder."[68]

The next night, Queen Emma met with delegations of the Chickasaw, Choctaw, and Cherokee who were also in Washington, D.C., conducting peace negotiations with the Federal government to end the Civil War, to reestablish treaty obligations that were disrupted by the divisions between the North and the South, and to stave off U.S. colonial attempts to use the occasion to open Indian Territory for further encroachment and settlement. Those present at this reception with the queen included some of the most prominent Southeastern Indian leaders at the time. Diplomats from the Chickasaw Nation included Governor Doughtery Winchester Colbert and ex-Governor Edmund Pickens; from the Choctaws, Principal Chief Peter Perkins Pitchlynn and Alfred Wade; and from the Cherokee, Judge Richard Field, W. P. Adair, and John Rollin Ridge. In addition to the Southeastern leaders, several Indian agents were present, including Charles E. Mix, chief clerk of the Indian Bureau, as well as a number of Pawnee, who had been brought to New England by two white men who had planned to display them to the public for money. What emerges in the account of the scene is a complex delineation of civilization and savagery. The delegates from the Southeast are described by the journalist reporting the meeting as civilized, while the Pawnee slip between "semi-civilized" and savage. Queen Emma herself is described as wearing "a dress of the finest quality of crape, and [she] wore no ornaments except of jet." There are a number of ways to unpack this scene with regards to how discourses of savagery and civilization play out under the watchful eyes of the U.S. governmental officials in the room, and in many ways the undercurrent of the exchange is paternalistic, as the queen is presented with Indians as trophies of empire.[69]

But within the scene another exchange occurs between Queen Emma and the Southeastern delegates. As the *Daily National Intelligencer* described the meeting:

> The Chickasaws were the first to enter the room, and were sever-
> ally presented by Mr. Mix; and they simply bowed and passed on.
> When Gov. Pytchlyn *[sic]* was introduced he extended his hand,
> remarking that he wished her Majesty to shake hands with a North
> American Indian, and he cordially welcomed her to this country. The
> proffered hand was gracefully taken, and the Governor then intro-
> duced his children and grandchildren, and the Queen expressed
> surprise that they should all have English names. The Governor
> then called them by Indian names, whereat her Majesty was much
> pleased.... Her Majesty then entered into general conversation
> with her visitors, and Governor Pytchlyn remarked to her that the
> wild Indians belonged to Mr. Mix, but the civilized ones belonged
> to themselves. At the request of her Majesty, the Governor then
> made a short address in the Choctaw tongue.... It was simply a
> word of congratulation at having met her Majesty. He wished her
> much happiness, and trusted that when she arrived at her island
> home she would remember her interview with the North American
> Indians with pleasure.[70]

There are a number of significant elements in this moment, not the least of which is that this scene is filtered through a journalist who observes the meeting between nations and reports it back to the colonizing settler society. The contrast between Chief Pitchlynn's welcome of Queen Emma to this country and his insistence that she "shake hands with a North American Indian" is striking, especially when juxtaposed with President Andrew Johnson's welcome. When Chief Pitchlynn remarks that "the wild Indians belong to Mr. Mix, but the civilized ones belonged to themselves," his words echo and refract President Johnson's facetious comments that "you will have none but Queens to associate with." The scene epitomizes the very stakes within the "politics of distraction" as Southeastern Indian leaders, the dowager queen of Hawaiʻi, and the Pawnee are presented within a competition of recognitions that occur in the heart of an imperial power that uses such competitions to diminish and curtail indigenous sovereignties. The affinities and claims to sovereignty and civilization that each of the nations deploys discursively in 1866 resonate with the politics of recognition that continue to pit indigenous peoples against each other in the present.

Chief Pitchlynn's career as principal chief and delegate for the Choctaw spanned almost his entire life, and he was an important diplomatic speaker for Chickasaws and Choctaws as they survived removal, rebuilt in Indian Territory, struggled to retain autonomy and control of communal lands in opposition to the United States' desire to allot those lands at the end of the Civil War, and negotiated modernity and cosmopolitanism in the distances between home, traditional culture, and Washington, D.C. As a young man, Pitchlynn was painted by George Catlin as "The Snapping Turtle—Choctaw" and was commemorated by Charles Dickens in a textual moment that, according to Gerald Vizenor, "preserved the only native he encountered as an obscure soliloquy of the other in *American Notes*."[71] Pitchlynn fulfills Vizenor's definition of a crossblood; his father was a white cotton farmer who owned slaves, and his mother was Choctaw. "These chance situations, the manners, poses, and *sovenance* of native stories, are continuous adventures," Vizenor writes, and Pitchlynn's ambivalent figure as statesman, slave holder, and cosmopolitan diplomat disrupts the desire to commemorate him as a tragic, noble figure waging a losing war against civilization. "The clever native reverse of the binary, savagism and civilization, is the combination of savagism as presence."[72]

The 1866 meeting between Queen Emma and the delegates and leading men of the Chickasaw, Choctaw, and Cherokee nations does not fully escape the articulations of political identity and sovereignty dependent on competing claims to exceptionalism and civilization. And Pitchlynn, to counter Queen Emma's surprise that "they should all have English names," is signaling the distinctions of Southeastern self-determination and nationalism by also undermining the same distinctions for the Pawnee. However, we do see a glimmer of "savagism as presence" within these civilizational shifts among all the participants in the moment, and that glimmer might provide a basis for a condition of possibility to turn those savagisms to subversive effect. Principal Chief Pitchlynn's insistence that Queen Emma shake hands with a "North American Indian" welcomes her through an acknowledgment of indigenous diplomacy, and in the act he performs protocols that situate the queen's arrival to the United States as foundationally an arrival to native lands. This historical moment is significant because it demonstrates the possibilities of simultaneous participation with and against colonialist discourses to offer us alternative ways of theorizing indigeneity grounded not just in specific geographies, communities, and histories but capable of forming what Leela Gandhi has described as horizontal affective communities across those specificities brought into relation by empire.[73]

The scene offers, then, a moment in which we can see how continental nations gestured toward diplomatic protocols that recognized indigenous trans-Pacific consciousnesses as a site of possible resistance to U.S. empire, and it speaks to the necessity for indigenous sovereignties to remain grounded in and responsible to the needs and struggles of our individual peoples while simultaneously looking outward and across to the responsibilities to and struggles of others. This moment cannot be romanticized, because the Pawnee are still abjected as wild others who belong to the United States through a complicit recognition between Dowager Queen Emma and Principal Chief Pitchlynn. But it does dramatically emphasize the need to reframe how certain peoples are designated sovereign, independent, and free, and others are cast off errants who must "steal weeping away" within the transits of empire.[74] Glen S. Coulthard has argued that the ability of the colonizing liberal state "to entice Indigenous peoples to come to *identify,* either implicitly or explicitly, with the profoundly *asymmetrical* and *non-reciprocal* forms of recognition either imposed on or granted to them by the colonial-state and society" reproduces the very structures of dominance embedded within Hegelian dialectics of recognition. The alternative for indigenous peoples is to "'turn away' from the colonial state and society and find in their own *transformative praxis* the source of their liberation."[75]

To this end, Joy Harjo's poem "Protocol," which first appeared in *A Map to the Next World* and in a revised form as *mele,* or song, on her blog, provides an example of how one might gesture towards affective—here in the context of Muscogee and Hawaiian—exchanges of kinship sovereignties in relation to literary imagination. The song version, which begins with a Hawaiian chant or *oli,* draws upon both Hawaiian protocols of welcome and the Southeastern ceremonial call and response of stomp dance. The first stanza is voiced to establish relationship and arrival on Hawaiian shores, and the rest of the poem responds with a detailed history of Muscogee migration, removal, war, and travel within the violences of empire and colonialism that disrupt the everyday intimacies of family and home. The poem traces a politics of protocol in which introductions, names, songs, and autobiography are necessary for international relations to occur, whether on a personal or state level. As the poem explains, the exchange of *tobacco* and Hawaiian *lei* made from *pikake* flowers and *maile* vines establishes Southeastern continental offerings within the logics of Hawaiian practices that order the place of peoples within relationship to land; in the process, these diplomatic protocols create a feeling of kinship between the ancestors of both lands in order to make the narrator and the subject of the poem responsive to each other's histories and genealogies.

In the poem, the narrator positions herself as a self-in-relation to Muscogee history—beginning within ceremonial time of creation and centering upon stomp ground rituals that draw out fire and water and then moving through the genocide of treaties and forced marches. Harjo enters into a dialogue through Pacific protocols and refigures international diplomacies into intimacies that do not depend upon conquest. The poem performs a creative and imaginative engagement even within a moment of tension—the lines from the first stanza, ". . . if I am to follow protocol I will introduce myself / and in that you might know that I did not find myself / here on your island by some coincidence," speak to the transgressions of colonialism that might frame the narrator's arrival as an act of imperialism rather than a consequence of continual displacements as Indians are forced to transit by empire.[76] Harjo's poem depends upon indigenous phenomenologies, in which "knowing" serves as a process through which Harjo others the self and selves the other to represent the movement toward amnesty, toward retaining relations that are responsible, right, and *pono*.

While the forms and procedures of Hawaiian protocol are most recognizable within the poem, Harjo's work also draws upon Southeastern institutions such as *iksas,* a structured network of relationships that had a similarly generative kinship function.[77] Ethnohistorian Patricia Galloway writes of the importance of the *fani mingo/fani miko* (squirrel chief) within Southeastern intertribal relations, framing it as a "native ombudsman" institution observed among eighteenth-century Chickasaw and Choctaw nations.[78] While Galloway's work delineates the institution within Chickasaw and Choctaw cultures, others have noted that the Muscogee Creek had similar institutions in which, according to Galloway, "tribes would adopt an advocate within a neighboring tribe, and it would be his duty to argue in favor of his adopted tribe whenever war threatened to break out. It is nowhere specifically stated that the adopted *fanimingo* would also be capable of speaking the language of the tribe whose interests he represented, but there are several instances in which this is implied."[79] The practice, which could perhaps best be understood as a generative kinship that "helped manage extravillage relationships," not only ensured diplomatic relations with other tribes but served to negotiate competition and difference.[80] In her song/poem "Protocol," Harjo gestures towards a similar diplomatic negotiation that emerges in the collision between Muscogee and Hawaiian genealogies of identity and history, and ultimately provides an adoptive link between the practices of the Hawaiian *hānai* and the Southeastern *iksas* through which the narrator of Harjo's poem can know herself both as other and as self.

What is instructive in evoking the *fani mingo* institution here at the end of this chapter and in conversation with the generative kinships of Harjo's song/poem that enacts the genealogies of protocol is that it provides a means to advocate for the need to maintain outwardness even as we delineate the necessity of drawing inward to look at specific indigenous nations and their particular struggles against colonization. Harjo's poem and the diplomatic institutions it enacts help to redraw the transit of empire into a new line of relation that shows the Indian in transit as site of relational sovereignties that do not depend upon conquest and Hegelian dialectics of self and other. As the United States continues to overthrow Hawai'i through the legislative and juridical discourses of Indianness, Harjo demonstrates that there are alternative roots through which to respond that do not reiterate the recognitions of nation-states to partition redress and status.

6

Killing States

Removals, Other Americans, and the "Pale Promise of Democracy"

The impression that I have now is the same one I had on the terrible two days when the first three hundred of you came—the impression of great physical discomfort, hardship, and of perfectly marvelous human spirit throughout the colony.

John Collier, speech at Poston, June 27, 1942

Sudden Removals

On June 27, 1942, John Collier, acting as administrator of the sole internment camp run by the Office of Indian Affairs, addressed the first group of 7,500 Japanese American internees at Poston, Arizona, on the Colorado River Indian Reservation (CRIR). His speech was the culmination of a policy vision of Indian self-management and economic self-sufficiency that stretched from the 1930s and collided headlong with the events that followed December 7, 1941. Poston, Arizona, and the Colorado River Indian Reservation, as Ruth Okimoto's research in *Sharing a Desert Home* has shown, spatialized the competing hegemonies that first carved the reservation out of indigenous lands through an act of Congress approved by Abraham Lincoln in 1865 and led to the incarceration of Japanese American citizens in relocation camps during World War II. John Collier's vision for the Colorado River Indian Reservation, even before the attack on Pearl Harbor, involved a 1940 proposal to "'colonize 10,000 American Indians' to the reservation and to develop an irrigation system to make the CRIR self-supporting."[1] With war looming, time running out, and a reluctant Congress unwilling to appropriate the monies necessary to approve such a project, Collier leaped at the opportunity the War Relocation Authority presented in the form of an incarcerated work force who could "improve" the land for future Indian, and then white and non-Indian, use.[2]

Though Collier claimed he was tongue-tied and embarrassed in the face of the hardships of relocation that those Japanese Americans who had already arrived at the camps had endured, he tried to frame their suffering within a larger purpose. "You are here," he assured the captive listeners, "in the capacity of full citizens of the American commonwealth. Being here in that capacity, it is for you to determine your own fashion of life, your own methods of cooperative action, to make your own life." Speaking as a representative of the Department of the Interior and gesturing towards the office he held as commissioner of Indian Affairs, Collier shared his philosophy and vision for both the American commonwealth and the version of democracy that underpins U.S. colonization and imperialism. "We in this country," he continued,

> join with the people of England, the people of Australia, with the Free French, China, etc., in asserting that Democracy is the right way of life. We are waging a war for Democracy. That war is going to be won. There is not the slightest doubt. But when we look around within our own country, whether it be on a national or local scale, we do not find that Democracy has been achieved. It has not been achieved in any of these countries and certainly not in the United States. Our Democracy is an imperfect, embryonic institution as yet.[3]

Collier's speech that summer day in the dusty and temporary Japanese American "colony" reflected an ambivalent administrator seeking to reassure his fellow citizens that though an injustice had been done, there was also an opportunity to undertake a great social experiment.

Though Collier was speaking to the internees from the ambivalent vantage point of the not-quite-yet-greatest-generation administrator of a wartime incarceration, his evocation of a "war for Democracy" eerily foreshadows George W. Bush's post-9/11 justification for the war on terror and the militaristic desire to inflict democracy the world over as panacea for a failing capitalism. At the same time, Collier's assessment that "our Democracy is an imperfect, embryonic institution" mirrors Barack Obama's delineation of the United States as a perfecting union, still struggling with racial divides and inequalities.[4] Captured within Collier's dualistic allegory of democracy as unfulfilled battleground and as promise for a more perfect union are the seeds of a fracturing neoliberalism that pulled conservative and liberal discourses into a biopolitical assemblage justifying recursive colonialisms that, during World War II, served to enjamb Japanese American detainees within the histories of containment and expropriation that strip lands and nations from American Indians. By naming the relocation centers and internment camps "colonies" within their internal documents, the United States revealed the deeper logics of removals and reservations, and Collier, who saw in Poston an opportunity to develop a social experiment that might innovate future management strategies within the Office of Indian Affairs, had already laid the groundwork so that Hopi and Navajo families might join those relocation colonies after the war ended to continue the work started by the Japanese American internees. In the process, the transformation of indigenous peoples from colonized to colonist within the historical record helps to lay the foundation for a double-barreled Korematsu "loaded weapon" that provides the basis for U.S. sovereignty dependent upon settler colonialism and its ability to enact a state of exception against its own citizens and citizens of other nations.[5]

Collier's moment of address raises for me some significant questions about how scholars might theorize the colonization of indigenous peoples in the face of settlers who are coerced and deployed by the nation-state to inhabit what Kevin Bruyneel provocatively has termed the third space of sovereignty. What does it mean for Collier to address Japanese American internees as citizens in a moment when the civil rights accorded them as U.S. citizens have been radically suspended, and why does he evoke democracy in a moment that is so clearly undemocratic? What tensions and patterns emerge from the historical matrix that produced World War II relocation and internment camps? And what might those historical convergences say about the state of exception theorized by Giorgio Agamben?

Both the bare life of the camps that Agamben identifies as the basis for sovereign power and the threshold between bare life and *homo sacer* haunt the colonial imaginings of the United States. At its most basic level, Agamben's definition of the state of exception centers on his point that the "fundamental localization *(Ortung)*, which does not limit itself to distinguishing what is inside from what is outside but instead traces a threshold (the state of exception) between the two, on the basis of which is outside and inside, the normal situation and chaos, enter into those complex topological relations that make the validity of the juridical order possible."[6] In the context of the ongoing settler colonizing project of the United States, those thresholds and chaotic systems, as I have argued throughout this book, depend upon the transit of Indianness to inscribe empire internally and externally. The one arena where postcolonial theory has made the most inroads into the emerging body of critical theory addressing indigeneity has been in the evocation of hybridity, particularly as Homi K. Bhabha has defined it as the threshold in-between, "where difference is neither One nor the Other but *something else besides.*"[7] Most controversial, at least in American Indian literary circles, is Elvira Pulitano's *Toward a Native American Critical Theory.* Pulitano valorizes hybridity in order to resist notions of reality, authenticity, and essentialism as she eschews, according to Jace Weaver and Craig Womack, sovereignty, governance, and the possibility for Native American literary nationalisms to emerge from the texts she critiques. Hybridity, as Pulitano uses it, depends upon an underlying colonialist assumption that indigenous peoples and their cultural productions exist in primitive excess and gain validity only in the exchanges with Western literary traditions.[8]

Within the legal discourses of indigenous sovereignty, however, hybridity, when understood as a process that creates a third space within the colonial dialectic, has proven a more fruitful site for articulating the potential usefulness of postcolonial theory to the development of indigenous critical theories. Scholars such as Paul Meredith, Kevin Bruyneel, Jay T. Johnson, Robert A. Williams Jr., and Eric Cheyfitz argue that the treaties between indigenous nations and the settler colonial nation-state, as well as the laws that emerged as a result, become the primary site for postcolonial analysis because they represent the resistant dialogics of indigenous responses to state-sponsored colonialism that transformed land into property, independence into dependency, foreign into domestic.[9] This work, and especially Bruyneel's *The Third Space of Sovereignty,* provides important insights into the negotiations between colonizer and colonized that, through the efforts of indigenous leaders to resist the encroaching United States, open a space between internal/external and foreign/domestic for indigenous articulations of sovereignty. As a site of refusal, the third space of sovereignty, according to Bruyneel, offers a productive location from which indigenous nations can assert political autonomy that is not dependent upon a settler society that continually asserts its totalizing authority over lands, space, and time. In other words, the third space offers a way for tribal sovereignty to exist concurrently with U.S. state sovereignty and functions as an anti-statist, postcolonial supplement that disrupts the logics of colonial rule.[10]

Bruyneel claims that this productive space emerges out of indigenous resistances and articulations of alternative governance strategies that remain in spite of the legal machinations of the occupying colonial nation-state. But as the last two chapters demonstrated in the discussions of Hawai'i and the Cherokee Freedmen, even the third space of sovereignty can become a colonial enactment that supersedes the desires of anticolonial resistances or is, in fact, produced by those resistances. As Bruyneel suggests, his articulation of the third space raises many directions for future research into alternatives to statist sovereignty. Foremost among them in this book is: What happens to the third space of indigenous sovereignty when others are injected into it through a process of what Brian Masaru Hayashi has identified as "democratizing the enemy?"[11] The goal of this chapter, then, is threefold. The first is to identify, by returning to the cultural and theoretical models of the 1980s and 1990s that were concerned with Los Angeles, multiculturalism, and postethnicity, the discursive colonialist traces of the transits of Indianness that haunt theorizations of race in the United States. Given the return of the ascendancy of multicultural liberal democracy as the best hope for a postracial United States founded on principles of *in*clusion, it is necessary to understand the affective desires underpinning current ideas such as commonwealth and planetary conviviality.[12] Understanding the third space of sovereignty as a perpetual motion of oscillation between the parallax gap of irreducible difference between internal and external, I will consider how the transits of empire use removal, deferral, and containment as processes of incorporation and assimilation.

The second goal of this chapter is to reframe Japanese American internment and the concomitant "yellow peril" that traps Asian Americans in a third space between immigrant threat/model minority, within those distortive parallactic effects that have been used to disrupt and deny indigenous sovereignty. By focusing on the internment of Japanese Americans at Poston and the role that John Collier, the father of the Indian Reorganization Act of 1934, played in promoting Japanese American wartime relocation as an experiment in self-governance toward assimilation, I hope to deepen our understandings of how U.S. colonial policies targeting indigenous nations inform the assumptions of multicultural liberal democracy that now exemplify current U.S. preoccupations with race and diaspora and serve to deterritorialize indigenous prior claims. And finally, I will draw upon Gerald Vizenor's work in *Hiroshima Bugi* to consider American Indian participation in and disruptions of conviviality within the transits of empire. Vizenor's unmapping of the nineteenth-century voyager and half-Chinook Ranald MacDonald's travels through the Pacific and into Ainu territory in Japan troublingly parallels, for Vizenor, the consequences of the atomic weaponry that violently ended World War II.

Giorgio Agamben links the political power of U.S. sovereignty to a series of states of exception that track how martial law and discourses of emergencies have led to the consolidation of executive power and its subsequent expansion into the legislative sphere. Agamben's theorization of sovereignty as that which determines and enacts the state of exception—understood as that which breaks the law to enforce the law—demonstrates the degree to which Western democracies exist in a dialectic with totalitarian regimes. Though Agamben typically theorizes sovereignty within Greco-Roman and European contexts, his *State of Exception* marks a notable shift. In his diagnosis of U.S. sovereignty and its deployment of the state of exception as a "conflict over sovereign decision" arising from a "dialectic between the powers of the president and those of Congress," the first example Agamben gives of a U.S. president appropriating dictatorial powers is Abraham Lincoln, who violated the law to suspend habeas corpus in 1861 and then, on his sole authority, declared the emancipation of slaves in 1862.[13]

The second president Agamben cites as an example is Woodrow Wilson, who during World War I appropriated even broader powers to the office of the presidency when Congress passed a series of espionage acts between 1917 and 1918. Agamben notes that "because the sovereign power of the president is essentially grounded in the emergency linked to the state of war, over the course of the twentieth century the metaphor of war becomes an integral part of the presidential political vocabulary."[14] By deploying the linguistic logic of waging war, according to Agamben, Franklin D. Roosevelt was able to appropriate extraordinary powers to deal with the economic crisis of the 1930s, and the New Deal represents Agamben's third example of the U.S. presidency locating in itself the ability to declare the state of emergency. The final example Agamben gives us is Franklin D. Roosevelt's Executive Order 9066 that Agamben describes as "the most spectacular violation of civil rights (all the more serious because of its solely racial motivation) [,which] occurred on February 19, 1942."[15] Roosevelt's order, which authorized the secretary of war and the military commanders he might designate to "prescribe military areas in such places and of such extent as he or the Military Commander may determine, from which any or all persons may be excluded," directed the U.S. war machine to define and enforce "regulations for the conduct and control of alien enemies."[16] Though it did not name them or any other ethnic communities specifically, and in fact allowed the secretary and those military commanders to exclude "any or all persons," the order interpellated Japanese American citizens of the United States particularly as "alien enemies" to be evacuated to relocation centers in the name of national defense.

Poston, Arizona, functions as a temporal and spatial site within these states of exception not least because it was one of the camps that represented "the most spectacular violation of civil rights." The state of exception as first theorized by Carl Schmitt and later developed by Agamben depends upon the sovereign's ability to order space as "not only a 'taking of land' *(Landesnahme)*—the determination of a juridical and a territorial ordering (of an *Ordnung* and an *Ortung)*—but above all a 'taking of the outside,' an exception *(Ausnahme).*"[17] This ordering of space begs a question, however: Why doesn't Agamben theorize the state of exception in relation to American Indians in the first place? It is striking, if not unanticipated, that all three of his presidential examples played a significant role in ordering the historical landscape that stretched beyond the text of Roosevelt's executive order instituting internment camps that in itself serves as exemplary exception within Agamben's text. The Colorado River Indian Reservation was created by an act of Congress signed into law by Abraham Lincoln in 1865, and on November 22, 1915, President Woodrow Wilson issued an executive order remapping the boundaries of the CRIR to steal 16,000 acres for miners and cattlemen in the region.[18] In 1933 Roosevelt appointed John Collier to the Office of Indian Affairs to implement the "Indian New Deal" in the form of the Indian Reorganization Act, and on February 19, 1942, his order set the stage for the Colorado River Indian Reservation to house an internment camp through which Collier planned to wage his war for democracy in the form of the doctrine of self-governance that was the basis for his administration over colonized indigenous nations.

Linking Japanese American experiences of the state of exception that was internment to American Indian history allows us to scrutinize the theoretical blind spots within critical philosophy and postcolonial theory and identify the discourses of colonialism that facilitated the violation of Japanese American civil rights. The bare life that the internment camps reveal is the life of U.S. colonialism laid bare in all its settler/native dialectical glory. Such an observation allows for a reordering of the colonial logics that underpin the United States' internment of Japanese Americans and locates its source in the prior colonization of indigenous peoples. As both captives and settlers, interned Japanese Americans are forced to play out in an abridged trajectory the U.S. frontier discourses, in which the only way to become "true" American citizens is to first go native and then carve democracy out of the wilderness. That Japanese American labor is used by Collier to tame the desert and make it productive allows the United States to enforce the frontier as the site of exception that proves the norm for U.S. colonial democracy and at the same time enacts in microcosm the progessivist history that leads civilization out of savagery.

But the problem of the sovereign is not necessarily just the state of exception but the project of democracy itself. Agamben hints at this in *Homo Sacer,* when he implies that "Western politics is a biopolitics from the very beginning, and that every attempt to found political liberties in the rights of the citizens is, therefore, in vain" and that observation supports Wendy Brown's critique of liberal politics that seek, through injury, recourse from the state and in the process serve to negate the originary violence in Benjamin's delineation of law-making and law-preserving violence.[19] Collier has come to epitomize the ambivalent colonial administrator whose efforts to reform the government-to-government relationship that provides the basis for the continued U.S. occupation of indigenous lands mark a fundamental shift in U.S. colonial administration. According to Vine Deloria Jr., John Collier was "probably the greatest of all Indian commissioners," and much of the scholarship about his role as commissioner of the Office of Indian Affairs tends to frame Collier as a liberal prophetic politician who embodied the social welfare vision of Roosevelt's administration—though in Deloria's case, that praise may be faint given that most Indian commissioners were devastating to indigenous nations.[20] Even Ruth Okimoto came to appreciate Collier and found his decision to use Japanese American internment to realize his plans for the Colorado River Indian Reservation to be a "brilliant organizational move."[21]

John Collier was ultimately contradictory in his fundamental support of indigenous communities and peoples. On the one hand, he greatly esteemed indigenous cultures, communities, and spiritual traditions, especially in the Southwest; on the other, he thought that there was a vacuum in indigenous governance in most communities that needed to be redressed through the imposition of democratic and bureaucratic structures.[22] Fundamentally, Collier, in his own words, believed American Indian democracies to be deeper and thicker democracies than those of the West, that they represented "the long hope" for humanity. "They had what the world has lost," Collier wrote at the beginning of his 1947 *Indians of the Americas*, "they have it now. What the world has lost, the world must have again, lest it die."[23] That lost ingredient for Collier was "the power for living" in the face of bare life, and he advocated that "if the modern world should be able to recapture this power, the earth's natural resources and web of life would not be irrevocably wasted within the twentieth century, which is the prospect now. True democracy, founded in neighborhoods and reaching over the world, would become the realized heaven on earth. And living peace—not just an interlude between wars—would be born and would last through ages."[24]

In many ways, then, this sentiment of "true democracy" that arises out of "the power for living" is what led Collier to address Japanese American internees at Poston Camp on June 27, 1942, and speak of a "pale promise of democracy" that would spark real Democracy out of the shadows of struggle and endurance. This pale promise resided in Collier's administrative vision and idea that the U.S. could manage difference best and most benignly by deploying self-management and indirect, bilateral colonialist regimes to construct a permanent security state to manage indigenous peoples, internal minorities, and overseas territorial holdings.[25] With only eight years separating the implementation of the Indian Reorganization Act from Roosevelt's Executive Order 9066, Collier expanded his vision of colonial administration to include indigenous and racial minorities alike as he advocated for reconsideration of self-government as a tool for assimilative incorporation. Collier's vision for the IRA, which provides the cornerstone for the federal recognition and nation-to-nation status of indigenous nations colonized by the United States, reveals the syllogistic fallacy at the heart of such policies, that because the IRA reestablished the language of self-governance, the act recognized indigenous nations as sovereign entities rather than as racial, ethnic communities who would one day be assimilated into the U.S. body politic. The implications for American Indian studies and our reliance on the Indian Reorganization Act to provide the language of government-to-government sovereignty and self-determination are profoundly eclipsed by the intersection of colonial and racist agendas that collude to oppress on the one hand and offer the seductive recognitions that maintain state hegemony on the other. The intersection of Collier's administrative colonialism with his affirmation of self-government served the larger agenda of furthering liberal democracy that sought to bring the world into U.S. alignment.

And as Justice Robert Jackson observed in his dissention to the *Korematsu* decision that upheld the constitutionality of Japanese American relocation, the loaded weapon in the law created in part by the juridical principle of stare decisis, which Robert A. Williams Jr. defines as "like cases should be decided alike," facilitates a transit of colonial subjectivities across which "Indianness" becomes a homology emptied of indigenous contexts and content.[26] These contexts are then, through the logics of settler colonialism, spatially, physically, and psychically mapped onto other arrivants and trajectories. Such processes lead to what Ruth Okimoto rightly recognizes as "a brief moment in history [in which] the Japanese American detainees experienced what the American Indians have endured for centuries" but absents why that might be.[27] And while many scholars locate those intersections in Dillon Myer's reign first in the War Relocation Authority and then in the Bureau of Indian Affairs, where he implemented policies of relocation and termination in the 1950s, Collier shoulders his own responsibilities for implementing and advocating a process of "democratizing the enemy" that sought to layer the U.S. colonial administration of colonized Indian nations onto first Japanese American citizens and then Pacific Island holdings at the end of the war.[28] Next stop, the world.

In other words, Collier intended to enact a third space of sovereignty that functioned as a state of exception, the establishing of the outside in order to facilitate its reincorporation, for indigenous nations, recent immigrants, and newly acquired territories at the end of the war that would allow not-quite-citizens to be formally recaptured through the maintenance of the colonialist logics that cohered U.S. territory into the nation-state. When Japanese Americans are forced by Collier into the third space of sovereignty, however, what happens to American Indians nations is an extension of the egalitarian processes that David Kazanjian has termed the colonizing trick, whereby Indians become colonists, Japanese Americans Indians.[29] And in the process, the entire territorial conquest that is the basis for U.S. hegemony is elided, and the colonization of indigenous peoples is then abjected outside the dialectics of settler/native and into a now movable and infinitely repeatable state of assimilation through exception.

Maps and Maps

Karen Tei Yamashita's *Tropic of Orange* spans a border, a week, and an orange. Time slows, space stretches and collapses as each of the seven characters try to locate themselves in an increasingly chaotic topography as the south is dragged northward along with the sun. The plot culminates on Sunday in the El Contrato Con América wrestling showdown between El Gran Mojado, a character based on performance artist Guillermo Gómez-Peña and occasionally known and rarely recognized as Arcangel, and SUPER-NAFTA in the Pacific Rim Auditorium at the Borders. All of the characters are being drawn through the narrative arc of one week, each facing a specific destiny tied to the larger showdown that El Gran Mojado will inevitably lose. But even before that Monday when the orange first falls from the tree, the characters are lost in a fragmented existence in a Los Angeles and Mexico that are starkly separate and distinct. That small, deformed citrus becomes the fulcrum of "a border made plain by the sun itself," and its very presence can warp geography and time to stretch the Tropic of Cancer and the southern hemisphere from Mexico to Los Angeles, from the Columbian discovery moment of 1492 to the virtual interwebs and back again, as if a map of the Americas had been graphically liquefied then smeared by dragging a small point through it, until a distorted, stretched, and blurred path remained of lands and borders that once seemed coherent.[30]

In Los Angeles a lone figure can be seen, if one were to pay any attention at all to lone figures in the middle of a city, waving his arms as he stands at the edge of an overpass above the freeways. This figure, it turns out, is a former surgeon named Manzanar Murakami, and what he does all day is conduct the unheard symphonies of the city. Manzanar, we find out later, was the first Sansei born in the captivity of internment camps. He spends his days recycling "residues of sounds":

> *There are maps and there are maps and there are maps.* The uncanny thing was that he could see all of them at once, filter some, pick them out like transparent windows and place them even delicately and consecutively in a complex grid of pattern, spatial discernment, body politic. Although one might have thought this capacity to see was different from a musical one, it was really one and the same.

For each of the maps was a layer of music, a clef, an instrument, a musical instruction, a change of measure, a coda.[31]

In rhizomatic detail, Yamashita documents the mapping layers that Manzanar imagines. They begin with the geology of the land itself, "the artesian rivers running beneath the surface, connected and divergent, shifting and swelling . . . the complex and normally silent web of faults." Then Manzanar's vision goes deeper below the surface to the

Man-made grid of civil utilities: Southern California pipelines for natural gas; the unnatural waterways of the Los Angeles Department of Water and Power, and the great dank tunnels of sewage; the cascades of poisonous effluents surging from rain-washed streets into the Santa Monica Bay; electric currents racing voltage into the open watts of millions of hungry energy-efficient appliances; telephone cables, cable TV, fiber optics, computer networks.

Finally, the passage concludes:

As far as Manzanar was concerned, it was all there. A great theory of maps, musical maps, spread in visible and audible layers—each selected sometimes purposefully, sometimes at whim, to create the great mind of music. To the outside observer, it was a lonely business; it would seem that he was at once orchestra and audience. Or was he indeed? Unknown to anyone, a man walking across the overpass at that very hour innocently hummed the recurrent melody of the adagio.[32]

The connections between the characters, histories, and borders are concrete and steel as much as they are digital and virtual. The characters are mythic allegories as well as mothers, sons, and husbands struggling to find the roads that will lead them across borders, nations, and oceans to find homes and each other in the abandoned cars on the freeway or at the wrestling match at the edge of the Pacific Rim.

Yamashita's novel was published in 1997 during the height of U.S.-based cultural studies' concerns with the pitfalls of multiculturalism in the breach between imperialism and globalization. Literary scholars have focused on how this novel extends the work of her first novel and speaks to Asian American experience, and how it might exemplify an ethnic postmodernism born through globalization. Caroline Rody has argued that Yamashita's work is shaped by a narrative strategy that is informed by border fictions that situate Asian Americanness within transnational Americas and ties postmodern interethnic ethics to nature.[33] In "Tropics of Globalization: Reading the New North America," Molly Wallace suggests that the novel, if read through globalization discourse analysis, might illuminate and complicate Fredric Jameson's discussion of the logics of late capitalism and extend Arjun Appadurai's discussions of globalization.[34] When the author's work is discussed within a U.S. context, the emphasis is on the ethnic postmodern. When the novel is placed into a conversation with globalization, which Michael Hardt and Antonio Negri have identified as "a process of economic *postmodernization,* or better, *informatization,*" a reading emerges through the globality that emphasizes the economic and the diasporic, the nation and the postnation.[35]

The map that Yamashita gives us of Los Angeles is a map consisting of transparent windows that open up to other transparent windows that then point to the next map and the map after that. The implication of Manzanar's infectious symphonies is that one should look for the maps and maps and maps that trace and mark the pre- and post-historical movements of peoples and information within the larger narratives that have consolidated those movements and collapsed maps into maps. An inner and outer space to the city contained within the "city" itself influences and haunts the land and creates residual sounds that, were one to listen carefully, would provide insight into how the cityspace consists of cacophonies that challenge and reinforce the institutional and historical logics that constructed the city in the first place.

Manzanar's symphonic Los Angeles, however, is only a microcosm of, a movement within, the orchestrations and patriotic songs of the United States—California and its redwood forest confirm that this land was made for you and me in an evocation of Manifest Destiny that lingers within and around the imagined community that has been consolidated as the United States. Manzanar's ability to conduct cacophony into polyphony within these larger movements arises from the political, spatial, and temporal boundaries that his very existence encapsulates. Caught against his will by and within the parallax oscillations of exception that arise from the discourses of Indian removal and reorganization and underpin the creation of Japanese American internment camps, Manzanar began his life as a captive within the larger forces of imperialism that attempt to continually consolidate U.S. control over Indian lands.

Chief Justice John Marshall declared in an opinion that would have lasting ramifications for indigenous sovereignty that indignous nations on the North American continent "may more correctly, perhaps, be denominated *domestic dependent nations.* They occupy a territory to which we assert a title independent of their will, which must take effect in point of possession when their right of possession ceases. Meanwhile, they are in a state of pupilage. Their relation to the United States resembles that of a ward to his guardian."[36] In a stunning moment of law-making and law-preserving violence, the U.S. government juridically transformed native nations from sovereign foreign states, whose governments and lands were independent of U.S. control, into domestic dependent nations existing within the boundaries of the United States and occupying, by grace of their guardian's permission, lands that rightfully belong to the United States. The impact of Marshall's opinion on behalf of the Court facilitated continued removals, forced diasporas, colonization, and assimilation through the establishment of a paternal relation between the United States and those peoples it deemed were its "children" or "wards." The superior claim to land that Marshall acknowledges in this statement addresses the "Doctrine of Discovery," which gave Europeans and by extension their agents in the new world a claim to native lands by the physical act of discovery. So long as indigenous peoples lived peacefully on the land, the question of title would not be forced; the only ways to cede title were through either treaty negotiations or "just war."[37] The borders standing between the United States and the Pacific coast were always, as we can see from Marshall's decision, flexible and disposable in the eyes of the federal government and its citizens. The founding fathers of the United States, including Thomas Jefferson, Benjamin Franklin and Thomas Paine, had visions of expansion even before the Revolution; the conquest of western lands was to some extent considered a fait accompli. It was only a matter of time in their eyes. The Pacific coast was only the beginning, and as early as 1771 Benjamin Franklin and hydrographer Alexander Dalrymple wrote a treatise on how best to benevolently bring civilization to the Māori.[38] In the minds of these founding fathers, the imaginative investment in the Pacific was an inevitable progression of civilization that would save indigenous peoples around the globe from themselves and usher in an exceptional world safe for Americans.

At the same time American exceptionalism was making new worlds safe for Americans, another narrative emerged during westward expansion that mapped the movements of peoples both pre-western historically as well as contemporarily. In order for the United States to have a fundamental right to land that superseded that of indigenous peoples and nations, the colonizing country needed to establish those nations and peoples as interlopers on their own lands, to ban them. As the judical branch enacted the state of exception just as much as the executive and legislative branches did through "a cultural process of 'jurisgenesis'—the creation of legal meaning"—imperial and national narratives cohered those creations into jurispathic supremacy, where Supreme Court justices continue to retain interpretive authority to kill "non-state-centered law" as a process of making law.[39] These two processes, according to Robert Cover, are constitutive of "*nomos*—a normative universe" in which "law and narrative are inseparably related."[40] According to Agamben, *nomos* is "the ordering of space," and "the camp—and not the prison—is the space that corresponds to this originary structure of the *nomos*."[41] For Mark Rifkin, the resultant *bare life* is also *bare habitance,* through which the "biopolitical project of defining the proper 'body' of the people is subtended by the geopolitical project of defining the territoriality of the nation, displacing competing claims by older/other political formations."[42]

In the mid-nineteenth century, as the phrase "Manifest Destiny" was innovated by the national print culture to justify the annexation of a huge swath of land from Mexico, there was a "scientific" investigation into the origins of the first Americans. Of the many stories of Indian migration to the Americas, the most popular included hypotheses that wandering Celts, Vikings, and other early Europeans were the true source of any prehistoric "civilization." Some "scientists" even claimed that Egyptians had built the mounds along the Ohio and Mississippi rivers, while others continued to gravitate to the observation that the structures were much too complex and had to be evidence that Europeans had been present in the landscape at some point to build cities and then abandon them.[43] Many cultural anthropologists, ethnologists, and linguists were convinced that Indians were in fact descendants of the Lost Tribes of Israel, and that the mounds and earthworks throughout the continent were built by anyone except indigenous peoples.[44] Among all these developing narratives to solve the "mystery" of the first Americans, however, Thomas Jefferson's articulation of the trans-Siberian migration solidified into scientific facticity once Clovis spear points were found early in the twentieth century.

Jefferson's hypothesis, now commonly referred to as "the Bering Strait Theory," had its origins in a speculation that Fray José de Acosta, a Jesuit missionary stationed in Mexico and Peru, offered in 1589. Acosta conjectured that "small groups of hunters, driven from their Asiatic homeland by starvation or warfare, might have followed now-extinct beasts across Asia into the New World. Acosta argued that this slow, mostly overland migration took place perhaps two thousands years before Spaniards arrived in the Caribbean."[45] In 1787 Thomas Jefferson published in *Notes on the State of Virginia* his own suppositions on the origins of the first Americans that reflects Acosta's:

> Great question has arisen from whence came those aboriginal inhabitants of America? Discoveries, long ago made, were sufficient to shew that a passage from Europe to America was always practicable, even to the imperfect navigation of ancient times. . . . Again, the late discoveries of Captain Cook, coasting from Kamschatka to California, have proved that, if the two continents of Asia and America be separated at all, it is only by a narrow streight. So that from this side also, inhabitants may have passed into America: and the resemblance between the Indians of America and the Eastern inhabitants of Asia, would induce us to conjecture, that the former are the descendants of the latter, or the latter of the former . . .[46]

Jefferson's theory of the trans-Siberian migrations of Asians and Indians helped establish the continuing question over the "true" origins of indigenous peoples as fair game in the emergent scientific discourses of anthropology and archaeology. These theories, too, provided a means to question aboriginal title to lands—if they were prior migrants from Asia, they had no aboriginal rights at all. But, significantly, a close reading of Jefferson's text reveals a slight difference from what is now accepted as the movement of peoples across the land bridge between Asia and the Americas. Jefferson, in counter to current popular discussions of American Indian origins that depend on an originary and a priori *terra nullius,* at least allows the possibility that migrations went both ways across the Bering Strait. Or, as Joy Harjo succinctly puts it: "There is no such thing as a one way land bridge."[47] The distinction is significant to mark, because it fractures the trajectory of peoples between America and Asia and initiates the indeterminacy within Asians in America as the site of foreignness, threat, model minority exemplar, and as a site for Asian settler colonialisms that have continued to inflect how scholars have started to interrogate how Asian arrivants in Pacific Island contexts construct their own local identities.[48]

Problematic Post Destinies

In *A Different Mirror,* Ronald Takaki makes note of residual sounds echoing back through Shakespeare and writes, "Caliban could have been Asian. 'Have we devils here?' the theatergoers heard Stephano declare in *The Tempest.* 'Do you put tricks upon's with savages and men of Inde, ha?'"[49] Spoken aloud, the final two words would evoke both Inde and India for the audience, mapping onto the new world a familiar Orientalism and acknowledging in the joke the cacophony emerging in the new/old world referents. That Orientalism within the "Indian" of the new world refracts and solidifies even further within the Bering Strait theory as it attempts to explain historical movements of peoples into (and, in the case of Jefferson's "the latter of the former," out of) the Americas. The constructed imaginary arrival of peoples in the Americas thousands of years ago across a land bridge from Asia performs nineteenth- and twentieth-century concerns over Asian immigrants and the perceived "threat" they posed to the United States. For American Indian nations in the twenty-first century, such assemblages suggest that not only were "Indians" not indigenous to the Americas, but that they were ultimately the first wave of a "yellow peril" invasion that infested the lands already (or destined to be) inhabited by Europeans. Such assemblages were underwritten by the colonialist discourses of the United States that allowed nothing within the continental sweep of its manifest aspirations to stand *outside.* Indians were either dead or they were remade entirely into newly arrived immigrants who illegally violated the sanctity of the United States' expanding borders as the prior specters and refugees of anti-Asian and anti-Mexican attitudes.

The introduction of Orientalism into the context of the Americas and the construction of "native" otherness as foreign to and excluded from the United States implies a colonial and imperial construct of the place and movements of peoples. But it is an implied colonial discourse that depends upon racial categories to incorporate native peoples as part of, though marginal to, the U.S. melting pot of immigrants that now exists on indigenous peoples' own lands. Edward Said argues that "the Orient is an integral part of European *material* civilization and culture. Orientalism expresses and represents that part culturally and even ideologically as a mode of discourse with supporting institutions, vocabulary, scholarship, imagery, doctrines, even colonial bureaucracies and colonial styles."[50] And though Said considers American Orientalism less dense and less established than the European variety, his definition is useful here in considering how such material culture shapes U.S. understandings of "native" peoples as part of a larger "Asiatic" influence and threat. But even if those knowledges that produce Orientalizing narratives about American Indians refer to colonial bureaucracies and colonial styles, the American Indian version of a remapped "Orientalism" also contains a racializing component that is necessary to contextualize. As a narrative of racist, colonialist, and imperialist supremacy, Manifest Destiny transformed indigenous peoples from citizens of separate, external sovereign nations into racial minorities within and subject to the internal structures of the United States. The orientalizing cacophonies that remap indigenous peoples as part of an early wave of Asian immigrants perform an originary racialization of indigenous peoples as they are recast as immigrants who may or may not be full citizens.

In *Race and Manifest Destiny,* Reginald Horsman identifies the narrative of Manifest Destiny as a process of racialization that constructed the "American" as inheritor of the Anglo-Saxon lineage. Accompanying that racialization of the "American" into Anglo-Saxon whiteness was the racialization of the other as the savage, inferior "Indian" who would, sadly, fall by the wayside as civilization advanced.[51] By identifying Manifest Destiny as primarily a narrative fixated on the process of constituting and cohering racial categories, Horsman establishes one of the tenets that has enabled the slippage between colonization and racialization to propagate within postcolonial, critical race, and critical whiteness studies. As the United States stretched and exceeded its own boundaries under the rubric of Manifest Destiny, indigenous peoples and nations, who were initially externally colonized, had to be imaginatively and legally incorporated into the internal of the U.S. nation-state. They had to be worlded as other and *worlded anew* as cultures and races that add to the distinctive mosaic of U.S. multiculturalism, with the additional distinction implied here that the United States does not and would not enter into treaties with its own citizens. On a fundamental level, then, the process of racialization that reinforced the U.S. destiny to spread from sea to sea served a larger function by turning indigeneity into a "racial" category, a transformation that equates the distinctions of indigenous nations as sovereign and independent with that of every other racialized and diasporic arrival to be mediated within U.S. citizenry. This process of racialization, embedded within the Orientalizing cacophonies justifying the transit of U.S. empire, has particular significance to how postcolonialism and altermodernity are articulated and discussed by European, American, and diasporic theorists concerned with creating intersectional insurrections that parallel class struggles with race, gender, and sexuality in order to create the common within the global.[52]

Often, theorists have returned to certain posts—postmodernism, postracial, postmetropole, or perhaps postnational—and the new alters that emerge from those to resolve the ontological dilemma indigeneity poses to the colonizing nation-state. Within U.S. empire, "postrace" and "colorblind" discourses circulate as evidence of U.S. exceptionalism on the one hand, and proof on the other that the U.S. historical destiny was and is a just and righteous destiny, despite its flaws. Those flaws, of course, are framed as easily remedied through the inclusion and incorporation of racial difference into the larger structures of power, though the process may be slow and marked by fits and starts. Second, within this paradigm of U.S. exceptionalism articulated through postracial liberalisms, the emphasis on the post- allows for a sanitized remembrance of the United States' origins as an imperial, enslaving and colonizing white supremacy to remain within liberal critiques of its neocolonial and superpower status even as those critiques precede in the urgency of now with the assumption that all those processes are safely ensconced in the past. Or, postracial liberalisms manage the disruptive consciousness of the United States' origins as colonial and imperial by cathecting the United States as exemplar within the historical development of worldwide governmentality that leads from natural and primitive man to civilized democracy that is then exported as commonwealth, freedom, and happiness to the world through capitalism, militarism, populism, or a combination of all three. Either way, the colonization of indigenous peoples through which the United States manifested its imperial intent is rendered unactionable within the very critiques that strive to challenge how the nation-state constructs a world defined through racialized constellations as if they have nothing to do with the ongoing colonization of indigenous peoples that are constitutive of the everyday for settlers and arrivants.

At the same time, cathecting an "after" to racialization and colonialism transforms the United States, or at least the lands it occupies, into a geopolitical space that offers asylum to global and transnational diasporas that resist or refuse the normativities of nation-states and nationalism that make "home" impossible. Nandita Sharma and Cynthia Wright, for instance, suggest that "for those defined as outside the new nationalized polity—or even as its 'enemies'—migration is one of the few available 'escape routes' for life."[53] In arguing against indigenous claims to land, sovereignty, and nation, they suggest that autochthony stands, in the face of global capitalism and migration that now inform the postcolonial world, as xenophobic elitism that traffics as neoliberal hatred of foreigners.[54] To resolve the dialectics of indigeneity that, for them, stand as regressive neoracism in light of the global diasporas arising from oppression around the world, Sharma and Wright cast indigeneity as untenable by arguing that colonialism and the resistances to it are better understood "as the theft of the commons, the agents of decolonization as the *commoners,* and decolonization as the gaining of a *global commons.*"[55] Autochthony and indigeneity in this view become regressive antimodern oppositional identities that stand as obstacle to the gaining of a commons as the means to the end of oppression within the lands that once did, but no longer can or should, belong to indigenous peoples.

Michael Hardt and Antonio Negri make a similar argument in *Commonwealth* when they state: "We are all entangled and complicit in the identities, hierarchies, and corruptions of the current forms of power. Revolution requires not merely emancipation, as we said earlier, but liberation; not just an event of destruction but also a long and sustained process of transformation, creating a new humanity." They continue: "Making the multitude is thus a project of democratic organizing aimed at democracy."[56] To resist the hierarchies of identity, class, and race that have demarcated the world through access to power requires that democracy be made anew, so that "democracy must not only be the goal of a multitude with the already developed powers necessary for self-government but also a learning mechanism, a *dispositif,* that expands those powers, increasing not only the capacity but also the desire to participate in government."[57] Hardt and Negri's multitudinous insurrectional parallelism that draws upon Deleuze and Guattari's "Indians without ancestry" is ultimately, despite its global vision for revolution against the normativities of property, family, and nation, a project not unlike the one John Collier delineated at Poston Relocation Center when he told the internees that democracy remained yet embryonic. "In this community of yours," Collier promised, "you will be not only gaining for yourselves satisfaction, and power, and fame, but will be rendering to this country and to the other countries, including Japan, a momentous sociological human service, lasting peace and a happy humanity."[58] There is, as Agamben points out, "an inner solidarity between democracy and totalitarianism."[59] This parallax gap makes locating the fascist and liberatory within democratic philosophies difficult to escape even as pluralizing discourses head towards restructuring political institutions to be more just, so they provide more life. Further, any notion of the commons that speaks for and as indigenous as it advocates transforming indigenous governance or incorporating indigenous peoples into a multitude that might then reside on those lands forcibly taken from indigenous peoples does nothing to disrupt the genocidal and colonialist intent of the initial and now repeated historical process.[60]

These delineations of the commons within altermodernity that simultaneously reveal and mask the colonization of indigenous peoples attempt, as they spread along the transit of empire, to make a commons out of internment camps. In the process, they reshape the U.S. project of democratic civilization as a paradigmatic epoch of exceeding and succedent sociopolitical experiments in self-governance that emerged in Collier's thought as finally and ultimately assimilative. Los Angeles has functioned in similarly paradigmatic ways within discussions of postmodern architecture and geography. Edward W. Soja positions Los Angeles as the space of "territorial consolidation" where, in the Los Angeles Times's slogan, "it all comes together." The city of Los Angeles, Soja suggests, is a "prototopos, a paradigmatic place; or, pushing inventiveness still further, a mesocosm, an ordered world in which the micro and the macro, the idiographic and the nomothetic, the concrete and the abstract, can be seen simultaneously in an articulated and interactive combination."[61] Yamashita's Tropic of Orange draws upon and engages established tropes of the postmodern cityscape that scholars such as Mike Davis and Soja have discussed in terms of the city's socio-geopolitical structurings and destructurings. The spatial ecology that emerges in these discussions of Los Angeles emphasizes the grids of human economic and social interaction, the nodalities that serve as urban localities, and call to mind Manzanar's observation that "There are maps and there are maps and there are maps." Soja's point that Los Angeles is a constant repetition of territorial consolidation activated through this spatial division of labor attempts to articulate a deeper historical consciousness of the physical land and space that has been appropriated and reorganized in ways that ultimately mask the "hard edges of capitalist, racist and patriarchal landscape." That historical consciousness contains, in addition to the hard edges he addresses, a colonial landscape that, quoting Marx quoting Shakespeare, "melts into air."[62]

If Soja's discussion of postmodern Los Angeles is an incomplete engagement with the colonial structures underpinning the capitalist, racist, and patriarchal normativities that he does address, then the postmodern, as it has been deployed in the United States, is an attempt to confront, even as the pastiche and fractures belie a deeper logic, the transits of empire that continually consolidate the United States beyond its own borders and limitations. K. Anthony Appiah argues in his essay, "Is the Post- in Postmodernism the Post- in Postcolonial?," that "Postmodernism can be seen, then, as a retheorization of the proliferation of distinctions that reflects the underlying dynamic of cultural modernity, the need to clear oneself a space."[63] Postmodernism, Appiah cautions, depends upon this dynamic of space clearing and as such does not necessarily disrupt the rationality and legitimations of modernism's need for the "primitive" or the other. Modernism is intimately concerned with colonial and imperial projects, as a "clearing of space" that then opens up new markets and new aesthetic influences to transform and extend the hegemony of the global North over the South.[64] That clearing of space, Appiah continues, is ultimately displaced into the "post-" of the postmodern *and* the postcolonial, and gestures to the dependence of the "post-" on that which it exceeds or follows, be it modernism or colonialism. The observation that Orientalism, "yellow peril," Manifest Destiny, and the jurisgenesis violation of treaties incorporate and exclude Asian American and indigenous bodies simultaneously from the U.S. imagination contextualizes further how colonial systems continue to reproduce and remap themselves anew and again through the space-clearing of "the taking of land" and "the taking of the outside" that Agamben denotes as the state of exception necessary for democracy to function.[65]

Even in its consolidation, the United States is haunted by the specters of its origins, and the displaced narratives that have been continually rewritten do not altogether disappear. America becomes obsessed with borders and its frontiers, with origins and legitimacy—its schizophrenic nature might then be said to ventriloquize the perspectives of previously denied "citizens" such as Yamashita's Manzanar through reenactments and dispersals of the foundational logic of borders and frontiers, indigeneity and foreignness.[66] This schizophrenia—defined by Fredric Jameson as a breakdown in the signifying chain that reduces one to "a series of pure and unrelated presents in time"—might also voice a fundamental tenuousness of U.S. national self-consolidations to the degree that foreignness itself challenges the fabric of the nation, every immigrant a threat, every treaty a "special right" given to native peoples over other citizens.[67] As the rewritings of the 1980s and 1990s in the United States play out in the post-9/11 twenty-first century, they address these possibilities and advance a celebration of the altermodern multitude that proffers and then contains the possibility of dissolution of originary colonial worlds. The underlying disruptions of the cacophonies initiated through colonialism could perhaps be understood, then, as an attempt to bear historical witness to the rewritings of the United States and its alter.

This Is Not America

The 1992 Columbian quincentennial was greeted in Los Angeles with a riot. That riot had nothing to do with a commemoration of Columbus's voyage to the new world, though it had everything to do with the 500 years since. The initial riot stretched across the country and touched cities in the Midwest as well as along the East Coast. In Los Angeles, the riot spread through neighborhoods, sparking fires, vandalism and beatings. After three days, at least fifty-four people were dead and another 3,000 were arrested. At least half of those arrested were Latino and another 40 percent African American. The seeds for the April 29 rebellion were sown in the the videotaped beating Rodney King suffered at the hands of four white police officers that was aired throughout the nation by the national media. But even before the videotaped beating of Rodney King on March 3, 1991, race relations in Los Angeles and in the national consciousness were strained. There had been a long, established, and well-documented history of white police brutality against African Americans, and in addition to a strong current of anti-black racism, there were fears that non-European immigrants were overrunning the country and that Japanese businessmen and corporations were poised to buy out the United States once and for all. The very social fabric of the nation, it was feared, was imperiled by a triad of African American, Latino, and Asian American populations who were rapidly becoming the majority. This fear made it all the way to a special issue of *Time* in 1993 in which the magazine, using then newly developed computer imaging technologies, claimed to "predict" what a multiethnic American might look like. That face was surprisingly "white," even as the magazine disavowed that "whiteness" would exist in this future America of postracial hybridity.[68]

David Palumbo-Liu's discussion of the riots, first published in 1993, focuses on how Korean Americans were figured as "vigilantes" in the national media coverage. He begins with a close reading of an image included with *Newsweek's* coverage of the events that foregrounded a young Korean American in a Malcolm X "by any means necessary" T-shirt holding a handgun pointed up in that cautious-yet-prepared-for-anything noir. In addition to the Malcolm X quotation, the T-shirt displayed an image of a black man in a suit and tie peering through window blinds and pointing a rifle outward and back towards the right. Palumbo-Liu characterizes the expression of the young man in the photo as "looking askance toward the left of the frame." Palumbo-Liu continues: "In the background of the *Newsweek* photograph, two red fire engines spray jets of water on a smoldering building; a street sign tells us this is Olympic Boulevard. *Newsweek's* caption, quoting a Korean American witness to the riots: 'This is not America.'"[69] In an argument now canonical to Asian American studies, he stresses that the hyphenated "Asian-American" is not sufficient to encapsulate the slippage between Asia and America that occurs in the configurations of Asianness within the U.S. imaginary. "I argue," Palumbo-Liu writes, "that the proximity of Asian Americans to that ideal [the signifier 'American'] should be read as a history of persistent reconfigurations and transgressions of the Asian/American 'split,' designated here by a solidus that signals those instances in which a liaison between 'Asian' and 'American,' a *sliding over* between two seeming separate terms, is constituted."[70] This "sliding over" emphasizes the historical indeterminacy of Asian/American status within the United States, while at the same time it destabilizes both the Asian modifier and the American baseline. That threshold between the two terms, then, identifies the dominant ideology that, during World War II, allowed second- and third-generation Japanese Americans to be interned in camps as if they were newly arrived agents of the Japanese government while it simultaneously accounts for the radical reconfiguration, in the case of the 1992 riots, that positioned Korean Americans as the quintessential "cowboys" holding the "savages" at bay.

That the Poston Relocation Center was overseen by the Department of the Interior and the Bureau of Indian Affairs, and many other relocation centers were built on or in close proximity to reservations in the west, only supports further the slippages Palumbo-Liu identifies in Asian/American.

The United States needs "cowboys and Indians" to inhabit the "frontiers" of its borders, and in the Asian/American body, it finds a convenient consolidation on which to perform each of these narratives. The space of the "/" that Palumbo-Liu offers as an intervention to the hyphenated "Asian-" or the less adorned "Asian American" reiterates the slippage inherent in the "space-clearing" movement of the state of exception. Because indigenous peoples are fundamentally foreign and threatening to the U.S. nation-state, they are continually emptied of any indigenous Americanness—that identity is reserved in such narratives for European immigrants—and repositioned as either invisible, unidentifiable, or collapsed back into Asian. Just as Asian American representations and reconsolidations exist somewhere within Palumbo-Liu's solidus between Asia and America, American Indians exist somewhere (or nowhere) between America and the Indies that Columbus encountered. With the advent of multiculturalism in the 1980s and its transformation into the postracial ideologies of the 2000s, American Indians were refigured as "Native Americans" to parallel the politically correct categorization of other racial and ethnic minorities who now belong to the United States—African Americans, Asian Americans, Italian Americans, Indian Americans, and. . . . The solidus between Asian and American that Palumbo-Liu identifies exists because the normative "American" is constantly modified by the "Asian," functioning as a means of social, economic, and cultural buffer through which dominant ideologies police and maintain racial bans between whites and everyone else.

Palumbo-Liu explains: "The use of Asians, again, as the fulcrum inserted between ethnic groups to leverage hegemonic racist ideology is rearticulated in the homology—Asians against blacks and Latinos as white settlers stood against 'pillaging' Indians. The Korean American 'cowboy' thus serves as a defamiliarized image of white America's manifest destiny."[71] Kandice Chuh draws upon Palumbo-Liu and the "uniqueness of the Asian/American dynamic" to articulate the necessity of a *subjectless discourse* to problematize identitarian politics and "to create the conceptual space to prioritize difference by foregrounding the discursive constructedness of subjectivity, by reminding us that a 'subject' only becomes recognizable and can act as such by conforming to certain regulatory matrices."[72] But because the solidus exists as a product, I would argue, of the transit of empire that depends upon the paradigmatic "Indianness in Asianness," which is tied to the beginnings of the United States that made indigenous peoples aliens in their own lands, the signification of "Asian" when it slants—with all of its onto-poetic meanings and racial alterities implied—towards "American," carries the supplement of "Indian" along with it in the stretch of the real, so that the Asian body is then made to bear cowboys *and* Indians. This additional matrix disrupts Asian American exceptionalism and resituates it within processes of subjectification/objectification that exist outside the self-construction and perform through repetition the ongoing significations that maintain settler and arrivant colonialisms. Indigeneity becomes incommensurable with the subjectlessness that Chuh enunciates, precisely because it becomes the very site of colonial enactment where both subject and object serve the jurisgenerative *nomos* that uses violence to exclude *and* include.[73]

Atomu Year Zero

Not insignificantly, subjectlessness begins to proliferate at this twenty-first-century moment marked by the rise in DNA testing to link identity to history and descent. Henry Louis Gates Jr. has made an industry out scientific obsessions with DNA markers in his PBS televisual edutainments that have tracked *African American Lives 1* and *2* and provided a genomic snapshot of prominent African American cultural and literary icons, ranging from Oprah Winfrey and Toni Morrison to Don Cheadle and Chris Tucker. By presenting his guest interviewees with a detailed genome-ography to return them to their pre-American, tribal pasts, Gates attempts through science to heal family pasts breached through the violences of history. His *Faces of America* expands his vision to include a multicultural range of prominent Americans, including Kristi Yamaguchi, Stephen Colbert, Elizabeth Alexander, and Louise Erdrich, in order to articulate a possible postracial Americanness that emerges once everyone recognizes their immigrant, hybrid ancestry.[74] According to the *New York Times,* however, and much to their consternation, "some celebrities . . . turn surprisingly emotional about remote ancestors, but one refuses to look too closely into ancient roots. Ms. Erdrich, a novelist *(Love Medicine)* and chronicler of American Indian life, declines to have her genome sequenced and decoded," the columnist writes, "possibly for fear that the DNA results would complicate her claim to Chippewa ancestry." Louise Erdrich, whose grandfather served as tribal chairman for the Turtle Mountain Band of Chippewa Indians, counters "that her relatives said that it was their DNA too, and not hers alone to share with the world."[75]

Elizabeth Povinelli, in discussing "the dynamic conditions that qualify one kind of lethality as 'state killing' and another as a more amorphous condition of 'letting die,'" distinguishes the settler state's privatization of loss to that of Aboriginal indigenous "cosubstantial distribution of life, health, and social being" where one's body is shared through ancestral being.[76] "'That is not your body; that is my body. When you die, my body will suffer and die,'" an aunt tells her nephew when he insists he has a right to do with his body as he sees fit, even if it risks death.[77] Where Povinelli emphasizes the kinship responsibilities of cosubstatiation, Aileen Moreton-Robinson makes the point that the multidirectionality of *inter*substantiation inherent in indigenous sovereignty involves ancestral beings, humans, and land, where ancestral being does not just pair metynomically, but reciprocally constitutes being as self-in-relation:

> Our sovereignty is embodied, it is ontological (our being) and
> epistemological (our way of knowing), and it is grounded within
> complex relations derived from the intersubstantiation of ancestral
> beings, humans and land. In this sense, our sovereignty is carried
> by the body and differs from Western constructions of sovereignty,
> which are predicated on the social contract model, the idea of a uni-
> fied supreme authority, territorial integrity, and individual rights.[78]

These intersubstantiations that Moreton-Robinson details place indigenous subjectivities as the necessary embodiment of sovereignty and relationship that cannot be made subjectless, because they are the site of difference from Western delineations of citizenship, rights, and inclusion that the settler state proffers as possession. Within these frameworks, and in the genomic refusal Erdrich presents to Gates and the American viewing public, indigenous subjectivity is *of* rather than *made to bear*.

In his novel *Hiroshima Bugi*, Anishinaabe novelist and theorist Gerald Vizenor confronts indigenous intersubstantiations within the transnational states of killing and letting die. With a narrative style that delights in the juxtaposition of the absurd to defamiliarize iconic figures, where characters are renamed Bogart, Sumo, Virga, and Orion in echoes of famous movie stars, wrestlers, and astronomical constellations, and through word choices that include "tease," "simulation," and "contrary," Gerald Vizenor plays tricks on his readers as he demands that they engage him on the terms he provides. At times, such tricks produce parodic humor: "Mister

Nightbreaker Butler, when did those nasty soldiers burn Atlanta? Why, Scarlett Okichi, you know it was the Civil War. The Japanese lost the war to the Union."[79] Other moments taunt with a syntax of associative meaning: "Mount Fuji was my first vision in black feathers. The ravens crashed through my window at the orphanage and together we soared around the country."[80]

Vizenor's novel plays within realms of interconnected referentialities in an attempt to make a world in which it is more possible to grieve as a means to disrupt the killing states of international "peace" dependent upon mutual assured destruction. Though his work has been criticized and dismissed for its inaccessibility, cosmopolitanism, and mixed-blood emphasis, his work also employs native aesthetics to challenge what he sees to be the traps of "bankable" Indianness which have more to do with identities constructed for and by the colonizers than resistance to those romantic expectations through the radical fluidity that remains grounded in embodied histories and traditions.[81] Vizenor's *Hiroshima Bugi* provides a possible model for coming to an ethical and aesthetic consciousness through which to engage domination and to recenter embodied indigeneity as counter to the logics of late capitalism that unhinge identity in the service of a parallel, inclusive, world-dominant liberal democracy.

"The Atomic Bomb Dome is my Rashomon," begins Ronin Mifune Ainoko Browne, the main character and the half-Anishinaabe cross-blood storier of Gerald Vizenor's *Hiroshima Bugi*. That phrase, often repeated throughout the text, sets the stage for what has been called a kabuki novel that challenges the simulations of nationalistic peace in the wake of nuclear technologies and revels in the cross-cultural allegories shared among American Indian, Japanese, and Ainu traditions. The novel deploys intertextual plays between critical theory, postmodernism, and Anishinaabe epistemological traditions, as well as Vizenor's own experiences when he was stationed in Japan at the end of the Korean War. The overtones of Akira Kurosawa's iconic post–World War II film *Rashomon* (1950) intentionally draw the characters and readers into a world where absences, conflicting realities, and dis/locatednesses trouble one's accepted notions of consciousness in order to address what the novel terms a "moral survivance" informed by samurai and trickster ethics. Vizenor's narrative confronts what he has termed elsewhere the complacent manifest manners—those poses, performances, and identities that reinforce Manifest Destiny and its devastation of indigenous peoples—that perpetuate dominance and a victimry dependent upon static identities created through nationalistic projections of Indianness. The Hiroshima Peace Park Museum, with its grotesque displays of burned hair, scarred skin, and tragic stories including that of Sadako Sasaki's cruel optimism in the faith that folding one thousand paper cranes would cure her radiation-caused leukemia—she folded five hundred more than required by tradition, yet still died—offers, according to Vizenor's main character, mere protestations of suffering that momentarily elicit the guilt of nations rather than offer any real strategies for the peace of nuclear de-escalation. Nor do they provide any avenues for an ethic of grievability that can address and apprehend a young girl's struggle to come to terms with her life made bare.

If, as he writes in his novel, Vizenor intends to give his readers a mode of moral survivance that contains "a vision and vital condition to endure, to outwit evil and dominance, and to deny victimry," then it is important to examine how Vizenor links Japanese and indigenous peoples who are drawn together and pulled apart by imperial, colonialist, and militaritistic violences as well as the uranium sourced from American Indian lands and exploded as "Little Boy" above Hiroshima.[82] The novel forces readers to ask questions about accountability. How can peace exist in the burnt-out ruins of war? By prioritizing a "moral survivance" rather than mere survival, Vizenor attempts through Ronin's cross-blood hybrid narrative in *Hiroshima Bugi* to resolve some of the problems he sees in uncritical poses of opposition that reinforce the dominant liberal democratic modes of justice that continue to destroy indigenous cultures in addition to celebrating death under the guise of promoting peace.

Elizabeth Cook-Lynn has written "that it is the responsibility of a poet like me to 'consecrate' history and event."[83] While her poetry and scholarship focus on national narratives of the Dakota people, Gerald Vizenor's writing positions stories and those who tell them as memories and survivancists within the global. "The marvelous, elusive tease of our many stories, and variations of stories," he writes, "became concerted memories. Our tricky metaphors were woven together day by day into a consciousness of moral survivance."[84] Rather than a mode of reflexive remembrance and commemoration, Vizenor emphasizes an intensive, collaborative performance of memory that gives rise to ambivalent and affective consciousnesses inspired and shaped by indigenous worlds and lived histories. "More than the commerce of reactive survivalists, mere liturgy, ideology, or the causative leverage of a sworn witness," Vizenor tells us, "survivance is a creative, concerted consciousness that does not arise from separation, dominance, or concession nightmares. Our stories create perfect memories of survivance."[85]

In this context, Kurosawa's *Rashomon* becomes the ideal shadow text for *Hiroshima Bugi*. The film is often evoked to describe situations in which there are competing narratives of truth, memory, and reality, and it presents a layered mystery that unravels rather than reveals as more stories are added to narrate the rape of a woman, the murder of her husband, and the arrest of a bandit who may or may not be guilty. As a reflection on memory and the impossibility of representing the truth, it is symptomatic of the post-Hiroshima Japanese landscape as well as the emergence of postmodernism in reaction to the breakdown of master narratives in the aftermath of mass destruction. Drawing structurally from the film, *Hiroshima Bugi* examines parallactic reality and the truth of Hiroshima from a number of different subject positions within and outside the U.S. and Japanese empires. Through the course of the novel, we are presented with American Indian soldiers who served as part of the occupying United States force and who were then later victims of nuclear testing in Nevada.

In order to create a mnemonic engagement with the ramifications of such trans-Pacific complicities, Vizenor's writing interplays Japanese poetic aesthetics with Anishinaabe oral tradition. Such a crosscultural aesthetic, as Kimberly Blaeser suggests, allows Vizenor to "creat[e] an 'open' text, a text that advertises its absences and requires the response of the reader to bring it to fruition."[86] According to Blaeser, that process "unfixes" the text, activates the readers' imagination, and allows Vizenor to transform the written into an oral aesthetic that works on the reader and gives life to the words beyond the page.[87] The narrative of *Hiroshima Bugi* demands a similar unfixing. Not only does the narrative function more like oral tradition, it compels the reader into a consciousness of interreferentiality that breaches the United States' historical narratives of Manifest Destiny, "yellow peril," and nuclear annihilation, as well as Japanese nationalism and imperialism.

Vizenor employs two narrators for his novel. Ronin, who lives in the shadow of the Atomic Bomb Dome, provides the first layer of the text as he writes meditative reflections on the ironies of peace within museum displays of horror. The second voice is that of an Anishinaabe from Leech Lake Reservation who was a friend of Ronin's deceased father. Named the Manidoo Envoy, this character is amorphous, connected to ancestral beings figured as plentipontentiary, with a seemingly omniscient awareness that allows him to describe Ronin's ideas, feelings, and motivations. In a parallel narrative, the Envoy reads Ronin's work every night to other American Indians living in the Hotel Manidoo somewhere near Nogales, Arizona, on the border with Mexico. The Envoy's voice in the text takes on the voice of the historian/literary scholar as he explains and contextualizes much of Ronin's narrative to the other soldiers. Early on in the novel, the Envoy remarks that Ronin's stories are structured as "dialogue in a kabuki theater style, short, direct, positional words and sentences."[88] He further describes kabuki as a tension between reality and unreality, where literal representations are often followed by the nonsensical. The Envoy suggests that Ronin's stories shift between fancy and reality, and the interpretation provided by the Envoy following each of Ronin's stories functions similarly to those stories with the authoritative scholarly mode of "reality." Such an aesthetic within kabuki theater, the reader is told, serves to remind the audience that what they view is a constructed performance. By interspersing Ronin's lyrical passages with the grounding voice of an informed translator who contextualizes Ronin's pastiche of cultural referents at play in modern Japan, the Manidoo Envoy provides an entry point for the reader, a place through which to activate the creative processes that, according to Vizenor, will undo the bankable simulations of otherness within domination.

Though there are shared sensibilities and ethics between Anishinaabe and Japanese narrative traditions in the verbal shift between the Anishinaabe trickster *naanabozho* and the Japanese water spirits signified by the *namazu*, for instance, Vizenor is careful in the novel to resist romanticizing either or equating them. In contrast to N. Scott Momaday, who has notoriously linked American Indians and Asians through the Bering Strait theory, Vizenor in his novel refuses what he has elsewhere described as "a tidy bit of cultural arrogance [that] denies the origin myths of natives."[89] Instead, Vizenor creates a cross-blood narrator to embody the links that histories of World War II, nineteenth-century trans-Pacific expeditions, and shared cultural resonances imply. Ronin bears the scars of Japanese ethnocentrism that ostracizes Hiroshima survivors, lepers, Ainu, and mixed-blood foreigners. Born in Japan, the son of a Japanese nationalist Bugi/Boogie dancer and an Anishinaabe U.S. soldier, Ronin is abandoned as an *ainoko*—a mixed-blood product of the occupation, one of "the untouchables of war and peace in two countries" at the threshold of exception (22). Orphaned and raised in the ruins of Hiroshima, Ronin is finally adopted by the tribal government at the White Earth Reservation as a means to work around the restrictive U.S. anti-Asian immigration laws and allow him to travel to the reservation in the hopes of finding his father and learning about Anishinaabe stories and traditions. He eventually returns to Japan when he learns his father had survived Hiroshima only to die later from cancer resulting from the military nuclear tests at Yucca Flat, Nevada. It is in his process of returning to Japan that he truly finds his father and becomes, in the transit, memory, the destroyer of the simulated peace commemorated at the Hiroshima Peace Park (24).

That process of returning, the reader learns through the course of the narrative, is one of the sources of indigenous survivance that Ronin performs. When confronted by the police after one of his protests, which involved pouring gasoline into the Pond of Peace and igniting it at 8:15 AM on August 6 in a tribute to the parade of ghosts that haunt the ruins of Hiroshima, Ronin provides a narrative of his life and his citizenship. "Mister Browne," the police interpreter says, "we know you are ainoko, and we respect you, but you left many years ago, a hafu adopted by Amerika Indians in United States. You stay, never return to Japan" (43). Ronin responds, and the dialogic exchange creates one of the many textual moments informed by haiku and kabuki:

> Japan is my country.
> How you return?
> By Ainu.
> By who?
> Ainu in Hokkaido.
> Ainu shaman.
> No Ainu.
> Ainu boaters.
> You joke me.
> Yes, yes, but truly. (43)

The Koban interpreter continues to insist that the Ainu are gone, and Ronin responds by noting that the bears are still there. "My resistance," he writes a few pages later, "was by tease and irony, not by deceptive tactics and practices. The police, as usual, would never believe that my ironic confessions and stories were true. So, my best defense was a tricky style of sincerity" (44). In these moments Vizenor offers a vision of possible strategies for embodied indigenous survivance in the ironic *hafu* truths that ultimately inform Ronin's "perfect memories" necessary for grievability (36). Ronin comes to consciousness through a Janus transit of empire that crosses the *nomos* of Japanese and U.S. bans on indigeneity. His "natural reason," "communal wit" and "ironic truths" allow Ronin to recognize that the only way to find and honor the spirit of his father is to return through the radical acknowledgment that authority and presence reside within the Ainu rather than the national Japanese citizenship laws. The police are unable to engage Ronin on the terms he provides, in his justifications for his right to return to the country by way of the Ainu after he had been repatriated to White Earth. However, because Ronin is a samurai of mnemonic "perfect memory," his return voyage to Japan must also retrace the previous journey of a half Scots–half Chinook man by the name of Ranald MacDonald. MacDonald (a real historical figure whose homophonous name evokes signs of clownish global capitalism) arrived in Japan in 1847 via a whaling ship named *Plymouth.* When the ship neared the northern island of Yagishiri, he asked the captain to give him a small boat that he then intentionally capsized so that the Ainu people there would rescue him. Arriving "by chance of nature, adventure, and plucky determination" six years before Commodore Perry and during imperial Japan's push to colonize Ainu lands in the north, Ranald MacDonald helped open Japan to the West (123–24, 139–41).

The specter of Ranald MacDonald haunts Ronin through the course of the novel. Convinced that his father was also aware of this native trace, Ronin uses MacDonald's travels as a way to commit himself to his work as a peace terrorist. While *Hiroshima Bugi* reclaims MacDonald as a *hafu* crossblood, the text also remains critical of his role in empire. The son of a Scotsman, MacDonald did not learn until later in life that his mother was Princess Raven of the Chinook. Vizenor writes, "He had accepted the native nicknames, 'Little Chinook,' and 'Little Chief,' as an affectionate tease, but did not think of himself as a native or mixedblood Chinook" (140). He decided to go to Japan because he believed that Indians originated there and because, as an educated man, he believed he might "make himself something of a personage among [the Japanese]" (140). That he arrived on a ship named *Plymouth* only repeats those forms of dominance inherited within the transits of empire. That his mother's name evokes the Raven trickster is an added bonus for Vizenor (140).

Ronin's own travels to the Ainu, then, repeat those of MacDonald—he gets a small boat that he intentionally capsizes and when he arrives he is warmly welcomed. However, his voyage is in many ways a reverse ethnography, informed by Anishinaabe stories and his experiences on White Earth rather than a desire to educate or save. Upon his arrival, he explains his own *hafu* parentage and discusses MacDonald's travels. The elders, Ronin writes, "were amused and wanted to explore the actual journey of MacDonald" (124). Though Ronin tells us that "the Ainu and the Anishinaabe honor bears as original totems in their creation stories," he does not assume any right or privilege based on those similarities (125). When the elders, independent of Ronin and his desires, undertake the journey, Ronin observes, "No one invited me to travel with them, but no one resisted my presence either" (125). His journey to and with the Ainu shadowed those of both his father and MacDonald, and it is through the Ainu and their bear creation stories and invisible tattoos that Ronin commits himself to serving as a mercenary against those simulations of peace that service domination after Hiroshima. The invisible tattoos become part of his perfect memory: on his chest, the words "eight fifteen Atomu One" in honor of the day and time the bomb exploded over Hiroshima; on his back, chrysanthemums, morning glories, and wild lettuce to represent his mother the nationalist, nuclear survivance, and the "fare of ruins" that feeds bare life (109). The tattoos appear only when his body, in true trickster fashion, becomes flush through sex, hot baths, or agitation—and they have the power to confront the denials of the everyday that absent the horrors of Hiroshima from consciousness. For instance, when he bathes at one of the natural hot springs in the north, "Atomu One" blazes across his chest. Later, we are told, there were stories of a *hafu hibakusha* (a Hiroshima survivor) "who poisoned the mountain water with the invisible words and flowers on his atomu body" (132).

Ronin's strategies of survivance as well as resistance take many forms in the novel, though each demand an "active sense of presence, the tease of the natural world in native stories" (36). The trickster stories Ronin writes as well as performs as protest in the Hiroshima Peace Memorial Museum and in the streets of the Ginza District force the reader to confront the ironies propagated by tributes to peace that involve dioramas of destruction. The dioramas of suffering within the halls of the Peace Memorial, Ronin explains, "only teased the horror with cultural manners and 'aesthetic victimry'" (135). In reaction to what he perceives as an affront to real peace after Japan has suffered the ravages of atomic weapons, Ronin contrarily supports an amendment to Article 9 of the Japanese Occupation Constitution to allow nuclear weapons, arguing that the "Japanese must vote to amend their constitution so the government can possess nuclear weapons as a theatrical balance of crucial, reductive rituals and pleasures" (14). Ronin's staged calls for nuclear weapons that he enunciates as protest within the halls of the Peace Memorial Museum disturb the tourists, who quickly head to the gift shop to buy souvenir T-shirts and in the process attract the attention of a Japanese nationalist disguised as a journalist. But lest one assumes that Vizenor and his character advocate nuclear escalation, the text makes it clear that Ronin's performance as trickster revels in the contrary; his support for an amendment to the constitution does not serve a nationalist Japan. Rather, his advocacy is similar to Einstein's, who said real peace could emerge only when a supranational organization had the sole authority to possess weapons of mass destruction.

In spite of the imperial chrysanthemum tattooed invisibly on his back in honor of his mother, Ronin reserves most of his trickster play and parody for the Japanese nationalists. Once Richie, the nationalist disguised as a journalist, realizes that Ronin resists the nationalist rhetoric that denies the Nanking massacre and demands that all foreigners be removed from Japan, Ronin joins forces with a reformed *kamikaze* pilot to commandeer one of the nationalist black vans to travel around the Ginza District and Imperial Palace. Mocking the imperialists who wear all black and use the vans to spread propaganda and nationalist hatred of non-Japanese, Ronin broadcasts rock and roll, blues, and gospel music from a loudspeaker.[90] Songs of choice for his subversive resistance include Johnny Cash's "The Man in Black," Chuck Berry's "Rock 'n' Roll Music," and Roy Orbison's "Pretty Woman." Cash's "Man in Black" drives home the disparities between the nationalists—who dress in black to support the return of imperial Japan, the denial of the Ainu, and the demonization of Hiroshima survivors—and Cash's reason for his choice of wardrobe: "And I wear it for the thousands who have died / Believin' that the Lord was on their side / I wear it for another hundred thousand who have died / Believin' that we all were on their side."[91]

Rather than relying upon narratives of destruction and victimization, Vizenor complicates the roles that Japan and American Indians have played in the service of empire to create a trans-Pacific indigenous ethic that confronts the inherited complicities of globalization. What he gives us in *Hiroshima Bugi* is an unsettling text that demands of its readers not only a leap of imagination but a turn to indigenously minded consciousnesses through which they will engage all the processes of domination produced by complicity and masked by avowals of oppression. It is not enough to reclaim (in the case of MacDonald) or to commemorate in the wake of nuclear destruction. Such narratives of identity and victimry produce simulated Indianness and false peace that has nothing to do, according to Vizenor, with survivance and the embodied intersubstantiation with ancestral beings, humans, and land. What Vizenor leaves readers with is a mode of chance, tricks, and irony that are constantly in motion and constantly resisting dominance. Movement and complexity, rather than static dioramas of tattered clothes, Vizenor argues, provide generative strategies though which one might confront the horrors of human violences that emerge from those killing states that proffer the illusion of peace in the place of life.

Conclusion

Zombie Imperialism

The apocalypse is the end of secrecy. Literally, it is the discovery, the
revelation when everything is said. It is the end of metaphors and secrets.
The nuclear bomb is the Sun cast on the Earth, of the end of the Sun as a
metaphor, as distance. It is the Sun materialized on Earth: the end.

Jean Baudrillard, *Radical Alterity*

The Transit of Empire has taken as its point of entry the constellating discourses that juridically, culturally, and constitutionally produce "Indians"
as an operational site within U.S. expansionism. "Indianness" circulates
within poststructural, postcolonial, critical race, and queer theories as both
sign and event; as a process of signification and exception, "Indianness"
starts, stops, and reboots the colonialist discourses that spread along lines
of flight that repeatedly challenge the multicultural liberal settler state to
remediate freedom despite the fact that such colonializing liberalisms
established themselves through force, violence, and genocide in order to
make freedom available for some and not others. As the liberal state and
its supporters and critics struggle over the meaning of pluralism, habita-
tion, inclusion, and enfranchisement, indigenous peoples and nations, who
provide the ontological and literal ground for such debates, are continually
deferred into a past that never happened and a future that will never come.
And as a system dependent upon difference and differentiation to enact
the governmentality of biopolitics, the deferred "Indian" that transits U.S.
empire over continents and oceans is recycled and reproduced so that empire might cohere and consolidate subject and object, self and other, within
those transits. In the process, racialization replaces colonization as the site
of critique, and the structuring logics of dispossession are displaced onto
settlers and arrivants who substitute for and as indigenous in order to
consolidate control and borders at that site of differentiation. Indigenous
peoples are rendered unactionable in the present as their colonization is
deferred along the transits that seek new lands, resources, and peoples to
feed capitalistic consumption.

For the Chickasaw, who have negotiated and survived such a system for over four hundred and fifty years, the intersubstantiations of sovereignty and relationship that connect community to ancestral place and belonging arise from the ontologies of reciprocal complementarity, Upper and Lower Worlds, that inflect and shape this world through balance and *haksuba*. Movement across land and time was tied to the night sky and a deep awareness of the celestial order of spiral galaxies even as that movement traversed rivers and mountain ranges on ceremonial cycles of death and rebirth. Sovereignty, in the context of such philosophies, is an act of interpretation as much as it is a political assertion of power, control, and exception. That interpretation is an act of sovereignty is something well known and practiced by the imperial hegemon that uses juridical, military, and ontological force to police interpretation and interpellate what is and is not seen, what can and cannot be said. Indigenous critical theory stands in the parallax gap created when U.S. empire transits itself in the stretch between perceptions of the real to *interpret* and will against the signifying systems that render "Indianness" as the radical alterity of the real laid bare.

Colonialism worlded the Americas into a planet, and as eighteenth- and nineteenth-century colonialisms continue into the present throughout the global North and South, indigenous peoples are forced into proximities they might not have chosen for themselves as they have become neighbors to arrivants they did not anticipate. Such enforced settler cohabitations demand the best of indigenous government traditions to imagine, innovate, and restructure kinship sovereignties in order to repair the violent breaches of family, history, and tradition that forced people into indigenous lands. And it requires, as we have seen in Wilson Harris, a recentering of indigenous authority to adjudicate the past and future on those indigenous lands. Māori poet Robert Sullivan, in his operatic libretto *Captain Cook in the Underworld,* imagines the need for repentance as the foundation through which to forge possible livable pasts and futurities in the aftermath of Cook's arrival. As Captain Cook wanders through an underworld peopled by the Pacific Islanders he had killed, the narrator of the poem explains: "For your soul / to rest, good captain, you must meet them, soul / to soul, until the earth in mercy / enfolds you—until then you're nursing / a zombie soul forever searching for its tomb."[1] For Captain Cook's zombie soul to rest, he must explain to his own descendants in the Pacific, as well as the descendants of those Māori he had tortured and killed in pursuit of discovery, what he has learned in the underworld, and he must face justice and apprehend the consequences of his propagated violence that knowingly denied the humanity of indigenous peoples to project the liberal good at the site of possession.

The U.S.–Pacific Imperium in Transit

In 1897 Lieutenant General John M. Schofield published his memoirs detailing the forty-six years he had served in the U.S. Army. The text, ostensibly written to document Schofield's memories of the Civil War, provides not so much a history lesson as it does reflections and opinions on the events of his military career. Memorialized by the army barracks on the island of O'ahu in Hawai'i that serve as one of the staging grounds for the urban combat Stryker vehicle brigade deployed in Iraq and Afghanistan, Schofield played an instrumental role in the development of U.S. colonial policy after the Civil War ended, serving as secretary of war in President Andrew Johnson's cabinet and as a U.S. envoy to the Hawaiian kingdom to help broker the plans for Pearl Harbor in 1877. He was a product of the U.S. Gilded Age and its imperialist longings, and his reflections on his life are less artful than self-serving. His *Forty-six Years in the Army* provides insights into the racist, colonialist, and imperialist logics that generated the rationales for U.S. expansionism. Schofield's military memoir serves as bridge to the twenty-first-century security state that links the violences of "Indian Wars" and Hawaiian overthrows, Jim Crow racisms and anti-Asian exclusions, to the current manifestation of what Robert J. C. Young has delineated as the genre conventions of the "'terror' effects" of the post-9/11 world that are "self-generating, uncontrollable, proliferating. Totally random."[2]

Despite the fact that his name is now commemorated throughout the U.S. military-industrial complex, Schofield is often overlooked outside military histories and his life in microcosm shadows the parallactic horizons that punctuate the imperial turns at the heart of *The Transit of Empire*. His life spanned 1831 to 1906, encompassing Southeastern Indian removal to the allotment of Indian Territory, along with the U.S. military's turns from the Civil War, to the genocidal subjugation of American Indian lands and nations, and then to the Spanish-American War and its territorial acquisitions in the Pacific and Caribbean. Along the way, his career's rhizomatic details are striking. He was, for instance, superintendent at West Point in 1880 when Cadet Johnson Chestnut Whittaker, the second African American to enter the academy, was brutalized by his fellow cadets in a racist profiling attack meant to terrorize the only African American at West Point.[3] Schofield's investigation and subsequent court-martialing of Whittaker ruled that the cadet himself was responsible for his own beating rather than his white peers, and following public outrage and presidential investigation, Schofield was finally reprimanded and dismissed. Schofield's reflection on the beatings and his dismissal give the measure of the man; his own zombie soul imagined a continent full of merciless savages who threatened the foundations of civilized white society. Even in his dismissal, he refused to accept any accountability and presented himself as both victim and paternalistic father who was horrified that "the over-kind superintendent should be sacrificed to that partisan clamor before the coming election."[4] Schofield deemed African Americans neither "mentally [n]or morally" fit for "the enjoyment of privileges in the nation's institutions."[5] He went on to command the Pacific Military Division and in 1888 became the commanding general of the army; Cadet Whittaker went on to teach Ralph Ellison's science courses in Oklahoma.[6]

The questions and methodological concerns that arise here at the intersection between indigenous critical theory and the most recent manifestations of a United States bent on defining whiteness not just as possession but as the proprietary domain for citizenship and human rights center on remembering that anti-immigration legislation, internments, and incarcerations are not exceptions but the rule for U.S. liberalism inaugurated through colonialism. The current century's surveillance of terrorism, homelands, and financial markets following 9/11 has been accompanied by the expansion of U.S. imperialism in the form of the global war on terror that has continued unabated for almost ten years. But within those expansions, we have also experienced a sea-change within the trajectory of race and power within the political traditions in the belly of the beast that reorients complicity along lines of access, money, and power as well as race, nativism, and status. In November 2008 the United States changed at least one aspect of its historical intent by electing its first African American president. By any standard of assessment, such a shift in the history of white supremacist imperial rule marks a turning point for understanding how race and identity underscore power within the United States, even if that shift proves fleeting or is limited still to only certain individuals, classes, or confluences of story and biography. Or even if, as suggested by the debates around health care and "death panels" and the rise of conservative nativism, that long legacy of racist nationalism has only fallen asleep temporarily to awaken reinvigorated and more powerful still for having dreamed at all.

Caution! Zombies Ahead!

With the onset of the twenty-first-century U.S. war on terror, American popular culture became obsessed (again and still) with zombies. From the 2004 remake of George A. Romero's 1978 *Dawn of the Dead* to Valve Corporation's 2008 video game *Left 4 Dead,* from Cormac McCarthy's *The Road* to the Seth Grahame-Smith/Jane Austen mash-up *Pride and Prejudice and Zombies,* the beginning of the twenty-first century is marked by an obsession with the living dead. The referent has proven useful. From flesh-consuming banks "too big to fail" (called zombie banks) to embodiments of Nazi fascism head-shot in video games such as *Call of Duty: World at War,* zombies now serve as a "moar brainz!" cannibalistic embodiment of conspicuous consumption that spans oil-guzzling SUVs and their global-warming-responsible drivers to the pResident Evil of the Bush II administration and its blood-for-oil invasion of Iraq in March 2003. And while the unthinking living dead have haunted the end of the last two centuries in vampiric, zombified, and Frankensteinian imperial allegories of gender, class, and race, there is a certain ghastly reveling in the not-quite-dead-yet-but-soon-to-be amnesias that drift now into political critiques in such forms, for instance, as the Jonestown specters haunting the evocation of "Kool-Aid drinkers" to describe mindless support for political candidates and any other marketing fads and fandoms. Zombie imperialism, at least as it seems in these moments, has emerged as the post-racial, liberal democratic apocalyptic vision of pluralistic cosmopolitanism gone viral.

But these zombie narratives have yet another function at the boundaries between human and inhuman, legal and illegal, sacred and bare life that exist in the no-man's-land that constitutes the states of nature and exception. Slavoj Žižek diagnoses in the U.S. imprisonment and torture machine a necromantic process in which captured political prisoners are placed "almost literally into the position of the living dead," where they occupy the threshold of *homo sacer.*[7] This state of the living dead, or "the undead," for Žižek, means that the "*differentia specifica* which defines a human being is not the difference between man and animal (or any other real or imaginary species like god), but an *inherent* difference, the difference between human and the inhuman excess that is inherent to being-human."⁸ By evoking Lacan's *lamella* as "the undead object" and identifying it as the "the product of the cut of castration, the *surplus* generated by it," Žižek understands "the undead" therefore as "the wound, the disfiguration/distortion, inflicted upon the body when the body is colonized by the symbolic order."⁹ The tortured captives of Guantánamo become the "living dead" excess to liberal democracy and have been made to bear, through historical juxtaposition and reiterative surplus, the Black Atlantic crossings that created *zombi* as a new world, African-Caribbean anti-imperialist assemblage that was quickly reappropriated by U.S. empire to allegorize its own anxieties about the threats that racial, sexual, and class "contaminants" posed to the nation. The living dead of empire exist within the juridical *corpus nullius* exception that Patrick Wolfe defines as "the ideological continuity that links the effacement of Indian subjecthood to the juridical nullification of Guantánamo Bay detainees."¹⁰

"Historical amnesia," Noam Chomsky writes, "is a dangerous phenomenon, not only because it undermines moral and intellectual integrity, but also because it lays the groundwork for the crimes that lie ahead." In writing about the Bush administration's "torture memos," Chomsky remarks that although the level of "viciousness and deceit of the administration" revealed in the memos is "shocking," it is not surprising, even though many in the media reported that it was. Rather, Chomsky goes on to argue:

> The conquest and settling of the West indeed showed individualism and enterprise. Settler-colonialist enterprises, the cruelest form of imperialism, commonly do. The outcome was hailed by the respected and influential Senator Henry Cabot Lodge in 1898. Calling for intervention in Cuba, Lodge lauded our record "of conquest, colonization, and territorial expansion unequalled by any people in the 19th century," and urged that it is "not to be curbed now," as the Cubans too are pleading with us to come over and help them. Their plea was answered. The US sent troops, thereby preventing Cuba's liberation from Spain and turning it into a virtual colony, as it remained until 1959.¹¹

Mapping the transit of U.S. empire between ongoing settler colonialisms and the twenty-first-century states of exception, one begins to understand why John C. Yoo's infamous March 14, 2003, torture memos cited the 1865

Military Commissions and the 1873 *The Modoc Indian Prisoners* legal opinions in order to articulate executive power in declaring the state of exception, particularly when *The Modoc Indian Prisoners* opinion explicitly marks the Indian combatant as *homo sacer* to the United States:

> It cannot be pretended that a United States soldier is guilty of murder if he kills a public enemy in battle, which would be the case if the municipal law was in force and applicable to an act committed under such circumstances. All the laws and customs of civilized warfare may not be applicable to an armed conflict with the Indian tribes upon our western frontier; but the circumstances attending the assassination of Canby and Thomas are such as to make their murder as much a violation of the laws of savage as of civilized warfare, and the Indians concerned in it fully understood the baseness and treachery of their act.[12]

In other words, the Modoc, and by extension all who can be made "Indian" in the transit of empire, can be killed without being murdered, yet they are held to the standards of U.S. law that make it a crime for such combatants to kill any American soldier. As a result, citizens of American Indian nations become in this moment the origin of the stateless terrorist combatants within U.S. enunciations of sovereignty.

The Modoc, a small northern California tribe whose traditional lands reside near Tule Lake and the Lost River, were in 1864 caught in a matrix created out of the aftermath of the Gold Rush that had brought white, Chinese, and African American settlers into their lands, the U.S. removal policies that were opening up more and more territories for settlement, and the Klamath nation in what is now Oregon, with whom they were supposed to share a reservation. The Modoc signed a treaty that same year in which they agreed to relocate to the Klamath's Oregon reservation, but a year later they complained "that they were treated like second-class citizens" there.[13] A small band, led by Captain Jack, left the reservation to return to their traditional lands and fishing grounds in California. Through a series of events that included treachery, violence, and failed negotiations, Captain Jack was convinced by some of the other Modoc leaders to kill General Edward Canby and two other military agents during peace negotiations in 1873. As a result, Captain Jack and his allies were tried and convicted of murder, and the Modocs were sent as prisoners of war to Indian Territory, where they lived in exile until they returned to the Klamath Reservation in 1909.[14]

Lieutenant General John M. Schofield, who was head of the Pacific Military Division at the time, reflected on the outcome of the Modoc War in his memoir: "If the innocent could be separated from the guilty, 'plague, pestilence, and famine,'" he wrote, "would not be an unjust punishment for the crimes committed in this country against the original occupants of the soil. And it should be remembered that when retribution comes, though we may not understand why, the innocent often share the fate of the guilty. The law under which nations suffer for their crimes does not seem to differ much from the law of retribution which governs the savage Indian."[15] Imagining "plague, pestilence, and famine" raining retribution on the innocent and guilty alike, Schofield presents us with the Indian deferred as zombie attack return of the repressed. Twenty-first-century zombies are no longer a critique of whiteness as conspicuous consumptive death, as Richard Dyer argued in his reading of George A. Romero's zombie films: "Living and dead are indistinguishable, and the zombies' sole raison d'être, to attack and eat the living, has resonances with the behaviour of the living whites."[16] Rather, I am arguing, zombie imperialism is the current manifestation of a liberal democratic colonialism that locates biopower at the intersection of life, death, law, and lawlessness—what Mbembe has termed necropolitics—where death belongs more to racialized and gendered multitudes and killing becomes "precisely targeted."[17]

Stop the World

This book has tried to detail how the United States transits itself transoceanically and transhemispherically through cacophonous representations that arise as the real is stretched through the distortive parallactic effects of empire and collapsed into competing struggles for hegemony. Indianness, within critical, poststructuralist, and postcolonial theories, exists on the threshold between past and present, life and death, and continues—even as it decomposes into an overfilled blank monstrosity of Caliban becoming–zombie—to inflect the metonymic narrative of the U.S. imperial torture state. As apocalyptic narratives of cannibalistic retribution rise to the fore in the early decades of the twenty-first century, the challenge for American Indian and indigenous scholars is to find ways to unmap the logics of conquest that underpin sovereign power conceptualized as the taking of space. The "Indian without ancestry" within Deleuze and Guattari's *A Thousand Plateaus* stops the world through the asignifying Indian Event that is death; and that asignifying "Indianness," reframed through indigenous critical theory, provides conditions of possibility for radical resistance to state formulations. Theorizing against the systematized necropolitics that U.S. empire deploys to manage the world and activating indigenous presences as the point of critical inquiry disrupts the *corpus nullius* juricides that have used Indianness as the cultural and legal precedent to police normativity at the threshold of making the living, dead.

Indigenous scholars engaged in indigenous critical theories that draw from the intellectual traditions of their own histories and communities to contravene in, respond to, and redirect European philosophies can offer crucial new ways of conceptualizing an after to empire that does not reside within the obliteration of indigenous lives, resources, and lands. Indians, as the originary necropolitical affect of the living dead brought back to haunt cosmopolitan colonialism, serve as the deferred melancholia of a lingering sense of retribution that hovers over a nation that forever strives to make native the foreign through an abandonment of the native to the foreign. If, as Donald E. Pease suggests, the state of exception repositions U.S. citizens "within the equivalent to that exceptional space that Justice Marshall had called a 'domestic dependent nation,'" then American Indians may be able to provide some insights into survivability, livability, and alternatives to the nativist sovereignty that carves U.S. homelands out of Indian territory and positions diasporic arrivals as zombie terrorists seeking to consume the proprietary domains of a forever threatened and embattled whiteness.[18] The generic and juridical conventions of terror, which affectively draw upon the deeply engrained colonialist discourses of what Jean M. O'Brien identifies as firsting and lasting, cannot stand in the face of the mnemonics of land, repentance, survivance, differentiation, kinship, and *haksuba* that writers like Wilson Harris, Gerald Vizenor, Joy Harjo, Karen Tei Yamashita, and LeAnne Howe among many others deploy to rewrite the story of the Americas from the other side. Rather than framing justice for American Indians as the fourth horseman accompanying the apocalyptic "plague, pestilence, and famine," it is time to imagine indigenous decolonization as a process that restores life and allows settler, arrivant, and native to apprehend and grieve together the violences of U.S. empire.

Acknowledgments

A book like this only comes into being through the help of many minds and the support of advisors, colleagues, editors, friends, and family who took the time to read, comment, and offer encouragement along the way. I owe a huge debt of gratitude across the Midwest and into the Pacific.

The book has been twelve years in the making and saw its beginnings in my dissertation project for the English department at the University of Iowa. I am grateful to my chair Mary Lou Emery and my advisor Anne Donadey for all their time, advice, and care in mentoring me and sending me off well prepared for a life in the academy. I must also thank Peter Nazareth, Florence Boos, Phillip Round, and Jacki Rand for supporting me in my pursuit of postcolonial theory as a way of addressing indigenous issues.

My career in the academy started with an interdisciplinary shift that was only feasible because of the imaginative, revolutionary, and challenging minds in the political science department at the University of Hawai'i at Mānoa, who were willing to risk hiring a literature scholar to teach Indigenous Politics. I must thank Noenoe Silva first for remembering me after just one meeting, and then for not holding that meeting against me. Noenoe's scholarship and dedication to the Native Hawaiian community have been an inspiration, and I am forever indebted to her for all her *mana'o* and *aloha*. This book would not have existed without all her knowledge. My two years at Hawai'i were amazing, and made all the better for having had the opportunity to draw upon the wealth of intellectual resources offered by my colleagues there, including Petrice Flowers, Jungmin Seo, James Spencer, Hoku Aikau, Jim Dator, Mike Shapiro, Sankaran Krishna, Jon Goldberg-Hiller, Nevi Soguk, Manfred Henningsen, Kathy Ferguson, Monisha Das Gupta, Ty Tengan, Elisa Joy White, Katerina Teaiwa, Robert Sullivan, Albert Wendt, Cindy Franklin, Laura Lyons, Rich Rath, Bianca Isaki, Melisa Casumbal-Salazar, Iokepa Salazar, and so many others.

Giving up such friends on the islands for the landlocked Midwest was one of the most difficult things I've ever done, but the transition was made easier by my colleagues across the Illinois campus community, who have shared their time and support through reading and responding to drafts. Of course, there is LeAnne Howe who I first met in Iowa before joining her anti-mascot opera at Illinois. Her Wagonburner Theatre Troop provided a community on those days when we felt overwhelmed, and her generosity and laughter kept me going through the days after my dad died. If this is a book that he would have been proud of, it is because she was there at every step to read and offer moral support. My colleagues in the American Indian Studies Program, including John McKinn, Debbie Reese, Matthew Sakiestewa Gilbert, Frederick Hoxie, Robert Dale Parker, Brenda Farnell, and Durango Mendoza, have time and again offered their support, knowledge, and careful reading attention and have made me a better scholar for having worked with them. I am also grateful to the Chancellor's Postdoctoral Fellows: Joseph Bauerkemper, Jill Doerfler, Tol Foster, Dustin Tahmahkera, Keith Camacho, and Manu Vimalassery especially gave up valuable time from their own research projects to read, copyedit, and share so generously their own thoughts on the questions at the center of this book.

Above all, I must thank Robert Warrior for his dedicated and tireless leadership of AIS and his vision in building an intellectual community at Illinois and within the larger field of American Indian and indigenous studies. The manuscript workshop he organized for a draft of this book was vital, and he brought together a number of colleagues on campus as well as Elizabeth DeLoughrey and María Josefina Saldaña-Portillo from outside our campus to provide feedback. I cannot thank Robert or them enough for their careful reading of each and every chapter and their serious engagement with my work. Their comments and insights were invaluable as they challenged me to rethink key components of my argument by asking me to clarify and own flat-footedly the interventions this book was seeking to make. I am not quite sure if I accomplished that last bit, but I gave it my best go—all the errors here are my own in spite of the sage advice everyone so generously shared.

I must also thank J. Kēhaulani Kauanui, who provided her *mana'o* and friendship, from the book proposal to the final version—her insights and suggestions have been invaluable. *Mahalo.*

I have wonderful colleagues in the English department here as well who have played a significant role in enriching this project, including Michael Rothberg, Stephanie Foote, Siobhan Somerville, Melissa Littlefield, Curtis Perry, Feisal Mohamed, Spencer Schaffner, Trish Loughren, and Lauren

Goodlad to name only a few who read pieces or full drafts along the way and offered their insights. Much of my initial research was supported by the Ford Foundation and the completion of the project was made possible by the Illinois Program for Research in the Humanities that provided a semester release from teaching and an energizing forum to consider issues of disciplinarity. I particularly thank Dianne Harris and Christine Catanzarite for creating an inspiring space to pursue projects in the humanities. From across the Illinois campus and the broader community of scholars outside Illinois, I have drawn upon and been inspired by a number of colleagues, friends, and students, including Lisa Nakamura, Christian Sandvig, Cris Mayo, Gabriel Solis, Antoinette Burton, Margaret Kelley, Ricky Rodríguez, Heidi Kiiwetinepinesiik Stark, Kevin Washington, Darren and Whitney Renville, Jeani O'Brien, Gwen Westerman, Jane Hafen, Patrice Hollrah, Benjamin, Vicki and Donald Ensor, Rajeswari Sunder Rajan, Aileen Moreton-Robinson, Scott Manning Stevens, Jeff Corntassel, Taiaiake Alfred, Monique Mojica, Leilani Basham, David Shorter, Konrad Ng, Chad Uran, Grant Arndt, Velana Huntington, Lisa Kahaleole Hall, Jessica Cattelino, Russell Benjamin, Gregory O. Hall, Bridget Orr, Larry Zimmerman, Bernadette Hall, Yona Catron, Joann Quiñones, Ashely Tsosie-Mahieu, Sarah Cassinelli, Katie Walkiewicz, and many others I'll wish I had named and thanked. I am also grateful to the First Peoples Initiative and Natasha Varner, the University of Minnesota Press, Alicia R. Sellheim, Mike Stoffel, Danielle M. Kasprzak, and particularly Jason Weidemann for supporting the project from start to finish.

I could not have written this book without my family supporting me every step of the way. To my mom who would always check to see how it was coming, cracking the whip if necessary, to my brothers Matt and Chad and their wives Cherie and Carrie, to my stepmom Phyllis and to my little brother Jay, to my nieces and nephews Sammi, Luke, and James, to my Aunt Kathie and my Uncle Roy, thank you so much for your support and love. And for your patience when I was not always able to be there in Oklahoma or at gatherings because of an ocean or a deadline.

Finally, this book would not have been possible without Elizabeth Tsukahara. All that is good here in this book, and in me, is because of her. She has been with me since the beginning, has traversed oceans with me, and in the process has made life livable in the creases of joy and sadness. She has always believed in me, and the project, no matter how much I tried to convince her otherwise. *Yakoke.*

Notes

Preface

1. Stephen Graham Jones, *Demon Theory* (San Francisco: MacAdam/Cage, 2006).
2. Robert A. Williams Jr., *Like a Loaded Weapon: The Rehnquist Court, Indian Rights, and the Legal History of Racism in America* (Minneapolis: University of Minnesota Press, 2005), 6.
3. *Buffy the Vampire Slayer,* episode no. 4.7, "The Initiative," first broadcast November 16, 1999, by the WB Television Network. Directed by James A. Contner and written by Douglas Petrie and Joss Whedon (creator).
4. Grace Nichols, *I Is a Long-Memoried Woman* (London: Karnak House Press, 1983).

Introduction

1. Steven Salaita, *The Holy Land in Transit: Colonialism and the Quest for Canaan* (Syracuse, N.Y.: Syracuse University Press, 2006), 15.
2. Gerald Vizenor, *Fugitive Poses: Native American Indian Scenes of Absence and Presence* (Lincoln: University of Nebraska Press, 1998), 15–16.
3. For more on indigeneity and prior, see for instance Elizabeth A. Povinelli, "The Governance of the Prior," *Interventions* 13, no. 1 (2011): 13–30; and Mary Louise Pratt, "Afterword: Indigeneity Today," in *Indigenous Experience Today,* ed. Marisol de la Cadena and Orin Starn (New York: Berg Publishers, 2007), 397–404.
4. Judith Butler, *Precarious Life: The Powers of Mourning and Violence* (2004; London: Verso, 2006), 33–34.
5. Aileen Moreton-Robinson, "Writing Off Indigenous Sovereignty: The Discourse of Secularity and Patriarchal White Sovereignty," in *Sovereign Subjects: Indigenous Sovereignty Matters,* ed. Aileen Moreton-Robinson (Crows Nest, NSW: Allen & Unwin, 2007), 89, 95.
6. Gayatri Chakravorty Spivak, *Death of a Discipline* (New York: Columbia University Press, 2003), 82.
7. Audra Simpson, "Paths toward a Mohawk Nation: Narratives of Citizenship and Nationhood in Kahnawake," in *Political Theory and the Rights of Indigenous*

Peoples, ed. Duncan Ivison, Paul Patton, and Will Sanders (Cambridge: Cambridge University Press, 2000), 114.

8. For more on planetarity, see Paul Gilroy, *Postcolonial Melancholia* (New York: Columbia University Press, 2005); Mary Louise Pratt, *Imperial Eyes: Travel Writing and Transculturation* (New York: Routledge, 1992); and Spivak, *Death of a Discipline.*

9. *United States Declaration of Independence.*

10. Jasbir K. Puar, *Terrorist Assemblages: Homonationalism in Queer Times* (Durham, N.C.: Duke University Press, 2007), xvi, 46.

11. *Cherokee Nation v. Georgia* (1831) 30 U.S. 1.

12. Joanne Barker, "For Whom Sovereignty Matters," in *Sovereignty Matters: Locations of Contestation and Possibility in Indigenous Struggles for Self-Determination,* ed. Joanne Barker (Lincoln: University of Nebraska Press, 2005), 14.

13. Ibid., 17.

14. Charles W. Mills, *The Racial Contract* (Ithaca, N.Y.: Cornell University Press, 1997), 20. Italics in original.

15. Vijay Mishra and Bob Hodge, for instance, discuss forms of complicit postcolonialism, particularly settler colonialism, in "What is Post(-)colonialism?" in *Colonial Discourse and Post-colonial Theory: A Reader,* ed. Patrick Williams and Laura Chrisman (New York: Columbia University Press, 1994), 284–85.

16. For more, see Wendy Brown, *States of Injury: Power and Freedom in Late Modernity* (Princeton, N.J.: Princeton University Press, 1995), 27.

17. J. Kēhaulani Kauanui, "Colonialism in Equality: Hawaiian Sovereignty and the Question of Civil Rights," *South Atlantic Quarterly* 107, no. 4 (2008): 635–50; Kauanui, *Hawaiian Blood: Colonialism and the Politics of Sovereignty and Indigeneity* (Durham, N.C.: Duke University Press, 2008); Jean M. O'Brien, *Firsting and Lasting: Writing Indians Out of Existence in New England* (Minneapolis: University of Minnesota Press, 2010); Jill Doerfler, "An Anishinaabe Tribalography: Investigating and Interweaving Conceptions of Identity during the 1910s on the White Earth Reservation," *American Indian Quarterly* 33, no. 3 (Summer 2009): 295–324; and Taiaiake Alfred and Jeff Corntassel, "Being Indigenous: Resurgences against Contemporary Colonialism," *Government and Opposition* 40, no. 4 (2005): 597–614.

18. Lisa Lowe, "The Intimacies of Four Continents," in *Haunted by Empire: Geographies of Intimacy in North American History,* ed. Ann Laura Stoler (Durham, N.C.: Duke University Press, 2006), 206.

19. Ibid., 207.

20. Ibid., 192.

21. Ibid., 206.

22. Ibid., 206.

23. Ibid., 193.

24. Aileen Moreton-Robinson, "Writing off Treaties: White Possession in the United States Critical Whiteness Studies Literature," in *Transnational Whiteness Matters,* ed. Aileen Moreton-Robinson, Maryrose Casey, and Fiona Nicoll (Lanham, Md.: Lexington Books, 2008), 84.

25. See Edward Said, "On Lost Causes," in *Reflections on Exile and Other Essays* (Cambridge, Mass.: Harvard University Press, 2000), 527–53.

26. Daniel Heath Justice, *Our Fire Survives the Storm: A Cherokee Literary History* (Minneapolis: University of Minnesota Press, 2006), 28.

27. LeAnne Howe, "The Chaos of Angels," *Callaloo* 17, no. 1 (1994): 108.

28. Ibid., 108.

29. Ibid., 114.

30. See Dale Turner, *This Is Not a Peace Pipe: Towards a Critical Indigenous Philosophy* (Toronto: University of Toronto Press, 2006); Sandy Grande, *Red Pedagogy: Native American Social and Political Thought* (Lanham, Md.: Rowman and Littlefield, 2004); Robert Warrior, "Native Critics in the World: Edward Said and Nationalism," in Jace Weaver, Craig S. Womack, and Robert Warrior, *American Indian Literary Nationalism* (Albuquerque: University of New Mexico Press, 2006), 179–223; and Chris Andersen, "Critical Indigenous Studies: From Difference to Density," *Cultural Studies Review* 15, no. 2 (September 2009): 80–100.

31. Brendan Hokowhitu, "Indigenous Existentialism and the Body," *Cultural Studies Review* 15, no. 2 (September 2009): 102.

32. Alfred and Corntassel, "Being Indigenous," 597.

33. The number of federally recognized tribes and nations are in flux and the U.S. Federal Register published a supplement on October 27, 2010, to officially list 565 federally recognized tribes after the Shinnecock Indian Nation gained recognition on October 1, 2010: http://www.bia.gov/idc/groups/xraca/documents/text/idc012025.pdf (accessed April 24, 2011).

34. Aileen Moreton-Robinson, "I Still Call Australia Home: Indigenous Belonging and Place in a White Postcolonizing Society," in *Uprootings/Regroundings: Questions of Home and Migration,* ed. Sara Ahmed (Oxford: Berg Publishers, 2003), 31.

35. Robert Warrior, "Native American Scholarship and the Transnational Turn," *Cultural Studies Review* 15, no. 2 (September 2009): 122.

36. Aijaz Ahmad, *In Theory: Classes, Nations, Literatures* (London: Verso, 1994); E. San Juan Jr., *Beyond Postcolonial Theory* (New York: St. Martin's Press, 1998); Benita Perry, "Problems in Current Theories of Colonial Discourse," *Oxford Literary Review* 9, nos. 1–2 (1987): 27–58; Anne McClintock, "The Angel of Progress: Pitfalls of the Term 'Post-Colonialism,'" *Social Text* no. 31/32 (1992): 84–98; Ella Shohat, "Notes on the 'Post-Colonial,'" *Social Text* no. 31/32 (1992): 99–113; and Arif Dirlik, "The Postcolonial Aura: Third World Criticism in the Age of Global Capitalism," *Critical Inquiry* 20, no. 2 (1994): 328–56.

37. Gayatri Chakravorty Spivak, *A Critique of Postcolonial Reason: Toward a*

History of the Vanishing Present (Cambridge, Mass.: Harvard University Press, 1999), 255–56.

38. Eric Cheyfitz, "The (Post)Colonial Predicament of Native American Studies," *Interventions* 4, no. 3 (2002): 406.

39. Ibid.

40. Teresia Teaiwa, "On Analogies: Rethinking the Pacific in a Global Context," *Contemporary Pacific* 18, no. 1 (2006): 73.

41. Teresia Teaiwa, "Native Thoughts: A Pacific Studies Take on Cultural Studies and Diaspora," in *Indigenous Diasporas and Dislocations*, ed. Graham Harvey and Charles D. Thompson Jr (Burlington, Vt.: Ashgate, 2005), 19.

42. For instance, in their conclusion to *De-Scribing Empire: Post-colonialism and Textuality*, ed. Chris Tiffin and Alan Lawson (London: Routledge, 1994), Tiffin and Lawson argue that "the invasive difference of colonial experience is observed nowhere more acutely than in that ambivalent figure, the settler subject.... the male settler is part of the imperial enterprise, its agent, and its beneficiary, without ever acquiring more than associate membership of the imperial club. He is both mediator and mediated, excluded from the unmediated authority of Empire and from the unmediated authenticity of the indigene" (231).

43. Moreton-Robinson, "I Still Call Australia Home," 30–31.

44. Spivak, *Death of a Discipline*, 80–81; Mahasweta Devi, "The Author in Conversation," *Imaginary Maps*, trans. and ed. Gayatri Chakravorty Spivak (New York: Routledge, 1995), xi.

45. Jace Weaver, "Indigenousness and Indigeneity," in *A Companion to Postcolonial Studies*, ed. Henry Schwarz and Sangeeta Ray (Malden, Mass.: Blackwell, 2000), 224.

46. Anna Lowenhaupt Tsing, *Friction: An Ethnography of Global Connection* (Princeton, N.J.: Princeton University Press, 2005), 9.

47. Sankaran Krishna, *Globalization and Postcolonialism: Hegemony and Resistance in the Twenty-first Century* (Lanham, Md.: Rowman and Littlefield, 2009), 122–23.

48. Gaurav Desai, "Editor's Column: The End of Postcolonial Theory? A Roundtable with Sunil Agnani, Fernando Coronil, Gaurav Desai, Mamadou Diouf, Simon Gikandi, Susie Tharu, and Jennifer Wenzel," *PMLA* 122, no. 3 (May 2007): 642.

49. Spivak, *A Critique of Postcolonial Reason*, 255.

50. Linda Tuhiwai Smith's *Decolonizing Methodologies: Research and Indigenous Peoples* (London: Zed Books, 1999), for instance, provides a sustained discussion of possible ways to indigenize research practices to be more responsive and accountable to indigenous communities.

51. Vizenor, *Fugitive Poses*, 15.

52. Ibid., 211.

1. Is and Was

1. Nicholas Thomas, *Cook: The Extraordinary Voyages of Captain James Cook* (New York: Walker and Co., 2003), 16.

2. R. J. Bray, "Australia and the Transit of Venus," *Proceedings of the Astronomical Society of Australia* 4, no. 1 (1980): 114–29.

3. Thomas, *Cook*, 17.

4. See especially Aileen Moreton-Robinson, "White Possession: The Legacy of Cook's Choice," in *Imagined Australia: Reflections around the Reciprocal Construction of Identity between Australia and Europe*, ed. Renata Summo-O'Connell (Bern: Peter Lang, 2009), 27–42.

5. See Marshall Sahlins, *How "Natives" Think: About Captain Cook, for Example* (Chicago: University of Chicago Press, 1995) and Gananath Obeyesekere, *The Apotheosis of Captain Cook: European Mythmaking in the Pacific* (1992; repr., Princeton, N.J.: Princeton University Press, 1997).

6. Noenoe K. Silva, *Aloha Betrayed: Native Hawaiian Resistance to American Colonialism* (Durham, N.C.: Duke University Press, 2004), 19.

7. For further discussion of the deterritorialized sovereignty of globalization that is empire, see Michael Hardt and Antonio Negri, *Empire* (Cambridge, Mass.: Harvard University Press, 2000).

8. Ibid., xi.

9. Amy Kaplan, "Left Alone with America: The Absence of Empire in the Study of American Culture," in *Cultures of United States Imperialism*, ed. Amy Kaplan and Donald E. Pease (Durham, N.C.: Duke University Press, 1993), 12–13.

10. Ibid., 17.

11. Peter Hulme, "Including America," *ARIEL* 26, no. 1 (1995): 118–19.

12. Martin Luther King Jr., "I Have a Dream," speech, Washington, D.C., August 28, 1963, in *A Testament of Hope: The Essential Writings and Speeches of Martin Luther King Jr.*, ed. James M. Washington (New York: HarperCollins, 1991), 218.

13. Achille Mbembe, "Necropolitics," trans. Libby Meintjes, *Public Culture* 15, no. 1 (2003): 11–40, offers necropolitics as a delineation of Foucault's biopower that deploys governmentality and sovereignty as the right to kill.

14. Jasbir K. Puar, *Terrorist Assemblages: Homonationalism in Queer Times* (Durham, N.C.: Duke University Press, 2007), 2.

15. Judith Butler, *Frames of War: When Is Life Grievable?* (London: Verso, 2009), 132.

16. Gilroy, *Postcolonial Melancholia*, 2.

17. Hulme, "Including America," 122.

18. Jacques Derrida, "Force and Signification," in *Writing and Difference*, trans. Alan Bass (Chicago: University of Chicago Press, 1978), 3.

19. Ibid., 29.

20. Ibid., 11.

21. Ibid., 8.

22. Spivak, *A Critique of Postcolonial Reason*, 430.

23. Ibid., 423.

24. Jacques Derrida, "Freud and the Scene of Writing," in *Writing and Difference*, 212.

25. Ibid., 197.

26. Vizenor, *Fugitive Poses*, 35.

27. Ibid., 4.

28. Slavoj Žižek, *In Defense of Lost Causes* (London: Verso, 2008), 272.

29. Jacques Derrida, *The Work of Mourning*, ed. Pascale-Anne Brault and Michael Naas, trans. Pascale-Anne Brault (Chicago: University of Chicago Press, 2003), 65.

30. David Kazanjian, *The Colonizing Trick: National Culture and Imperial Citizenship in Early America* (Minnesota: University of Minnesota Press, 2003), 155.

31. Vizenor, *Fugitive Poses,* 35.

32. For more on Pacific Islander epistemological practices of *tatau, moko*, and *uhi*, see Juniper Ellis, *Tattooing the World: Pacific Designs in Print and Skin* (New York: Columbia University Press, 2008); Ngahuia Te Awekotuku, *Mau Moko: The World of Māori Tattoo* (Honolulu: University of Hawai'i Press, 2008); and Albert Wendt, "Afterword: Tatauing the Post-Colonial Body," in *Inside Out: Literature, Cultural Politics, and Identity in the New Pacific*, ed. Vilsoni Hereniko and Rob Wilson (Lanham, Md.: Rowman and Littlefield, 1999), 399–412. Southeastern Chickasaw and Choctaw also had tattooing traditions pre- and post-contact. Some of the tattoos included clan, *iksa*, designations, genealogical information, as well as battle honors. Some Choctaw tattooed the corners of their mouths blue. One possible word for tattooing in Choctaw is *inchunwa*, though most of the anthropological data on Southeastern body scriptings uses "tattoo." For more information, see James Adair, *The History of the American Indians* (1775; Tuscaloosa: University of Alabama Press, 2005); and John R. Swanton, *Source Material for the Social and Ceremonial Life of the Choctaw Indians* (1931; Tuscaloosa: University of Alabama Press, 2001).

33. Moreton-Robinson, "White Possession," 27.

34. See Giorgio Agamben, *State of Exception*, trans. Kevin Atell (Chicago: University of Chicago Press, 2005), 1–32; Lauren Berlant, "Cruel Optimism," *differences* 17, no. 5 (2006): 21–36 and "Slow Death (Sovereignty, Obesity, Lateral Agency)," *Critical Inquiry* 33, no. 4 (2007): 754–780; Brown, *States of Injury*, 174–96; Achille Mbembe, *On the Postcolony* (Berkeley: University of California Press, 2001), 66–94; and Elizabeth Povinelli, *The Cunning of Recognition: Indigenous Alterities and the Making of Australian Multiculturalism* (Durham, N.C.: Duke University Press, 2002), 1–34.

35. Philip J. Deloria, "Broadway and Main: Crossroads, Ghost Roads, and Paths to an American Studies Future," *America Quarterly* 61, no. 1 (2009): 11.

36. Gilles Deleuze and Félix Guattari, *A Thousand Plateaus: Capitalism and Schizophrenia,* trans. Brian Massumi (Minneapolis: University of Minnesota Press, 1987), 98.

37. Ibid., 19.

38. Ibid., 20.

39. I use Janus America here to expand on Deleuze and Guattari's formulation of an America that puts its west in its east and its east in its west. The phrase signals the bidirectional discord of imperialism that the United States deploys to manage its imperial projects. In *The Break-up of Britain: Crisis and Neoliberalism* (Altona, Australia: Common Ground, 2003), Tom Nairn discusses "The Modern Janus" as a form of nationalism that looks to the past and to the future to cohere the nation.

40. Amy Kaplan, *The Anarchy of Empire in the Making of U.S. Culture* (Cambridge, Mass.: Harvard University Press, 2002), 18.

41. Ibid., 18.

42. Ibid.

43. In "The Significance of the Frontier in American History," given first as a speech at the World's Columbian Exposition in 1893 and published in 1921. See the University of Virginia's Hypertext Projects, which reproduces the 1921 publication: http://xroads.virginia.edu/~Hyper/TURNER/chapter1.html (accessed January 13, 2010).

44. Michael J. Shapiro, *Cinematic Political Thought: Narrating Race, Nation, and Gender* (Edinburgh: Edinburgh University Press, 1999), 93.

45. Ibid., 22.

46. Louis Owens, *I Hear the Train: Reflections, Inventions, Refractions* (Norman: University of Oklahoma Press, 2001), 207.

47. Gilles Deleuze, "What Children Say," in *Essays Critical and Clinical,* trans. Daniel W. Smith and Michael A. Greco (Minneapolis: University of Minnesota Press, 1997), 64.

48. Deleuze and Guattari, *A Thousand Plateaus,* 12.

49. Ibid., 20.

50. Spivak, *A Critique of Postcolonial Reason,* 255.

51. Ibid., 279.

52. Deleuze and Guattari, *A Thousand Plateaus,* 115.

53. Ibid., 117.

54. Ibid., 116.

55. Ibid., 113.

56. Christopher L. Miller, "The Postidentitarian Predicament in the Footnotes of *A Thousand Plateaus*: Nomadology, Anthropology, and Authority," *diacritics* 23, no. 3 (1993): 19.

57. The phrase "we are the ones we've be waiting for" is more properly attributed to June Jordan, "Poem for South African Women," *Passion: New Poems, 1977–1980* (Boston: Beacon Press, 1980), 42–43. However, according to Mary Francis Berry, Theodore C. Sorenson, and Josh Gottheimer, *Power in Words: The Stories behind Barack Obama's Speeches from the State House to the White House* (Boston: Beacon Press, 2010), Barack Obama's speech writer Jon Favreau took inspiration for the line from Maria Shriver's evocation of the new age prophecy issued by the anonymous Hopi "elders of Oraibi" in many of the speeches she gave as first lady of California. While "some commentators attributed the line to the late black feminist poet June Jordan," they write, "Favreau, however, said that he borrowed the line from Maria Shriver, a member of the Kennedy clan who had endorsed Obama a week earlier" (170). For more on Shriver's use of the "Hopi Prayer," see Jodi A. Byrd, "'In the City of Blinding Lights': Indigeneity, Cultural Studies, and the Errants of Colonial Nostalgia," *Cultural Studies Review* 15, no. 2 (September 2009): 13–28.

58. Deleuze and Guattari, *A Thousand Plateaus,* 116.

59. Ibid.

60. Giorgio Agamben, *Homo Sacer,* trans. Daniel Heller-Roazen (1995; Stanford, Calif.: Stanford University Press, 1998). See for instance, Scott Richard Lyons, *X-Marks: Native Signatures of Assent* (Minneapolis: University of Minnesota, 2010) and Robert Warrior's essay "Native Critics in the World," in Weaver, Womack, and Warrior, *American Indian Literary Nationalism,* 179–223, for cautions against the excesses of nationalism that turn on faciality and regimentation.

61. Deleuze and Guattari, *A Thousand Plateaus,* 282–83.

62. Of Carlos Castaneda's faux and fictional narrative of encounter with Yaqui Don Juan, Philip J. Deloria writes, "This brand of countercultural spiritualism rarely engaged real Indians, for it was not only unnecessary but inconvenient to do so. . . . Even in the quest for fixed meaning, Indian people were basically irrelevant. Indianness—even when imagined as something essential—could be captured and marketed as a text, largely divorced from Indian oversight and questions of authorship." *Playing Indian* (New Haven, Conn.: Yale University Press, 1998), 169–70.

63. Deleuze and Guattari, *A Thousand Plateaus,* 138–39.

64. Ibid., 139.

65. Ibid., 117.

66. Brian Massumi, *Parables of the Virtual: Movement, Affect, Sensation* (Durham, N.C.: Duke University Press, 2002), 19.

67. Arun Saldanha, "Reontologising Race: The Machinic Geography of Phenotype," *Environment and Planning D: Society and Space* 24 (2006): 20–21.

68. Puar, *Terrorist Assemblages,* 222.

69. Moreton-Robinson, "I Still Call Australia Home," 30–31.

70. For more on errant, see Slavoj Žižek, "'Ode to Joy,' Followed by Chaos and Despair," *New York Times,* December 24, 2007, http://www.nytimes.com/2007/12/24/opinion/24zizek.html (accessed February 6, 2010).

71. Puar, *Terrorist Assemblages,* xviii; on September 18, 2001, the *New York Post* ran a story that took inspiration from President Bush's evocation of Wild West rhetoric when he said he wanted Osama bin Laden "dead or alive." The story provided Wanted posters of famous "outlaws" alongside bin Laden, including Chiricahua Apache leader Geronimo, who, according to the article, "raided settlements for a decade." For more, see Robert Hardt Jr., "Terror Big in Bad Company," *New York Post,* September 18, 2001, http://www.nypost.com/p/news/terror_big_in_bad_company_ksyBEqm7s3oHoVRvkZqRZK (accessed May 2, 2011). That association of Osama bin Laden with Geronimo solidified into popular imagination and military code, and on May 2, 2011, U.S. journalists began to report that the manhunt for Osama bin Laden was over when President Obama heard "We've IDed Geronimo" and "Geronimo, E KIA." See Michael Scherer, "After Uncertainty, a Moment of Triumph in the Situation Room: 'We've IDed Geronimo,'" *Time Swampland,* May 2, 2011, http://www.swampland.time.com/2011/05/02/inside-the-situation-room-weve-idd-geronimo/ (accessed May 2, 2011), and Mark Mazzetti, Helene Cooper, and Peter Baker, "Behind the Hunt for Bin Laden," *New York Times* May 2, 2011, http://www.nytimes.com/2011/5/03/world/asia/03intel.html (accessed May 2, 2011), for more on the Geronimo code word usage in the operation to kill Osama bin Laden. Although journalists attempted to damage-control the association of bin Laden with Geronimo by suggesting that Geronimo was code for the operation and not bin Laden himself, President Obama made clear in his *60 Minutes* appearance to discuss the death of bin Laden that "there was a point before folks had left, before we had gotten everybody back on the helicopter and were flying back to base, where they said Geronimo has been killed. And Geronimo was the code name for bin Laden." President Barack Obama, interviewed by Steve Kroft, "The Complete Interview," *60 Minutes Overtime,* May 8, 2011, http://www.cbsnews.com/8301-504803_162-20060530-10391709.html.

72. Ibid., 90. Paul Gilroy, in *Darker than Blue* (Cambridge, Mass.: Belknap Press of Harvard University Press, 2010), discusses how the U.S. military represents cultural diversity "more comprehensively than any other institution." Shoshana Johnson, also part of the same unit as Lori Piestewa and Jessica Lynch, was the first African American woman in U.S. military history to be held as a prisoner of war. "What kind of measure of America's racial nomos," Gilroy asks, "do these discrepancies suggest? Was a degree of conviviality produced by the humanizing powers of class and gender solidarity, interdependence, and ordinary transcultural contact perhaps evident among these American women in the multicultural belly of the military beast?" (165–66). Jessica Lynch named her daughter Dakota in honor of her Hopi friend Piestewa. What kind of nomos exists in that intimacy?

73. Puar, *Terrorist Assemblages*, 38–39.

74. Gilles Deleuze, *The Logic of Sense*, trans. Mark Lester, ed. Constantin K. Boundas (1990; repr., London: Continuum Books, 2004), 169.

75. Derrida, *The Work of Mourning*, 192.

76. Deleuze, *The Logic of Sense*, 170.

77. Ibid., 194; Howe, "Chaos of Angels," 108.

78. Cyrus Byington, John Reed Swanton, and Henry Sale Halbert, eds., *A Dictionary of the Choctaw Language* (Washington, D.C.: Smithsonian Institution, 1915), 133.

79. Joy Harjo, "The Place the Musician Became a Bear," *The Woman Who Fell from the Sky* (New York: W.W. Norton, 2004), 51.

80. Mark Twain, *Roughing It* (1872; Berkeley: University of California Press, 1993), 489–90.

81. Ibid., 490, 491.

82. Brandy Nālani McDougall, "On Cooking Captain Cook," in *The Salt-Wind: Ka Makani Pa'akai* (Honolulu, Hawai'i: Kuleana 'Oiwi Press, 2008), 52.

83. Thomas, *Cook*, 17.

84. Sunera Thobani, *Exalted Subjects: Studies in the Making of Race and Nation in Canada* (Toronto: University of Toronto Press, 2007), 9.

85. Moreton-Robinson, "White Possession," 28–32.

86. Twain, *Roughing It*, 490.

87. See Edward G. Gray, *The Making of John Ledyard: Empire and Ambition in the Life of an Early American Traveler* (New Haven, Conn.: Yale University Press, 2007).

88. In a letter to John Adams dated April 8, 1816, Thomas Jefferson writes about Ledyard and his plan "to go to Kamschatka, and cross over thence to the Western coast of America, in order to penetrate across our continent in the opposite direction to that afterwards adopted for Lewis and Clarke" (Thomas Jefferson, *Jefferson: Political Writings*, ed. Joyce Appleby and Terence Ball [Cambridge: Cambridge University Press, 1999], 49–50).

89. Mark Twain, *Letters from Hawaii*, ed. A. Grove Day (1966; Honolulu: University of Hawai'i Press, 1975), 219.

90. Kaplan, *The Anarchy of Empire*, 52.

91. Ibid., 91.

92. Ned Blackhawk, *Violence over the Land: Indians and Empires in the Early American West* (Cambridge, Mass.: Harvard University Press, 2006), 275.

93. Twain, *Roughing It*, 129.

94. Mark Twain, "Our Fellow Savages of the Sandwich Islands," Paul Fatout's Composite Text from *Mark Twain Speaking, 1869–1870*, http://etext.virginia.edu/railton/onstage/savlect2.html (accessed February 7, 2010).

95. Ibid.

96. John Ledyard, *The Last Voyage of Captain Cook: The Collected Writings of*

John Ledyard, ed. James Zug (Washington, D.C.: National Geographic Society, 2005), 98–99.

97. George E. Lankford, *Reachable Stars: Patterns in the Ethnoastronomy of Eastern North America* (Tuscaloosa: University of Alabama Press, 2007), 226–39.

98. Pratt, *Imperial Eyes,* 39–40.

99. Eli Maor, *Venus in Transit* (2000; Princeton, N.J.: Princeton University Press, 2004), 94–96.

100. Ibid., 44–45.

101. Slavoj Žižek, *The Parallax View* (Cambridge, Mass.: MIT Press, 2006), 4.

102. Ibid., 10.

103. Ibid., 281.

104. Ibid., 4. See Žižek's note 25 on page 391 for his critique of hybridity and nomad subjectivity in relation to the parallax gap.

105. Jodi Dean, *Žižek's Politics* (New York: Taylor and Francis Group, 2006), 54.

106. Slavoj Žižek, *First as Tragedy, Then as Farce* (London: Verso, 2009), 154.

107. Alexis de Tocqueville, *Democracy in America,* trans. Henry Reeve (1838; New York: The Colonial Press, 1900), 1:346.

108. Michelle Obama, 2009 Commencement Speech (University of California–Merced, Merced, Calif., May 16, 2009). Transcript at http://www.huffingtonpost.com/2009/05/16/michelle-obama-commenceme_n_204302.html (accessed February 7, 2010).

109. Berlant, "Cruel Optimism," 21.

110. Ibid.

111. Ibid., 35.

112. Ibid., 23.

113. Ibid., 33.

114. Ibid., 34.

115. Ibid., 35.

116. Geoff Ryman, *Was: A Novel* (New York: Penguin, 1992), 209.

117. Ibid., 215.

118. Ibid., 60.

119. Ibid., 246.

120. L. Frank Baum, "Editorial," *Aberdeen Saturday Pioneer,* December 20, 1890, and January 3, 1891.

121. Berlant, "Slow Death," 754.

122. Butler, *Frames of War,* 96–97.

2. "This Island's Mine"

1. Jacques Rancière, *The Politics of Aesthetics: The Distribution of the Sensible,* trans. Gabriel Rockhill (London: Continuum Press, 2004), 39.

2. Rob Nixon, "Caribbean and African Appropriations of *The Tempest,*" *Critical Inquiry* 13, no. 3 (1987): 576.

3. Ania Loomba, *Shakespeare, Race, and Colonialism* (Oxford: Oxford University Press, 2002), 165.

4. William Sanders, "The Undiscovered," collected in *East of the Sun and West of Fort Smith* (Winnetka, Calif.: Norilana Books, 2008), 64.

5. Coco Fusco, *English Is Broken Here: Notes on Cultural Fusion in the Americas* (New York: New Press, 1995), 39.

6. Ibid.

7. Ibid., 44.

8. Ibid., 50.

9. Diana Taylor, *The Archive and the Repertoire: Performing Cultural Memory in the Americas* (Durham, N.C.: Duke University Press, 2003), 66.

10. Fusco, *English Is Broken Here,* 6.

11. Ibid., 7.

12. Taylor, *The Archive and the Repertoire,* 71.

13. Mikhail Bakhtin, "From the Prehistory of Novelistic Discourse," in *The Dialogic Imagination: Four Essays,* ed. Michael Holquist, trans. Caryl Emerson and Michael Holquist (Austin: University of Texas Press, 1981), 51, 55.

14. Ibid., 61.

15. José Esteban Muñoz, *Disidentifications: Queers of Color and the Performance of Politics* (Minneapolis: University of Minnesota Press, 1999), 187–88.

16. Fusco, *English Is Broken Here,* 40.

17. Mikhail Bakhtin, *Rabelais and His World,* trans. Hélène Iswolsky (Bloomington: Indiana University Press, 1984), 305.

18. Taylor, *The Archive and the Repertoire,* 74–75.

19. Ibid., 72.

20. Fusco, *English Is Broken Here,* 50.

21. Ibid., 53.

22. Ibid.

23. Ibid., 59. This parenthetical note on the use of surveillance cameras was supposed to highlight the irony of the placard and raise suspicions among the audience members. However, it is interesting to note that MTV's *The Real World* started the same year as Fusco and Gómez-Peña's performance and that a growing market for voyeuristic reality television ever since has naturalized the presence of cameras filming the everyday.

24. Linda Hutcheon, *Irony's Edge: The Theory and Politics of Irony* (New York: Routledge, 1995), 180.

25. James Luna, "The Artifact Piece," in *The Sound of Rattles and Clappers: A Collection of New California Indian Writing,* ed. Greg Sarris (Tucson: University of Arizona Press, 1994), 33.

26. Jean Fisher, "In Search of the 'Inauthentic': Disturbing Signs in Contemporary Native American Art," *Art Journal* 51, no. 3 (Fall 1992): 48.

27. Ibid., 192.

28. Scott Manning Stevens, "Mother Tongues and Native Voices: Linguistic Fantasies in the Age of the Encounter," in *Telling the Stories: Essays on American Indian Literatures and Cultures,* ed. by Elizabeth Hoffman Nelson and Malcolm A. Nelson (New York: Peter Lang, 2001), 14.

29. Fusco, *English Is Broken Here,* 59–60.

30. See Vine Deloria Jr. for an engagement with the Buckskin Curtain in *Red Earth, White Lies* (Golden, Colo.: Fulcrum Press, 1997), in which he argues against the common misconception on the part of mainstream anthropologists and others that native peoples arrived in the Americas from Asia by way of the Bering Strait.

31. The early 1990s saw a proliferation of movies like *Rising Sun* (1993), in which anxieties over Japan's growing economic and technological presence in the global economy were played out in popular culture.

32. Homi K. Bhabha, *The Location of Culture* (London: Routledge, 1994), 37.

33. Ibid., 39.

34. Ibid., 37.

35. Anne McClintock, *Imperial Leather: Race, Gender, and Sexuality in the Colonial Context* (New York: Routledge, 1995), 64.

36. Michael Rothberg, *Multidirectional Memory: Remembering the Holocaust in the Age of Decolonization* (Stanford, Calif.: Stanford University Press, 2009), 3.

37. Žižek, *The Parallax View,* 20.

38. Chadwick Allen, *Blood Narrative: Indigenous Identity in American Indian and Maori Literary and Activist Texts* (Durham, N.C.: Duke University Press, 2002), 9.

39. William Shakespeare, *The Tempest,* ed. Frank Kermode (London: Routledge, 1987), II.ii.24–37.

40. Fusco, *English Is Broken Here,* 42.

41. Ronald Takaki, *A Different Mirror: A History of Multicultural America* (Boston: Little, Brown and Company, 1993), 32.

42. Bill Ashcroft, Gareth Griffiths, and Helen Tiffin, *The Empire Writes Back: Theory and Practice in Post-Colonial Literatures* (London: Routledge, 1989), 190.

43. See, for instance, Alden T. Vaughan and Virginia Mason Vaughan, *Shakespeare's Caliban: A Cultural History* (Cambridge: Cambridge University Press, 1991).

44. Vaughan and Vaughan, *Shakespeare's Caliban,* 120.

45. Ibid., 118. A significant amount of work places *The Tempest* in the Americas, including Peter Hulme's *Colonial Encounters: Europe and the Native Caribbean, 1492–1797* (London: Routledge, 1992); Ronald Takaki's essay, "*The Tempest* in the Wilderness: The Racialization of Savagery," *Journal of American History* 79, no. 3 (1992): 892–912; and Roberto Fernández Retamar's *Caliban and Other Essays,* trans. Edward Baker (Minneapolis: University of Minnesota Press, 1989), among others. As for the indigenous origins of Ariel's songs, Harold Bloom speculates

after Frank Kermode in his *Bloom's Shakespeare through the Ages: The Tempest* (New York: Infobase Publishing, 2008), that "the curious 'Bowgh, wawgh' refrain in Ariel's first song" might be from "a contemporary account of an Indian dance" (193). "Bowgh, wawgh" in the song refers to barking dogs.

46. Vaughan and Vaughan, *Shakespeare's Caliban*, 131–32.

47. Thomas Cartelli, *Repositioning Shakespeare: National Formations, Postcolonial Appropriations* (New York: Routledge, 1999), 2.

48. José Enrique Rodó, *Ariel*, trans. Margaret Sayers Peden (Austin: University of Texas Press, 1988), 31.

49. Octave Mannoni, *Prospero and Caliban: The Psychology of Colonization* (Ann Arbor: University of Michigan Press, 1990).

50. Retamar, *Caliban and Other Essays*, 14.

51. Ibid., 9, 14.

52. Aimé Césaire, *A Tempest*, trans. Richard Miller (1969; New York: Theatre Communications Group, 2002), 26.

53. Shakespeare, *The Tempest*, II.ii.184–85; Kamau Brathwaite, *The Arrivants: A New World Trilogy* (Oxford: Oxford University Press, 1973), 192.

54. Abena P. A. Busia, "Silencing Sycorax: On African Colonial Discourse and the Unvoiced Female," *Cultural Critique* 14 (Winter 1989–90): 85, 99.

55. Shakespeare, *The Tempest*, III.ii.132–34.

56. Ibid., 108.

57. Ibid., 107.

58. Hulme, *Colonial Encounters*, 3.

59. Ibid., 109.

60. Barbara Fuchs, "Conquering Islands: Contextualizing *The Tempest*," *Shakespeare Quarterly* 48, no. 1 (1997): 45–46.

61. Ibid., 62.

62. Fusco, *English Is Broken Here*, 47.

63. Paul Chaat Smith, *Everything You Know about Indians Is Wrong* (Minneapolis: University of Minnesota Press, 2009), 26.

64. Edward Said, *Orientalism* (New York: Vintage, 1979).

65. Spivak, *A Critique of Postcolonial Reason*, 117.

66. Ibid., 118.

67. Ibid., 211, 118.

68. Ibid., 211.

69. Ibid., 423–24.

70. Ibid., 426.

71. Bakhtin, *Rabelais*, 26.

72. Shakespeare, *The Tempest*, II.ii.1–108; Fuchs, "Conquering Islands" 48.

73. Shakespeare, *The Tempest*, II.ii.39.

74. Fuchs, "Conquering Islands," 48.

75. The *Oxford English Dictionary* defines "gaberdine" as follows: "b. As a garment

worn by Jews, perh. orig. a reminiscence of Shakespeare's phrase. 1596 Shaks. *Merch.* I.iii.113 You . . . spet upon my Jewish gaberdine" (*OED*, second edition 1991, 302). In *Shakespeare, Race, and Colonialism,* Ania Loomba notes the overlap between Irish and Jewish gaberdine that transform vocabularies across literary contexts (167).

76. George Lamming, *The Pleasures of Exile* (Ann Arbor: University of Michigan Press, 1992), 109.

77. Spivak, *A Critique of Postcolonial Reason,* 303.

78. Ibid., 305n.

79. Ibid., 154.

80. For more on Baudelaire and afterimage see Walter Benjamin, "On Some Motifs in Baudelaire," in *Illuminations: Essays and Reflections,* trans Harry Zohn, ed. Hannah Arendt (New York: Schocken, 1968), 155–200. Benjamin argues that Henri Bergson's philosophy provides a clue to Baudelaire's poetics: "In shutting out this experience the eye perceives an experience of a complementary nature in the form of its spontaneous afterimage, as it were. Bergson's philosophy represents an attempt to give the details of this afterimage and to fix it as a permanent record. His philosophy thus indirectly furnishes a clue to the experience which presented itself to Baudelaire's eyes in its undistorted version in the figure of his reader" (157).

81. Louis Owens, "As If an Indian Were Really an Indian," in *I Hear the Train,* 224.

82. Jack D. Forbes, *The American Discovery of Europe* (Urbana: University of Illinois Press, 2007), 11–21.

83. John Cummins, *The Voyage of Christopher Columbus* (London: Weidenfeld and Nicolson, 1992), 17–18; Miles H. Davidson, *Columbus Then and Now: A Life Reexamined* (Norman: University of Oklahoma Press, 1997), 109–12.

84. Cummins, *The Voyage of Christopher Columbus,* 17. See also John F. Moffitt and Santiago Sebastián, *O Brave New People: The European Invention of the American Indian* (Albuquerque: University of New Mexico Press, 1998), 242.

85. Gerald Vizenor, *Manifest Manners: Postindian Warriors of Survivance* (Hanover, N.H.: Wesleyan University Press, 1994), 11.

86. See Taiaiake Alfred, *Peace, Power, Righteousness: An Indian Manifesto* (Oxford: Oxford University Press, 1999.) Alfred notes that at the time of Columbus's voyage, "India" was still referred to as "Hindustan" (xxvi).

87. Jack D. Forbes, *Africans and Native Americans: The Language of Race and the Evolution of Red–Black Peoples* (Urbana: University of Illinois Press, 1993), 2–3.

88. See Kim F. Hall, *Things of Darkness: Economies of Race and Gender in Early Modern England* (Ithaca, N.Y.: Cornell University Press, 1995). Hall suggests that many of the texts of Early Modern England depended upon a confusion or conflation between the West Indies, India, Africa, and the Americas (80–81, 85n).

89. Smith, *Everything You Know about Indians Is Wrong,* 17.

90. Fusco, *English Is Broken Here,* 62.

91. Ibid., 48.

3. The Masks of Conquest

1. *Stabroek News,* "Remembering Jonestown," November 22, 1998, http://www.guyana.org/features/jonestown_20.html (accessed October 18, 2011).

2. Neville Annibourne, "Remembering Jonestown," *Stabroek News,* December 10, 2008, http://www.stabroeknews.com/2008/guyana-review/12/10/remembering-jonestown/ (accessed October 18, 2011).

3. Provenance for the phrase "drinking the Kool-Aid" is a bit hard to track. Some argue it is a reference to Ken Kesey and the Merry Pranksters immortalized in Tom Wolfe's *The Electric Kool-Aid Acid Test* (New York: Picador, 1968) and certainly such earlier iterations of "Kool-Aid" inform its usage to critique the LSD, hippie 1960s and 1970s. The first use of "drinking the Kool-Aid" inside the Beltway appears in the *Washington Post,* "Dick Gephardt's Weekend Whirl; 125 Constituents Pay $850 Each for the Congressman's Washington Tour," September 23, 1985, which quotes Don Foley explaining that Gephardt's campaign manager did not want "what I call the politics of Jim Jones, you know, that 'let's drink the Kool-Aid' kind of downer" to predominate the congressman's tour. *Oxford English Dictionary* identifies the phrase's etymology as tied to Jonestown and not Ken Kesey.

4. Rebecca Moore, *Understanding Jonestown and Peoples Temple* (Westport, Conn.: Praeger Publishers, 2009), 119.

5. Žižek, *The Parallax View,* 19.

6. Moore, *Understanding Jonestown,* 6.

7. Ibid., 6.

8. See Moore, *Understanding Jonestown* (13), for more on adoption within Peoples Temple, and especially Jim Jones's transnational and interracial additions to his own family in the 1950s.

9. Fred D'Aguiar, *Bill of Rights* (London: Chatto and Windus, 1998), 74.

10. Ibid., 1.

11. See, for instance, the Guyana Ministry of Amerindian Affairs' brochure, *The New Amerindian Act: What Will It Do for Amerindians?* Distributed by the Guyana Government Information Agency (http://www.Amerindian.gov.gy/documents/AmerindianAct_Briefing.pdf), the brochure explains the "special rights" delineated for Amerindian communities within the Amerindian Act of 2005 that secures communal land tenure for Amerindian communities and ensures that sub-surface rights are retained by the nation-state (11). The Amerindian Act passed the National Assembly, and President Bharrat Jagdeo assented to the bill on March 14, 2006.

12. Moore, *Understanding Jonestown,* 6.

13. Tim Reiterman, *Raven: The Untold Story of the Rev. Jim Jones and His People* (1982; repr., New York: Penguin, 2008), 15.

14. Robert Lindsey, "Jim Jones—From Poverty to Power of Life and Death," *New York Times,* November 26, 1978.

15. Dennis Banks with Richard Erdoes, *Ojibwa Warrior: Dennis Banks and the Rise of the American Indian Movement* (Norman: University of Oklahoma Press, 2004), 316.

16. Reiterman, *Raven,* 281.

17. Banks, *Ojibwa Warrior,* 320.

18. Deloria, *Playing Indian,* 161.

19. Vizenor, *Manifest Manners,* 4.

20. Vizenor, *Fugitive Poses,* 15. For more on terminal creeds, see Gerald Vizenor, *Bearheart: The Heirship Chronicles* (1978; Minnesota: University of Minnesota Press, 1990).

21. Moore, *Understanding Jonestown,* 95.

22. Mary McCormick Maaga, *Hearing the Voices of Jonestown* (Syracuse, N.Y.: Syracuse University Press, 1998), 152.

23. Jonestown had an extensive video inventory of 267 films that included a wide range of documentaries, children's entertainment, and popular films focused around social issues. For more, see San Diego State University's website *Alternative Considerations of Jonestown and Peoples Temple,* accessed April 6, 2011, that is managed by Rebecca Moore at http://jonestown.sdsu.edu, and particularly the video inventory list included in the resource documents about Jonestown organization and its entertainment and guests: http://jonestown.sdsu.edu/AboutJonestown/JTResearch/organization/Entertain_Guests/2-VideosFromJT.pdf.

24. David L. Eng, *The Feeling of Kinship: Queer Liberalism and the Racialization of Intimacy* (Durham, N.C.: Duke University Press, 2010), 22.

25. Wilson Harris, *The Palace of the Peacock* (London: Faber and Faber, 1960), 10.

26. Wilson Harris, *Jonestown* (London: Faber and Faber, 1996), 5.

27. For more on Guyanese colonialist discourses and their effect on Amerindians in Guyana, see Shona N. Jackson, "The Contemporary Crisis in Guyanese National Identification," in *Ethnicity, Class, and Nationalism: Caribbean and Extra-Caribbean Dimensions,* ed. Anton L. Allahar (Lanham, Md.: Lexington Books, 2005), 85–120.

28. Paget Henry, *Caliban's Reason: Introducing Afro-Caribbean Philosophy* (New York: Routledge, 2000), 104.

29. Ibid., 104.

30. Paula Burnett, "Memory Theatre and the Maya: Othering Eschatology in Wilson Harris's *Jonestown,*" *Journal of Caribbean Literatures* 2, nos. 1–3 (2000): 215.

31. Harris, *Jonestown,* 103.

32. Sandra E. Drake, *Wilson Harris and the Modern Tradition: A New Architecture of the World* (New York: Greenwood Press, 1986); Hena Maes-Jelinek, "'Numinous Proportions:' Wilson Harris's Alternative to All 'Posts,'" in *Past the Last Post,* ed. Ian Adam and Helen Tiffin (Calgary: University of Calgary Press, 1990), 47–64; Stuart Murray, "Postcoloniality/Modernity: Wilson Harris and Postcolonial Theory," *Review of Contemporary Fiction* 17, no. 2 (1997); 53–58.

33. Mary Lou Emery, "Reading 'W. H.': Draft of an Incomplete Conversation," in *Wilson Harris: The Uncompromising Imagination*, ed. Hena Maes-Jelinek (Sydney: Dangaroo Press, 1991), 170.

34. See Kirsten Holst Petersen and Anna Rutherford, "Some Intimations of the Stranger," in *Wilson Harris: The Uncompromising Imagination*, 28.

35. Glyne A Griffith, *Deconstruction, Imperialism, and the West Indian Novel* (Kingston: Press University of West Indies, 1996), 57.

36. Ibid., 120.

37. Ibid., 58.

38. Ibid., 61.

39. Wilson Harris, "Tradition and the West Indian Novel," in *Selected Essays of Wilson Harris*, ed. Andrew Bundy (London: Routledge, 1999), 140–41.

40. Ibid., 141.

41. Antonio Benítez-Rojo, *The Repeating Island: The Caribbean and the Postmodern Perspective*, trans. James E. Maraniss (Durham, N.C.: Duke University Press, 1996), 189.

42. Hena Maes-Jelinek, *Dream, Psyche, Genesis: The Works of Wilson Harris*, http://www.l3.ulg.ac.be/harris/whintro.html (accessed February 9, 2010).

43. Gilroy, *Postcolonial Melancholia*, 2.

44. Harris, *Jonestown*, 4.

45. Benítez-Rojo, *The Repeating Island*, 189–90.

46. Jamaica Kincaid, *The Autobiography of My Mother* (New York: Plume, 1996); Kamau Brathwaite, *Contradictory Omens: Cultural Diversity and Integration in the Caribbean* (Mona, Jamaica: Savacoa, 1974). Jamaica Kincaid, for instance, describes the Carib people as extinct in *The Autobiography of My Mother*. "They were like living fossils, they belonged in a museum, on a shelf, enclosed in a glass case" (197–98). Harris, while locating depths of conquest onto Amerindians themselves, still seeks to activate them as presence rather than place them in stasis within Caribbean literature.

47. Deleuze and Guattari, *A Thousand Plateaus*, 19; Deleuze, "What Children Say," 64.

48. Wilson Harris, "Merlin and Parsifal: Adversarial Twins," in *Selected Essays of Wilson Harris*, 64.

49. Ibid., 65.

50. Harris, *Jonestown*, 225.

51. Edward W. Said, *Culture and Imperialism* (New York: Vintage, 1994), 66–67.

52. Harris, *Jonestown*, 21.

53. Ibid., 18–19.

54. My use of "postcolonizing" is here informed by Aileen Moreton-Robinson's discussion of the Australian settler society as a postcolonizing society in her essay, "I Still Call Australia Home," 30–31.

55. Harris, *Jonestown*, 112.

56. Stephanos Stephanides, "Goddesses, Ghosts, and Translatability in Wilson Harris's *Jonestown*," *Journal of Caribbean Literatures* 2, nos. 1–3 (2000): 238.

57. Harris, *Jonestown*, 26.

58. Hena Maes-Jelinek, *The Labyrinth of Universality: Wilson Harris's Visionary Art of Fiction* (Amsterdam: Rodopi, 2006), 426 n14.

59. Monica Pozzi, "A Conversation with Wilson Harris," *Journal of Caribbean Literatures* 2, nos. 1–3 (2000): 262.

60. Harris, *Jonestown*, 19.

61. Ibid., 46.

62. Wilson Harris, "The Age of the Imagination," *Journal of Caribbean Literatures* 2, nos. 1–3 (2000): 17.

63. Harris, *Jonestown*, 199.

64. Ibid., 163.

65. Ibid.

66. Ibid., 192–93.

67. Ibid., 216.

68. Mount Roraima was "discovered" by the German explorer Robert Schomburgk in 1838. Schomburgk is the name of one of Harris's characters in *Palace of the Peacock* as allusion.

69. Harris, *Jonestown*, 227.

70. Maes-Jelinek, *The Labyrinth of Universality*, 435.

71. Harris, *Jonestown*, 233.

72. Elizabeth DeLoughrey, *Routes and Roots: Navigating Caribbean and Pacific Island Literatures* (Honolulu: University of Hawai'i Press, 2007), 238.

73. A revealing yet perplexing statement within the Guyana Ministry of Amerindian Affairs' brochure, *The New Amerindian Act: What Will It Do for Amerindians?* maintains that to define indigenous so it applies only to Amerindians "means that other Guyanese would no longer be able to call themselves indigenous and this would breach the principle set by international law. All people have the right to call themselves 'indigenous peoples' if they want" (7).

74. Ibid., 237.

75. Wilson Harris, *The Dark Jester* (London: Faber and Faber, 2001), 27; Wilson Harris, *The Resurrection at Sorrow Hill* (London: Faber and Faber, 1993), 102.

76. Wilson Harris, "The Amerindian Legacy," in *Selected Essays of Wilson Harris*, 169.

77. Jackson, "The Contemporary Crisis in Guyanese National Identification," 112.

78. Harris, *Jonestown*, 4–5.

79. Hena Maes-Jelinek, "'Numinous Proportions': Wilson Harris's Alternative to All 'Posts,'" in *Past the Last Post*, 59.

80. Alfred J. Lopez, *Posts and Pasts: A Theory of Postcolonialism* (Albany: State University of New York Press, 2001), 45.

81. Ibid., 55–56.

82. Ibid., 64.

83. Andrew Bundy, "Introduction" to *Selected Essays of Wilson Harris*, 18, emphasis added.

84. Harris, *The Dark Jester*, 46.

4. "Been to the Nation, Lord, but I Couldn't Stay There"

1. Quoted in Keith Basso, *Wisdom Sits in Places: Landscape and Language among the Western Apache* (Albuquerque: University of New Mexico Press, 1996), 4.

2. Ibid., 5.

3. Quoted in Angela Cavender Wilson, *Remember This! Dakota Decolonization and the Eli Taylor Narratives* (Lincoln: University of Nebraska Press, 2005). On the importance of place as opposed to time within American Indian sacred geographies and oral histories, see, among others, Vine Deloria Jr., *God Is Red* (New York: Putnam, 1973); Basso, *Wisdom Sits in Places*; Craig Howe, "Keep Your Thoughts above the Trees: Ideas on Developing and Presenting Tribal Histories," in *Clearing a Path: Theorizing the Past in Native American Studies* (New York: Routledge, 2002); and Lisa Brooks, *The Common Pot: The Recovery of Native Space in the Northeast* (Minneapolis: University of Minnesota Press, 2008).

4. Brooks, *The Common Pot*, 3–6.

5. Joy Harjo, "The Place the Musician Became a Bear," in *The Woman Who Fell from the Sky* (New York: W. W. Norton, 2004), 51.

6. Ibid., 52.

7. See Paul Oliver, Tony Russell, and Robert M. Dixon, et al., *Yonder Come the Blues: The Evolution of a Genre* (Cambridge: Cambridge University Press, 2001); and Robert Palmer, *Deep Blues: A Musical and Cultural History of the Mississippi Delta* (New York: Penguin, 1981).

8. Clyde Woods, *Development Arrested: Race, Power, and the Blues in the Mississippi Delta* (London: Verso, 1998), 108.

9. Ibid., 289–90.

10. Charles Peabody, *Exploration of Mounds, Coahoma County, Mississippi* (Cambridge, Mass.: Peabody Museum of American Archaeology and Ethnology, 1904).

11. Ibid., 23, 28.

12. Charles Peabody, "Notes on Negro Music," *Journal of American Folk-Lore* 16, no. 62 (1903): 105.

13. Ibid., 149.

14. LeAnne Howe, "Ohoyo Chishba Osh: The Woman Who Stretches Way Back" in *Pre-removal Choctaw History: Exploring New Paths*, ed. Greg O'Brien (Norman: University of Oklahoma Press, 2008), 26–47. Howe uses this story to articulate a

Choctaw literary nationalism and suggests that "it's time Choctaw scholars interrogate these ancestral stories. We have a great deal to learn from them—even if they have been written down by an invited tribal guest such as Cushman" (28).

15. H. B. Cushman, *History of the Choctaw, Chickasaw, and Natchez Indians* (Greenville: Headlight Print House, 1899), 276–78.

16. Ibid., 276.

17. Salaita, *The Holy Land in Transit.*

18. Elizabeth Cook-Lynn, *New Indians, Old Wars* (Urbana: University of Illinois Press, 2007), 204.

19. See James Welch with Paul Stekler, *Killing Custer: The Battle of Little Bighorn and the Fate of the Plains Indians* (1994; New York: W. W. Norton, 2007), 58. See also Walter C. Rodgers, *Sleeping with Custer and the 7th Cavalry: An Embedded Reporter in Iraq* (Carbondale: Southern Illinois University Press, 2006). His reports often alternated between casting Iraqi peoples as either Bedouins shocked by "camels like they've never seen with 120-millimeter guns sticking out" ("Strike on Iraq: 7th Cavalry Rolls across S. Iraq, Largely Unopposed," *CNN Live Event/Special,* March 20, 2003) or as Iraqi cowboys who might shoot Apache helicopters out of the sky ("3–7th Cavalry Moving Toward Baghdad," *CNN American Morning with Paula Zahn,* April 3, 2003) in echoes of what Richard Slotkin, in *Gunfighter Nation: Myth of the Frontier in Twentieth-Century America* (New York: Atheneum, 1992), diagnosed as the frontier mythology of U.S. history and what Amy Kaplan suggests served as crucible for U.S. foreign and domestic imperialism.

20. Spivak, *A Critique of Postcolonial Reason,* 211.

21. See Priscilla Wald, *Constituting Americans: Cultural Anxiety and Narrative Form* (Durham, N.C.: Duke University Press, 1995); Amy Kaplan, *The Anarchy of Empire*; and Jonathan Elmer, *On Lingering and Being Last: Race and Sovereignty in the New World* (Bronx, N.Y.: Fordham University Press, 2008), for discussions of how included/excluded, foreign/domestic, territorialized/deterritorialized persons respectively constituted an epistemic violence at the core of American nationalism.

22. Antonio Gramsci, "Some Aspects of the Southern Question," (1926) in *The Antonio Gramsci Reader,* ed. David Forgacs (New York: New York University Press, 1998), 171–85. Mark Rifkin, in "Representing the Cherokee Nation: Subaltern Studies and Native American Sovereignty," *boundary 2* 32, no. 3 (2005): 47–80, provocatively demonstrates how subaltern and subalternization provide important insights into how pre-removal Cherokee established elite structures of national governance and citizenship that created fractures between statist and traditional practices of kinship, identity, and consent.

23. See Patrick Wolfe, "Land, Labor, and Difference: Elementary Structures of Race," *American Historical Review* 106, no. 3 (2001): 866–905; Frederick E. Hoxie, "What Was Taney Thinking? American Indian Citizenship in the Era of Dred Scott," *Chicago-Kent Law Review* 82, no. 329 (2007): 329–59.

24. In the context of the Cherokee, Choctaw, Chickasaw, Creek, and Seminole,

the term Freedmen refers to descendants of African American and African Indian slaves owned by those nations.

25. Robert Warrior, "Cherokees Flee the Moral High Ground over Freedmen," *News from Indian Country,* August 7, 2007, http://indiancountrynews.net/index. php?option=com_content&task=view&id=1106&Itemid=74 (accessed September 1, 2007).

26. For more on Freedmen history, see David A. Chang, *The Color of the Land: Race, Nation, and the Politics of Landownership* (Chapel Hill: University of North Carolina Press, 2010); Daniel Littlefield, *The Cherokee Freedmen: From Emancipation to American Citizenship* (Westport, Conn.: Greenwood Press, 1978) and *The Chickasaw Freedmen: A People without a Country* (Westport, Conn.: Greenwood Press, 1980); Tiya Miles, *Ties That Bind: The Story of an Afro-Cherokee Family in Slavery and Freedom* (Berkeley: University of California Press, 2006); and Circe Sturm, *Blood Politics: Race, Culture and Identity in the Cherokee Nation of Oklahoma* (Berkeley: University of California Press, 2002).

27. On May 14, 2007, the Cherokee Courts issued a temporary order and injunction that reinstated Freedmen's citizenship rights while the courts consider appeals against the March 3, 2007, special election results.

28. *Native American Housing Assistance and Self-Determination Reauthorization Act of 2008,* Public Law 110–411, U.S. Statutes at Large 122 (2008), Stat. 4319; Jerry Reynolds, "Housing Amendment Would Punish Cherokee over Freedmen," *Indian Country Today,* July 27, 2007, http://www.indiancountrytoday.com/ archive/28201654.html (accessed July 5, 2009).

29. Jerry Reynolds, "Watson Bill over Freedmen Could Fall Hard on Cherokee If Compromise Cannot Be Reached," *Indian Country Today,* June 22, 2007, http://www.indiancountrytoday.com/archive/28147184.html (accessed February 10, 2010); Murray Evans, "Cherokees Vote to Revoke Membership of Freedmen," *Indian Country Today,* March 12, 2007, http://www.indiancountrytoday.com/ archive/28150249.html (accessed February 10, 2010).

30. Will Chavez, "CN Files Freedmen Lawsuit in Federal Court," *Cherokee Phoenix,* February 5, 2009, http://www.cherokeephoenix.org/3321/Article.aspx; "Watson Files Bill to Cut Cherokee–US Ties," *Cherokee Phoenix,* June 10, 2009, http://www.cherokeephoenix.org/3744/Article.aspx (accessed July 5, 2009); Reynolds, "Housing Amendment Would Punish Cherokee over Freedmen."

31. Jennie Lee-St. John, "The Cherokee Nation's New Battle," *Time,* June 21, 2007, http://www.time.com/time/nation/article/0,8599,1635873,00.html (accessed July 5, 2009); Diane Watson, "Jim Crow in Indian Country," *Huffington Post,* October 25, 2007, http://www.huffingtonpost.com/rep-diane-watson/jim-crow-in-indian-countr_b_69927.html (accessed July 5, 2009).

32. Warrior, "Cherokees Flee."

33. Eric Cheyfitz, "The Historical Irony of H.R. 2824," *Indian Country Today,*

August 10, 2007, http://www.indiancountry.com/content.cfm?id=1096415548 (accessed August 13, 2007).

34. Diane Watson, John Conyers Jr., Barney Frank, Barbara Lee, John Lewis, and Sheila Jackson Lee, House of Representatives, "Letter to Eric Holder, Attorney General of the United States, Washington D.C.," April 30, 2009, http://thehill.com/images/stories/news/2009/may/letter--att%20gen%20holder-4-30-09.pdf (accessed July 5, 2009).

35. Spivak, *A Critique of Postcolonial Reason*, 172.

36. Michael Hechter, *Internal Colonialism: The Celtic Fringe in British National Development* (1975; New Brunswick: Transaction Publishers, 1999), 8.

37. Gramsci, "Some Aspects," 171.

38. Hechter, *Internal Colonialism*, 9.

39. Ibid., 2.

40. Ibid., 32.

41. See ibid., 30–32.

42. See Hechter, *Internal Colonialism* (1975); Martin Luther King Jr., "The Chicago Plan," in *Sing for Freedom: The Story of the Civil Rights Movement through Its Songs*, ed. Candi and Guy Carawan and Julian Bond (Montgomery: New South, Inc., 2007), 227–28; Robert Blauner, "Internal Colonialism and Ghetto Revolt," *Social Problems* 16, no. 4 (1969): 393–408; Robert K. Thomas, "Colonialism: Classic and Internal," *New University Thought* 4 (1969): 37–44; María Josefina Saldaña-Portillo, *The Revolutionary Imagination in the Americas and the Age of Development* (Durham, N.C.: Duke University Press, 2003); Ramón A. Guitiérrez, "Internal Colonialism: An American Theory of Race," *Du Bois Review* 1, no. 2 (2004): 281–95.

43. Hechter, *Internal Colonialism*, xxviii.

44. Blauner, "Internal Colonialism and Ghetto Revolt," 396.

45. bell hooks, *Teaching to Transgress* (New York: Routledge, 1994), 109.

46. bell hooks, *Killing Rage: Ending Racism* (New York: Henry Holt, 1995), 199.

47. Aileen Moreton-Robinson, "Writing off Treaties: White Possession in the United States Critical Whiteness Studies Literature," in *Transnational Whiteness Matters*, 84.

48. According to Jeff Corntassel, "Toward Sustainable Self-Determination: Rethinking the Contemporary Indigenous-Rights Discourse," *Alternatives: Global, Local, Political* 33, no. 1 (2008): 105–32, the Salt Water Thesis, implemented by U.N. General Assembly resolution 1514 (1960), "stipulat[ed] that only territories separated by water or that were geographically separate from the colonizing power could invoke self-determination" (108).

49. Will Kymlicka, "Theorizing Indigenous Rights," in *Politics in the Vernacular: Nationalism, Multiculturalism, and Citizenship* (Oxford: Oxford University Press, 2001), 123.

50. Anne McClintock, "Angel of Progress: Pitfalls of the Term 'Post-Colonialism,'" in *Colonial Discourse, Postcolonial Theory*, 294.

51. Jenny Sharpe, "Is the United States Postcolonial?" in *Postcolonial America*, ed. C. Richard King (Urbana: University of Illinois Press, 2000), 106.

52. Ibid.

53. Ibid., 111.

54. Kevin Bruyneel, *The Third Space of Sovereignty: The Postcolonial Politics of U.S.–Indigenous Relations* (Minneapolis: University of Minnesota Press, 2007), xvii.

55. *Cherokee Nation v. Georgia* (1831) 30 U.S. 1.

56. David E. Wilkins and K. Tsianina Lomawaima, *Uneven Ground: American Indian Sovereignty and Federal Law* (Norman: University of Oklahoma Press, 2001), 61.

57. Ann Laura Stoler, "Tense and Tender Ties: The Politics of Comparison in North American History and (Post)Colonial Studies," in *Haunted by Empire*, 56.

58. This is one of the memes circulating as the Cherokee nation and its spokespeople respond to the media and question regarding their March 3, 2007, vote.

59. Diane Watson, interview by Tony Cox, *News and Notes*, NPR, June 22, 2007.

60. See Deloria, *Playing Indian*, and Shari Huhndorf, *Going Native: Indians in the American Cultural Imagination* (Ithaca, N.Y.: Cornell University Press, 2001).

61. Cherokee Nation, "Citizenship Status of Non-Indians." Official Site of the Cherokee Nation, http://freedmen.cherokee.org (accessed July 5, 2009).

62. Spivak, *A Critique of Postcolonial Reason*, 62.

63. Ibid., 65.

64. Sydney Smith, *Wit and Wisdom of the Rev. Sydney Smith, Being Selections from His Writings and Passages of His Letters and Table-Talk* (New York: Redfield, 1856), 187.

65. O'Brien, *Firsting and Lasting*, xv.

66. John L. O'Sullivan, "Introduction," *United States Democratic Review* 1, no. 1 (October 1837): 14.

67. Robert J. Scholnick, "Extermination and Democracy: O'Sullivan, *The Democratic Review*, and Empire, 1837–1840," *American Periodicals* 15, no. 2 (2005): 124.

68. Walt Whitman, *Uncollected Poetry and Prose of Walt Whitman*, ed. Emory Holloway, 2 vols. (New York: Doubleday and Page, 1921), 2:215, quoted in Scholnick, "Extermination," 125.

69. Scholnick, "Extermination," 124–25.

70. John L. O'Sullivan, "The Supreme Court of the United States. Its Judges and Jurisdictions," *Democratic Review* 1, no. 2 (January 1838): 167

71. Craig S. Womack, *Red on Red: Native American Literary Separatism* (Minneapolis: University of Minnesota Press, 1999), 6–7.

72. Smith, *Decolonizing Methodologies*, 14.

73. Warrior, "Native Critics in the World," in Weaver, Womack, and Warrior, *American Indian Literary Nationalism*, 179–223.

74. Charley Patton, "Down the Dirt Road Blues" (Paramount 12854, 1929). For more about Patton, see David Evans, "Charley Patton: The Conscience of the Delta," in *The Voice of the Delta: Charley Patton and the Mississippi Blues Traditions*, ed. R. Sacré (Liège: Presses Universitaires Liège, 1987), 111–214. For a discussion of blues songs that engage the idea of "the Nation" and Indian Territory, see Chris Smith, "Going to the Nation: The Idea of Oklahoma in Early Blues Recordings," *Popular Music* 16, no. 1 (2007): 83–96.

75. Pura Fé, "Medley: Going Home/Stomp Dance," *Follow Your Heart's Desire* (Music Maker, 2004).

76. Warrior, "Cherokees Flee."

77. Clifton Adcock, "Cherokee File Federal Suit in Freedmen Dispute," *Tulsa World*, February 3, 2009, http://www.tulsaworld.com/news/article.aspx?subjectid=298&articleid=20090203_14_0_TeCeoe853145 (accessed July 5, 2009).

78. Gavin Off, "Freedmen Granted Tribal Citizenship," *Tulsa World*, January 15, 2011, http://www.tulsaworld.com/news/article.aspx?subjectid=11&articleid=201101 1511A1CUTLIN723811&allcom=1 (accessed January 15, 2011).

5. Satisfied with Stones

The epigraph at the beginning of the chapter is a version and translation of "Kaulana Nā Pua" from Kanaka Maoli political scientist Noenoe K. Silva's *Aloha Betrayed* (Durham, N.C.: Duke University Press, 2004), 135. The song was written after the overthrow of Queen Lili'uokalani and gave voice to Native Hawaiian resistance to the haole plantation owners' Republic of Hawai'i that was lobbying to annex Hawai'i to the United States as a territory. The song continues to express Kanaka Maoli ideas of sovereignty and righteousness in the face of the illegal overthrow and illegal annexation of the Hawaiian kingdom by the United States.

1. Victor Bascara, *Model Minority Imperialism* (Minneapolis: University of Minnesota Press, 2006), xviii, xix, xix–xx.

2. Ibid., 13.

3. Named so after U.S. senator Daniel Akaka, who first introduced and sponsored a version of the bill in 2000. Since its first introduction, the bill has gone through various revisions and a multitude of designations. In 2006, when a draft of this chapter was presented as a talk for American Indian Studies at the University of Illinois at Urbana-Champaign, the Akaka Bill was designated S 147 as it moved its way through the 109th Congress. The Native Hawaiian Reorganization Act (NHRA) of 2007 was designated S 310 and HR 505 in the 110th Congress. On October 24, 2007, HR 505 passed a House vote with 261 ayes, 153 nays, and 18

present/not voting. The Senate did not put the bill to vote in the 110th Congress. The NHRA of 2009 was reintroduced to the 111th Congress as S 1011/HR 2314 with new controversies surrounding timing, appropriations, and revisions that have turned former supporters such as then governor of Hawai'i Linda Lingle against the bill. As of this writing, the NHRA has been considered in committee and recommended for a full vote, but it has since stalled. Time will tell.

4. For more information on the arguments of Hawaiian kingdom activists who resist "indigeneity" as a political category, see http://www.hawaiiankingdom.org/ (accessed February 24, 2008) and the *Hawaiian Society of Law and Politics,* available online at http://www2.hawaii.edu/~hslp/ (accessed February 24, 2008). J. Kēhaulani Kauanui examines these contrapuntal strategies for sovereignty claims in "The Multiplicity of Hawaiian Sovereignty Claims and the Struggle for Meaningful Autonomy," *Comparative American Studies* 3, no. 3 (2005): 283–99.

5. Alfred and Corntassel, "Being Indigenous," 597–614.

6. "Talk of the Town: 'Squaw,'" *New Yorker,* March 13, 1935, 19.

7. For more about the interplay of racial and hegemonic colonizing forces at work during this time period, see Eric Love, *Race over Empire: Racism and U.S. Imperialism, 1865–1900* (Chapel Hill: University of North Carolina Press, 2004).

8. See http://thomas.loc.gov/cgi-bin/bdquery/z?d103:SJ00019: for the full text of the 1993 Apology, officially known as United States Public Law 103–150, S.J.Res.19 for the 103rd Congress.

9. United States Public Law 103–150 (1993 Apology).

10. *Rice v. Cayetano, Governor of Hawaii,* 528 U.S. 495 (2000), 146 F3d 1075.

11. Senator John McCain of Arizona, *Native Hawaiian Government Reorganization Act: Hearing before the Committee on Indian Affairs,* March 1, 2005, 109th Cong., 1st sess. (2005): 40.

12. Neal Milner and Jon Goldberg-Hiller, "'Feeble Echoes of the Heart': A Postcolonial Legal Struggle in Hawai'i," *Law, Culture, and Humanities* 4, no. 2 (2008): 229.

13. *Native Hawaiian Government Reorganization Act of 2007.* S 310, 110th Cong., 1st sess. (Sec. 2, 15), http://akaka.senate.gov/public/documents/S310.pdf. (accessed February 25, 2008).

14. *NHGRA of 2007,* S 310, Section 7, B(8).

15. *NHGRA of 2007,* S 310, Section 3(10).

16. Jonathan Kamakawiwo'ole Osorio, "'What Kine Hawaiian Are You?': A Mo'olelo about Nationhood, Race, History, and the Contemporary Sovereignty Movement in Hawai'i," *Contemporary Pacific* 13, no. 2 (2001): 359–79.

17. Ralph Z. Hallow, "Akaka Bill Seeks Ethnic-Hawaiian Government," *Washington Times (D.C.),* May 30, 2005, A03.

18. Senator Daniel Inouye of Hawai'i, *Report from the Committee on Indian Affairs, to Accompany S 746,* September 21, 2001, 107th Cong., 1st sess. (2001), 23.

19. *Native Hawaiian Federal Recognition Joint Hearing before the Committee on Indian Affairs*, August 28, 2000, in Honolulu, Hawai'i, part 4 (77), 106th Cong., 2nd sess. (2000).

20. Ibid., 78.

21. There is another possible interpretation of this moment in the hearing, though, and one might read the unnamed Indian's words at the hearing as an attempt to articulate indigenous solidarity in the face of U.S. juridical and legislative colonialism by affirming the abjected violence that subsuming oneself to "Indianness" entails within the transit of empire.

22. Leela Gandhi, *Affective Communities: Anticolonial Thought, Fin-de-Siècle Radicalism, and the Politics of Friendship* (Durham, N.C.: Duke University Press, 2006), 7–8.

23. In fact, the August 28, 2000, hearings were published under the title *Native Hawaiian Federal Recognition Joint Hearing before the Committee on Indian Affairs*, though the long heading includes, in typical legislative precision, the phrase "to provide a process for the reorganization of a Native Hawaiian government and the recognition by the United States of the Native Hawaiian Government." The large, bold typeface of the document proclaiming the joint hearing is directly below the equally bold and underlined, "Native Hawaiian Federal Recognition" title that demonstrates an intent to bait and switch.

24. See David E. Wilkins, *American Indian Politics and the American Political System* (Lanham, Md.: Rowman and Littlefield, 2006), 19. According to Wilkins, prior to 1978, recognition was "bestowed by congressional act or presidential action" (19). The BIA's 1978 guidelines and criteria for recognition, as Wilkins delineates them, include establishing that the nation seeking recognition had: (1) a long history of cultural and governmental continuance as an American Indian or Aboriginal community; (2) the continued inhabitance of tribal lands; (3) a functioning government; (4) a constitution; (5) criterion for citizenship that meets those required by the secretary of the interior; (6) not been terminated under House Resolution 108 that Congress adopted in 1953; and (7) members who did not belong to other tribes.

25. For more on the Indian Reorganization Act, see Vine Deloria Jr., ed., *The Indian Reorganization Act: Congresses and Bills* (Norman: University of Oklahoma Press, 2003).

26. For more, see Brian Masaru Hayashi, *Democratizing the Enemy: The Japanese American Internment* (Princeton, N.J.: Princeton University Press), 2004.

27. Vine Deloria Jr., *Behind the Trail of Broken Treaties: An Indian Declaration of Independence* (1974; Austin: University of Texas Press, 1985), 204.

28. *Cherokee Nation v. Georgia* (1831) 30 U.S. 1.

29. Silva, *Aloha Betrayed*.

30. For more on how Native Hawaiians were considered wards of the state, see

R. Hokulei Lindsey, "Akaka Bill: Native Hawaiians, Legal Realities, and Politics as Usual," *University of Hawai'i Law Review* 24 (2001-2): 693-727; and Haunani-Kay Trask, "Settlers of Color and 'Immigrant' Hegemony: 'Locals' in Hawai'i," in *Asian Settler Colonialism: From Local Governance to the Habits of Everyday Life in Hawai'i*, ed. Candice Fujikane and Jonathan Y. Okamura (Honolulu: University of Hawai'i Press, 2008), 45-65.

31. S. James Anaya, "The Native Hawaiian People and International Human Rights Law: Toward a Remedy for Past and Continuing Wrongs," *Georgia Law Review* 28, no. 309 (1993-1994): 326-28.

32. Bruce Granville Miller, *Invisible Indigenes: The Politics of Nonrecognition* (Lincoln: University of Nebraska Press, 2003), 113. See J. Kēhaulani Kauanui, "Precarious Positions: Native Hawaiians and U.S. Federal Recognition," *Contemporary Pacific* 17, no. 1 (2005): 1-27, for an excellent discussion of the problems inherent with the Akaka bill and the imperialist discourses of recognition that the United States deploys to further subjugate the Hawaiian kingdom and American Indian nations.

33. Julie Kitka, president of Alaskan Federation of Natives, *Native Hawaiian Government Reorganization Act: Hearing before the Committee on Indian Affairs*, March 1, 2005. 109th Cong., 1st sess. (2005): 61.

34. Lili'uokalani, *Hawaii's Story by Hawaii's Queen* (1897; Honolulu: Mutual Publishing, 1990), 251. Emphasis in the original.

35. Lili'uokalani, *Hawaii's Story*, 369.

36. See Silva's *Aloha Betrayed*. Her chapter on Queen Lili'uokalani, especially pages 173-80, addresses some of the cartoon representations of the queen and the discourses of race and savagery that were being used to depict Hawai'i at the time of the overthrow.

37. Samuel Manaiakalani Kamakau, *Ruling Chiefs of Hawai'i* (1961; Honolulu, Hawai'i: Kamehameha Schools Press, 1992). Quoted in the revised edition's introduction by Lilikala K. Kame'eleihiwa, ix.

38. Lili'uokalani, *Hawaii's Story*, 309.

39. Ibid., 310.

40. Philip J. Deloria, *Indians in Unexpected Places* (Lawrence: University Press of Kansas, 2004), 16.

41. Mary Jane Warde, *George Washington Grayson and the Creek Nation, 1843-1920* (Norman: University of Oklahoma Press, 1999), 178.

42. Kauanui, *Hawaiian Blood*, 87.

43. Quoted in Rona Tamiko Halualani, *In The Name of Hawaiians: Native Identities and Cultural Politics* (Minneapolis: University of Minnesota Press, 2002), 74.

44. Ibid., 74.

45. See Kevin Bruyneel, "Challenging American Boundaries: Indigenous People

and the 'Gift' of U.S. Citizenship," *Studies in American Political Development* 18 (Spring 2004): 30–43, for more on how Indian citizenship debates reveal how "dominant institutions and boundaries of American Politics are still deeply defined by their colonial practices toward the 'First American Citizens' or, alternatively, the 'original North Americans'" (43).

46. Dudley O. McGovney, "American Citizenship," *Columbia Law Review* 11, no. 4 (1911): 328.

47. Ibid., 337.

48. Ibid.

49. Ibid., 333.

50. *Dred Scott v. Sandford,* 60 U.S. (19 How.) 393, 403–4 (1857).

51. Ibid., 404.

52. Hoxie, "What Was Taney Thinking," 358–59.

53. Left Quarter Collective, "White Supremacist Constitution of the U.S. Empire-State: A Short Conceptual Look at the Long First Century," *Political Power and Social Theory* 20 (2009): 189.

54. *Dred Scott v. Sandford,* 405.

55. Brown, *States of Injury,* 27.

56. Governor Linda Lingle of Hawai'i, *Native Hawaiian Government Reorganization Act: Hearing before the Committee on Indian Affairs,* March 1, 2005. 109th Cong., 1st sess. (2005): 46.

57. Ibid., 47.

58. Spivak, *A Critique of Postcolonial Reason,* 255.

59. Senator Daniel Akaka of Hawai'i. *Native Hawaiian Government Reorganization Act: Hearing before the Committee on Indian Affairs,* March 1, 2005. 109th Cong., 1st sess. (2005): 61.

60. Tex Hall, president, National Congress of American Indians, *Native Hawaiian Government Reorganization Act: Hearing before the Committee on Indian Affairs,* March 1, 2005. 109th Cong., 1st sess. (2005) 61.

61. Senator Daniel Akaka of Hawai'i, *Native Hawaiian Federal Government Reorganization Act of 2005,* PowerPoint slide presentation, notes for slide 28. Though this PowerPoint presentation has since been removed from Senator Akaka's current website, it can still be downloaded at http://web.archive.org/web/20060923031740/http://akaka.senate.gov/public/index.cfm?FuseAction=Issues.Home&issue=Akaka+Bill&content_id=24 (accessed February 25, 2008).

62. *Native Hawaiian Government Reorganization Act of 2007,* S 310, 110th Cong., 1st sess. Sec. 8(b)(3), http://thomas.loc.gov/cgi-bin/query/F?c110:3:./temp/~c1102PETzt:e40851: (accessed April 9, 2011).

63. *Side-by-Side Comparison of HR 2314 and S 1011 Substitute Amendment, The Native Hawaiian Government Reorganization Act of 2009,* revised January 14, 2010,

Office of Hawaiian Affairs, http://www.oha.org/index.php?option=com_content& task=view&id=1045&Itemid=224 (accessed February 9, 2010).

64. Herbert A. Sample, "Lingle Fights Akaka Bill Changes," *Honolulu Star-Bulletin,* December 16, 2009, http://www.starbulletin.com/news/20091216_Lingle_ fights_Akaka_Bill_changes.html (accessed February 9, 2010).

65. Epeli Hau'ofa, "Our Sea of Islands," *Contemporary Pacific: A Journal of Island Affairs* 6, no. 1 (Spring 1994): 152–53.

66. "An Ex-Queen of the Kanakas on Her Travels," *Chicago Tribune,* August 12, 1866, 3.

67. "Our First Royal Lady Visitor," *New York Times,* August 9, 1866, 5.

68. "The President's Welcome to Queen Emma," *Chicago Tribune,* August 19, 1866, 1.

69. "Our Royal Guest," *Daily National Intelligencer* (Washington, D.C.) Friday, August 17, 1866; issue 16,845; col B.

70. Ibid.

71. Vizenor, *Fugitive Poses,* 84.

72. Ibid., 81, 83.

73. Gandhi, *Affective Communities.*

74. Žižek, "'Ode to Joy' Followed by Chaos and Despair."

75. Glen S. Coulthard, "Subjects of Empire: Indigenous Peoples and the 'Politics of Recognition' in Canada," *Contemporary Political Theory* 6 (2007): 439, 456.

76. Joy Harjo, "Protocol," in *A Map to the Next World: Poems and Tales* (New York: W. W. Norton and Co, 2000), 116–117. Song version published at *Joy Harjo's Weblog,* July 18, 2006, http://www.joyharjo.com/news/2006/07/protocol.html (accessed February 9, 2010).

77. See Valerie Lambert, *Choctaw Nation: A Story of American Indian Resurgence* (Lincoln: University of Nebraska Press, 2007), 23–26 for more information on Southeastern and specifically Choctaw (though the Muscogee Creeks share many similar institutions) kinship moieties, phratries, subphratries, and houses that structured social groupings: "Especially during the eighteenth century, a Choctaw's placement in a structured network of kin defined his or her obligations and responsibilities in a wide range of political, economic, and social activities, including ceremony and ritual (the funerary ceremonies described above being one example), justice (which for years was controlled by clans), and agriculture" (26). My definition of kinship sovereignty depends upon these structured networks as counter to state-centered articulations of sovereignty that depend, in Enlightenment humanism, on the centrality of the sovereign individual.

78. Patricia Galloway, *Practicing Ethnohistory: Mining Archives, Hearing Testimony, Constructing Narrative* (Lincoln: University of Nebraska Press, 2006), 230.

79. Ibid., 230.

80. Lambert, *Choctaw Nation,* 27; Galloway, *Practicing Ethnohistory,* 231.

6. Killing States

1. Ruth Okimoto, *Sharing a Desert Home: Life on the Colorado River Indian Reservation, Poston, Arizona, 1942–1945, A Special Report of News from Native California* (Berkeley, Calif.: Heyday Books, 2001), 7.

2. Ibid., 8–9.

3. John Collier, "Speech to Poston Camp Evacuees," June 27, 1942. Wade Head Collection MS FM MSS 118, box 1, folder 1, Arizona Historical Foundation. Available online at http://azmemory.lib.az.us/cdm4/browse.php?CISOROOT=/ahfreloc.

4. See Barack Obama, "A More Perfect Union" (speech, Philadelphia, Penn., March 18, 2008), http://blogs.wsj.com/washwire/2008/03/18/text-of-obamas-speech-a-more-perfect-union/tab/article/ (accessed February 12, 2010).

5. See *Korematsu v. United States* (1944); and Williams Jr., *Like a Loaded Weapon*.

6. Agamben, *Homo Sacer*, 19.

7. Homi K. Bhabha, *The Location of Culture*, 313.

8. Elvira Pulitano, *Toward a Native American Critical Theory* (Lincoln: University of Nebraska Press, 2003).

9. See Bruyneel, *The Third Space of Sovereignty*; Paul Meredith, "Hybridity in the Third Space: Rethinking Bi-Cultural Politics in Aotearoa/New Zealand," (paper presented to Te Oru Rangahau Maori Research and Development Conference, 7–9 July 1998); Jay T. Johnson, "Indigeneity's Challenges to the White Settler-State: Creating a Thirdspace for Dynamic Citizenship," *Alternatives: Global, Local, Political* 33, no. 1 (2008): 29–52; Williams Jr., *Like a Loaded Weapon*, 146–48; and Cheyfitz, "The (Post)Colonial Predicament of Native American Studies," 405–27.

10. Bruyneel, *Third Space*, 218–22.

11. Hayashi, *Democratizing the Enemy*.

12. See Michael Hardt and Antonio Negri, *Commonwealth* (Cambridge, Mass.: Harvard University Press, 2009); and Gilroy, *Postcolonial Melancholia*.

13. Agamben, *State of Exception*, 21.

14. Ibid.

15. Ibid., 22.

16. Exec. Order No. 9066, 3 C.F.R. 1092–1093 (1942).

17. Agamben, *Homo Sacer*, 19.

18. For more history about the creation of the CRIR, see the Colorado River Indian Tribes Official Website, "About the Tribes" http://www.crit-nsn.gov/crit_contents/about/ (accessed February 12, 2010); Woodrow Wilson, Executive Order—Colorado River Indian Reservation, November 22, 1915. Text available at *The American Presidency Project*, ed. John T. Woolley and Gerhard Peters. University of California, Santa Barbara, http://www.presidency.ucsb.edu/ws/index.php?pid=76623 (accessed February 12, 2010).

19. Agamben, *Homo Sacer,* 181; Walter Benjamin, "Critique of Violence," in *Reflections,* ed. Paul Demetz (New York: Schocken Books, 1986), 286; Brown, *States of Injury,* 3–29.

20. Vine Deloria Jr., *Custer Died for Your Sins: An Indian Manifesto* (1969; Norman: University of Oklahoma Press, 1988), 48. For more assessments of Collier, see Kenneth R. Philp, *John Collier's Crusade for Indian Reform, 1920–1954* (Tucson: University of Arizona Press, 1977); Richard Drinnon, *Keeper of the Concentration Camps: Dillon S. Myer and American Racism* (Berkeley: University of California Press, 1989); Elmer R. Rusco, *A Fateful Time: The Background and Legislative History of the Indian Reorganization Act* (Reno: University of Nevada Press, 2000); and David W. Daily, *Battle for the BIA: G.E.E. Lindquist and the Missionary Crusade against John Collier* (Tucson: University of Arizona Press, 2004).

21. Okimoto, *Sharing a Desert Home,* 23.

22. Rusco, *A Fateful Time,* 282–83.

23. John Collier, *Indians of the Americas: The Long Hope* (New York: New American Library, 1947), 7.

24. Ibid., 7–8.

25. For more on Collier's understanding of bilateralism in American Indian policy, see John Collier, "The United States Indian," in *Understanding Minority Groups,* ed. Joseph B. Gittler (New York: John Wiley and Sons, 1956), 33–57.

26. See Williams Jr., *Like a Loaded Weapon,* 23, for more on stare decisis as it pertains to the figuration of American Indians in U.S. law.

27. Okimoto, *Sharing a Desert Home,* 23.

28. See Hayashi, *Democratizing the Enemy,* 1–10.

29. See Kazanjian, *The Colonizing Trick,* 1–34.

30. Karen Tei Yamashita, *Tropic of Orange* (Minneapolis: Coffee House Press, 1997), 71.

31. Ibid., 56–57.

32. Ibid., 57.

33. Caroline Rody, *The Interethnic Imagination: Roots and Passages* (Oxford: Oxford University Press, 2009), 127–28, 137.

34. Molly Wallace, "Tropics of Globalization: Reading the New North America," *symplokē* 9, no. 1–2 (2001): 145–60.

35. Hardt and Negri, *Empire,* 280.

36. *Cherokee Nation v. Georgia* (1831) 30 U.S. 1.

37. For more on the Doctrine of Discovery and "just wars," see Robert A. Williams Jr., *The American Indian in Western Legal Thought* (New York: Oxford University Press, 1990).

38. Benjamin Franklin and Alexander Dalrymple, "Plan for Benefiting Distant Unprovided Countries" (August 29, 1771), in *The Writings of Benjamin Franklin,* vol. 5, ed. Albert Henry Smyth (London: Macmillan Company, 1907), 340–44.

39. See Williams Jr., *Like A Loaded Weapon*, 20–21. Williams Jr. evokes Robert Cover's concepts of the "jurisgenesis" and "jurispathic" functions of the law to explain how languages of racism function within the Supreme Court's claim to interpretive authority over law-making and law-killing.

40. Robert Cover, "Nomos and Narrative," in *Narrative, Violence, and the Law: The Essays of Robert Cover*, ed. Martha Minow, Michael Ryan, and Austin Sarat (Ann Arbor: University of Michigan Press, 1993), 95–96.

41. Agamben, *Homo Sacer*, 19–20.

42. Mark Rifkin, "Indigenizing Agamben: Rethinking Sovereignty in Light of the 'Peculiar' Status of Native Peoples," *Cultural Critique* 73 (Fall 2009): 94.

43. See David Hurst Thomas, *Skull Wars: Kennewick Man, Archaeology, and the Battle for Native American Identity* (New York: Basic Books, 2000), for a detailed discussion of how and why these stories emerged in the mid-nineteenth century as part of scientific racism.

44. See Adair, *The History of the American Indians*, for an earlier Enlightenment articulation of this idea.

45. Thomas, *Skull Wars*, 132.

46. Thomas Jefferson, *Notes on the State of Virginia*, ed. William Peden (1787; New York: W. W. Norton and Co., 1954), 100–101.

47. Joy Harjo, "There's No Such Thing as a One-way Land Bridge," in *A Map to the Next World*, 38–39.

48. For more on Asian settler colonialism, see Candace Fujikane and Jonathan Y. Okamura, ed., *Asian Settler Colonialism*.

49. Takaki, *A Different Mirror*, 191.

50. Said, *Orientalism*, 2.

51. Reginald Horsman, *Race and Manifest Destiny: The Origins of American Racial Anglo-Saxonism* (Cambridge, Mass.: Harvard University Press, 1981).

52. See Hardt and Negri, *Commonwealth*, vii–xiv, 360–75.

53. Nandita Sharma and Cynthia Wright, "Decolonizing Resistance, Challenging Colonial States," *Social Justice* 35, no. 3 (2008–9): 123.

54. Ibid., 124. Sharma and Wright's discussion of autochthony is a critique of an essay by Bonita Lawrence and Enakshi Dua, "Decolonizing Antiracism," *Social Justice* 32, no. 4 (2005): 120–43. Lawrence and Dua critique antiracism struggles in Canada for collusion and complicity with the juridical and legislative structures that colonize First Nation peoples in Canada. They write, "Thus, critical race and postcolonial scholars have systematically excluded on-going colonization from the ways in which racism is articulated. This has erased the presence of Aboriginal peoples and their ongoing struggles for decolonization, precluding a more sophisticated analysis of migration, diasporic identities, and diasporic countercultures" (130).

55. Ibid., 133.

56. Hardt and Negri, *Commonwealth*, 361, 363.

57. Ibid., 377.

58. Collier, "Speech," June 27, 1942.

59. Agamben, *Homo Sacer*, 10.

60. Throughout *Commonwealth*, Hardt and Negri draw upon indigenous writers such as Leslie Marmon Silko and Keri Hulme to articulate the resistant possibilities of altermodernity. Of Silko, they write: "The novelist Leslie Marmon Silko is one of the most interesting theorists of altermodernity.... Native American practices, knowledges, and ceremonies constantly need to be transformed to maintain their power. Revolution is thus, in Silko's world, the only way not simply to rebel against the destroyers and guarantee our survival but paradoxically to preserve our most precious inheritance from the past" (105–6). They end their book with an evocation of laughter in the face of Silko's destroyers: "And in the struggles against capitalist exploitation, the rule of property, and the destroyers of the common through public and private control, we will suffer terribly, but still we laugh with joy. They will be buried with laughter" (383).

61. Edward W. Soja, *Postmodern Geographies: The Reassertion of Space in Critical Social Theory* (London: Verso, 1989), 191.

62. Ibid., 246.

63. K. Anthony Appiah, "Is the Post- in Postmodernism the Post- in Postcolonial?" *Critical Inquiry* 17, no. 2 (1991): 346.

64. Ibid., 356.

65. Agamben, *Homo Sacer*, 19.

66. Although this is now the common identification for the camps, there is also another important layer to this history with internment camps positioned as U.S. War Relocation Centers. It is yet another remapping of relocations transferred from native peoples onto Japanese American citizens.

67. Fredric Jameson, *Postmodernism, or The Cultural Logic of Late Capitalism* (Durham, N.C.: Duke University Press, 1991), 27.

68. See "The New Face of America: How Immigrants Are Shaping the World's First Multicultural Society," *Time*, November 18, 1993.

69. David Palumbo-Liu, *Asian/American: Historical Crossings of a Racial Frontier* (Stanford, Calif.: Stanford University Press, 1999), 183.

70. Ibid., 1.

71. Ibid., 188.

72. Kandice Chuh, *Imagine Otherwise: On Asian Americanist Critique* (Durham, N.C.: Duke University Press, 2003), 11, 9.

73. Scholars in native studies have started to interrogate subjectless critique and its usefulness to indigenous critical theory. See for instance Andrea Smith, "Queer Theory and Native Studies: The Heteronormativity of Settler Colonialism," *GLQ* 16, no. 1–2 (2010): 41–68. In her discussion of subjectless critique arising from the

intersections of queer studies and native studies, Smith argues that native studies might decenter native peoples as subject/object of the field and recenter the field on queer of color critique and the larger processes of settler colonialism (44). In the process, she argues that subjectless critique within native studies "enables an indigenous critique of queer of color projects that do not directly engage Native studies but do depend ideologically on the disappearance of Native peoples" (54). As I am discussing subjectless critique here, I am very much in alliance with David L. Eng, Judith Halberstam, and José Esteban Muñoz's deployment of the concept in "What Is Queer about Queer Studies Now?" *Social Text* 23, no. 3–4 (Fall-Winter 2005): 1–17. They argue that "'subjectless' critique of queer studies disallows any positing of a proper subject *of* or object *for* the field by insisting that queer has no fixed political referent" (3). But what I am arguing as point of distinction from Eng et al. and Smith is that subjectlessness is impossible within indigenous critical theory because "Indian" and "Indianness" are the fields through which subject and object might be approached as parallax. Such an argument is very much attuned to the processes of settler colonialism, but understands discursive normativities as affecting every subject and object adjudicated inside *and* outside subjectivity. There can be no subjectless critique because subjectlessness has already formed itself in relationship to "Indianness" within the transit of empire.

74. *Faces of America with Henry Louis Gates Jr.*, 4 episodes. PBS, February 10–March 3, 2010.

75. Alessandra Stanley, "Genealogy for a Nation of Immigrants," *The New York Times,* February 9, 2010, http://tv.nytimes.com/2010/02/10/arts/television/10faces. html (accessed February 12, 2010).

76. Elizabeth Povinelli, "The Child in the Broom Closet: States of Killing and Letting Die," *South Atlantic* 107, no. 3 (2008): 511, 517.

77. Ibid., 516.

78. Moreton-Robinson, *Sovereign Subjects*, 2.

79. Gerald Vizenor, *Hiroshima Bugi: Atomu 57* (Lincoln: University of Nebraska Press, 2003), 9.

80. Ibid., 143.

81. Vizenor, *Manifest Manners*, 11.

82. Vizenor, *Hiroshima Bugi*, 36.

83. Arnold Krupat and Brian Swann, ed., *I Tell You Now: Autobiographical Essays by Native American Writers* (Lincoln: University of Nebraska Press, 1987), 59.

84. Vizenor, *Hiroshima Bugi*, 9.

85. Ibid.

86. Kimberly Blaeser, *Gerald Vizenor: Writing in Oral Tradition* (Norman: University of Oklahoma, 1996), 113.

87. Ibid., 12–13.

88. Vizenor, *Hiroshima Bugi*, 12.

89. Gerald Vizenor and A. Robert Lee, *Postindian Conversations* (Lincoln: University of Nebraska Press, 1999), 128.

90. I am indebted to Petrice Flowers here for her help in articulating the interventions Johnny Cash's song is making to the nationalist movement in Japan.

91. Johnny Cash, "Man in Black," *Man in Black* (Columbia Records 1971).

Conclusion

1. Robert Sullivan, *Captain Cook in the Underworld* (Auckland: University of Auckland Press, 2002), 37.

2. Robert J. C. Young, "Terror Effects" in *Terror and the Postcolonial*, ed. Elleke Boehmer and Stephen Morton (Oxford: Wiley-Blackwell, 2010), 307.

3. Donald B. Connelly, *John M. Schofield and the Politics of Generalship* (Chapel Hill: University of North Carolina Press, 2006), 261–65.

4. Lieutenant General John M. Schofield, *Forty-six Years in the Army* (New York: Century Co., 1897), 446.

5. Ibid., 446.

6. Ibid., 268; See Lawrence Patrick Jackson, *Ralph Ellison: Emergence of Genius* (Athens: University of Georgia Press, 2002), 44–45.

7. Žižek, *In Defense of Lost Causes*, 49.

8. Žižek, *The Parallax View*, 123.

9. Ibid., 123.

10. Patrick Wolfe, "*Corpus Nullius*: The Exception of Indians and Other Aliens in U.S. Constitutional Discoures," *Postcolonial Studies* 10, no. 2 (2007): 129.

11. Noam Chomsky, "The Torture Memos," *chomsky.info*, May 24, 2009. http://www.chomsky.info/articles/20090521.htm (accessed August 19, 2009).

12. *The Modoc Indian Prisoners* 14 Op. Att'y Gen. 252 (1873); John C. Yoo, *Memorandum for William J. Haynes II, General Counsel of the Department of the Defense,* March 14, 2003: 7.

13. R. David Edmunds, Frederick E. Hoxie, and Neal Salisbury, *The People: A History of North America* (Boston: Houghton Mifflin Company, 2007), 309.

14. For more information, see R. David Edmunds et al., *The People*, 308–12; and Patricia Nelson Limerick, *Something in the Soil: Legacies and Reckonings in the New West* (New York: W. W. Norton, 2000), 34–64.

15. Schofield, *Forty-six Years in the Army*, 438.

16. Richard Dyer, *Matter of Images: Essays on Representation* (London: Routledge, 2002), 142.

17. Mbembe, "Necropolitics," 29.

18. Donald E. Pease, *The New American Exceptionalism* (Minneapolis: University of Minnesota Press, 2009), 181.

Index

Abercrombie, Neil, 175
Aberdeen Saturday Pioneer, The, 36
Abu Ghraib, 19
Acosta, Fray José de, 200
Adair, James, 240n.32
Adair, W. P., 178
Afghanistan, 223
African Americans: *Dred Scott* decision and, 168–69, 170; and internal colonization, 133–34; nationalism as mode of resistance for, 133; Peoples Temple in context of, 80; police brutality against, 207; racialization and, xxvi, 12, 16, 27, 73; resistance and agency of, 82–83, 119–22; Twain's attitudes toward, 24–26; at West Point, 223–24
After Race (Gilroy), 18
Agamben, Giorgio, 10, 22, 144, 205, 240n.34, 242n.60; *Homo Sacer,* 16, 192; on *nomos* (normative universe), 199; state of exception theorized by, 187, 190, 191, 206
Ahmad, Aijaz, xxx
ainoko, 215, 216
Ainu, 212, 215, 216, 217–18
Akaka, Daniel, 153, 173, 174, 175, 259n.3, 263n.61
Akaka bill. *See* Native Hawaiian Government Reorganization Act
Alaska Federation of Natives, 173

Alaska Natives, 124, 127, 150, 162, 172, 173
Alfred, Taiaiake, xxix, 150, 249n.86
Allen, Chadwick, 54
allotment, federal Indian policies of, 141, 149, 159–60, 165; Dawes General Allotment Act (1887), 127, 128–29, 139, 141, 155, 159, 164, 166
Aloha Betrayed (Silva), 259
altermodernity, 203, 205, 207, 268n.60
American exceptionalism, 5, 133, 198–99; Manifest Destiny and, 148; postracial, 203; Queen Liliʻuokalani's use of, 165; Rodó's reading of *The Tempest,* 57–58; Twain and, 23; U.S. imperialism as function of, 5. *See also* state of exception
American Indian(s): as aliens, 166–70; BIA's guidelines for recognition of, 159, 261n.24; as domestic dependent nations, 136, 152, 173; in *Dred Scott* decision, 168–69; internal colonization and, 136, 137–38; in liminal space, 136–37, 168; Marshall on, xxi–xxiii, 136–37; Orientalism about, 63, 73, 201–2; Queen Liliʻuokalani on, 162–63, 165; racialization vs. colonization, xxiii–xxiv, 125–26, 137; as soldiers, 19, 214, 216, 243n.72; Spivak on, 70–71; as

271

Rothberg, Michael, 53
Roughing It (Twain), 21–23, 24
Rousseau, Jean-Jacques, 27
"Run Children Run" or "Run Johnny
  Run" (song), 121
Ryan, Leo, 77
Ryman, Geoff, 35–36, 38

Sahlins, Marshall, 239n.5
Said, Edward, 4, 63, 237n.25, 248n.64,
  252n.51; contrapuntal reading de-
  fined by, 93; on Orientalism, 201–2
Salaita, Steven, xvi, 122, 235n.1
Salazar, Ken, 146
Saldaña-Portillo, Maria Josefina,
  257n.42
Saldanha, Arun, 18
salt water thesis, 135, 148, 257n.48
Sanders, William, 41–42
San Juan, E., Jr., xxx, 237n.36
Sasaki, Sadako, 213
savagery: savage other, 27; "tattooed
  savages," 7, 8–10, 13, 17, 21; Vizenor's
  savagism as presence, 180–81
Schmitt, Carl, 191
Schofield, John M., 223–24, 228
Scholnick, Robert J., 143
Schomburgk, Robert, 253n.68
Sebastián, Santiago, 249n.84
self: Hegelian dialectic of self/other,
  141–42; in-otherness, 65, 98–100,
  106–8, 109, 211; recognition of, 99
self-determination, xxiv, 74, 127, 135,
  137, 144, 152–54, 160–61, 173–74, 180,
  193, 257n.48; as contagion, 156. *See
  also* sovereignty
self-governance: Collier's project of,
  160, 191, 205; reorganization and,
  160–61
Seminole, 12, 128, 138, 144
Senate Committee on Indian Af-

fairs, 154, 162, 261n.19–21, 261n.23;
  Lingle's testimony before, 172–73
Seneca, 160
settler colonialism, xix, xxvi, 27, 74,
  111, 113, 117–18, 226–27, 236n.15;
  Asian, 201; Caliban and, 66–67;
  coerced complicity of, xvii, xxiii,
  71, 187; competing claims to indigeneity, 122, 150; distortive parallactic effects of, 171–72; indigeneity
  as inclusive remediation of, 54,
  59; maps of, 13; multicultural, xx,
  39, 53–54; normativities of, 20;
  property ownership within logics
  of, 2; racializations of, xxiii–xxiv,
  54, 75–76, 170; settler subject in,
  238n.42
7th Cavalry, 123, 255n.19
Shaffer, Barbara, 81
Shakespeare, Race, and Colonialism
  (Loomba), 248–49n.75
Shakespeare, William, xxxvi, 39, 56,
  201, 206, 247n.39; in Sanders'
  "The Undiscovered," 41–42; as
  U.S. "founding father," 57. *See also
  Tempest, The*
Shapiro, Michael J., 13, 241n.44
Sharing a Desert Home (Okimoto), 185
Sharma, Nandita, 204, 267n.53–54
Sharpe, Jenny, 135–36
Shinnecock Indian Nation, 237n.33
Shohat, Ella, xxx, 237n.36
Shriver, Maria, 242n.57
Silko, Leslie Marmon, 268n.60
Silva, Noenoe K., 3, 239n.6, 259,
  262n.36
Simpson, Audra, xx
slavery: blues and, 118; Cherokee Na-
  tion and, 126, 128, 138; as coeval
  contradiction for freedom, xxv;
  Dred Scott decision and, 168–69,

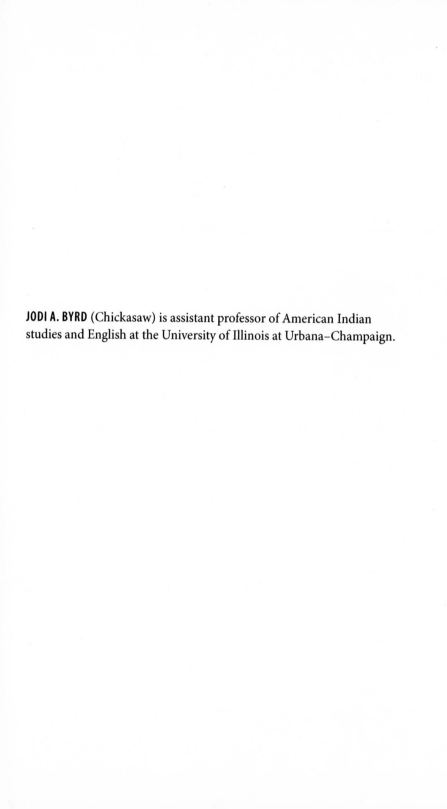

JODI A. BYRD (Chickasaw) is assistant professor of American Indian studies and English at the University of Illinois at Urbana–Champaign.